PENGUIN BOOKS

# THE LAST LINGUA FRANCA

Nicholas Ostler is the author of *Empires of the World: A Language History of the World* and *Ad Infinitum: A Biography of Latin*. He studied Greek, Latin and Philosophy at the University of Oxford and holds a PhD in Linguistics from MIT. With a working knowledge of twenty-six languages, Nicholas now runs an institu... the protection of endangered languages.

# THE LAST LINGUA FRANCA

*The Rise and Fall of World Languages*

NICHOLAS OSTLER

PENGUIN BOOKS

PENGUIN BOOKS

Published by the Penguin Group
Penguin Books Ltd, 80 Strand, London WC2R ORL, England
Penguin Group (USA) Inc., 375 Hudson Street, New York, New York 10014, USA
Penguin Group (Canada), 90 Eglinton Avenue East, Suite 700, Toronto, Ontario, Canada M4P 2Y3
(a division of Pearson Penguin Canada Inc.)
Penguin Ireland, 25 St Stephen's Green, Dublin 2, Ireland (a division of Penguin Books Ltd)
Penguin Group (Australia), 250 Camberwell Road, Camberwell, Victoria 3124, Australia
(a division of Pearson Australia Group Pty Ltd)
Penguin Books India Pvt Ltd, 11 Community Centre, Panchsheel Park,
New Delhi – 110 017, India
Penguin Group (NZ), 67 Apollo Drive, Rosedale, Auckland 0632, New Zealand
(a division of Pearson New Zealand Ltd)
Penguin Books (South Africa) (Pty) Ltd, 24 Sturdee Avenue, Rosebank, Johannesburg 2196, South Africa

Penguin Books Ltd, Registered Offices: 80 Strand, London WC2R ORL, England

www.penguin.com

First published in The United States of America by Walker Publishing Company, Inc. 2010
First published in Great Britain by Allen Lane 2010
Published in Penguin Books 2011
1

Copyright © Nicholas Ostler, 2010

Printed in England by Clays Ltd, St Ives plc

ISBN: 978-1-846-14216-1

www.greenpenguin.co.uk

MIX
Paper from
responsible sources
FSC   FSC® C018179
www.fsc.org

Penguin Books is committed to a sustainable
future for our business, our readers and our
planet. This book is made from paper certified
by the Forest Stewardship Council.

To Steve,

the Master.

само собою разумеется.

*Wer fremde Sprachen nicht kennt, weiß nichts von seiner eigenen.*

He who is not acquainted with foreign languages knows
nothing of his own.

—Goethe, *Maximen und Reflexionen*

# Contents

## PART IV: WHO'S IN CHARGE HERE?

# Big Beasts:

## Official Zones for the World's Major Languages in 2010

—

### KEY
—

ENGLISH

SPANISH

RUSSIAN

ARABIC

PORTUGUESE

FRENCH

These languages do not necessarily have the largest speaker populations in their territories and some states have more than one official language.

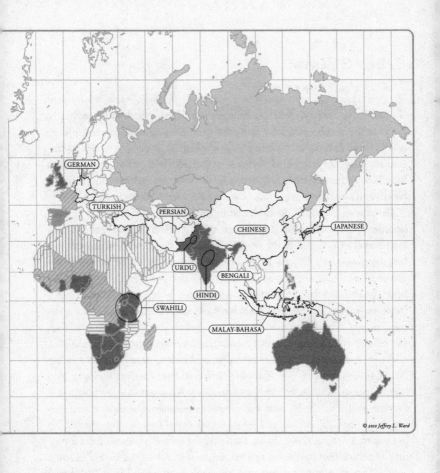

GERMAN

TURKISH

PERSIAN

CHINESE

JAPANESE

URDU

BENGALI

HINDI

SWAHILI

MALAY-BAHASA

© 2010 Jeffrey L. Ward

# Acknowledgments

I BENEFITED EARLY FROM the antiquated grading system at my prep school. At Yardley Court in Kent in the 1960s, performance either in Latin or in French—English's two predecessors as a global lingua-franca— was as highly prized as expertise in mathematics, or all other subjects (including English) combined. Studies associated with English were seen somehow as free extensions of growing up with this mother tongue, combined, and so undervalued. This bias suited my own talents just fine.

Perhaps as a result, I never shared in the local reverence for the "special beauties" perceived in the language that the English (and in fact the lowland Scots) have "given to the world." What can they know of English as a language, who only English know, after all? But evidently, without the predominance of English, this book would not exist; nor would I, in all likelihood, be able to subsist on writing such things. My first acknowledgment, then, must go to the English language past and present—which means the collaborative speech community that has spoken it, and made it available, and ever more widely useful and even attractive, these last fifteen centuries.

After that I must confess comparable, and rather more sincerely felt, indebtedness to so many other languages that had previously developed into lingua-francas. Curiously many in this book have initial *P*—Phoenician, Persian, Pali, Portuguese, and various pidgins—and a few more initial *S*— Sanskrit, Sogdian, Syriac, and (at a pinch) *sermo Latinus*. But there have been so many more. Once again, a language principally means the community of people that have been moved to speak it. As a good friend of mine once enthused over the existence of "so much good music" from Hildegard of Bingen even unto Andrew Lloyd Webber, so I feel a bubbling up of joy at the thought of so many good languages. Blessings upon their diversity!

More specific human debts are much plainer. My agent Natasha Fairweather accepted my curious ideas and conveyed them with added charm to hard-headed but (let us hope) perceptive publishers, George Gibson at Walker & Co. and Will Goodlad at Penguin. At Walker & Co., Jackie Johnson and Mike O'Connor have worked valiantly with an intricate manuscript. And thanks to Carl Masthay for enthusiasm, and close reading, alike. Matthew Young designed the mesmeric cover for the English paperback.

Before and while writing it, I have learned much from Harold Schiffman and assembled sages, especially Birgit Schlyter, at the UPenn symposium in 2001 on *Languages in and Around Afghanistan*; later, the library at London University's School of Oriental and African Studies was fundamental to progress. From Douglas Streusand I learned of the military organization of the Mughals, from Ian Bradley of British missions and hymns, and from Eisel Mazard and Ken Kawasaki of the Pali tradition, ancient and modern. Various written works by Wheeler Thackston and P. Oktor Skjærvø have inducted me into the history of Iranian languages. None, of course, are responsible for what I have made of what I think I have learned. Hakim Elnazarov, ably arranging the conference for the Foundation for Endangered Languages in Tajikistan in 2009, allowed me to see some of the modern reality in the valleys where Sogdian and Tajiki have long been spoken.

Other stimuli for useful thinking, largely about the future of English, have come from John Timpane at the *Philadelphia Inquirer*, Elisabeth Eaves at Forbes.com, Harry Somers and Lluís Màrquez at the European Association for Machine Translation, and Richard Ishida at the Unicode Consortium. Koos du Toit and Hermann Gilliomee at Stellenbosch, Henry Thipa and S E Ngubane at Port Elizabeth, Wynn Chao at SOAS, Salikoko Mufwene and William Wimsatt at the University of Chicago, and John Alcorn at Trinity College Hartford have all generously provided invitations, and discussions with students and faculty, that have had an impact here.

I thank Eisel Mazard for his beautiful renditions of some Southeast Asian scripts in chapter 6. I wish there had been scope to display more of them.

My wife, Jane, and daughter, Sophia, and many more in my ever-sprouting wider family, have supported and encouraged this work throughout. Other friends, notably David Nash and Jane Simpson, have drawn my attention to curiosities in odd corners of the world, as well as offering laconic comment on the passing show.

The book as a whole I dedicate to my elder brother Steve, who—as a budding scientist—was less well served by Yardley Court's idiosyncrasies. The early rivalry I had with him is the good earth from which the dogged, but I hope truthful, perversity of my thesis here has sprung. He came to the first languages I learned before I did, and shaped many of my thoughts about them before I knew a single foreign word. Like me he is a determined language learner when he chooses to be. As he crosses the brook to our seventh shared decade, his steadfast resilience and technical originality still leave me gasping. This is his tribute from "Linguistic Nic."

# Preface

The Moving Finger writes; and, having writ,
Moves on: nor all your Piety nor Wit
Shall lure it back to cancel half a Line,
Nor all your Tears wash out a Word of it.

—Edward Fitzgerald combining
Daniel, chapter 5, with Omar Khayyám

THE DECLINE OF ENGLISH, when it begins, will not seem of great moment.

International English is a lingua franca, and by its nature, a lingua franca is a language of convenience. When it ceases to be convenient—however widespread it has been—it will be dropped, without ceremony, and with little emotion. People will just not get around to learning it, not see the point, be glad to escape a previously compulsory subject at school. Only those who have a more intimate relation to it, its native speakers, may feel a sense of loss—much as French people do today when their language is passed over, or accorded no special respect. And those who are conscious of having made a serious investment to learn the language—having misread the signs of change afoot in global communication—may also feel cheated, even disappointed, when others seem to be excused from having to know it. But the world as a whole will shrug and go on transacting its business in whatever language, or combination of languages, next seems useful.

In AD 100 a Greek speaker could travel from Spain to the Hindu Kush with influential people all along his route to talk to in his own language. Likewise in AD 1300, this same compass of the world was open to Arabic. And by the Hindu Kush, that very extremity achieved by Greek and Arabic, another language had been born, in the early first millennium BC. Known as Sanskrit, it did not do too badly itself. In AD 1200, temples in Cambodia, twenty-five hundred miles to the southeast, were being inscribed with the verses of a queen, Indradevi, written in Sanskrit; by then it had already been spoken for a thousand years in most of India and Indochina. But such large-scale languages were known in the West too: in London, in AD 1600, the foremost English intellectual of his age, Francis Bacon, was claiming that if his writings had any hope of a future, it lay in their translation into Latin, a language of southern Europe then over two millennia old.

World languages are not just a modern phenomenon: they are at least as old as world empires, global trade routes, and proselytizing religions. Many, many more can be found in the world's history. But they are strangely fleeting: Greek is now restricted to the small country of its origin; Arabic (outside the mosque) is not current north of Morocco or west of Iraq; and neither Sanskrit nor Latin are in active use outside small priestly enclaves. Despite the appearance of permanence that they always offer in their heyday, global languages tend to wane after they wax. To understand the changes looming in the world's pattern of languages, in the past as in the present, one must learn to take the long view.

This book will consider the place of English in this global perspective: can it look forward to a more extended tenure than these, its august predecessors?

In the present era, the progress of English is hard to exaggerate. Recent history—a mere four centuries—has seen it expand from confinement in some out-of-the-way off-continent European islands to become the world's preferred medium for business, science, and, to some extent, even entertainment. This was not just generated by Britain's unequaled imperial expansion on every continent, and its pioneering industrial revolution, but by its ability to keep clear of the political revolutions that have derailed all its major rivals in the last three hundred years, while its greatest scion, the USA, was exploiting vast virginal resources to emerge independently as a global power and cultural icon. As a result, education in English has become an industry in its own right; and its current scope is so vast, taking it apparently so far beyond the reach of any competitor, that a scholar such as David Crystal can write, "It may be that English . . . will find itself in the service of the world community for ever"; and a business analyst such as David Graddol sees English now less as a lingua franca, more a basic educational skill, comparable to math or computing.

This book challenges this dominant, indeed commonsense, view of English, accusing it both of memory failure, and of signal lack of imagination.

In assessing the situation, we are more fortunate than the Greeks, the Romans, or the Renaissance Europeans before us: we have far wider and deeper knowledge of language histories, and so we can hope to understand, as our predecessors could not, both the predicament and its likely outcome. We can apply a long-term view, derived from the past of other world languages, not to illuminate their own present, but identify which factors will nourish and foster influence, and which poison and endanger it.

It is important to distinguish the uses of English as a lingua franca from its continuing status in many countries as a mother tongue, and this is emphasized in Part I, where we look at the role of English in recent history, and whether global English may disintegrate one day into a family of languages. But when English is seen as a lingua franca, it becomes possible to compare it with many languages that had this function to a greater or lesser extent in the past. What forces spread them, and how did they fare in the long term? Answering these questions is the purpose of Parts II and III, which aim to give some historical sense of these languages that have seemed to defy history but, ultimately, could not. Part IV then looks at language politics in the modern world and applies this historical sense to English and its competitors. What are the linguistic implications for the future in a world configured as ours is?

✥

Elitism is a weak point in the profile of every global language. Every lingua franca is a partial language—in the sense that not everyone knows it: it is a skill that needs to be acquired consciously by those who do not grow up with it, and that education often comes at a high price. Global languages divide the societies that make use of them. Inevitably, some end up mastering them, and others do not—and this often makes a decisive difference to life chances. A sense of injustice can easily be associated with a language, and the resistance this generates can easily lead, ultimately, to linguistic collapse.

Despite its proffered links with democracy and popular taste, English is no exception to this. The "English-speaking elite" is a fact of life in every continent except North America—and typically, in the present "globalized" age, its members get to make the decisions and reap whatever surpluses are available.

They are currently, then, in a strong position. But in the long term, such elites—and their languages—often fight a losing battle. By the first millennium BC, Akkadian tablet-writers had for many centuries held a monopoly of writing skills—so much so that their language was not only the Assyrian imperial standard, but also the lingua franca for diplomacy from Egypt to Elam. But they were swept aside by lower-class Aramaeans, who had been scattered across the Middle East, but had a writing system—the alphabet—that did not need a whole childhood of apprenticeship to master. Aramaic, not Akkadian, inherited the Middle East. Afterward Aramaic letters provided the foundation for every writing system in Asia.

Many more stories are to be told, of power languages that died away as the position of elites came to be resented. This was the reason that Persian retook Iran from Arabic as the language of government and literature in the ninth century AD. This was why Greek died out as a language of education in the western Roman Empire, even as Latin died out—as a language of officialdom—in the east. Elite languages are always widely resented, and it is hard to inherit the future in the teeth of such resentment. One of the most famous, and indeed recent, cases of such a fall is the ultimate loss of Latin itself. The universal language of European culture for two thousand years—a position it retained despite assaults from Greek intellectualism, Gothic Arianism, French Romance, and the German Reformation—could not nevertheless hold its own once the middle classes learned to read and write, and buy books, in the vernacular.

◇◇◇◇

An evident objection to these rumors of decline for English is the lack of any alternative. What language can the world use in future if not English? Globalization, surely, cannot be undone, and how shall nation speak unto nation—or company to company, individual to individual—in a world that has instantaneous communication links point to point from and to virtually anywhere?

Ironically, this seems to be one aspect where too rigid adherence to the traditional ground rules for language history may lead us astray. In the past, large territorial units, and widespread communication, have always called for wide-scale languages. This was as true for the Persian Empire as it was for the Roman Catholic Church, the Soviet Union, or the United States of America. But just as the print revolution changed the ground rules of communication among Europeans in the sixteenth century, so modern electronic technology is set to change the ancient need for a single lingua franca. When electronics removes the requirement for a human intermediary to interpret or translate, the frustrations of the language barrier may be overcome without any universal shared medium beyond compatible software. Recorded speeches and printed texts will become virtual media, accessible through whatever language the listener or speaker prefers. In such a world, English might have—and might need—no successor as the single language of the future mass-connected world.

But then, what role will be left for English, no longer the world's lingua franca? Here, the hints from history are more encouraging. What seems to be true is that a vast lingua franca, when it declines, will survive only if it is the official and current language of a great institution, typically a state or an organized religion. Latin, despite its vast range, died out because it had no major state to sustain it—and many more stories can be told of once great languages that went the same way—but its equals and successors live on in the parts of the world where governments call them their own: French in the states of northwestern Europe, Persian in Iran and its neighbors to the east, Russian in Russia. On this reckoning, English will have an undiminished future as the national language of many states, even when it is no longer in contention to be the world's language of choice.

This book contends that the world is moving not to English monolingualism, but a much more multilingual, diverse, and potentially incalculable future. The forces making for the spread of English will soon peak, and the sequel will be a long retrenchment, as auxiliary English comes to be less widely used, but no single language takes its place. There is no convincing reason to think that the future of English will diverge from the pattern of all the great world languages that have preceded it, once that pattern is revealed.

Besides promoting realism about the prospects of English and other languages currently dominant in the world, this book also aims to promote a new, more judicious way of looking at human affairs. An analogy may explain this. In the nineteenth century, with Lyell's revolution in geology, and Darwin's in biology, the world was induced to see the world's history measured in millions, rather than thousands, of years; to see how small, incremental changes could combine over aeons to change the balance of landforms and life-forms; and to understand how there could also be world-shattering events—such as impacts between continents, and the origin of vision—even on this inconceivably longer time-scale.

None of us live long enough to see the course of development of a global language, although we may witness some of the salient events in one, such as the revival of Hebrew in Israel, the abolition of Russian from schools in the Baltic, or the growth of competence in English in Japanese students. This inevitably gives the impression that these relatively sudden changes are where the action lies; by contrast, we are led to believe that a development that has taken centuries, such as the rise of English, is ultimate and unstoppable. These impressions are deceptive.

The world is more various than that, as we can see if only we are ready to look at the historical record. Trends, even those we have ourselves witnessed throughout our lives, may be fleeting. The outcomes of long-term developments may in an even longer term be unsustainable. What now seems barely possible, if conceivable, may one day be inevitable, even obvious. We are not at the end of history.

# PART I

# LINGUA-FRANCA PRESENT

English is the Kiswahili of the world.

—Julius Nyerere, retiring president
of Tanzania, 1990

꘎꘎꘎

# CHAPTER I

# The Edges of English

> The basis of any independent government is a national language,
> and we can no longer continue aping our former colonizers . . . I do
> know that some people will start murmuring that the time is not right
> for this decision; to hell with such people! Those who feel they
> cannot do without English can as well pack up and go.
>
> —Jomo Kenyatta, president of Kenya, 1974

THE ONLY WAY TO understand the future is to think of the past. And so it is that all pathbreakers are seen, first and foremost, in terms of their predecessors. Julius Caesar wept comparing his own deeds in his early thirties with those of Alexander the Great. Jesus, in the Gospels, was repeatedly and explicitly compared with Elijah from the Old Testament. And Newton, in lessening his own role as a discoverer of nature's laws, claimed to stand on the shoulders of giants; in this, he harked back to Bernard of Chartres, a French philosopher of the twelfth century.

Likewise the English language, now viewed throughout the world as the preeminent medium of international communication, and possessed of a truly global status that is unprecedented in human history, is accorded the recognition of being compared with Latin. To echo a host of parallel quotes, it has "become the Latin of its time / our age / the modern world / the 20th (or 21st) century / the New Millennium / the masses." But common as this metaphor is, a search on Google suggests that it has only one thirtieth of the currency of a less august equation, namely the concept of English as a *lingua franca*. English is also "the lingua franca of international scientific publications / of the global marketplace / of world communication / of an increasingly interdependent and globalized world / of business and politics from Berlin to Bangkok."

Both of these metaphors relate English to a concrete forerunner, which somehow tells us what to expect. Latin is well-known as an ancient, and largely obsolete, language in its own right. It needs no introduction here. But the original "Lingua Franca" was once a particular language too, the common contact language of the eastern Mediterranean in the first half of the second millennium, the pidgin Italian in which Greeks and Turks could talk to Frenchmen and Italians. The 1204 fall of (Greek) Constantinople to "Franks" (who were largely from Venice and other Italian cities) meant that westerners in the eastern Mediterranean became conscious of being addressed in a broken version of their own language. Byzantine Greeks knew it as *phrángika* and the westerners referred to it, perhaps ironically, as *lingua franca*.[1]

Yet in modern English the term *lingua franca* is much less likely to be felt as a concrete metaphor than *Latin* is: it has become a hackneyed, irrelevantly colorful word to mean a language of wider communication, used to bridge language barriers. It was not always this way round. In the High Middle Ages, when even little birds were said to sing "in their own Latin," Latin was rather the cliché for a universal language, while *lingua franca* was a striking new turn of phrase.

Human life has been moving noticeably faster for some centuries now, opening up possibilities that we know to be unprecedented. We have a sense, absent in the eras of Caesar, Christ, or Isaac Newton, that something really is new under the sun, that inventions are taken up and change ways of life, that innovations accumulate and move life as it is lived all over our planet into quite different pathways.

To quote just one example—striking because its elemental significance is already almost forgotten—consider the technology of horsepower. This had provided a sustained and sustainable basis for long-distance overland transport since the dawn of recorded history, in a variety of human civilizations, over at least 150 generations: one thing that the worlds of Sennacherib, Ashoka, and Alexander had in common with those of the Duke of Wellington, Simón Bolívar, and Robert E. Lee. But horsepower was superseded by combustion engines—almost simultaneously, all over the world—just five generations ago, and now (outside the races) horses play a smaller role in our economies than sniffer dogs.

If we fear the end of the world—as by and large, we always have—we now expect it not through divine retribution or some exogenous event, but as the predictable consequence of our own ungovernable behavior, through warming the atmosphere with our exhausts, poisoning or crowding out our fellow creatures, or simply unleashing a conflagration that some have devised for all.

In such an era, there is understandable skepticism about the guidance for our future that is to be derived from the study of history. The Roman historian Livy might well write, at the dawn of the first millennium AD, "This is what is beneficial and good for you in history, to be able to examine the record of every kind of event set down vividly. Here you can find for yourself and your country examples to follow, and here too ugly enterprises with ugly outcomes to avoid."

In those days, the principle of the uniformity of nature was assumed: the future would be no more marvelous than the past. But what about now, when the terms of world history have clearly changed? The past was simply on a different scale. Never before has it been possible for human beings anywhere on earth to hold conversations with each other, without ever meeting physically at all. In principle, any pair of humans at all can be in each other's presence within at most a few days. Through electronic or physical media, these people can share a large part of their cultural intake—from ephemera to literature, in oral and written language, as well as music and imagery that may involve no language at all.

That such communication is increasingly cheap and feasible makes it hard to believe that the ground rules for the life of languages, which applied to the great languages of the past, will still be true of the languages that flourish in our own era. World languages today (and notably English) have first survived to dominate on a truly global stage; then communications technology has advanced to the point where all can take part in a single speech-community, even at the level of direct conversation. The powers that be (or those that have been over the last two centuries) have projected a few languages all over the world, and electronic technologies have increased the maximum size of a dialect group to encompass the world itself.

Surely such a language has simply outgrown the constraints that made Latin shatter into a host of Romance languages across Europe in the first millennium AD? How can such frictions be relevant to a language that is today current and effective across not a continent but a globe? Yet two things the historical record shows quite invariably about the long-term future of any language: one, that it is never in the end determined by simply following the early trends that first spread a language; and two, that it is not restricted to what contemporary speakers can imagine. In the case of Latin, the spread of the language to northern and central Europe after the fifth century AD was powered by the missionary zeal of the Catholic Church. This force was quite different from the armies of the Roman Empire, which had accounted for the main early expansion of Latin out of Italy over the previous five centuries. And in the fifteenth and sixteenth centuries, just as the printing presses were making Latin books and pamphlets so much more cheaply available, and the whole world beyond the Atlantic was becoming open to discovery and exploitation by western Europe and its Latin-using elite, no one foresaw that Latin would face a sudden decline.

Yes, the limits to language growth and survival are extending: modern language communities can pulsate and interact on a global scale whereas three thousand years ago they might have been restricted to a single district. But languages are still the products, and the living media, of human societies. These, as ever, change and compete. The only trustworthy guide we have to the long-term outcomes for real languages in real societies is the historical record. In this, we are assured that the complexity of the outcome is the genuine net effect of all the social forces at play. If we can make sense of what arose from what, we may indeed find some inkling of what awaits our own very different languages in our own very different period in world history.

The past can give scale, since it is far enough distant for its shape to have fallen into perspective: the figures that stand out with a magnitude that still looks tall must have been great indeed. The past also has the advantage of time depth, so that long-term effects can be traced, identified, and weighed against one another. Caesar's contemporaries were better advised to compare him with Alexander the Great, three centuries before, than with his actual political opponent (and peer) Pompey. They could not know the dynasties that would claim descent from Caesar, whose survival and glory would go on to make his name synonymous with *emperor* in languages yet unknown to any Roman;* but Alexander's continuing fame could at least have shown them what it was to found a legend, and a vast, apparently permanent, extension to a war-built empire.

By examining the historical record of many languages, we can get a feel

---

* Gothic and Germanic *kaisar* (e.g., German *Kaiser*); Slavic *cĕsari* (giving, e.g., Russian *tsar*); Lithuanian *ciesorius*; Armenian *gaysr*.

for the kinds of forces that shape the long-term future of all large-scale languages used internationally, what we usually call a lingua-franca.*

English is so familiar to its mother tongue speakers, a vast community who largely speak nothing else, that it hardly seems a distinct language at all. Since it is also well-known to be used all round the world, the natural tendency is to take it for granted, to expect that it will be available and accepted as a default means of expression for whatever might need saying. Hence the irate tourist's despairing shout of "Don't you speak *English*?" when this expectation is disappointed. It's nothing fancy to know English; indeed (as Cicero once said of Latin[2]) it is not so much creditable to know it as it is a disgrace not to. When the "ordinary language" philosophers of the 1950s and '60s talked about "ordinary language," this was the language that they quoted and argued from, or more specifically the literate British variety of it that they themselves spoke. There is a sense that speaking English is the least one can do, and for native speakers to learn another language is to give themselves airs; hence the urban myth of the preacher in Texas truculently claiming that English had been "good enough for Jesus."

This kind of presumption is not peculiar to English; indeed it has been characteristic of speakers of widely spoken and respected lingua-francas down the ages. Latin is a good example. Romans of the Classical era had used the adverb *latine* 'in Latin' to mean 'speaking quite plainly'. To an early language enthusiast such as Pliny the Elder, it seemed that Latin's common currency had "united in conversation the wild, discordant tongues of so many peoples," allowing Rome to give them nothing less than common *humanitas* itself.[3] Sometime after that, and for most of the first Christian millennium,

---

* Now is the time to set some ground rules for our use of this key word, or at least its spelling. The word's etymology is confused: it seems to be a retranslation of some eastern-Mediterranean term for 'language of the Franks', but into what—Italian, the commercial vernacular, or Latin, the learned universal? It makes no difference until we try putting it into the plural: but should that be *lingue franche* or *linguae francae*? For the latter, there are even competing pronunciations: *liŋgwai fraŋkai* versus *liŋgwī fransī*. Even if we stick chastely to English, *lingua francas* looks wrong, with the plural *s* attached only to the last word of what is a very un-English-looking phrase. My solution (when the word is a technical term of linguistics, not a proper name) is to write it always with a hyphen: *lingua-franca*, plural *lingua-francas*. For me, this settles all unease, both in spelling and in pronunciation.

Latin was the only language in which the Bible and the Church Fathers' writings were available to western Europe. This brute monolingualism in our early tradition is especially striking since most of these writings had been originated in some other language (usually Greek or Hebrew); and this "good enough" monolingualism reigned even among scholars of the era, despite the critical importance in western Christianity of verbal disputes based on these key texts. At the turn of the thirteenth century Dante Alighieri himself had characterized the Latin taught at school as "nothing but a kind of sameness of speech unalterable for diverse times and places."[4] So speakers of Latin too once found it difficult to take other languages seriously as competitors to it for conveying serious content.

However, monolingualism poses a problem. Goethe once wisely remarked, "He who is not acquainted with foreign languages has no knowledge of his own."[5] But the success of English since Goethe's time has driven out much of the opportunity for such prior acquaintances, and the kind of orientation in time and space that they could give. In practical terms, the English-reading world, as represented by its publishers, seems to presume that there is no other world, as evidenced by the fact that translations into English make up every year just 2–3 percent of the world's translated texts, a rate that has halved in the last three years.[6] Note that this disregard for other languages' cultures is not mutual: as source language, English consistently represents the lion's share of all translations published (60–70 percent in Europe, the biggest translation market); i.e. twice as many as all the other source languages put together.

There is little point in trying to treat English as "just another language" since, quite unlike any other language in our era at least, anyone who wants to participate directly in business beyond the nation will have to use it or come to terms with it. This status may be accepted by its speakers smugly, as if it reflected some attractive values that have powered its advance, or it may engender concern stemming from two quite opposite fears, either that its acceptance has not gone far enough—even in their home country not all residents might speak it—or that its advance is relentless and may in time drive out the use of all other languages, together (implicitly) with the cultural values and knowledge that they convey. Whatever the reaction, it is hard to lay aside emotion and simply reflect.

How can we be decentered from our anglophone assumptions? How to get a disinterested sense of the particular profile of English as a global lingua-franca when we know it so well and have none other with which to compare it? Later in this book, we shall enhance our sense of what English's lingua-franca peers have been like; but inevitably, those languages flourished and spread in past ages, when the world and its style of connectedness were very different. Here at the outset we are still trapped in an English-speaking bubble: we know that, like no other language, in the modern world it seems to be everywhere, but we lack independent tools to take its measure. What is a prior, and involuntary, commitment to English doing to our understanding of the world? Could there have been a world like the present but without English? How is English to be rated in its solitary glory as world lingua-franca? "How shall we extol thee, who are born of thee?" Can we conceive a future where the world as we know it might go on without English? If not, does that mean it is impossible or just unforeseeable?

We are not talking about logical possibilities and necessities here. After all, English is a human language, outwardly simple and originally quite humble, with a past career and pathways of historical spread that are well-known and have, besides, been fairly short. Its origin is not, like that of Chinese, Sanskrit, or Arabic, buried in the sands of time, but datable to a few centuries before and after AD 900 in an island off the Atlantic coast of Europe, when the main settlement pattern of the Continent had already been set. It neither attracts nor tolerates adoring claims, unlike some of those languages, that it might hold some sacred value in its use, or in its expressive power. Nonetheless, the striking extremity of its progress so far tends to undercut any forebodings of future limits and brings to mind cosmic analyses, or analogies. "*The limits of my language* signify the limits of my world," wrote Ludwig Wittgenstein in 1921 (in German—though with a parallel English translation).[7] True, English is coming close to involving itself in all the world's business, yet there would be no paradox of Wittgensteinian self-reference, or logical impossibility, in referring in English to the boundaries of its world role. It is just difficult to pin them down. But perhaps we can take the hint from Wittgenstein's philosophy and look for facts that have *shown* effective constraints on its spread, even if it would have been difficult to *state* those limits in advance, from within an English-language mind-set.

∞∞∞

If we consider English historically, as the language of Anglo-American colonialism and commerce—clearly the initial drivers of its spread round the world—what events in its career look intrinsically exceptional or irregular? Are there peoples by whom English seems to have been gratuitously rejected? Or are there others to whom it has passed unexpectedly, as if following unseen contours of language gravity? What has perturbed the even flow of English as it has spread along with the interests of its speaker communities, making it seem to have a life of its own, or rather a life constrained and defined by interests and activities expressed in other languages?

Looking round the world for places where English is notable for its rarity, our gaze first lights on three countries that had once hosted massive use of the language, since they were colonies within the British Empire, but have since moved to promote other languages in its place. They are distributed round the Indian Ocean: Malaysia in the east, Śri Lanka centrally, and Tanzania in the west. Each of these countries had multiple language communities when the British took over, and so in each of them English might have been considered able to go on playing a convenient, almost natural, role as a neutral lingua-franca for the whole country.

This, after all, is what has been decreed for many of the closest neighbors of these countries, such as Brunei, India, and the African countries Zambia, Malawi, Uganda, and Kenya. The value of English in all these countries has been as a lingua-franca, first to secure access to the wider world where it is a common currency, but often also to reconcile differences between different mother tongue groups, without obvious favoritism.

In the east, even though Brunei takes the Malay language as one of its national pillars (with its slogan *Melayu Islam Beraja* 'Malay—Islam—Monarchy'), it chooses to educate its people mostly in English. In fact Malay is the mother tongue for a large majority (just over 70 percent), including all the political elite, and it is officially the national language; so there would have been little call for English as a compromise. In fact, the option taken is defended as "primarily instrumental in nature," "since a small country could not afford to isolate itself from the rest of the world." Yet evidently the relations in view were primarily economic, and with a very much wider world than Southeast Asia: after all, the close neighbors, Malaysia and Indonesia, both use Malay.[8] Of these, Indonesia was a Dutch, not a British, colony, but Malaysia was on a par with Brunei. Why has it come to a different conclusion about the role of English?

In Malaysia, unlike Brunei, a significant dispute came from other powerful groups than the Malays, namely the Chinese (26 percent) and the Indians, mostly Tamils (7 percent). In the negotiations leading up to independence (achieved in 1957), these groups would have approved the choice of English as a neutral compromise. But precisely because of this significant difference, the dominant Malay majority felt the need to assert a greater right, claiming Malay not English as the official language. Crucially, this established a link with the history of the region, with the indigenous empires based on Palembang and Malacca long before the advent of British colonialism (and conveniently, before so many Chinese and Tamils arrived to trade and make their living in what is now Malaysia). *Bahasa jiwa bangsa*, as they liked to claim: 'Language is the soul of the nation'.* The deal was done with the non-Malay groups via a concession in a different direction, allowing (for the first time) all resident noncitizens to achieve full citizenship even if they could not pass a test in Malay.

Language has remained an issue ever since, especially in determining the syllabus of school education. Malay has spread in official spheres, notably administration and the courts. Parliament proceedings switched from English to Malay in 1967, and the last simultaneous interpreters were withdrawn in 1980. Malay also spread as the language of instruction in the schools. Though multifarious concessions to education in other languages have been made in this multilingual country (including Arabic, as well as Mandarin Chinese and Tamil), few of them were made to English until 2003. Then, in response to fears that Malaysians were losing a major potential asset for international and scientific discourse, it was reintroduced as a language of instruction for mathematics and science. This decision is still controversial and could be repealed, since many feel that the quality of actual instruction has declined as a result.[9]

Overall, Malaysia has shown that the role of English in national life, in a nation where it was always a minority language for an elite, can quite quickly be diminished—say, over two generations—by a consistent government policy. Nationalism, and a determination to make a new start after colonial domination, can be sufficient motives. A price will be paid, at least over the transition period, in terms of language facility. "But what," the Malaysians asked, "would using English *say* about us as a nation?"

Secondly, at the center of the Indian Ocean coastline, the policies of

---

* This is a simple sentence in Malay, but all its words are derived from Sanskrit: *bhāṣā jīvanam vaṃśaḥ* 'speech-life-stock'. This reflects the influence of Indian traders and adventurers in the early first millennium AD. Malay's roots are ancient, but they are not purely indigenous.

India stand in contrast to those of Sri Lanka: English (with some reluctance) affirmed versus English denied.

India's constitution divides the country up into states primarily on the basis of the official local languages, called "scheduled languages." There are currently eighteen of these. Only one of them, Hindi, is also the official language of the country as a whole. It is the language of nine states in the north as well as the capital territory, Delhi. It is, however, partnered by English as "subsidiary official" language for the whole country. According to the constitution of 1950, English was going to be dropped by 1965 in favor of universal Hindi. But this was blocked by the southern states and West Bengal—essentially the non-Hindi-using states—so the use and official status of English has continued. The Official Languages Act of 1963 guarantees that the use of English cannot be ended until a law abolishing it is passed by the legislature of every state that has not adopted Hindi as its official language, and also by each house of the Indian Parliament. At the same time, in an interesting curiosity, a constitutional requirement of India is that every law be drafted exclusively in English, though every law must also have a non-authoritative translation into Hindi. English in India, then, continues its official status as a means of maintaining an uneasy balance between the linguistic interests of the Hindi and non-Hindi states; meanwhile in practice, its use is ubiquitous in graduate-level communication throughout the country.

To the south, in Sri Lanka (formerly known as Ceylon),[10] a more radical decision was made in 1956, with the passing of the Sinhala Only Act, the principal electoral commitment of the Sri Lanka Freedom Party under Solomon Bandaranaike, which swept to power in that year. The act mandated Sinhala as the sole official language of the country, replacing English in that role. In British Ceylon, Tamils (some 18 percent) had benefited from their higher levels of education and played a disproportionate role in the colony's civil service, which functioned in English. The Sinhala-speaking majority (74 percent) had tolerated this for the first eight years of independence, but then used their electoral majority to strike at its root: the Tamils had just done too well out of an English-dominated system for English to be seen as neutral. Sure enough, by 1970 the civil service was largely staffed by Sinhala speakers. But a major rift had been created in Sri Lankan society, and a bloody civil war resulted, which lasted from 1973 to 2009, despite the fact that since 1987 Tamil had been recognized as a national and official language on a par with Sinhala, and English was even reintroduced as a "link language."* It was much too late when quite literally battle lines had been drawn.

Sri Lanka shows that a foreign lingua-franca such as English has no magic to create a neutral medium of communication for competing language communities within a state if one group becomes too closely associated with it. The ills of British colonial policy can live on after the end of empire, and the English language may bear the resulting stigma. Having been seen by the Sinhala speakers as a proxy for Tamil domination, English was ruled out as an acceptable official language. But then no practical compromise was left between Sinhala speakers fearing submergence beneath a Tamil community with much of south India behind it, and Tamil speakers resenting discrimination that was calculated to demean them in this one island. An association with past injustice can create feelings of deep resentment for a lingua-franca, and such baleful associations can stick.

Completing this triptych on its western side, we turn to eastern Africa.[11] In the British colonial states here, there has been, as almost everywhere else in the continent, a profound mismatch between linguistic boundaries and national frontiers. This is because the nation-states derive ultimately from competing European land grabs in the nineteenth century "scramble for Africa," irrespective of social alliances that might have arisen among African tribes. With far more languages than states, attempting to pick out one majority language within a country and declaring it the national language is dangerously divisive. Some kind of lingua-franca—with sufficient development of its vocabulary to serve all the needs of a modern state—has been needed, and the natural choice by default in a former British colony was English. This explains the official language situations in Zambia, Malawi, Uganda, and Kenya, although in all these countries Swahili has also been widely used.

In the area that became Tanzania, however, this Swahili language (named from Arabic *sawāḥil* 'coasts', and referring to itself as *kiSwahili*) had spread particularly widely as a lingua-franca, originally from the coastal region round Zanzibar. It had been picked up and reinforced by European (mainly German) missionaries' schools in the nineteenth century and carried on under British administration after 1918. Essentially, it was the de facto

---

* Even then, passions still extended beyond the community mother tongues. In 1990 the *Daily News* saw fit to comment: "English has always been a social killer, shedding no blood but maiming the many who did not have it."

lingua-franca in the country that had preceded the British Empire's widespread introduction of English. Ever since the country became an independent and united state (over the period 1961–64), its first president, Julius Nyerere, had been keen to promote it as the national language, and an effective lingua-franca for all Tanzanians, bridging the gaps among the more than a hundred languages they spoke with a distinctively African medium that avoided any recourse to the colonial language English.* Luckily for Swahili, in Tanzania there was no tribe or tribes much larger or more dominant than the others, as the Luo or Kikuyu were and are in Kenya, or the Baganda in Uganda. Such groups have languages that tend to provide an unofficial, but competing, African lingua-franca for some parts of the country and so make the use of English seem desirable to level the playing field in the country as a whole. The ancestral speakers of Swahili in Tanzania, the WaSwahili, have not been contenders for domination, and so their language was uncontested as a national resource. Tanzania extended the use of Swahili in primary schools from four to seven years in 1967, and many have suggested that it should be used at more advanced levels too. But hitherto, the government has not opted to replace English with Swahili in secondary schools or colleges.

Tanzania, therefore, unlike its neighbors, has given English no official status. The reason, apparently, is that only here was it practically and politically possible to do so, giving the country a single linguistic medium, and an African one at that, without causing serious social imbalances among the tribes that make up the country. To do this, Tanzania's government rejected the status quo at independence, when English had already been used for a couple of generations as the official language of the state.

These three cases of Malaysia, Sri Lanka, and Tanzania, with their different circumstances, suggest that—despite its foreseen and well-known practical benefits—English must have faced considerable challenges to be retained as any official language in any country where it is not the mother tongue. Its historical associations with British colonial power mean that it will be used where necessary or useful, but avoided wherever possible. The Malays, even though they had to negotiate with sizable and influential

---

* This promotion as a lingua-franca has required Tanzania to efface Swahili's special links with its historical native speakers in the coastal region round Zanzibar, the WaSwahili, particularly their links with Islam. This denial of any cultural overlay to a language is one mark of an established lingua-franca.

minorities within Malaysia, preferred to substitute their own language for it; the Sinhala found the advantages it was giving to the Tamil minority unacceptable, and when they had the power to do so, abolished it, regardless of consequences;* the Tanzanians had the easiest time of it, being spared the need for negotiation, given the absence of any heavyweight minorities. But all three went out of their way to displace English as their official language. It may be accepted, but is seldom embraced.

◇◇◇◇

In many places English has spread effectively when, a priori, one might have expected it to have no right to be there. In the most extreme case, these will be places with no historical—usually colonial—connection with English speakers, yet the demand for the language as an adjunct to the community has proved irresistible, places where the use of English was demanded as a "one-way option" or a "no-brainer": a language choice that "went without saying," so to speak.

Nowadays, it is quite difficult to find a part of the world with no historical connection with English-speaking powers, but a good candidate would be Mongolia, 1.5 million square kilometers sandwiched between Russian Siberia and Chinese "Inner Mongolia." This has never been part of any UK or U.S. sphere of influence, at any time in its history. Nevertheless, in the 1990s the attempt was being made to retrain half of its Russian-language teachers to be competent in English; and in 2004 its prime minister, Tsakhia Elbegdorj (admittedly, a Harvard-educated man), announced that English would be substituted for Russian as the first foreign language in Mongolian schools. The explicit motivation of the government is economic, with aspirations to make Ulan Bator, the capital, some kind of center for outsourcing and call-center services, to be modeled on Singapore or India's Bangalore.[12]

It remains to be seen if the aspirations can be translated into reality, but the idea is now rife that English is the natural choice for those seeking access to the world's wealth. For such wealth seekers, there are some good omens.

Singapore itself, though founded by the British in 1819, has a population 77 percent Chinese, the majority of the rest being speakers of Malay (14

---

* Unfortunately, they failed to negotiate this change, causing a massive reaction from the losers, with a dreadful ultimate cost to all concerned.

percent) and Tamil (up to 8 percent). English had always been recognized along with Chinese, Malay, and Tamil as an official language, but after Singapore achieved independence in 1959, the prime minister, Lee Kwan Yew, placed much greater emphasis on English than Mandarin (though personally he liked to promote them both). In that era China was not among the world's fastest-growing economies, and even if overseas Chinese were already a massive reservoir of capital, his strategy was aggressively to build the Singapore market in the short and medium terms, to be part of a U.S.-dominated world economy. In 1966 compulsory bilingual education in English was introduced at the primary level, and in 1969 at the secondary. The early results in building widespread competence in English had been disappointing, but then Singapore had been starting from a low base: at independence no more than a quarter had been able to understand it.[13] By 1975, more than 87 percent of 15-to-20-year-olds claimed to have this skill, even if the government's more rigorous tests assessed that its bilingual policy "had not been universally effective," with under 40 percent of students attaining the minimum level. The official response was to focus education with even more determination on English, dropping the other languages for the weaker students. English has uncompromisingly been adopted as the sole working language of government, administration, and the judiciary. This push appears to have been successful and has even extended to the increasing use of English in Singaporean homes, as it were a foster mother tongue. This new domestic use seems to have come largely at the expense of Chinese.[14]

English in this case has succeeded as a language of compromise among different native-language groups, as well as a spearhead for the advance of Singaporean international business. Unlike in Malaysia, no concessions were needed to a Malay-speaking majority, nor (unlike in Sri Lanka) was English denied to a minority who seemed to have gained by their history a natural advantage in using it. If anything, the use of English seems like a gratuitous concession made by the Chinese majority to guarantee a level playing field between them and the Malay and Indian minorities: English, after all, is equally foreign for all. That Singapore was founded ex nihilo by British imperial enterprise perhaps allays just a little the indignity of using a language derived from the city-state's colonial past.

To the east, in the Philippines, the use of English has also spread as a clear heir of imperialism—in this case, for once, the imperialists being the Yankees who took control of the colony from Spain in 1898. This is something of a surprise too, in that the USA has been able to spread its language over the turbulent twentieth century, despite an intervening Japanese occupation (1942–45)—which proved well able to dissipate Dutch influence in the neighboring East Indies—and in a place where the Spanish empire had already ruled unopposed for more than three centuries—beginning in the latter half of the sixteenth century, before English had ever been heard in North America.

In fact, the Spanish had spread their language in the Philippines very little. Although Manila, consistently the capital, was founded in 1572, less than 3 percent of Filipinos came to speak Spanish in the first three centuries; all education up to that point had been in the hands of the monastic orders of the Roman Catholic Church, who outside the capital used local languages. Although there were vast numbers of these, they tended to be closely related, and three lingua-francas that predated Spanish rule (Ilocano, Tagalog, and Cebuano, from north to south) had made contact tractable. In the last four decades of the nineteenth century, a new policy emanating from Madrid had encouraged the spread of Spanish, with primary schools being opened throughout the islands (though limited by inadequate financial provision). Scions of rich families (especially Chinese mestizos) were educated in Spain and returned as *ilustrados*, i.e. 'the enlightened', primed with all sorts of inconvenient liberal political ideas. It was these ideas that led to the armed revolt in 1896, which unsettled Spanish control, a revolt that was crucially aided, then crushed, by intervention from the USA, which was at war with Spain at the time. By 1902, the whole country was in U.S. hands, and the last resistance had died out by 1906.[15]

The USA, plunged into controversy from the outset about the ethics of becoming an imperial power like all the European powers of which it so disapproved, was determined to provide widespread education within its new colony, even (and in the Philippines, for the first time) to the masses. Spanish and the various Filipino languages were soon rejected as media for the new schools, since so few Filipinos were found to speak Spanish and there was little preexisting literacy in any other language. English was introduced as the natural alternative, which at least meant that volunteer teachers from the USA (called Thomasites, since the first shipload arrived on U.S. army transport *Thomas*) could directly be employed. An American clergyman was writing in 1905 that the Thomasites could "give the children an healthy outlook towards life . . . and explain to them the principles of hygiene and sanitation," and that more Filipinos spoke English after three years with American teachers than spoke Spanish after three hundred years with Spaniards.[16]

In general, the only resistance to the new education came from the pre-existing class of *ilustrados*, as well as the priests, who used their influence to rebut American secularism and discouraged school attendance in country districts. But when the United States brought in English-speaking Catholic priests from North America to work in the elite schools, and also the rural areas, even they were won over. Learning English turned out to be quite compatible with Catholic devotions. By 1923, all schools, even those for the elite in Manila, were working in English. The American spirit, attractive because more inclusive than the Spanish tradition, won them over. By the 1918 census, 28 percent of those already literate said they could read English. But twenty-one years later, just four decades after the advent of the Americans, 26.3 percent of the population as a whole claimed to speak English; by now, it was overall the country's most widespread single language.

As the memory of Spanish faded, however, a new indigenous lingua-franca was being proposed. The Philippines had been promised independence since the beginning of the U.S. takeover, but the Republican administrations that dominated the early decades of the twentieth century in the USA had kept deferring the prospect. This changed with the election of Franklin D. Roosevelt; on November 15, 1935, the Philippines were constituted a commonwealth, with independence promised by 1946. (The constitutional convention had still conducted its proceedings in Spanish.) Its new president, Manuel Quezón, deliberately chose Tagalog from among the indigenous languages of the Philippines to act as a new national language. This was the vernacular of the Manila region, and lingua-franca of southern Luzon island, and always the most prominent of the country's indigenous languages.* (It had, for example, been the first to be described in a missionary grammar, Fray Francisco de San José's *Arte y reglas de la Lengua Tagala*, published in Bataan as early as 1610.) Tagalog was soon introduced into the school system as a subject and has grown in coverage ever since. From 1939 English had to share the primary-school curriculum with Tagalog, and other vernacular languages were taught at the primary level too. Emphasis on English re-

---

* Tagalog was not clearly more populous than Cebuano, the main lingua-franca of the southern islands, centered on Mindanao, and Tagalog's use has continued to be resisted in the south. In this, its fate has been typical of a language selected to be the preeminent official language in a recently formed multilingual state in postcolonial Asia or Africa.

mained stronger in expensive private schools, and so a good command of English became a mark of the Filipino social elite, as it is to this day.

The educational system was disrupted by the Japanese occupation of 1942–45, but although the Japanese attempted to ingratiate themselves as anticolonial by banning Spanish and declaring Tagalog the sole national language, they were actually compelled to communicate with the population largely through English. The Japanese found little anti-American sentiment on which to build solidarity, and after the war the main problem for the resurgence of English lay not in reestablishing the credibility of Americans, but in overcoming the damage that had been done to libraries, and the broken succession of language acquisition from native speakers. National independence was conceded by the USA, as promised, in 1946; yet a resurgence in enthusiasm for English occurred over the next three decades, Americans collaborating again with Filipinos to rebuild their school system. This was not dogmatically English-based. Among other measures recommended from 1958 to 1974 was that the first two grades in primary schools should be in vernacular languages. Popularity of English, and competence in it, soared over this period, while Tagalog was mired in controversy, on how to define an appropriate standard for it, and over its right to be the national language at all.

Political pressure for the Philippines to have its own language, however, finally won out, through a combination of popular nationalism, and unease, outside elite circles, at having to rely on the metropolitan—if not exactly foreign—language English. Tagalog found its feet in the end, and after two rebrandings,* at last with an inclusive "no worries" approach to loan vocabulary, it became accepted as an authentically indigenous national language. A bilingual program of school education with a far greater role for Tagalog was introduced in the schools from 1974 to 1982. As a result, English has found itself fighting a losing battle to retain its substantive identity on Filipino lips, as more and more it is used to talk not to English speakers, but to other Filipinos familiar with urban Tagalog, and impatient of standardized English. The languages once defined and propagated, fairly clearly, by the school and university system have been subverted by popular use of a mixed

---

* In 1961 it was given the name *Pilipino*, basically the national adjective pronounced in Tagalog phonology: the message was it was national, but with a Tagalog flavor. Then in 1973, it was renamed *Filipino*, showing by its *F* that it would not be restricted by the constraints of Tagalog, but was universally Philippine.

language, Taglish, which combines elements of Tagalog and English, and many ingrained loans from Spanish.

The career of English to date in the Philippines throws into relief some more aspects of English as a potential lingua-franca for the world. Far more than Spanish ever could, it can offer the Filipinos an open door to contact with the wider world. Filipinos can even accept this language while rejecting the USA's sovereignty. But only a restricted elite in the Philippines (or any other foreign country) can truly keep in touch with this kind of authentic English; if the language is accepted fully as a national language, it will have to coexist with other kinds of national language, as well as local vernacular, in a way that will make sense in this part of the world.

This need to come to terms with the social realities of alien peoples, and the other languages they may use, is a real limit to the English language, especially now that it has become detached from the zone controlled by English speakers. The linguistic standard that by and large fits the United Kingdom, and its settlement colonies from the USA to New Zealand, cannot accommodate a linguistically fluid situation such as that of the Philippines. People whose first language is not English, in trying to make the language their own, will subvert and violate this standard. This constraint on the effective spread of English is independent of, and additional to, the hang-ups that many ex-colonies of the United Kingdom feel about relying on a language derived from their former colonial masters. The Philippines, as we have seen, had rather little trouble allying itself with a heritage from the USA, as its model and kindly schoolmaster, if not as its master and commander. But the Filipinos still cannot hold on to their English, at least if they try to integrate it into their own linguistic and social realities.

In our terms, the Philippines has been able to accept English as a lingua-franca, but not as a mother tongue. The Philippines' long-term link with the English language will remain precarious. There is a will to maintain it as a channel of communication with global culture beyond the Philippine islands; but it is less and less acceptable—unless merged into the melting pot of indigenous Philippine expression—as a means of social interaction among Filipinos.

◊◊◊

A completely different instance of surprising take-up of the English language is its advance as the principal lingua-franca within the European

Union (EU). This has happened since the 1950s, and especially over the past thirty years since the British entry to this organization in 1973. The progress has been paradoxical because historically English had no pretensions, or entrenched position, as a lingua-franca for Europe.

Although clearly a European language, English had, until the twentieth century, always been purely an offshore phenomenon. Besides the British Isles, where it originated on one island after the fifth century AD and spread into the other islands through Norman colonial activity from the twelfth, English was only spoken on the margins of Europe, in the isolated Mediterranean outposts of Gibraltar (since 1704), Minorca (1708–1802), Malta (1800–1964), and Cyprus (1878–1960). All the while, it was gaining a much bigger speaker community on other continents. But it was never spoken in any substantial enclave of Europe, even from the eleventh to fourteenth centuries when Norman and Angevin kings with a base in England ruled much of France.

The lingua-franca of western and central Europe, in a tradition that goes back to the beginning of the Christian era, had been Latin. For fifteen hundred years this had largely been unchanged because Latin was handed down through a common school curriculum for the elite. After the sixteenth century, though, this role was more and more filled by the modern language French, reflecting the long-standing prestige of the French state in Europe as a whole.* After the French Revolution, however, France's political dominance and its cultural influence were increasingly challenged by Prussia and Great Britain. Nevertheless, the leading political/commercial role of the French language survived for another century. Only with the Treaty of Versailles (1919), when Great Britain and especially the USA played the key roles as victorious powers in Europe, was English first asserted as an official diplomatic language on a par with French.

At the same time the global dominance of the British, and soon the U.S., economies were beginning to speak for themselves in Europe too. English

---

* Spain, a comparable power, was also making more use of its vernacular in the same period. It had dependencies (due to Hapsburg inheritance) in northern and central Europe. But Spanish was not really used by non-Spaniards outside the Iberian Peninsula, despite the well-known quip of Charles V, who reigned 1516–56. In its longest form, it runs: "I speak Latin with God, Italian with musicians, Spanish with the troops, German with lackeys, French with ladies, and English with my horse." This sounds like an extended piece of irony, a telling comment on the powers who spoke these tongues.

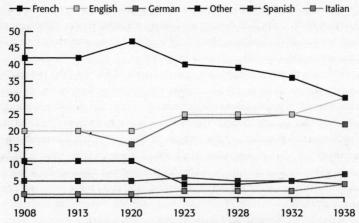

*Foreign languages in European schools 1908–38. Percent of foreign language teaching hours. (Adapted using data from* Post-Imperial English *by Joshua A. Fishman, Andrew W. Conrad, and Alma Rubal-Lopez [Verlag Walter de Gruyter])*

began to predominate among foreign languages studied in western Europe. The accompanying chart shows the changing balance of European schools' time devoted to studying different foreign languages in the period 1908–38 (though it excludes Austria-Hungary and Russia). English added over 50 percent to its classroom time in the period, moving from parity with German to parity with French. (After World War II it went on to vastly exceed them both.) Crucial turning points came in 1937, when German schools switched from French to English as their first foreign language for study; and just after World War II, when a number of Nordic countries downgraded German from first place in their school curricula and put English in its place.[17]

Europe's traditional choices among various lingua-francas had long indicated its structuring into political regions. But they have died away in the last fifty years. Thus the western Mediterranean from Portugal to Italy, traditionally the playground of French foreign policy, had been accessible in French, while the eastern shores and islands, through the commercial influence of the Venetians and Genoese, had been approached in Italian (or its creolized version, Lingua Franca itself). Inland, the age-old presence of the Orthodox faith and Greek merchants, which went back to the Byzantine

Empire, had kept Greek as a widespread language of the Balkans.* In the north and east of Europe, including Scandinavia, the Baltic, and much of central Europe, it was German that had been current, its familiarity derived from various sources. These included the Hanseatic League, based in Lübeck, which had dominated Baltic and North Sea trade from the thirteenth century for over three hundred years; the Teutonic Knights in much the same period of the Baltic states, bringing German monks to convert the people, and settlers to control territory; and of course the Holy Roman and later Austrian empires, German-speaking powers that had controlled the interior since the beginning of the second millennium. After World War II, there was a major linguistic projection of Russian onto the states of eastern Europe; but this is already dissipating—to the benefit of English—after only fifty years.

By contrast with the small number of these historical lingua-francas, Europe has remained seriously rich in mother tongues. Some sixty languages are spoken in the area of the present European Union. Of these, twenty-three are "official," a status granted not by the EU but by member states: an official language is one that some acceding state has declared to have this status within its own borders.† These become thereby "working languages" of the EU. Official communications with EU institutions can be conducted in any of these languages. Regulations have to be drafted in all these languages, and so does the *Official Journal*. In practice, however, only a small number of these languages are used for EU business as effective lingua-francas.

This narrowing down of languages is no coincidence. In fact, the paradox has emerged that as the number of languages current in the EU has increased—so that participants are drawn from ever wider language backgrounds—the number of real lingua-francas in use among their speakers has actually diminished. When the count of official languages was at its

---

* Curiously, the Ottoman Empire only disseminated Turkish in small pockets, notably creating the Gagauz community of modern Moldova.

† These are (in order of speaker numbers in Europe) German, French, English, Italian, Polish, Spanish, Rumanian, Dutch, Hungarian, Czech, Portuguese, Greek, Bulgarian, Swedish, Danish, Slovak, Finnish, Lithuanian, Slovene, Latvian, Estonian, Maltese, and Irish. In addition, three minority languages of Spain (Catalan, Gallego, and Basque) have been given semiofficial status: representations to the EU can be made and answered in them, but the costs of doing so (through Spanish translation) are undertaken by the Spanish government.

initial four (from 1951 to 1972), two languages were used, in practice, for internal discussion within the community, namely French and German. When the number of languages increased to six in 1973, English was added, and for a time three languages were in practical use. However, there was soon pressure to use less German, even though this has throughout remained the language with the greatest population of native speakers in the EU.

Other states (and languages) have since been added, first at moderate speed, growing the total to seven (in 1981), nine (in 1986) and twelve (in 1995), but then meteorically (mostly through the sudden access of much of eastern Europe), to twenty (in 2004) and then to twenty-three (in 2007). As the community has grown, the use of French too has become disputed. Although the recently acceded countries, mostly from central and eastern Europe, might have been expected to be more familiar with the use of German, or indeed Russian, in practice they seem to prefer to use English; and with more and more target languages requiring translation into them, there is a premium on reducing the number of languages from which the translation is done. The result has been increasing pressure to use English, and English only, as a common medium. Meanwhile, the other established lingua-francas of the Continent's regions (including French and German, but also Spanish, Italian, and Russian) have enjoyed no special status as such, although it is recognized that they are the languages that—besides English—are most widely understood.*

German is the native language of 18 percent of the EU population, but has been acquired as a lingua-franca by another 14 percent. By the same measure, French manages only 12 and 14 percent. English weighs in at 13 percent native speakers, but a massive 38 percent of lingua-franca speakers.[18] In the light of this apparent injustice to German, which holds as it were "the people's plurality" in the EU, it might be thought that speaker numbers

---

* Pragmatically, it might also be noted that, in the states where these are sole national languages (with the honorable exception of German), people are less likely to be competent in any other language: their mother tongue speakers are less likely than other Europeans to have access to any other lingua-franca. In a 2005 survey of the then twenty-five European member states' degree of conversational competence in at least one foreign language, the bottom seven places are held by France (51%), Spain (44%), Portugal (42%), Hungary (42%), Italy (41%), United Kingdom (38%), and Ireland (34%). So, as hotbeds of monolingualism, only Portugal and Hungary compete with the traditional lingua-franca-providing countries. The top score (99%) is for Luxembourg, and the median (69%) gained by Finland. (Eurobarometer 2006, 9)

outside the EU—i.e. global ranking—is what determines the status of languages within it. Why, after all, have all those Europeans chosen to acquire enough English to use it as a lingua-franca, rather than German?

But in the event, global ranking is a poor predictor of European language status. Both Spanish and Portuguese have (through their former colonies in Latin America) global speaker populations that, like English, vastly outnumber French and German worldwide; yet they are not accorded any special status. Only English cashes in its global standing for enhanced popularity within Europe. Why is this?

The rise of English to preeminence among official languages at the EU must be attributed above all to the global prestige of its speakers; that is to say, the perceived dominance of the United Kingdom and USA in both economic and later political power, as well as technologies of production and communication, clearly established by the end of the nineteenth century. Some economic figures are eloquent here. In the 150 years from 1750 to 1900, as shown on the chart on page 27, France, the economic pacemaker of the European Middle Ages, which had built French as the language of world diplomacy, almost doubled its share of world manufacturing, going from 4 to 7 percent, while the German-speaking powers, Germany and Austria-Hungary, taken together trebled from 6 to 18 percent. This was testimony to the force of colonialism and the industrial revolution, both emanating from Europe.* But these growth figures pale in comparison with those of the English-speaking powers. In the same period, the United Kingdom's share multiplied over ten times, from 2 to 23 percent (before falling off a little), while that of the USA grew even more massively, from 0.1 to 24 percent. When asked in 1898 for the defining event of his times, the former German chancellor Otto von Bismarck had famously replied, "North America speaks English."

But why should so many others then strive to take up the language, even if trying to emulate its speakers' economic success? Fundamental is the role of business, specifically the traders who wished to deal with the English-speaking world. It is a cliché that business is conducted in the customer's language. To take the initiative in gaining new customers one has to be able to make one's pitch in a language that they understand. But both the UK

---

* The great powers of the old world, China and India, were the principal losers in this process. China's share declined from 33 to 6 percent in the same period, India's from 25 to 2. The figures are derived from Kennedy 1988, 149.

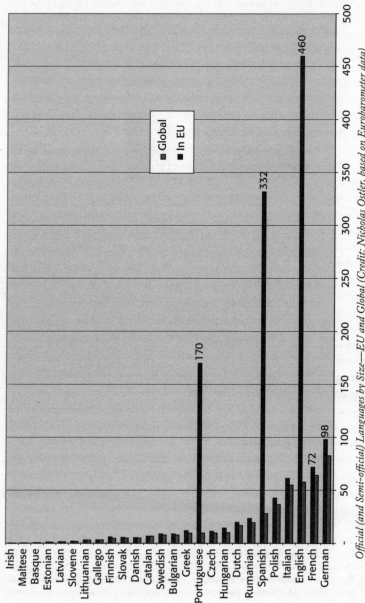

*Official (and Semi-official) Languages by Size—EU and Global (Credit: Nicholas Ostler, based on Eurobarometer data)*

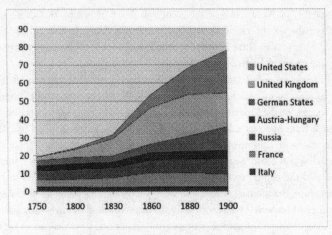

*Western Powers' Shares of World Manufacturing, 1750–1900.*
*(Credit: Nicholas Ostler, based on data from Kennedy 1988)*

and U.S. markets, and especially the latter, had been developed at home; the industrial revolutions that drove them were domestic, and the resources that they exploited were likewise largely mined or grown at home, or (in Britain's case) in colonies that were under their own management. Outside India and China, these developments that favored English-speaking powers had not required them to solicit the cooperation of foreigners who did not speak their language.* By contrast, third parties who wanted to join in had to make themselves understood. Just as Indians and other British colonial citizens who wanted to get a piece of the action in the British Empire had to strive to learn English, so other foreigners too had to take an interest in the language to make contact.

Another cliché of nineteenth-century Britain was that "trade follows the flag": imperial control of a territory was a useful precursor to getting British business to take an interest in it, as witness Hong Kong for Far Eastern

---

\* Early on, an exception to this had been Persian, spoken by traders in the Mughal Empire, in the deals which laid the foundation for the East India Company's wealth. But this remained a rare accomplishment for Englishmen. Most negotiations were handled through the medium of Portuguese, the lingua-franca for Indian Ocean trade in the seventeenth and eighteenth centuries. Bilingual Indians (called *banyan* or *dubash*) were usually involved too.

commerce, or New Zealand for wool and dairy products. But those who had not the good fortune to be born British did not have this option: they could only make their resources available for profitable trade with the English-speaking leviathans by learning to speak their language.

This was soon reflected by speaker numbers worldwide capable of using the English language as a lingua-franca. But boosterism also contributed to the success of the language in European education. English succeeded because it was expected to. English, rather than French, was learned by rising generations of European schoolchildren in the twentieth century because English was the language of the countries with the ideas, the proven know-how, and the capital to develop the future. Their ultimate victories in two testing, and devastating, European wars—although they shattered the economic (and imperial) basis for the older country's leadership—only proved that Anglo-Saxons would win through: linguistically too they must be the way to bet. Increasingly, as the twentieth century wore on, it became clear that others, all over the world, were making the same bet; and by implication English was elected as a lingua-franca for the world as a whole.

There is a doubly wry irony of fate in this current European preference for English as its lingua-franca. The EU is, after all, an organization many of whose members would still very much like to limit the global dominance achieved by the USA; and in favoring English, it makes life easier, above all, for the United Kingdom, the European member state whose public is least enthusiastic for the political development of the Union.

∞∞

This review of instances of "the edges of English" in the modern world prompts some first generalizations. In each case, the language has either disappointed, or else overfulfilled, its apparently appointed—but thereby limited—potential as a lingua-franca created by the spread of British power. English clearly has a recognized potential in a country with powerful linguistic minorities to serve as a neutral, because alien, lingua-franca among them. But this potential is not always fulfilled. One reason is that the frictions between minorities may have been seen as effects of British policy in the first place.

The attractiveness of the language is often reinforced by a sense that it can reward its speakers with the indispensable key to world markets and hence quicker economic development. English offers an entry card to the world's Executive Club. But this too can be vitiated if knowledge of English is seen as giving unjustified advantages to some sections of society, or if other sections feel that the language was once imposed on them in clear disregard of their right to choose, and to demean or devalue their own lin-guistic traditions.

This aspect of English—its attractiveness to those who want to be taken seriously by the world, and especially by global economic players—has caused a new phenomenon of the twentieth and especially the twenty-first centuries, the quest for English in communities that historically have little or no link with an English-speaking community. So far, this has only really established itself in a most unlikely location, the continent of Europe—the home of most of the lingua-franca competitors to English. But the per-ceived value of English—whether for neutrality or as a key to riches—is so great at the moment that it will no doubt attract many more to learn it and employ it for their internal or international needs.

All these uses of English in remote parts of the modern world show it functioning as a lingua-franca, a general means of contact between those whose mother tongues may be quite different. The attempt to adopt English as something more intimate than this, as a generally available mother tongue, has not been successful, as the Philippines have shown. (Other Southeast Asian nations have had similar incipient problems: the English that people speak fluently and naturally is too heavily influenced by the other languages they speak.) A country's government may well find it a good policy to pro-mote use of English, to gain direct access to centers of power and wealth in the modern world, and even, simultaneously, as a neutral medium within its own borders; but this makes sense only if it adopts the international stan-dard for English, not a colorful local version. And to do this, English needs to be kept at a healthy distance.

In recent works,[19] David Graddol has suggested that English is becom-ing so widely taught in the world's classrooms, and so widely used in the world's businesses, that its instrumental importance—as a business tool, the international medium of communication, comparable to mathematics, or a technical standard for computing such as Unicode—will totally expunge any sense of its historical origins in Britain or the USA. This new sense of English's universality should dissolve any special rights that its origins might have given to those who speak it natively. Perhaps also the democratic sense of joint ownership of a vast shared good could allay any resentment harbored by reluctant users too, those who, for one reason or another, might have preferred to be speaking another language for business purposes.

Could English really become so pervasive that its identity would disappear, as a language that stands in contrast to any other, as a disembodied skill, and standard of best practice? The brief and selective survey in this chapter has already suggested that this apolitical view of English—true as it may be for the aspirations of vast numbers of learners and users—simply diverts attention from many aspects of the impact of this language in the world today. Ultimately, and for the foreseeable future, the use of English will be a political issue. Many people will love it or loathe it, and many in power will see it as a policy objective or a legitimate target.

# CHAPTER 2

# How Various in the Future?

We must all hang together, or assuredly we shall all hang separately.

—Benjamin Franklin, at the signing
of the Declaration of Independence, July 4, 1776

T HE SPREAD OF ENGLISH from the British Isles across a network of
foreign homes has happened in just four centuries—a small fraction of
the five thousand years of the world's recorded history, and a mere blink
of the eye within the one hundred thousand years that human languages
have been spreading round the world. The complexities of history that have
caused it are various, a multiplicity of stories of religious utopians, rapacious
privateers, hopeful homesteaders, wide-ranging merchants, speculative in-
vestors, dreamy explorers, ambitious soldiers, indentured laborers, rivalrous
statesmen, transported prisoners, exploited slaves, mutinous sailors, dedicated
missionaries, and many more classes of adventurer, supporter, and victim,
all ultimately driven by a certain impatience with the geographic bounds of
living on Europe's offshore islands, and with traditional agricultural methods of earning a living at home.

The pattern of English use that has resulted is as various as the motives
that drove this history. English comes to many, in every continent, as a
mother tongue, often in a monolingual environment; but it is just as often
acquired in the classroom, either as an official language, with uses that may
be required by organizations of every size from national government down
to village schools, or as a lingua-franca that is expected to be useful for some
purpose later in life, perhaps for contact with people far away. By now English can, without contest, be described as *the* global language par excellence. Every continent has major English-speaking communities, and the

language is by far the most widely used lingua-franca among speakers of other languages. It seems even to be receiving the submission of its greatest rivals: the new French global TV service is to be available in English, and all Chinese children now study English at school, a compliment that is not returned in anglophone countries.

There might seem to be no way to grasp the diversity of situations in which English is present, and the roles that it is asked to play: the mix of mother tongue, official language, and speculative lingua-franca may easily give different motives for using English to three people within a single conversation, or to three communities within a single country (such as India or Canada), all using what sounds like the same dialect of English. But in practice, this tripartite division has been used (originally, and highly influentially, by the sociolinguist Braj Kachru in 1985) to conceive the world spread of English in three circles:

> The current sociolinguistic profile of English may be viewed in terms of three concentric circles . . . The Inner Circle refers to the traditional cultural and linguistic bases of English. The Outer Circle represents the institutionalised non-native varieties (ESL [English as a Second Language]) in the regions that have passed through extended periods of colonisation . . . The Expanding Circle includes the regions where the performance varieties of the language are used essentially in EFL [English as a Foreign Language] contexts.[1]

The virtue of this is that circles can contain one another; so, for example, in some sense the Inner Circle is within the other two, and English influence (at least historically) has flowed outward into them. Geographically, the circles can be shown on a map of the world and so given a concrete reference. A reasonable listing of countries so classified runs as follows.

The lists are ragged at the edges, especially between Inner and Outer circles. But the lists do have certain virtues, at least in reminding us of certain strong tendencies.

One virtue is to show the net linguistic effect of the different styles of colonization, something that has been emphasized by another sociolinguist, Salikoko Mufwene.[2] He distinguishes settlement colonies from exploitation colonies. In settlement colonies, most of the population are settlers from the mother country and their descendants. Exploitation col-

| INNER CIRCLE (ENGLISH NATIVE) | OUTER CIRCLE (ENGLISH OFFICIAL) | EXPANDING CIRCLE (ENGLISH FIRST FOREIGN LANGUAGE) |
|---|---|---|
| Anguilla, Antigua and Barbuda, Australia, the Bahamas, Barbados, Bermuda, Belize, British Indian Ocean Territory, British Virgin Islands, Canada, Cayman Islands, Falkland Islands, Gibraltar, Grenada, Guernsey, Guyana, Isle of Man, Jamaica, Jersey, Montserrat, New Zealand, Ireland, Pitcairn Islands, Saint Helena, Saint Kitts and Nevis, Saint Vincent and the Grenadines, South Georgia and South Sandwich Islands, Trinidad and Tobago, Turks and Caicos Islands, United Kingdom, U.S. Virgin Islands, and United States of America. | American Samoa, Aruba, Bangladesh, Botswana, Brunei, Cameroon, Cook Islands, Dominica, Fiji, Gambia, Ghana, Guam, Hong Kong, India, Kenya, Kiribati, Lesotho, Liberia, Malawi, Malaysia, Malta, Marshall Islands, Mauritius, Micronesia, Namibia, Nepal, Nigeria, Pakistan, Papua New Guinea, Philippines, Rwanda, Saint Lucia, Samoa, Seychelles, Sierra Leone, Singapore, Solomon Islands, South Africa, Sri Lanka, Suriname, Swaziland, Tanzania, Tonga, Zambia, and Zimbabwe. | E.g., continental states of the European Union (Bulgaria, Czech Republic, Denmark, Estonia, Finland, France, Germany, Greece, Hungary, Italy, Latvia, Lithuania, Netherlands, Poland, Portugal, Rumania, Slovakia, Slovenia, Spain, Sweden), China, Japan, Russia, South Korea, Mongolia, Taiwan, Thailand, Vietnam, and all states of Latin America (except Guyana). |

*Note: English is also spreading in many of the other states of Africa (including French-speaking and Portuguese-speaking colonies), but it would not be exact to say it is yet the "first foreign language" there.*

onies, by contrast, were held as sources of profit, with minimal and temporary presence of people from the mother country. In the language communities that resulted, the tendency is clear. British settlement colonies implanted English fully formed from its native source, the United Kingdom, and have become the Inner Circle of English users. The classic examples are the

USA, and also Canada, Australia, and New Zealand. British exploitation colonies, on the other hand, required local administrators; of these, senior roles were filled by UK nationals, but many of middling and junior rank were supplied from other colonies, especially India; there was also a program of education that attempted to train local populations, too, including instruction in English. The long-term effects were the institution of English as the language of administration and often strongly local varieties of the English spoken. Hence the status of English in countries such as India, Kenya, and Nigeria.

But this historical explanation only really applies to the larger territories that were once colonized. Most of the smaller countries of the Inner Circle, if their English has come from the imperial surge of the last four centuries, are neither exploitation nor settlement colonies, but rather "outposts of empire," held as bases for the Royal Navy to guarantee strategic linkages among the exploitation colonies, and back to the mother country. A few others, notably those round the Caribbean, are better classed as exploitation colonies, basically economic bases from which to export sugar. Such Inner Circle exceptions—where mother tongue communities for English have grown up in sites that were not major settlement colonies—remind us that the empire's military and business activities, at least in small islands, were capable of spreading the language ultimately as effectively as massive emigration of English speakers from the United Kingdom.

However, this exposes a major fault in this classification, at least if it is intended as revealing different paths that have led to divergent status for English-language communities—i.e. to be a kind of natural taxonomy, analogous to a pedigree in biology or even historical linguistics. Looking critically at the lists, one sees that the presence of a country in the Outer or Inner Circle depends on whether it hosts any other language communities bigger in size than the English one. South Africa contains an English-speaking community of UK-emigrant origin, quite comparable to the majority populations in Canada or Australia, but they are outnumbered there by three other communities, Zulu, Xhosa, and Afrikaans. So South Africa, as a whole, is in the Outer Circle.* To take another kind of example, many of

---

* Canada would have been Outer Circle too until English speakers came to outnumber French speakers in the mid-nineteenth century. Large indigenous languages such as Cree or Inuktitut had still matched French or English at the end of the eighteenth century, but they did not grow thereafter.

the countries have developed distinct forms of English vernacular quite different from the general standard. This is true of the Caribbean countries Belize, Guyana, Jamaica, and Barbados, where it is the majority language, and is also true of Papua New Guinea or the Philippines, where it is not. In the first group, a form of standard English has status as the unique official language; in the others, it only shares this status. Countries such as Nicaragua or Panama have similar, though smaller, communities with English-based vernaculars, but English is not an official language at all. These essentially political differences, which stem from the current balance of populations, mean that the first group (Belize et al.) are classed in the Inner, the second (Papua New Guinea and Philippines) in the Outer, while countries in the third group (e.g., Nicaragua) are excluded altogether, not even figuring in the Expanding Circle.

The three circles, then, are a convenient fiction for sketching the overall pattern of English spread through the world, and even, as Mufwene has shown, as an organizing framework to begin to understand the various linguistic effects of colonial policies. However, they are not an adequate basis for our attempt to fit the spread of English into some more general theory that would characterize lingua-francas in general, and not just English as it is currently spoken round the world. Besides, the theory of the three circles makes crucial reference to the pedagogical terms *English as a Second Language* and *English as a Foreign Language*. These are well-known, but too specific to just one language tradition, that of English.

For such a more general theory, we need to fall back onto a more elemental analysis of how languages are acquired. Essentially, a person can gain command of a new language in two ways. He or she either acquires it in a home environment, essentially "at mother's knee," or through recruitment to an organization of some kind in which it is used. In this book, the first will be called a *mother tongue*, or a vernacular.* We shall be referring to the second process of language learning as acquisition of a *lingua-franca*. The implicit contention is that all language deliberately acquired outside the home environment is a kind of contact language, consciously learned for social or

---

* This term has been used for "home-bred" language since the Roman linguist Terentius Varro (*de Lingua Latina* v) distinguished some words as *vernacula vocabula*. Ultimately, it can be derived from *verna* 'home-born slave', but it is no more specifically servile than the word *family*, derived from the Latin for a company of slaves (*familia*). The Romans just had a rather stratified idea of what made for a home or a family.

pragmatic reasons—essentially so as to cope in a wider society outside the community one was born to. The term *lingua-franca* has already been widely used in this book, but hitherto we have relied on the simple definition of it as a contact language, used for communication among those who do not share a mother tongue. In practice, there is no conflict between the two definitions: the term always refers to a language that, by most of its users, has been learned outside the home environment.

Evidently, mother tongues and lingua-francas overlap: if you are lucky and your mother tongue has been spread abroad in previous generations, you may use your mother tongue as a contact language to reach people whose mother tongue is quite different. But if any language is used as a lingua-franca, some, and usually most, of the people who use it as such have acquired it specifically to overcome the bounds of their own mother tongue speech community. A lingua-franca that is spoken exclusively by mother tongue speakers is a contradiction in terms.

English is a textbook example of a language with a large mother tongue community that is also widely used as a lingua-franca; modern Persian is another; and most lingua-francas of the modern era are of this kind, mother tongues pressed into wider service. But it has not always been so: classical languages, such as medieval Latin, ancient Greek, classical Chinese, Sanskrit, and classical Arabic, are all examples of languages long spoken by no one *en famille*, but transmitted through school systems down the generations and used as a means of communication among speakers of many different mother tongues.

Applying this simple, if radical, concept to the three circles of English, we see that the Inner Circle is just the set of those countries where English is predominantly spoken as a mother tongue. But we have greater difficulty in distinguishing the Outer from the Expanding Circle because English as an official language has no particular status in relation to the distinction of mother tongue versus lingua-franca. A lingua-franca is deliberately learned, and often explicitly taught too, so it is clear that the Expanding Circle is made up of countries where English is taught as a lingua-franca. But what of a classic Outer Circle country such as India? We should want to say that official English is maintained by law as a lingua-franca for use within the country; other than that, it is no different from any other language learned for contact among different mother tongue groups. In a country with one or more official languages, such a language will usually be known to some as a mother tongue, but (by definition) to more people as a lingua-franca;

when it is a mother tongue to a majority, and the language is English, the country is classified within the Inner, not the Outer, Circle.

For us, then, there is no crucial difference between English learned as a Second Language (ESL, for official wider contact within a country) and English learned as a Foreign Language (EFL, to contact people in other countries). There are differences, and perhaps important ones, for those attempting to organize language teaching, and that is why these two terms are established. But in this book the key question is what determines whether a language will survive in the long term. And as we shall see, for this it matters very much whether a language is acquired by large populations as a mother tongue, and hardly at all whether it is accorded official status by a state.*

⋈

An interesting question about the future of English spoken round the world is whether it will continue to cohere as a single language or come apart and so develop into a family of related languages, which gradually become ever more distant in their substance and style. Should we expect the future of global English to turn into a tale of many "Langlishes" or "the Ingo-lingos"?

In history, most well-known widespread languages, if they became media of communication for more than one polity and were given enough time to change (say, a few centuries), did split up into daughter languages.

The best-known case is Latin, apparently a unitary language as long as the Roman Empire continued in the west of Europe and the Mediterranean, but changing into the Romance languages (French, Italian, Portuguese, etc.) when the common administrative hierarchy was broken in the early fifth century to be replaced by a small number of Germanic-ruled states (states that, with some coalescences, have remained remarkably stable ever since and developed into half a dozen modern nations). Already by the eighth century it was difficult for speakers of the different vernacular dialects to understand one another. For various reasons, the transition to different written standards, and hence full recognition of different languages, did not

---

* Still less, whether it is taught by native speakers, or on a native-speaker model. This book makes no contribution to the debate on whose English should be taught, or who owns the language. But it does suggest that the existence of native speakers, not their role in teaching, will ultimately be crucial to the future of English. (Cf. Graddol 1999.)

come about until the twelfth or thirteenth centuries. And only in the late fifteenth and sixteenth centuries did they reach the final step of "grammatization," and a clear and crisp set of formal rules characterizing the resulting languages.[3]

But similar processes, though less well attested in their intermediate stages, can be recognized in many parts of the world.

The Indian subcontinent currently boasts some hundred languages of Indo-Aryan origin, of which eighteen have modern literary standards. All these are believed to descend from some one language rather like Vedic Sanskrit, which could have entered this area from Central Asia perhaps three thousand years ago. Classical Sanskrit itself, closely related to Vedic, has a defined literary standard that is at least twenty-five hundred years old. But although a fairly full written record exists of Indian languages since the fourth century BC, few inscriptions directly represent how people were speaking at the time. So the intermediate history by which these languages have arisen in their current positions is—to say the least of it—obscure.[4]

Similar obscurity attends the actual relation of Classical Arabic to the various vernaculars that *seem* to derive from it in the Levant and North Africa, arising in the millennium or so after the Arab conquests in the latter seventh century, which had originally debouched from Saudi Arabia and brought with them their language, which is documented in no less a source than the Koran. Some of differences seen in the North African languages (Tunisian, and perhaps Algerian, even Moroccan) may come from a (related) Semitic language that preceded Arabic in these regions, the Punic language of Phoenician traders (derived from Canaan, in northern Palestine).[5] A follow-up invasion in the tenth and eleventh centuries, led by the Banū Hilāl, originally from Syria, also affected mainly this same Maghreb, viz the west of North Africa.

These forms of vernacular Arabic (often called dialects even in linguistically expert sources, even though they are not mutually intelligible) provide a clear example of our distinction between mother tongue and lingua-franca, since they are always learned informally at home; Classical Arabic, often now known as Modern Standard Arabic, *fuṣḥā*, the common medium used by speakers of most of the vernaculars, is always acquired in a formal environment, namely a madrassa or a school. It can be claimed that they are not distinct languages at all, since they all (with the exception of Maltese) are spoken with heavy influence from *fuṣḥā* when the subject matter of the conversation becomes more serious or high level and so requires it. A willed, and hence perceived, social reality holds that all these vernaculars are just local varieties, more or less corrupt ways of speaking a single perfect language. And this continues to triumph over the perhaps more objective facts of the phonetic, grammatical, and vocabulary differences among them, and the practical difficulty of communicating in one variety to a native speaker of another.

Another language that is believed to have split in this way and so created a set of languages that in a sense dare not speak their name is Chinese. But in practice, a completely different conceptual problem exists in presenting the history of Chinese as one more instance of such fission. The Chinese writing system *hànzì* 漢字 is phonetically opaque: it provides signs for words, rather than phones or syllables. It originally coded an ancient language, Classical Chinese, usually known as *wényán* 文言 'literary talk'. But the signs are still in use and have modern pronunciations. The only way we can tell how they were pronounced in ancient times—which is the closest that we can get to *wényán*'s phonetic reality as a language—is to reconstruct them, i.e. to reason what original sounds would most likely have given rise to the profusion of different sounds they indicate in modern Chinese "dialects."* Certainly, we believe that ancient Chinese has split into the current languages that dominate modern China, but our only evidence for this original comes from the current languages themselves. This is a petitio principii, an assumption of what needs to be proved. Hence although the development of Chinese probably is a corroborating example, it is not exactly evidence.

In looking for more simple and direct examples of the splitting up of ancient languages when they spread so widely as (in a military metaphor) to exceed their lines of communication, we may be luckier if we turn to the New World, since the whole process from widespread empire to scattered communities has proceeded over the last four hundred years under the inspection of a western-European power. When the Spanish conquered Mexico and Peru in the sixteenth century, they found that each of these empires had an official language that had spread to the limits of their

---

* The earliest we can systematically reconstruct is Early Middle Chinese (EMC) of the fifth century AD, although classic *wényán* (the language of the age of Confucius) seems to be at least a thousand years older than this. For what it's worth, it is reckoned that 漢字 was in EMC pronounced *xan^h-dzi^h* and 文言 *mun-ŋian*. In those days, Chinese was not yet a tone language. (See Pulleyblank 1991.)

control, namely Nahuatl in Mexico, as well as Quechua in the Inca Empire, which extended from modern Ecuador to Bolivia and the north of Chile. Both of the languages survive to this day, but each has been split into many variant dialects or languages.

Nahuatl had not been spoken as a mother tongue over the whole territory of the Aztec Empire, but was rather a lingua-franca. Key individuals in subject peoples were designated as *nauatlato*, i.e. bilinguals, who could mediate between their own people and the ruling Aztecs. The Spanish dispossessed the Aztecs as imperial leaders, but continued from the sixteenth century to the eighteenth centuries to use, and indeed to spread, Nahuatl as a convenient *lengua general* 'common tongue' in their own empire. After the *Real Cédula* Royal Decree of 1770, however, which explicitly expressed the hope that it would die out (along with all the other indigenous languages of Spain's overseas colonies), official use of Nahuatl was withdrawn. In practice, Nahuatl, like the other languages of the country, declined in status to become exclusively the speech of Mexican villagers. There was no premium on maintaining a single standard (such as the Aztecs and Spaniards had used), and little motivation or opportunity for Nahuatl speakers in different villages to communicate with one another. Nahuatl is now spoken in at least nineteen quite different forms, according to systematic tests of mutual intelligibility conducted by the Summer Institute of Linguistics (SIL) in the 1980s.[6]

But here again there is controversy on whether these divergent forms, which are certainly now in existence after the demise of Nahuatl as a functioning lingua-franca, are really to be considered a family of languages rather than an ample spread of dialects. Some doubt whether SIL's quasi-objective tests of intelligibility should be followed in total oblivion of Nahuatl's common cultural past, which is no secret to its speakers in Mexico and actually gives them some sense of solidarity.[7] In this respect, it should perhaps be considered more like the union of dialects and languages seen in Chinese, united by acceptance of a common ancestral speech, even though no one in practice speaks it anymore.[*]

Farther south, Quechua had been spread much more thoroughly than this by its imperial sponsors, the Incas, especially in the fifteenth century;

---

[*] "He is not at home" is expressed as *x-aak* in Guerrero, *amo-hka* in Tezcoco, *am-iga* in Morelos, *amo yetok* in Puebla Sierra, and *mach nikaan kah* in Vera Cruz. In Classical Nahuatl, this would have been expressed as *amo i-chaan-ko (kah)*, literally 'not his-home-at (is)'. (Flores Farfán 2008, and in a personal letter)

this all happened over a few generations well before the advent of the Spaniards. The language had originated in central Peru, around Ancash, where it had already split into various dialects; but through an alliance, one such dialect became the official language of the Incas (newcomers from the south) and was then spread both northward into Ecuador, and southward, e.g., to the empire's capital city, Cuzco, and beyond. Language spread had been deliberate, with distribution of Quechua-speaking settlers far and wide, and favored princes from the provinces summoned for education in the capital. The result was widespread use of a common language, first as a lingua-franca, but increasingly as a mother tongue, for most of the length of the temperate zone between the Andes and the Pacific Ocean. After 1536, it was also conveniently adopted and spread by the Spanish as a *lengua general*. Like Nahuatl, the language subsequently became a literate (and literary) medium under Spanish and enjoyed even more currency after the sixteenth and seventeenth centuries, even among landholders, as a flaunted token of the independence of rural areas from the major cities, but it was officiously crushed after 1781 with the failed indigenous revolt of Túpac Amaru.

As in the Nahuatl case, the language community had no way to keep its coherence independently of the (Spanish-dominated) cities, so it has tended to split into dialects, often now considered distinct languages, not least because there are now national boundaries (among Ecuador, Peru, and Bolivia) dividing the major varieties, but also because the divergent Ancash dialects, and the totally distinct language Aymara, have split the main Quechua area into three discontinuous zones. Even so, the consciousness of a common source of the language under Inca domination is still widespread; and the different dialects that prevail in the Quechua-speaking states have not been codified into divergent national standards with different (national) names.

One could draw the conclusion from the cases of Nahuatl and Quechua that when the fission of a language area occurs under the full glare of historical witness—which is likely to be a feature of any future disintegration of English—it is difficult for different varieties to gain acceptance as distinct languages in their own right.

We have seen that in all these plausible cases where a breakup of a single widespread language into divergent sublanguages has clearly happened in documented history, only the example of the Romance languages in western Europe is straightforward, resulting in a clutch of daughter languages that are recognized as such. In every other case (Indo-Aryan, Arabic, Chinese, Nahuatl, or Quechua)—where we actually know an ancestral language that has spread, with several centuries having passed to allow divergence, and a host of related languages left in the area to tell the tale—something, often many things, spoil the story. There is an unwillingness to accept that the old language has gone, a total absence of intermediate history, a failure to record the sounds of the original language, and above all a continuing solidarity among speakers of all the descendant forms of speech, which makes their speakers happier to think of them as dialects rather than new languages.

Yet despite this failure to clinch these examples that should have occurred in recorded history, this kind of breakup is universally believed in by historical linguists, as a repeated phenomenon of human prehistory. With it, they account for the origins of all the language families in the world, and notable examples are the Indo-European languages, whose homelands cover a vast and contiguous zone (neatly) bounded north to south by Donegal and Bengal, east to west by Siberia and Iberia; the Bantu languages, which cover the whole of central and southern Africa; the Polynesian languages, over the islands of the Pacific; the Algonquian languages, which are widespread across the northern temperate zones of North America; and the Semitic languages, of southwestern Asia and Ethiopia. As August Schleicher, the original exponent of this theory of language origin, put it in 1871, "Through different developments, at different points in the province of one and the same language, the self-same tongue branches out . . . and diverges into several languages (dialects); this process of differentiation may repeat itself more than once . . . All the languages which are derived from one original-language form together a class of speech or speech-stem; these again are subdivided into families or branches of speech."[8]

What it means, for example, when it is claimed that the Ket language of central Siberia is related to the Navajo language of Arizona, i.e. that they come of the same stock or same family, is that both these speech communities share a set of their far ancestors. Two chains of descendants came from those ancestors, a social language community in each generation, each of whom transmitted the language down from parent to child as mother tongue, or among collaborators, as a lingua-franca. Afterward, whether gradually or suddenly, changes have occurred to transform the languages of the two chains, and one chain resulted in the Ket language, another the Navajo language. The chains, over many thousands of years and kilometers, cannot have been the only ones to split off from a lineage that evidently expanded or moved to switch from one continent to another. Many chains will have died out as extinct languages; but taking the surviving end languages of a number of different chains together gives you a family of languages. The longer ago those chains have diverged, the more distant are the relations among the languages in the family.

At this point, it makes sense to recall the distinction between mother tongue and lingua-franca. By its very nature, a lingua-franca is less likely than a mother tongue to split into mutually unintelligible regional dialects, or sublanguages. Command of one's mother tongue is a natural development, and among other things a mark of one's origins and close kin; if the identity aspect becomes stressed, it may readily develop to be distant from other varieties, even those that are quite nearby. But a lingua-franca is explicitly learned for a reason: one joins a speech community into which one is not born, for some profit or benefit. If that speech community is allowed to fragment, it will become less attractive to new recruits, and so an effort is likely to be made to keep the wider lines of communication open.

The native speakers of Latin in the latter centuries of the first millennium allowed it to fragment into local dialects, and ultimately regional and national languages; those who learned it at school (whatever their home language) maintained its rules, and its identity as a language, so that it remained essentially unchanged from its classical grammar, and a unitary language, over this same period (and indeed on throughout the second millennium AD).

Likewise, with modern English, the communities who speak it natively— in England, the Caribbean, Southeast Asia, or anywhere else—innovate distinctively in their English. The Expanding Circle of those who learn English as a Foreign Language—inevitably, as a lingua-franca—do not establish competing norms. There is no accepted, self-consciously asserted special style of English, in any part of Europe, China, or Latin America, such as there might be in Australia, Jamaica, or any Inner Circle country.

For this, the crucial issue is whether speakers consciously assert their difference. Is the way they talk English not only recognizable but "in your face"? Evidently, there may often be systematic influence from their mother tongues in pronunciation, sporadic interference in grammar, and some conspiracy, here and there, to use local words or concepts when English is being spoken among foreigners who share a cultural background. But despite all this, when the language is being used in an international situation (so that mutual comprehensibility is at a premium), the evidence is that Expanding Circle English speakers largely talk a neutral English, i.e. in a style close to the British or American standard. (This is true of Outer Circle speakers of

English too.)* This sets apart Inner Circle speakers, be they Glaswegians, inner-city African-Americans, or Australian drovers; they naturally feel that the language is theirs, that their English is as good as anyone else's, and that, if comprehension seems to fail, the problem lies with the international audiences, not them.

The record of the Outer Circle speakers of English in these international contexts gives some indication of where they fit. Do they, like the Inner Circle, have the potential to start off new dialects, and ultimately perhaps new languages, of English origin? They may, but probably only if they include enough mother tongue speakers. In a country such as Pakistan, many know English natively, but many more know it because they have studied it at school. When they use it together, such different types of speakers may create a distinct dialect; but the presence of native speakers in the mix is crucial, giving the variety a kind of authority. Without them, as in an Outer Circle country such as Papua New Guinea, where only 1 percent of the population speaks English, it is highly unlikely that a distinct variety of English will get established. More likely, either English will die out altogether or be spread through formal instruction, essentially as a foreign language.

It is precisely in the Outer Circle countries, which have a history of colonial use of the language, that a deviant version of English can have strength enough to be seen as a threat, either to the purity of the official language, or to the country's retention of English as a lingua-franca. "Manglish" in Malaysia, "Singlish" in Singapore, and "Taglish" in the Philippines are all the subjects of frequent deprecation in the policy discussions of those countries. "Anglikaans" in South Africa and "Hinglish" in India are also noted, but probably with less concern. So we read of the special concern of the prime minister of Singapore:

> Last year, in my National Day Rally speech I highlighted the problems that will arise if Singaporeans continue to speak Singlish instead of good English. This sparked off a spirited debate . . . Some supported

---

* The evidence from Meierkord 2004 (respectively that 95 percent and 94 percent of such utterances conform to a native-speaker norm) is cited by Kirkpatrick 2007, 167–68. Kirkpatrick, in his wide-ranging survey of World Englishes, seems to be committed to the belief that some Expanding Circle varieties of English (notably, English as spoken in China) are in transition to becoming established with their own standards (p. 183). But he presents no evidence that shows more than the informal variation that I have mentioned, created involuntarily or opportunistically.

the need to speak good English but others defended the place of Singlish in our society. Some said that Singlish, with its smattering of Chinese and Malay words, is unique to Singapore. Singlish allows us to identify each other as Singaporeans.

If Singlish were only "a smattering of Chinese and Malay words," there would be no problem. Unfortunately, this is not the case. Singlish uses Chinese syntax, and Singlish speakers often use literal translations of Chinese phrases. This means that the sentences are not only ungrammatical and truncated, but often incomprehensible, especially to foreigners. Classic examples would be "You got money, sure can buy one" or "This is my one," derived from *zhe shi wo de*.

The ability to speak good English is a distinct advantage in terms of doing business and communicating with the world. This is especially important for a hub city and an open economy like ours. If we speak a corrupted form of English that is not understood by others, we will lose a key competitive advantage. My concern is that if we continue to speak Singlish, it will over time become Singapore's common language. (Goh Chok Tong, at the launch of the "Speak Good English" Movement, April 29, 2000)

In the Philippines, money is being spent to improve the quality of English on citizens' lips:

Education Secretary Fe Hidalgo said her department has allocated 581 million pesos to implement its English-proficiency program among teachers, saying the results of a recent English-proficiency test among them was not very encouraging.

Her department is now looking at the factors contributing to the decline in the Filipinos' English proficiency. But Hidalgo said "this culture of Taglish that has emerged in the last few years has contributed to the problem." (*Manila Standard Today*, April 19, 2006)

In Malaysia, a doubly complementary policy is being tried, punishing the inadequate not to improve their English, but to deter the use of bad Malay:

Kuala Lumpur, Malaysia (AP) — Malaysia will levy fines on those incorrectly using the national language, and will set up a specialized division to weed out offenders who mix Malay with English . . .

Culture, Arts and Heritage Minister Rais Yatim said fines of up to 1,000 ringgit ($271) can be imposed on displays with any wrong or mutated form of Malay, the *Star* newspaper reported. The move was to ensure "the national language was not sidelined in any way," Rais said, according to the *Star* . . . English is widely spoken but a mutated form, known as "Manglish"—a mishmash of English, Malay and other local dialects is commonly used in the Southeast Asian nation. The government will attempt to swap commonly used English language words with Malay substitutes . . . "It has to be admitted that a mixture of Bahasa Malaysia and English sometimes cannot be helped, but we hope these measures can arrest the decline," Rais said. (October 5, 2006)

Meanwhile, the tone of language pundits on the situation in India is decidedly more flippant:

*Kyon na Hindi men likhen?* [Why not write in Hindi?] This question reminds me of the following lines from Ghalib's poetry:
    *Kyon na Firdous men Dozakh ko mila len ya Rabb!*
    *Sair ke liye thodi si faza aur sahi!*\*

These days, this generation communicates in mixed Hindi and English, or to say "Hinglish," and it is up to the individual to maintain the purity of the language. Of course, it depends on the individual's choice or comfort with the language to express his or her inner feelings and views in English or Hindi medium. (Raj Shekhar, *Patna Daily*, January 22, 2005)

To get an idea of what the *tamasha* (ruckus) is all about, listen to a typical Hinglish advertisement. Pepsi, for instance, has given its global "Ask for more" campaign a local Hinglish flavor: "*Yeh Dil Maange More*" (The heart wants more). Not to be outdone, Coke has its own Hinglish slogan: "Life *ho to aisi*" (Life should be like this). Domino's Pizza, which offers Indian curiosities such as the chicken tikka pizza, asks its customers "Hungry *kya*?" (Are you hungry?), and McDonald's current campaign spoofs the jumbled construction of

---

\* "Why not join hell onto heaven, O God? It would give a bit more space for a stroll." (From Ghalib's *Urdu-i-Mu'alla*)

Hinglish sentences with its campaign, "What your *bahana* is?" (*Bahana* means excuse, as in, "What's your excuse for eating McDonald's and not home-cooked food?")

None of this would have happened 10 years ago, says Sushobhan Mukherjee, strategic planning director for Publicis India. "My grandfather's generation grew up thinking, 'If I can't speak English correctly, I won't speak it,'" says Mr. Mukherjee. "Now, power has shifted to the young, and they want to be understood rather than be correct." (Scott Baldauf, *Christian Science Monitor*, November 23, 2004)

Although different degrees of language mixing are going on in these cases, each is potentially a new dialect or language, resulting from the insistent influence on the speakers' spoken English of other languages that they know as mother tongue. These are also spontaneous growths of language (with the possible exception of those cute advertising slogans) and as such are more comparable to mother tongue than lingua-franca use. None of them, however, has been dignified with any kind of official standard and hence been recognized as a separate language. Instead, if they are not officially disregarded (as they are in India), the attempt is often made by governments to suppress their use because it seems to be generally felt that in practice they cannot be kept separate from standard English. This is probably a misconception, given the evidence just mentioned that nonstandard features are rather thoroughly suppressed when Outer Circle speakers use their English to foreigners. Outer Circle speakers, in fact, retain a surprisingly clear concept of the English that they learned as a lingua-franca, before they began to reconcile it with their mother tongue.

The very idea of a lingua-franca—considered for its communicative value, rather than how it is learned—militates against the likelihood of its splitting up into distinct languages. If a lingua-franca is in danger of splitting, this is fairly good evidence that it is no longer serving its fundamental purpose, to bridge linguistic barriers between mother tongues. In this case, if it is not becoming a mother tongue itself (by being transmitted to the next generation in the family), it is more likely to die out altogether, along with its raison d'être.

What then are the prospects for the unity of English?

As a formal language of international communication, used for business, politics, and academic exchanges, it would be hard for English to change in a fissiparous way, so that different regions or disciplines would go off in different directions. Vocabulary and phrases can be added, and different domains will make different selections from the vast word-hoard that is available; but in principle—and especially with the common reference materials now available in printed or electronic form—it is all a shared resource for all its speakers, with accessibility limited only by what they want to talk about.

More informal use of international English, on the other hand, is far less unitary. This is the English found in newspapers, magazines, printed literature, and the vast variety of broadcast entertainment, as well as films, popular music, video games, etc., and even, most recently, in the untrammeled world of e-mail and messaging systems. Despite its availability worldwide, much of it remains close to the day-to-day outpourings of mother tongue English users. (This closeness is the main reason why the opposition that we have been stressing, between mother tongue and lingua-franca, tends to be so widely overlooked.) This kind of English is often not bland and universal but highly distinctive. In principle, it should be as easy to identify its place of origin, and sometimes its social milieu, as the local speech of mother tongue speakers at ease in their own neighborhoods—though to pick it out calls for an encyclopedic knowledge of linguistic characteristics probably greater than what George Bernard Shaw imagined for Henry Higgins.*

There is some scope then for international English, even when used as a lingua-franca, to be dialectalized, in some way and to some extent split up into distinguishable varieties. The varieties of English mother tongue speech cannot and will not be totally cloaked, hidden from the experience of those who consume of English internationally, the so-called Expanding Circle, as well as many in the Outer Circle too. All competent users of English, especially in the modern era, have to come to terms with some degree of local variety in what they hear and read.

But this does not mean they are free to develop varieties of their own. Here I can introduce a personal anecdote. As a learner of various foreign languages, I have noticed that native speakers are not happy for me in con-

---

* In the play *Pygmalion* (scene 1), Higgins claims to be able to place any man within six miles, and within two miles in London. But in the Edwardian age, before electronic broadcasting and recording, his range of information is mostly restricted to the United Kingdom. Worldwide English now provides a vaster universe of discourse.

versation to play with their language, e.g., to invent new words, or self-consciously abuse its grammar. Even if they know I am erring deliberately, their reaction is always to correct, not to laugh and accept the novelty as people do when I behave similarly unconventionally in speaking my native language, English. From this I infer there is some principle, perhaps a universal of human society, that only mother tongue speakers of a language have a natural right (given them by their language community) to innovate in it. One implication of this is that it is impossible for those who have consciously learned a language to establish a new dialect of it.

If this rule is violated, and some distinctive variety of nonstandard English comes to be used actively, and consistently, by nonnative speakers, it will have to be considered a species of pidgin. A pidgin is a lingua-franca that is incompletely learned by the community that needs to use it and so is supplemented with other elements, often drawn from the original mother tongues of the people who come to speak it. The most familiar pidgins have been trade languages, formed on the margins of speech communities, by people who have regular dealings with those who speak another language, but who do not get fully recruited into those alien groups. Hence the popular etymology of *pidgin* as a Chinese pronunciation of *business*.*

Of many other, well-thumbed examples of trade pidgins, three, far-flung among them, are the Lingua Franca of Italian merchants in the Mediterranean; Russenorsk, used in the eighteenth and nineteenth centuries among Russian and Norwegian traders on the arctic shores of Siberia; and Chinook jargon, established for trade in the Pacific northwest of America well before European contact. Such pidgins seem to arise everywhere when there is trade, but not much other contact, between distinct language groups. "Bazaar Malay" was a constant feature of coastal Southeast Asia for the past five hundred years; many forms of pidginized Portuguese were spoken all along the Indian Ocean coasts in the sixteenth and seventeenth centuries; and many other pidginized forms of English arose in Australasia and the Pacific in the nineteenth century, two of which were later developed

---

* The word, first attested according to the *Oxford English Dictionary* in 1850, was usually written *pigeon* in the nineteenth century. It certainly seems to have arisen to mean the jargon then used for Anglo-Chinese trade and has another plausible etymology in Cantonese *péi ts'ìn* 畀錢 'give money'. Hobson Jobson (Yule 1886) contrasts it with "Butler English," a similar jargon used in south India: "masters used it in speaking to their servants as well as servants to their masters."

into fully fledged creole languages: Bislama (Biche La Mar)* in Vanuatu, and Tok Pisin (Talk Pidgin) in Papua New Guinea. Creoles are mother tongues rather than lingua-francas, since rising generations learn these languages from childhood.

But not all pidgins are created in a commercial context. Another common situation where such lingua-francas arise is in working settlements for large numbers of resident workers, usually males. The linguist Mark Sebba lists several: military or police settlements, plantation life, mines or construction, and immigration.[9] Police forces in the Juba area of Sudan pidginized the Arabic language there, as did police in Papua with the Hiri Motu language. Indentured laborers living together on plantations created many pidgins around the Pacific in the nineteenth century, in Hawaii, Samoa, New Guinea, and Queensland. (Slave colonies, by contrast, mostly in the Caribbean area and Brazil, produced creoles.) Mining and construction workers in South Africa spread Fanakalo, based on Zulu, English, and Afrikaans, apparently an extension of what had been a trade lingua-franca. In the early years of Italian immigration to Argentina, the Cocoliche pidgin sprang into existence, mixing Spanish and Italian; likewise, in the hostels of Germany, a limited form of German known as Gastarbeiterdeutsch (guest-worker-German) could be heard. But in every case, we are talking about a form of a lingua-franca that is specialized, and often radically limited, for use in a subgroup.

Another kind of situation that can lead to the development of a pidgin language is religious contact. In this, one group adopts some features of scripture from another tradition.

A tantalizing example of this comes from Iran. The language of the Avesta, the oldest set of texts of Zoroastrianism, is actually identical with Vedic Sanskrit systematically transformed according to the Old Persian sound-system. It is just too regularly related to be an independent production in a sister language; it looks much more like an Iranian attempt to naturalize Vedic Sanskrit for their own use. A likely way that this might have happened is if Iranians—who in any case spoke a language closely related to Vedic—memorized a set of Vedic texts, then continued to recite them (conservatively) over centuries as their own language changed. (The actual transcription of the texts did not take place until the end of the tenth

---

* Named after the sea cucumber (French *bêche de mer* / Portuguese *bicho do mar*), which was the main trade item.

century AD, about two millennia later.) Effectively, the Zoroastrians would have adopted the ancient, and prestigious, Vedic language for ritual uses, then gradually naturalized this part of the language on their own lines, independently of what was happening to Sanskrit elsewhere. On this theory, the Avestan language is an Iranian-Sanskrit pidgin, based on a fixed corpus of texts.[10]

At the other end of the Sanskrit zone, early Mahayana Buddhists in northeastern India (around the second century BC) adopted a loose form of Sanskrit for their scriptures, in effect a Sanskritized version of their own language. Presumably their motive was to give their scriptures some of the resonance of the ancient Hindu tradition without losing accessibility to the vernacular language. This pidgin is usually called Buddhist Hybrid Sanskrit.[11] It continued in use for many centuries. In the Zoroastrians' creation of Avestan, a set of texts had been adopted, then gradually naturalized. Here by contrast, the Buddhists adopted a Sanskritized style as an overlay on their ordinary vernacular languages, giving them a fully functional, but some what stilted, language in which to discuss religion.

As a religious tactic, this self-conscious Sanskrit tushery has an analogue in the modern world with the Book of Mormon. Although this was written down by Joseph Smith in the late 1820s, its use of language is familiar from the King James Bible, which goes back to 1611, and actually used text mostly drafted by William Tyndale for his version, which came out in 1525.

In these religious cases, fragments of someone else's language (Sanskrit or early modern English) have been adopted, not to communicate to some extent with speakers of that language (as they would be in a trade or plantation pidgin), but to use the atmosphere they convey for one's own purposes among one's own people.

These specialized lingua-francas, the pidgins, do not seem to persist indefinitely. They have their times and their places, sometimes surviving over long periods, and wide spaces, but then they disappear. They do not, like the Romance languages of Europe for example, establish themselves and perhaps divide further into other dialects and languages. This impermanence is a first hint of what we shall find with lingua-francas more generally. Lingua-francas are creatures of time and circumstance and may flourish while they serve a certain purpose. Unlike mother tongues, they do not get passed on automatically to the next generation, for the purpose itself may be transient. Purposes do not beget subpurposes. Creoles have progeny, but pidgins don't. A pidgin is a sometime thing.

As a lingua-franca, then, English—specifically, international English—is unlikely to split into a family of dialects and languages. Even if pidgins of English arise, here and there, in contexts where English is used for some special purposes, or in a restricted area, they are unlikely to be long-lived, and even less likely to be fertile of other languages in the long term.

But what of English as a mother tongue, as spoken in Inner Circle and Outer Circle countries and passed on, with a fair amount of diversity, to new generations of native speakers? In principle, it seems possible—at least more possible than for English as a lingua-franca—that these different English-speaking communities could begin to go different ways. Will it happen?

Here the key is the degree to which the different communities of mother tongue speakers live distinct lives, as opposed to sharing common concerns and so keeping in dialogue with one another. Are the English-speaking peoples, as George Bernard Shaw once put it, divided by a common language? Or are they not? One significant indicator here may be that the distinction between mother tongue and lingua-franca English is so often overlooked. This suggests that these different mother tongue communities are in fact very much in contact with each other. They do sense their differences, and over the centuries some have created boundary markers to signalize them, notably authoritative dictionaries.* But they share what could be called "a common English-speaking life," letting the accepted lingua-franca aspect of English efface much concern for differences in the language as they actually acquire it. As a result, as common sense about human relations[12] suggests, participants in shared dialogue are striving—even involuntarily—to bring their own style of communication closer to what they perceive to be coming from the other side.

Unlike lingua-franca speakers, mother tongue speakers of English do have the freedom to diverge collectively from an established standard with-

---

* For British English, the *Oxford English Dictionary* has sustained this role since its first complete publication in 1928, replacing the proverbial status of Samuel Johnson's dictionary, which had come out in 1755. For American English, the authority, now diffused over a number of dictionaries, goes back to Noah Webster, whose magnum opus, *An American Dictionary of the English Language*, first came out in 1828. Australian English has aspired to something similar in *The Macquarie Dictionary*, since 1981. Other dictionaries could be used in this way, e.g., *Dictionary of Jamaican English* (Cambridge University Press, 1967), *Dictionary of the Scots Language* (www.dsl.ac.uk, 2005). But most varieties of English (e.g., Indian, Canadian) have coped without this kind of independent authority.

out endangering language survival. Their language is, after all, nothing other than what they acquired at home and developed over a lifetime, only to be passed, by similar means, to the next generation. When whole communities of mother tongue speakers of Latin lost touch with any external norm for the language over a few centuries and just spoke as they had learned, the result was the Romance family of languages. Likewise the different regions in Germany and the Netherlands have given rise to a profusion of dialects, which continue to be spoken into the twenty-first century, even though everyone respects the well-defined German or Dutch standards for spelling and grammar when they write their language down.*

A written standard (being transmitted formally, through classroom teaching) is relatively immune to change; but it is difficult for a spoken mother tongue to escape some degree of drift, given enough time, even if one clear written standard is used alongside it. This can be seen in the case of ancient Egyptian. The language of the hieroglyphic writing system persists unchanging in religious inscriptions from the third millennium BC to the fourth century AD, but more informal documents (stories, school texts, records) clearly show a new manner of expression after 1330 BC (perhaps due to pharaoh Akhenaten's attempts at a popular reform); and it is different again in the third century AD, after Coptic Christians start writing down Egyptian texts in the Greek alphabet. These reflect two radical attempts by scribes to bring the written language back into line with the way Egyptian was actually being spoken. Once the alphabetic system was in use (a full phonetic transcript, rather than the words and consonants shown by the hieroglyphs), we can even see a divergence between Bohairic in the north and Sahidic in the south.

Mother tongue speakers have the power to change, then. But will they use it? Clearly, many accents, dialects, and creoles of English (three terms that place a speech community at increasing distances from any of the standards) flourish in many parts of the world, all of them acquired in the natural way as mother tongues, and in no way dependent on any norm of official or international English. Wikipedia currently lists 125 "dialects" (including different accents) and a further 34 "creoles," though there is certainly some

---

* Choice of a written norm is a political rather than a linguistic act. For example, the sounds of spoken Low German are closer to Dutch, but its speakers all write in the national standard, Hochdeutsch.

overlap.[13] A fair basis exists here for a range of new languages, with relatives in every continent.

If for some reason the sense and knowledge that they are parts of "World English" were to fail, some at least would undoubtedly emerge as new languages. Russell Hoban's *Riddley Walker* is built on the premise that nuclear apocalypse has long since shattered world communications and tries to imagine the linguistic, as well as other, consequences. Here he imagines how life before the catastrophe might be remembered:

> Wen Mr Clevver wuz Big Man uv Inland thay had evere thing clevver. Thay had boats in the ayr & picters on the win & evere thing lyk that. Eusa wuz a noing man vere qwik he cud tern his han tu enne thing . . . he noet how tu bigger the smaul & he noet how to smauler the big.[14]

There is a maelstrom of changes here, and English has clearly churned up its twentieth-century spelling in the meantime, without quite losing it. It looks as if the language has been thrown back on its own resources, with some verbs made regular (*noet* past tense of *know*) and constructed as needed (*tu bigger, tu smauler*). Yet somehow the sense of the English text is still there.*

But could the shared sense of World English fail? Provided that modern communications survive, it certainly seems unlikely. The most extreme scenario would be a general holocaust taking us "back to the Stone Age," which would make long-distance contact between peoples for a long time as hard and as indirect as it used to be before spread of global navigation. A less extreme disaster with linguistic implications would be if some English-speaking countries were somehow to fall under foreign domination: if the age of empires should return, but under new management. This could mean that (as when the Spanish took over the Aztec and the Inca domains) speakers of another language would for a long time take all positions of power and keep English speakers in subjection. Even if English survived in such countries (as it did once, after all, during the three centuries of French-speaking domination that followed 1066), it might lose contact with other

---

* Deeper down there are problems: Hoban toys with sound changes that have theological consequences. So Eusa here is St. Eustace, who will confront a mystical stag; but he is also the USA engaged in splitting the atom. When he finds "the littl shynin man the Addom," it is also Adam, father of the human race.

people speaking it in other parts of the world and so begin to develop separately. This is beginning to happen already between the speech varieties of North and South Korea, even though there was no major difference in dialect in the first half of the twentieth century, before the partition of the country in 1953. The differences are most concentrated from deriving loan vocabulary from different sources (Russian or Chinese rather than English), and from some different policies in spelling (though using the same Korean alphabet). But phonetically too differences are arising, as a result of different views on whether the accent of Pyongyang or of Seoul should be the model for the national language. The outcome will depend on political progress, which is currently stuck, along with the project for a joint Korean dictionary, begun in 2005.

If such breakdowns in communications do happen, they would seem likely only to maroon a few isolated pockets of English, not to break the vast network of interconnected links among the major mass of Inner and Outer Circle territories. Meanwhile, these—and indeed all—parts of the world are now exposed to a stream of sound, video, and text from English-language media from distant parts of the world, all of which tends to exercise a pressure on the various dialects to accommodate to each other, however they may be changing under their own internal trends. Taglish may be different today from any other English, as native speakers in the Philippines first develop its potential, but it will not be left to its own devices. This linguistic stream of English diffusion has replaced the human stream of fresh English-speaking migration, which was the major force tending to keep English integrated all round the world in the seventeenth, eighteenth, and nineteenth centuries.

❧

The balance of all this diverse English—the question of which features, accents, and genres tend to be favored amid the vast gallimaufry—is hard to determine in general terms, or to predict. Initially the influence will have come mostly from the dialects, the places, the cultures, that are most closely associated with those who invented, marketed, and first propagated all these media. That has meant that the characteristic dialects of British English spread by railway travelers and radio telegraphy gradually lost out internationally to General American, in the era of airplanes, globally distributed movies, broadcast television, and networked computers. But once the media are established, it becomes clear that content can be generated anywhere. Australian soap operas, Indian Bollywood movies, Jamaican reggae videos, all have their effects on overall English.

News reporting and commentary is often delivered in the accents of the region originating the news. Furthermore, one feature of the end of colonial power has been a massive increase in migration flows from former Asian and African colonies to metropolitan countries, which in practice include all the white settlement colonies of the Inner Circle, as well as the United Kingdom. Hence, in the countries with traditionally massive output of English media, native productions show increasing linguistic variety, as recent immigrants, with creolized or even halting English, have their contributions to the national media fed into broadcast or otherwise accessible output. Traffic between centers remains asymmetrically skewed with a bias for flows from North America and Europe to Asia, and even more so to Africa, but one effect of general globalization is gradually to diminish this imbalance between traditional and more or less creolized English, making the positions of the long-term equilibriums, if there are going to be any, still unpredictable.

We face the prospect of a system with considerable diversity among English standards, dialects, and creoles, all spoken with mother tongue authority, and all communicating with one another through population contact and electronic media. There will be large-scale accommodations, surprisingly often by those at the traditional center to conform to what was once the periphery—as when UK speakers adopt new patterns of young, often female, Americans or Australians, e.g., the flapped pronunciation of dental consonants (so that *better* sounds more like *bedda*, *twenty* more like *twenny*), or the rising final intonation of sentences, so-called *uptalk*, which can make assertions sound a bit like questions: "Oh, yes, I totally agree?" But there will also be deliberate or involuntary holdouts against a tide of perceived difference from abroad: separatists, and many others with a developed sense of belonging or patriotism, may become sensitive about the retention of local features of their speech. Some may find an advantage in not accommodating their speech, or in even exaggerating its differences, when they change their local environment, as when speakers who have British Received Pronunciation (RP, aka BBC English) find themselves abroad in moneyed or educated environments in the USA.

The fact is that all mother tongue speakers of English are more or less sociolinguistically sophisticated: they can recognize some foreign accents and dialects, and have attitudes to them, which are probably only partly related to their actual experience of people who use them. These attitudes will in quite complex ways condition their propensity to accommodate and imitate others. Traditionally, where sense of social class was strong, members of lower classes who aspired to be upwardly mobile affected features of higher-class speech; but if they did it too much for their peers, they might have been called affected or la-di-da; yet if they did it too little, they might have been called common, rustic, or down-home. With comparable motives but in opposite direction, many people, often adolescents (sometimes individually, sometimes as a group) now have a contrarian, rebellious tendency to diverge from their own elders, whom naturally—by the usual process of language acquisition—they might have been expected to imitate. Instead, they adopt speech features (along with other behaviors) of some group whom they admire, especially if they think those elders disrespect or fear it. They may too misjudge their imitation and end up offending those they hoped to flatter. All these mimics are in effect trying to adopt aspects of someone else's mother tongue as a useful lingua-franca for themselves, and mistakes can be made.

The effect is a vast network of possibilities for social unease, moderated by mutual ignorance about what the full set of possibilities are, and perhaps some mutual indulgence and goodwill. The resulting interplay of performances and attitudes creates what is known to linguists as a dia-system, a kind of multidimensional interweaving of varieties of a single language, each of which is a full language system in its own right. Speakers know something (implicitly) about many of the others, and where they contrast with their own normal patterns. Dimensions of the dia-system include physical space (the different regional dialects of English), social class and line of work (which can be a minefield, and a differently laid minefield, in every different geographical region of English worldwide), and expressive level (having to do with different degrees of familiarity versus formality, and coarseness versus politeness).

The dia-system makes itself felt in popular culture through stereotypes of the speakers of different dialects. These are revealed, and no doubt reinforced, by their appearance in mass-circulation media. So Hollywood puts it about that speakers of British Received Pronunciation are well educated, but potentially unscrupulous. A character with this accent will pose a credible threat as a villain, but will not attract too much sympathy from a U.S. mass audience.* But RP speakers who find themselves in authoritative jobs in the USA (doctors, academics, business consultants) are under no pressure at all to conform to local speech norms. Conversely, in the United Kingdom, characters with General American accents are commonly represented as earnest, but doctrinaire or naive. The London accent, once called cockney, but now more amply characterized as (Thames) Estuary English, sets up an expectation, at least in the United Kingdom, that the speaker is self-consciously cunning, but possibly overconfident, likely a rogue, though maybe a lovable one. These are pretty widespread accents, and close to being standards. Many regional and foreign accents and dialects have the advantage in the United Kingdom that it is hard for most to assign them to a social class; but if they are far from the southeastern norms (as, say, Welsh, Glaswegian, Indian, or Jamaican are), they will tend to be seen as rather comical, an advantage for comedians, but a bit of a liability for those who want to be taken seriously.

This use of perceived linguistic differences as a kind of literary shortcut to establish character is ancient and widespread in the world. Over three thousand years ago goddesses in southern Iraq were represented as speaking in a separate dialect of Sumerian from anyone else. In classical Indian drama, basically written in Sanskrit, only the higher male characters had their lines in this, literally the 'perfected'—and geographically nonspecific—language; the ladies spoke in a related dialect historically associated with the city of Mathura, but sang in yet another variety, Maharashtri, both western dialects; some minor authority characters such as innkeepers and watchmen have the Magadhi style of speech, a dialect of the east and a forerunner to modern Bengali.

In other traditions, particular dialects have come to be associated not so much with social classes as with literary genres. The Germans refer to dialects so used as *Kunstsprachen* 'art languages'. In the Greek of the eighth to fifth centuries BC, different types of literature were expected to be written in different dialects, epics in a mixture of Aeolic and Ionic (as Homer had done), lyric poetry in Aeolic (after Alcaeus or Sappho) or in Doric (follow-

---

* This is copiously illustrated at "The Queen's Latin," one of the Web pages at tvtropes .org. But there it is attributed to a belief that any American accent in a historical drama set before the seventeenth century must sound inauthentic. This is not quite the same thing. By contrast, the site says nothing on the impression that General American accents make on those who find other accents more natural.

ing an early exponent Alcman), history in Ionic (after Herodotus), and tragedy in Attic. Comedy might be in Attic or Doric. In plays, for example, the dialect would change as between the dialogue and the sung interludes.* Literary dialects, though, are a kind of perverse lingua-franca largely put on by foreigners, and for foreigners' appreciation. So they should not be over-done, and they tend to be inconsistently kept up. The sound and shape of individual words get changed, but not so much the choice of words, or the way that sentences are put together.

This Greek practice was a baroquely elaborate dia-system; but it has sim-pler analogues in other traditions. Chinese novels in the sixteenth to eigh-teenth centuries were written in *báihuà* 'white speech', based on the colloquial used in the capital, Beijing, even though most other literature was steadfastly (as it had been for two millennia) in the classical dialect *wényán*. On the other side of the world, in the eleventh to thirteenth centu-ries, when Romance vernaculars were first being written down for purposes alien to Latin, they soon became specialized to different genres: in Spain, Castilian was for heroic verse, and for prose too, while Galician or Portu-guese was required for lyrical love poetry. In the south of France, Occitan was used for courtly love, while stories in prose were written in Catalan, whose geographical base was over to the west.

Back in English, the same phenomenon can be seen to this day, naturally enough in popular music. The different styles of music called gospel, blues, jazz, and country all had their origins in the southeast USA. The musicians developing them were long segregated by skin color, but nonetheless black and white all sang in much the same dialect, at least in sounds and gram-matical quirks, if not necessarily in vocabulary. Most of the traditions that grew up during the twentieth century were heavily influenced by one or other of these: gospel led to soul and funk; blues to jump, rhythm and blues, reggae; country to rockabilly and Nashville; all together to rock 'n' roll. Southern American became the "standard" language for singing rock mu-sic. This meant that when non-American singers, such as the Beatles, the Rolling Stones, or the Bee Gees (and many, many more), produced their own

---

* Later on, though, from the fourth century BC, all these were increasingly swept away by a tide of uniform Attic, a humorlessly unchanging standard that endured for the next two millennia. Clever-clever exceptions, such as Theocritus' pastoral sketches from the third century BC, composed in a crafted Doric of Sicily (or Lesbian, if he was imitating Sappho), are vanishingly rare.

rock songs in the 1960s and '70s, they tended to sing not in their own accents, but (possibly unconsciously) with a faux Southern American twang. No Englishman would naturally promise a girlfriend to "lurve her truleh," but when singing, that is almost the only way to pronounce it. There is a similar effect on Australians singing "folk," as if they can't get the country-and-western style out of their heads: the Ltyentye Apurte Band of aboriginals sing that their home is "San'a T'resa." More recently, new styles have come about, now inspired by urban models, but again from black neighborhoods, so hip-hop and rap, wherever in the world they are performed, if the language is English, tend to be chanted in African-American vernacular.

This story of pop-music accents shows us that minority mother tongues can get global exposure, and so (within the given cultural domain) become obligatory. They move to being the standard, in a sense, in one area of the dia-system. Given a few films such as Disney's 1950 *Treasure Island* (featuring Dorset man Robert Newton as Long John Silver), West Country English becomes established as a stereotype for pirate speech: "Oo arr." We can expect this to go on happening sporadically, with different dialects becoming (as Andy Warhol put it) "famous for fifteen minutes," and occasionally, when enough people with the same accent become famous for the same thing, converting this into a status as linguistic fixture. The global reach of media access to stories, and the global news agenda, mean that they could come, literally, from anywhere. The worldwide renown of Arnold Schwarzenegger made an Austrian/South German accent summon up ideas of a certain type of superhero, incorruptible but implacable (though this may be a distraction when listening to Boris Becker's tennis commentary); and Oliver Stone, in his film *Alexander*, ensured that all the Macedonian characters spoke with Irish accents, intending subtly—but viscerally—to connote the social attitudes among Greeks that would have surrounded King Alexander's winning team.*

---

\* This finesse does not seem to have been widely appreciated, or indeed successful, among the mainstream American audience, who have generally found the accents distracting, and out of line with the usual rule that non-American actors should speak "the Queen's Latin," i.e., British English, affected to show that they were foreign to the central characters. Possibly the social analogy only made sense to Britons, and the Irish themselves.

The world media keep the various mother tongue communities that grow up in English in touch with one another. And so—to a limited and artificial, but probably sufficient, extent—they keep knowledge alive, within the dia-system of each language speaker, of at least some features of other dialects spoken far away. One-way or two-way traffic means that no English-speaking community is without regular contact with the rest of the anglophone world.

Standards for such mutual knowledge (or interest) are never going to be equal in both directions. It should not be surprising that the Australian films *Mad Max* (1979) and *The Road Warrior* (1981) and likewise the Scottish *Gregory's Girl* (1981) and *Trainspotting* (1996) were dubbed for the U.S. market, whereas the converse, dubbing or subtitling U.S. films for Australia or Scotland, is a laughable idea. Every native speaker of whatever mother tongue version of English gets to understand General American, even if any reverse competence may be much more rarely achieved by Americans. (This lack of symmetry could be called the metropolitan effect, since in states too where a plurality of languages is spoken, the universal tendency is for native speakers of the language of the metropolis (be it Mandarin Chinese, Latin, Greek, Arabic, Persian, French, Swahili—not just English) not to learn any of their state's peripheral languages; all the linguistic accommodation is made in one direction.)*

In this overall situation, any changes that occur in any of the mother tongues are not likely to be kept secret from the other dialect areas. Either the changes will propagate to them, or (more likely) they will be noted by bilingual individuals, people who are conducting conversations, or sampling material, across the boundaries of different dialect areas. Such individuals, sometimes called language mavens, are usually journalists or linguists, but may just as easily be politicians, random bloggers, or members of the public sending their observations to some organs of the mass media. They will make the emerging differences explicit somewhere; they will broadcast and record them, as new details of the dia-system.

⌘

---

* This tendency can be mitigated by central decision, as witness the BBC's policy, begun as long ago as World War II, of using announcers, both locally and centrally, who speak with regional accents of English. It remains slightly controversial, but has no prospect of being reversed. On January 16, 2008, the BBC director general even called for more regional accents on the corporation's television and radio programs. Even if passive comprehension (and popular solidarity with linguistic varieties) are broadened by this, it does not seem to lead to broader active use of other people's dialects.

Overall, the scope for English to break up in the future is limited. A shattered lingua-franca is no lingua-franca at all, and a part of a lingua-franca specialized to a particular area is a pidgin, which tends to die out when contact situations change. Any mother tongue spoken in various territories can evidently find its parts developing in diverse directions, but the chance of any of these variants changing so as to be unintelligible to any other is slight, given the vast real-time communications network that spans every major region of the English-speaking world, and given that all mother tongue speakers are in command of a range of English varieties, in various relations to one another. Contact is ubiquitous, and people are acquainted with far more English than they naturally use. All this tends to keep the overall language community in touch with itself.

Even if a region were to become so cut off as to develop a variety unintelligible to any other (as one could imagine happening in a state such as Burma/Myanmar, if lively use of English is maintained there), this would not be enough in itself for the variety to be recognized as a separate language. We have seen the reluctance—even where such varieties have moved far apart, as in the Arab world or the old pre-Hispanic empires of America—to accept claims, despite a clamor from linguists, that new languages are here. For that to be recognized, a will to political separateness needs to be present, outweighing any sense of historic unity, and the political unit would have to claim ownership of the new variety of English (something that is less likely to happen in Burma/Myanmar). Ultimately, only politics can set the seal on linguistic difference.

This is not to deny that change will occur, all over the English-speaking world, and faster in mother tongue communities as they are relayed down the generations, than in the standard form taught and consciously used as a global lingua-franca. But for breakup to occur, rather than a certain elasticity in the relation between native-speaker English and the global standard, communication links must fall, and there is little prospect of this in the foreseeable future.

# PART II

# LINGUA-FRANCAS PAST

سوز گوهرى دور كه رتبه سى نينك

شرحى دا دور اهل نطق عاجز

آندين كه ايرور خسيس مهلك

كورگوزگوچه دور مسيح معجز

*söz guhari-dur ki rutbah say-ïng*

*šarḥi-da dur ahl nuṭuq-e ʿājiz*

*andïn ki erür ḥasīs muhlik*

*körgüzgüči dur masīḥ muʿjiz*

A language is a gem whose value humanity cannot express.
Bad ones are poison, but the good revive the weary and the dead.[1]

—Mir ʿAli Shēr Nawāʾi, December 1499
*Muḥākamat al-luğatain* 'Verdict on the Two
Languages', p. 2 (quatrain in Chagatay Turkic)

# CHAPTER 3

# The Pragmatism of Empire

... and we have written the law not in the paternal voice (Latin),
but this common Helladic one (Greek), so that it be known to all
for ease of interpretation.

—Roman emperor Justinian (native speaker
of Latin, writing in Greek), ca 535[1]

We are too few to teach the language of Castile to Indians. They do not
want to speak it. It would be better to make universal the Mexican
language, which is widely current, and they like it, and in it there are
written doctrine and sermons and a grammar and a vocabulary.

—Fray Juan de Mansilla, Comisario General,
in Guatemala, to Emperor Charles V, 1551[2]

ENGLISH IS ESTABLISHED IN many parts of the world as a mother tongue and also enjoys global reach as a lingua-franca. Mother tongues, once established, are self-replicating entities, transmitted to each new generation as part of growing up. Too many exist to set up even a representative comparison, and besides, as long as the home community flourishes and escapes foreign domination, there is no secret to their survival. But a lingua-franca, especially a widespread one, is more of a puzzle. What can cause a language to be spoken more widely than in its home community? Does the reason for the spread have any permanent effect on attitudes to the language, or its wider status? Ultimately, does it determine how long a lingua-franca will last, or at least set up a pattern of vulnerability?

The first of these questions is not hard to answer. The great lingua-francas of history have been spread by quite a small number of causes. For Europeans, the most salient among these is military conquest, the expansion of empire. This is because many of Europe's languages are descendants of Latin, once spoken as a mother tongue uniquely in central Italy, but which Roman armies originally projected across the rest of Italy, France, the Iberian Peninsula, and into the Balkans. Even before it became widespread there as a budding mother tongue, the administration of taxes and the army must have ensured that it was far-flung as a lingua-franca.

But although well-known, such a requirement for imperial administration, imposed by conquest, is not the only way lingua-francas arise. Others include commerce, and religious missions. Merchants are often wide-ranging and evidently need to negotiate about demand and supply, ways and means, costs and prices; this can create the need for an auxiliary language that goes beyond mother tongues. Missionaries too need to spread knowledge about their faith, narratives, rituals, and ethics, sometimes also their distinctive styles of administration. Particularly if they have a traditional body of scriptures, one or more particular languages may become associated with a spreading religion.

Each of these modalities has played a significant part in the worldwide spread of English. In this part of the book, some other previous lingua-francas that have been spread by these different means are considered in some detail, to shed a rather different light than usual on the dynamic forces involved. There is not space for a full review of all the comparable languages, and their contrast with the career of English. But even a selection of the major lingua-francas of western and southern Asia leads to some surprising insights.

✥

What are the links between language spread and the most literal understanding of *empire*: the imposition of power on alien peoples? English owes much of its global reach to actions undertaken by the British military (notably the conquest of the French colony Canada in 1754–63 and of various Dutch-ruled colonies in South Africa during the nineteenth century), and to more recent exertions of the United States of America (notably the Mexican War in 1846–48 and the Spanish-American War in 1898). English is just the latest in a series of world languages that were put there by political imperialism, the expansion by force of a state's territory, and so of the population that it administered. A growing empire evidently needs some means to communicate with its newly acquired subjects, and this is one motive for the spread of a lingua-franca.

Persian was another such language whose spread (from the ninth century AD to the seventeenth) was almost always militarily inspired—though strangely enough, largely not through the campaigns of the language's own speakers. Campaigns of Arabs, Turks, and Mongols would make Persian into a world language, a lingua-franca used widely as a second language by people with a different mother tongue. Persian is a world language that has overwhelmingly owed its currency to the needs of multinational states.

However, the career of Persian is particularly vivid in showing the difference between a shared mother tongue and a lingua-franca. Persian has been a widespread and widely used language for all of its recorded history—more than a hundred generations; yet in the early centuries, from the sixth to the fourth BC, when Persians were creating and ruling their own autonomous empire, alien languages, not Persian, served as lingua-francas. In this period Persian was not—or only to a limited extent—a cosmopolitan language.

Yet for most of the last millennium it was to become a lingua-franca itself, something which only happened when others, non-native-speakers, took it up and spread it. When they did so, its use created a kind of cultural unity in western Asia, the *qalamrau-e-zabān-e-fārsī*, quite literally 'where the writ of Persian ran'. This was always under the banner of Islam, but conceived socially, rather than theologically. This wider cultural use, although it lasted for over eight centuries, could not survive political change, while its use as a mother tongue clearly could and has. To become a lingua-franca, a language must transcend its ethnic base, appeal to third-party learners. But transcending, rather than extending, this base is a dangerous step for the long-term future of the language.

The six stages of the documented history of Persian, with their durations, are set out here:

| TITLE | PERIOD | LENGTH | EVENTS |
|-------|--------|--------|--------|
| Latent | . . . 550–150 BC | 4+ centuries | Persian is represented through documents written in other languages (Elamite, Aramaic); monumental inscriptions are in the real language; there is rapid change in the substance of the language. |
| Emergent | 150 BC–AD 650 | 8 centuries | This is a time of transition from Aramaic to explicit Persian in writing; Persian is dominant in Iran and spreads as lingua-franca into the Indian Ocean. |
| Islamized | 650–1000 | 3+ centuries | Arabic replaces literary and administrative functions; Persian, borrowing heavily from Arabic, supplants neighboring languages and becomes the cultural language of Iran. |
| Resurgent | 1000–1250 | 2+ centuries | Adopted by Turkic dynasties, Persian is used in administration and is spread through West, Central, and Southern Asia. |
| Cultural | 1250–1850 | 6 centuries | After Mongol conquests, Persian remains established as language of culture throughout its traditional zones. |
| National | 1850–present | 2 centuries | Persian is displaced in Turkey and India, but remains official in 3 states (Iran, Afghanistan, Tajikistan); it is in diglossia with Pashto in Afghanistan, and Russian in much of Central Asia. |

Complicating its recorded history, Persian has often been in important cultural and practical contact with some other language. Before the founding of the multinational Persian Empire in the sixth century BC, this language was Elamite, the indigenous language of the territory where Persians had settled (broadly, the west of modern Iran), providing written services to an aristocratic community. When the community achieved control of western Asia as a whole, it adopted Aramaic, long the de facto lingua-franca of the Babylonian empire, for written communications. Then, from the mid-fourth to mid-second centuries Greek became the language of the administration of Iran; but after its deposition, Persian reemerged in the written record, with heavy admixtures of Aramaic. In this period Persian was the language of trade round the Indian Ocean, and in an archaic form (Avestan) it was consciously revived to support the Zoroastrian faith. After the collapse of the Persian Empire under Arab assault, Arabic for a time became the sole language of serious, secular writing.

Subsequently, Persian was reasserted as "New Persian" and rewritten in Arabic script. Although this form of the language was "Islamized" through vast numbers of Arabic loans, it did not become a sacred language of Islam. Instead, as Turkic invaders largely took control of its territory, it was transformed into a language of high Islamic culture. But now, although sacred and intellectual use of Arabic did not cease, Persian became the dominant language of the Turkic, and later (briefly) Mongol, courts of southwestern Asia, with many other languages, principally Turkic and Indo-Aryan, in the background. As such, Persian exercised a major influence on them all, to form Ottoman Turkish and Chagatay, as well as Urdu and Sindhi. Persian remained a cultural lingua-franca until it was ousted (by determinedly secular governments) in India and Turkey; but beside Iran, where it continues as the mother tongue, it remains an official language in Afghanistan and Tajikistan.

To appreciate the dynamics of Persian's long career first among lingua-francas, and latterly as a lingua-franca itself, we first review two millennia of its history.

❈❈❈

In the beginning was the steppe. The Medes and the Persians, properly *Māda* and *Pārsa*,* speakers of different dialects within the language generally known as Old Persian, had prehistoric ancestors in the second millennium BC who had been nomads herding, riding, and driving about the

---

* The long *a* notable in the indigenous versions was converted to a long *e* in Herodotus' Ionic Greek accent. *Mēdoi*, *\*Pērsai*. The long vowel before the consonant cluster *rs* was then shortened, by a common Greek rule, to *Persai*; whence our *Medes*, *Persians*.

great grassy plains of Siberia. We place the Medes in the northwest, and Persians in the southwest of Iran (the area once known, in Greek, as Persis, and for the last millennium and a half, in Arabic, as Fārs). But the only evidence we have suggests that speakers of this language were already spread out much farther afield: Strabo the Greek geographer, writing for the Roman Empire of first century BC, stated that all the peoples of the Iranian plateau (Ariana) spoke "much the same language, close enough,"[3] explicitly including even the Bactrians and Sogdians (in Central Asia). If he knew what he was talking about, he must have had a fairly broad idea of "the same language," but he may have been right in stating that Iranian languages were spoken throughout. With the exception of Elamite, there is no trace of any other family of languages spoken in this vast area.

Elamite is, however, interesting. It was to have a cooperative relationship with Old Persian for at least the first half millennium while the two languages were in contact.

Elamite is a language with no known close relatives, the only contenders as its cousins being the Dravidian languages of the Indian subcontinent.[4] But Elam (now Khuzestan), the Iranian side of the lands at the outflow of the Tigris and Euphrates, is an ancient home of agriculture and literacy, with a history as long as Sumer itself, a capital known as Shusim (Greek Susa, Persian Shushan), and a hinterland called Anshan up to its east and south in the Zagros Mountains. Until the advent of the Persians in the early first millennium BC (when Anshan became Pārsa/Persis/Fārs), it had been a state, often independent of, and always in contention with, the civilizations across the Tigris marshes. Quite soon after this, in 646 BC, it succumbed to Assyrian attack and ceased to figure politically. But for two thousand years it had already been a literate society, originally with its own script, and since 1300 BC using a version of Assyrian cuneiform. It was this system that became of service to the Persians.

After the Persian invasion, the Elamites' settled civilization was ruled—essentially parasitized—by an aristocracy of Persian knights. One feature of their coexistence was for the Elamites to offer scribal services to the Persians. The details are obscure, but the basic ingredients are comparable to what was to happen in western Europe a millennium later, when after the end of the Roman Empire scribes educated in Latin were soon at the service of illiterate Germanic farmer-warriors. Persians indeed early made a virtue of illiteracy, reportedly holding that the only subjects fit for a noble to learn were to ride a horse, to shoot a bow, and to tell the truth—though this training, curiously, occupied them from the ages of five to twenty.[5] When a Persian needed to send written communication or to store records, it was done for him in Elamite, this being the beginning of a tradition of alloglottography (writing down Persian by the use of some other language), which was to continue in Persia—almost unbroken, and despite the spread of literate education—for the next millennium, and perhaps even after the Arab conquest in 650.

This did not mean that Elamite was widely learned, or even heard, by Persians. Rather Elamite-Persian bilinguals would be employed to use their writing skills, protecting their employers from the disconcerting experience of an unknown language by routinely translating the texts on request into, or out of, spoken Persian. Elamite remained central to Persian organization, but it could hardly be called a lingua-franca, since probably its currency was less widespread than that of Persian itself: very likely, all Elamites were bilingual in Persian, but not vice versa. However, this use paved the way for another language that certainly was to be a lingua-franca, all across the realms of the Persian 'King of Kings'.*

By the end of 522, with the new domains that included the Assyrian-Babylonian Empire, and also Anatolia and eastern Iran, the territory that had been under Median/Persian control had been quadrupled and its boundaries secured. The empire would last for two hundred years, extending in an arc, as the contemporary Book of Esther proclaimed, "over 127 provinces (*medīnāh*) from Hōdû to Kûš," i.e. from Hindustan to the land of Kush, south of Egypt, or as the Persian king Darius† himself described it, by its two diagonals, "from the Scythians beyond Sogd to Kush, and from the Indus to Sardis," i.e. from Central Asia to beyond Egypt, and from India to western Anatolia.[6]

This was a considerable area to coordinate, even if the main purpose was just to raise armies and tribute for the center. Was this vast conquest of Persian arms, then, the first domain for the Persian language as a lingua-franca? Actually, no. Persian certainly played a prestige role in this state, known as the Empire of the Achaemenians.‡ Persian was after all the language of the royal family and the ruling elite, and (in some broad version) most likely used as vernacular in much of the territory to the north and east

---

* This is an ancient and distinctively Persian way of referring to the head of the empire—from *xšāyaθiya xšāyaθiyānām* used of Darius and Xerxes to *šāhan-šāh* used of Mohammad Rezā Shāh Pahlavi (1941–79).

† *Dāraya-vahu-* 'holding virtue'.

‡ This is a Greek rendering of Cyrus's family name, *Haxā-maniśiya-* 'friendly disposed'.

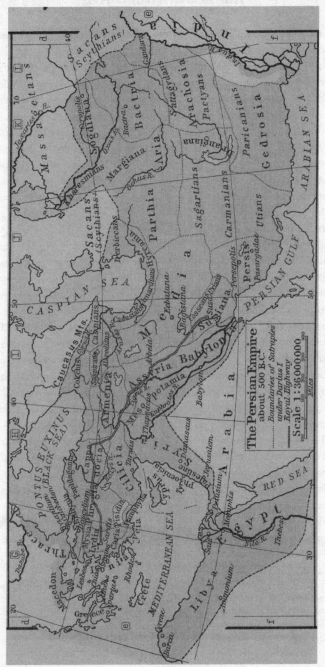

(Credit: University of Texas at Austin, Perry–Castañeda Library Map Collection)

of Pārsa. But it had no scribal tradition of its own, let alone a secretarial corps capable of administering and coordinating all the new provinces.

The regions where Persian might have been understood were the less developed, less civilized, and less wealthy regions of the empire. For all the rest—most of them previously ruled by Assyria or Babylon—there was Aramaic. This Semitic tongue, a close relative of Hebrew and Phoenician, had been the administrative language of the Babylonians for the past four hundred years. Elamite had sufficed to record Persian before Persian power had spread beyond their common home in Pārsa; but when the new Persian empire was to take in the whole civilized realm of the Middle East, the solution was to substitute Aramaic and continue it in service as the common medium of imperial communications.

One aspect of language politics as they were felt is illustrated by the monumental royal inscriptions that survive from the Persian empire, all apparently originated in Elamite,[7] but with translations added into Persian and Akkadian. Elamite was a script that could actually be read out (even if this was usually done in Persian), while the other two were both there for Persian "vanity" publishing. The really Persian versions were written in a unique alphabetic script, likely invented for the purpose, a means of writing that never caught on and so would never have been widely legible, even to the educated. Akkadian was the distinguished language of antiquity, once (five hundred years before) the official language of the Assyrian and Babylonian empires that had once dominated Persia, but were now subject to it. It was a pleasant irony to use it, but it had for many centuries been a moribund system, known only to scholars even in the land of its birth.*

The absence of Aramaic is striking here. But this language, despite its currency all over the empire, was never used for the king's monumental inscriptions. As a lingua-franca, used for interlingual communications and contracts, it was preeminently a practical medium; its status was just not adequate to win it a place alongside Elamite, Persian, and Akkadian.

The Empire of the Achaemenians was a highly multilingual place. These monumental Persian inscriptions describe the empire as *vispazana* (in Median)

---

* It was as if those invaders from Friesland and Denmark who established themselves in England in the fifth century AD had left inscriptions in Welsh, Anglo-Saxon, and Latin, and so simultaneously claimed attachment to their adopted homeland (British— hence Welsh), linguistic identity (Germanic—hence Anglo-Saxon), and (with Latin) aspirations to universal domination on a par with Rome.

*Royal Achaemenid inscription at Behistun, set up by Darius I (r. 522–486 BC). (Credit: Hamid Najafi)*

or *visadana* (in Persian), words whose literal meaning is 'of all peoples'.*[8] Besides Akkadian, Aramaic, Elamite, Median, and Persian in use on either side of the Tigris, contemporary inscriptions show that farther west in Anatolia, every one of the languages Greek, Lycian, Lydian (in Sardis), and Sidetic and Carian (in Cappadocia) continued to be used in public inscriptions, though often alongside Aramaic. A recent invention at the time, borrowed from the Lydians, had provided a new place to put monumental text—namely, the faces of coins. On these, Aramaic tends to predominate, though even here Greek and Lydian legends persist.[9] In Egypt, Egyptian hieroglyphs were still current, often found inscribed on contemporary objets d'art. So great was the diversity in the western provinces. To the east of Pārsa, there was little literacy within the empire, but also much less diversity, on the evidence of today's pattern of languages on the ground. Other than the Turkic languages Khalaj and Qashqa'i (which must have arrived in the first or even second millennia AD),[10] this area now contains only one language that is unrelated to Persian: Brahui, in Baluchistan, a Dravidian language that is certainly ancient and probably marks the trail linking Elamite with its relatives in southern India.

In the Persian Empire then, which flourished from 522 until it was overthrown by Alexander of Macedon in 332 BC, Persian was widely spoken (and especially so in the eastern provinces); but Aramaic, an unrelated language promoted by practical utility and wide currency, was the lingua-franca for official, hence written, business, bridging the substantial language barriers that divided up the west. To use Aramaic made no statement about your identity, nor even literacy. Messages could be dictated in the sender's language, written down in the Aramaic language and alphabet, and the letter would be presented for oral delivery by local heralds in whatever language the recipient understood. This process was known in Aramaic as *paraš* 'declaration', and in Persian as *uzvārišn* 'understanding'. Aramaic was, in the precise sense now used in machine translation systems, an interlingua, a communication code familiar to all scribes and heralds of any language within the empire, but unnecessary for anyone else to recognize.[11]

Politically, after the fall of the Achaemenids to Alexander in 332 BC, the story is one of three successive empires. The Greek (Seleucid) kingdom founded after Alexander's death persisted for two centuries; then, in the mid-second century BC, the dynasty of Aršak (known to the west as the

---

* Compare the related Sanskrit word *viśva-janam* 'all humanity'.

*Parthian coin of Artabanus II (r. ca AD 10–38) with a bowman enthroned,
surrounded by a largely legible Greek legend. The inscription can be translated:
"King of kings, Artabanus, benefactor, just, manifest, pro-Greek."
(Credit: Smithsonian National Numismatic Collection)*

*Parthian coin of Vologases III (r. AD 105–47), with same intended legend, but an
inscription largely illegible. (Credit: Smithsonian National Numismatic Collection)*

Arsacids, or the Parthian Empire) spread from the northeast to overwhelm
the Greeks; it successfully, and rather gloriously, resisted the depredations of
the Roman Empire over the next four centuries, but in AD 224 succumbed
to one of its vassals, Ardashir of Pārsa, the first of the Sassanians. His dynasty, more centralized politically than the Parthians, but no less successful
in its campaigns against the Romans and Byzantine Greeks, then continued
for a further four centuries, until Iran was overrun by the Arabs in 642.

The first of these kingdoms, the direct successor to Alexander, gave rise to a rather singular interlude of domination by Greek. It became preeminent among official languages, appearing on the coinage everywhere, and in Anatolia at least there came to be significant settlement by Greek speakers. For a time it may well have been a lingua-franca in Iran, giving those who learned it access in principle to the wider Greek *oikouménē* 'inhabited world', which (at the time) extended from the Mediterranean to the borders of India. However, the penetration of Greeks into Iranian life and the recruitment of Iranians into Greek-speaking strata of government seem to have been shallow. But even after the Parthians permanently detached Iran from the Greek empire, use of the Greek language continued in early royal inscriptions. Afterward it faded away fast, except on the coinage: that was still being issued—by Parthian kings—in garbled Greek until the mid-second-century AD.

Over this long period of some ten centuries from the fall of the Achaemenians to the fall of the Sassanians, use of the Aramaic lingua-franca declined, and use of (Middle) Persian—usually known as Pahlavi (a phonetic development of *parthavi*, i.e. 'Parthian')—correspondingly increased. Pahlavi as a dialect appears to have been a direct continuation of Median, so the geographical range—and the source of the linguistic ingredients—of standard Persian changed little over the period.

The actual content of the language may, however, have changed. It has long been noted that since this era Persian has been an exceptionally simple language among its Iranian relatives, in the sense of having relatively few grammatical inflections, and few irregularities in what it does have. In this, it differs not only from its ancestors, Old Persian and Avestan,* but also from its peers, northeastern languages such as Khwarezmian, Sogdian, or Bactrian of the pre-Islamic era, but also Pashto, Kurdish, or Balochi, which are major languages still spoken to this day. Persian has been distinctive in this way since the Middle Persian period.

To see the difference between Persian as it had been in the fifth century BC and what it was already becoming at the turn of the millennium, compare the three sentences that follow.

---

* Avestan is the name given to the language of Zoroastrian scriptures (Avesta), which was only written down in the ninth or tenth centuries AD, but records a state of Persian at least as old as the Old Persian monumental inscriptions (sixth to fourth centuries BC) and possibly, in part, as old as the prophet Zarathushtra (Greek Zoroaster) himself, taking it back to the tenth century BC. Some have suggested it is really Old Indic, recorded with an Iranian accent. (See pages 50–51.)

| NUMBER | 1 | 2 | 3 | 4 |
|---|---|---|---|---|
| Avestan (ca 1000 BC) | *aēuua* | *duua* | *θraii* | *čaθvar* |
| Pahlavi (ca 100 BC) | *ēk* | *do* | *sē* | *čahār* |

## Old Persian—ca 490 BC

*θātiy Dārayavauš xšāyaθiya imaiy martiyā <u>tayaiy</u> adakaiy avadā*
*[ā]hatā yātā adam Gaumātam <u>tayam</u> magum avājanam <u>haya</u> Bardiya*
*agaubatā*

says Darius(**Nom.**) king these(**Acc.**) men(**Acc.**) who then there were
while I Gaumata(**Acc.**) whom magus(**Acc.**) I-slew who Bardiya
(**Past**)was-called(**Middle**)

"King Darius says that these men were present then and there when
I slew Gaumata the Magus who called himself Bardiya."

—Darius inscription at Behistun (DB 4.80–86)

## Middle Persian—ca AD 245

*patkar-i-ēn mazd-yasn bag-i-Šāpur Šāhān šāh Ērān ud Anērān kē čhr*
*az yazdān . . .*

monument_this Mazda-worshipping god_Shapur of-kings king of-
Aryans and of-non-Aryans, which origin from deities . . .

"This monument (is of) Mazda-worshipping god Shapur of-kings
king of-Aryans and of-non-Aryans, whose origin (is) from deities . . ."

—King Shapur's rock inscription at Naqsh-i-Rajab

## Archaizing Middle Persian—ca AD 950

*U pas, gujasteh, gannâ [minu] druwand, gumân kardan i mardomân be*
*in den râ, ân gujasteh Aleksandar i Arumyi i Muzrâyi-mânišn wiyâbâ-*
*nid u be garân sezd u nabard u biše be Eran-šahr frestâd*

"But then, the sinful, corrupt, and deceitful (one), in order to cause
people to doubt this religion, led astray that sinful Alexander the

| 5 | 20 | 30 | 40 | 50 | 100 |
|---|---|---|---|---|---|
| *pañča* | *visaiti* | *θrisatəm* | *čaθvarəsatəm* | *pañčasatəm* | *satəm* |
| *panj* | *wīst* | *sīh* | *čehel* | *panjā* | *sad* |

Roman, the resident of Egypt, and sent him to Eran with heavy tyranny, anger, and violence."

—*Arda Wiraz Nâmah* 'The Book of the Righteous Wiraz'

The intricate endings of Old Persian, which marked number and syntactic role for nouns, and tense and mood for verbs (all marked here in bold), have largely disappeared in the later forms of the language: only *-ān* marking oblique plurals, and *(i)d* for past tense have survived. Meanwhile the frequent and multifarious, almost empty, relative pronouns of Old Persian (underlined) have been honed down to just *e* or *i*, the all-purpose joiner for noun phrases, which has continued into modern Persian (now called *ezāfe*).

The numerals, too, show evidence of the massive phonetic reduction that affected almost all words. (And as another extreme example, consider *xšāyaθiya* and *šāh* above, both meaning 'king', one the reduced form of the other.)

For McWhorter 2007, this loss of inherited irregularities and complexities is evidence that the language was subject to "interrupted transmission," i.e. acquired at some point in their histories by so many adult learners (who never attained full command of the traditional languages) that imperfect knowledge of the language became the standard, and the languages were radically simplified.* This makes sense in an era when the previous linguafrancas (Aramaic and Greek) were losing currency, if disturbances of traditional communities induced people to try to make contact with new neighbors in a kind of pidgin, or creolized, Persian.†

---

* This property he discerns in many of the world's widely spoken languages, including Chinese, English, vernacular Arabic, and Malay.

† More prosaically, the traditional explanation for this kind of massive loss of suffixes is to appeal to a change in the stress pattern of words: if a heavy stress is going on word beginnings, the vowels at the end of words are likely to be reduced—and this could potentially cause new generations of learners not to notice their full variety and ultimately to simply ignore them. E.g., Hale 2004, 770, refers to "serious 'erosion from the right' in

However, the possibility that Persian may have had a high percentage of nonnative adult learners at this early stage in its development is not an argument that the language was at this stage established as a lingua-franca, as we have defined that term in this book. For this the language must be a second language (L2) learned deliberately for purposes of wider communication. This definition fits Aramaic in the Achaemenian Empire and thereafter, and we shall see it later fits Arabic as learned in Iran, but there is no evidence that it was ever a good fit for Persian itself in Iran. If large numbers of nonnative speakers acquire the language in this way, it will—for that generation—be a lingua-franca. But if they then go on to bring up their descendants in the language, it ceases to be a lingua-franca and becomes a mother tongue.*

◇≫◇◇

The status of Persian, established over nine centuries as the language of power in Iran, and the whole Sassanian empire's only approximation to a single language, was shaken to its foundations in a decade and a half, 635 to 651, from the lost battle of Qāsidiyya on the Euphrates to the assassination of the last Sassanian king, Yazdgird III, near Merv on the borders of Central Asia. In these years, the empire collapsed under the sustained assault of the Muslim invasions, and armies under Arab command became the authorities throughout its former territories. It was no less than the opening of a new world, in religion, in script, and in language, and one of far greater complexity than what had gone before.

Evidently, the language spoken on the streets and in the fields did not change immediately. Nor was a great deal of Arabic to be heard even in army camps. Although the supreme authority of the Persian *shāhanshāh* 'king of kings' had been destroyed, to be replaced by the overlordship of an Arab

---

Pahlavi—the final syllables (or at least their codas) having more or less uniformly disappeared . . . a function of the development of strong dynamic stress . . . clearly implicated in the massive morphological (and syntactic) restructuring." This is, in itself, not uncommon; e.g., it happened to both English and French around the end of the first millennium AD.

* See chapter 7 for this kind of development of a lingua-franca. This is not to say that Persian in this period was not also a true lingua-franca in some places; it is just that these were mostly outside Iran. It was used by the traders of the Indian Ocean through the first, and well into the second, millennium AD. This is discussed in chapter 5.

*khalīfat* 'vicar' (of God, or of God's prophet\*), the conquest after the first few shocks of battle had come about largely through power-brokerage and negotiation with the existing nobility, and the bulk of marauding forces that spread out to take control were Iranians recruited in Persia and moved en masse over to the northeast, called by the Arabs *mawālī* 'clients'. This recruitment happened not just to individuals, but to whole units of the Persian army. Their presence was crucial to the linguistic developments that were to come.

Although the Arabic language was an utter novelty outside Arabia, the intent of the new rulers was to promote it as the new medium of government, in addition to its primacy as the language of the faith. However, both these roles for the new language were subject to a drag on progress.

First, Arabic had never been more than the language of a tribal society. It was inevitable that, at the outset, administration should continue to be conducted in Pahlavi in Iran, as it was in Greek in the newly conquered western provinces of Palestine and Egypt. Meanwhile, linguistic conversion continued. The order to use Arabic for financial records went out from the caliph in 697, after two generations of Arab rule. But only in 742, two generations after that, and almost a century after the conquest, did the governor of Iraq require Naṣr bin Sayyār, governor of Khorasan,† to "seek no assistance from pagans in office work." The official accounting was changed to Arabic medium.[12]

Second, although Arabic was always essential to Islam, the Arabs were not in the first few generations actively imposing, or even seeking, conversions to the faith. Arab ambivalence centered on the fear that excessive conversions by Arab missionaries (since Muslims were exempt from the *jizya* poll tax) could undermine the tax base. Certainly the *mawālī*, being young men displaced from their homes, with prospects of booty to urge them on, were likely prospects for early conversion. But in general, besides Jews and Christians, Persian Zoroastrians were recognized as monotheists and *ahl-al-kitāb* 'people of the book', officially tolerated but heavily taxed. Pahlavi continued as the language of this faith, written as ever by *mowbed* 'priest', *dibīr* 'scribe', and *dehqān* 'landed gentleman', and Zoroastrian families would only gradually yield to pressure to convert to Islam.

Nonetheless, Arabic became established, over the century 650–750, as Iran's high-level language in religion, state, and (to a large extent) in intellectual

---

\* These tellingly different interpretations of the title (*Khalīfat Allāh* versus *Khalīfat Rasūl Allāh* ) were both proposed at different times (Lewis 1991, 43–46).

† Pahlavi for 'sunrise', i.e., the Iranian east.

writing. Persian culture for a time lost its leading role, even if its writers continued to produce traditionalist fulminations and nostalgic religious texts. A new lingua-franca had been imposed on Iran, the first since Aramaic, but this time the imposition was effected by outsiders, and for ideological reasons (namely, the presumed superiority of Islam).

The immediate effect was apparently extremely positive, both for Persians growing up with the new language, and indeed for the Arabic language tradition itself.* A new generation of Persian scribes such as 'Abd al-Ḥamīd (d. 750, Persian secretary to the Caliph Marwān II), Ibn al-Muqaffaʻ (d. ca 757, translator of the animal fables *Kalīla wa Dimna*), and al-Faḍl bin Sahl (converted 805, vizier to the Caliph Ma'mūn) made early contributions to Arabic prose literature, with didactic epistles, and translations from Pahlavi. Persians also went on to provide the first formally explicit analyses of the Arabic language itself, Sībawaih (d. ca 796) writing his *al-Kitāb* 'Book' of Arabic grammar, and al-Khalīl bin Aḥmad (an Arab writing in collaboration with Persians in Khorasan) his *Kitāb al-ʻAin* 'Book of ʻAin,' an Arabic dictionary.†[13] Such Persians were lauded by Arabs for the special purity of their Arabic, especially since they were punctilious in pronouncing the case inflections that had already largely dropped out of spoken Arabic (except among Bedouin of the desert). But this was ironic since, at the same time, written Arabic (as seen in contemporary literature, e.g., the work of Abu Nuwās, who had a Persian mother and died in 810) was actually accepting many loans from Persian. And most Persian writers would have continued to converse in Persian, even as they kept their literary work (and recitations) largely in Arabic. (This was famously the case under the Tahirid dynasty, who ruled in Khorasan from 821 to 873 and sponsored much literature in Arabic.) Later on, toward the end of the tenth century, the Arab geographer al-Muqaddasī, noted for his attention to linguistic details, would remark that the residents of Khorasan spoke the purest Arabic he heard in all his travels of the Muslim lands.[14]

---

* This, to be sure, is the winners' view, from the perspective of the following millennium of dominant Islamic culture. It has been suggested that the breakdown in Persian literacy for a century or more, until its resurgence through the medium of Arabic script, stifled the development of Persian fiction, of which, nonetheless, many echoes can be found in the *Thousand and One Nights*. (Irwin 1994, 74–75)

† A curious feature of this early Persian achievement is that it stemmed from no tradition of writing grammar for Persian itself (rather as if the Romans were to have analyzed Greek, with no thought for Latin).

The standout performers here were, not surprisingly, members of ancestral scribal families, since they had traditionally included, besides accountants and recorders of government and judicial decisions, the physicians, poets, and astronomers of Persian society. New generations took easily to the new language, and 'Abd al-Ḥamīd outlined the way to go about it: "Begin with knowledge of the Qur'ān and religious obligations; then proceed to Arabic, for that sharpens your tongue; then master calligraphy, the ornamentation of your writings. Get to know poetry, its rare words and ideas, and know also the battle-days of both the Arabs and the Persians, their history and biographies, all of which serves to inspire you."[15]

*Banū* 'the sons of' is the name for a dynasty in Arabic, and the Banū Barmak, Sahl, Naubakht, and Jarrāḥ, all distinguished themselves in the eighth and ninth centuries, whether in power politics (where vizier to the caliph was the highest available post for a scribe) or in Arabic literature.* This is a classic example of the ease with which an elite adopts—and comes to be identified with—a lingua-franca. Al-Jāḥiz (781–869), an Arab critic of the era, thought it a mark of the people's ignorance that they saw scribes as pillars of excellence, but had to admit that their rhetorical style was second to none. With a certain symmetry, he also notes (as an example of mixed Persian and Arabic) a brief and risqué Persian verse set down by Yazīd bin Mufarrigh, an Arab poet resident in Khorasan (d. 689), which has thereby the honor of being the first record of Persian in Arab script, i.e. the New Persian language:

آب است نادیذ است عصارات زبیب است سمیه روسپید است

*āb ast,* **nadīð** *ast;*  It's water, it's wine;
**'uṣārāt**-*i* **zabīb** *ast;*  It's juice of raisin;
**sumayyah** *rūspīd ast.*  Sumayya is a whore.

—quoted in Al-Jāḥiz,
*Book of Eloquence and Exposition,* i, 143[†]

---

* The Banū Barmak are none other than the Barmecide family, which produced Vizier Ja'afar to Caliph Hārūn al-Rashīd (763–809), both famous through *A Thousand and One Nights*. The very word *vizier* may be by origin a borrowing from Pahlavi, whether *wuzurg* 'great' or *wizir* 'judgment' but it has been arabized (*wazīr*) to resemble an agent noun from *wazara* 'carry'—viz 'the office bearer'.

† Here the whole is in Persian syntax, but words in bold are actually in Arabic, something that would remain quite natural in New Persian. *rūspīd* may be a slight mistake for Pahlavi *rōspīg*; and **zabīb** 'raisin' is from the same root as Arabic **zubb** 'penis'.

At the same time as Persian intellectuals were adopting Arabic for their politics and literature, others were giving Persian itself a makeover. The pervasive control of Iran gained by the Arabs seems to have been accepted without widespread political resistance, and the clerical elite of Iran was largely enlisted to work in Arabic. Thus naturally large numbers of Arabic words became current in the speech of Iranians, and these began to be accessible to many who never learned Arabic beyond what was needed for worship.

The vast amount of Arabic vocabulary that decorates Persian took some time to accumulate. It has remained concentrated in more learned language, hence words with lower frequency, despite the universal exposure of the population to the Arabic used in Islam. In the first written documents (in the tenth century) the proportion is already about 25 percent of the whole stock of words in the dictionary, although only about 10 percent of words on any page are of Arabic origin. Over the next two centuries these two proportions increased markedly, to 50 percent and 20–25 percent respectively, where they have since held steady until the present day.[16]

These figures are comparable, say, to the Romance element in Middle and Modern English (since 1450). Like French (or Latin) in English, enough Arabic has been borrowed directly into Persian to create subsystems of related words in the vocabulary. So, for instance, as English owes the -ess ending that marks feminines to French (abbesse, duchesse, laundresse, princesse, prioresse, etc., giving rise to actress, goddess, waitress, etc.), so Persian owes the comparable -e ending to Arabic (actually written with a final -ah, or in the script ه ): malek-e 'queen', amm-e 'paternal aunt', etc., gave rise to hamšir-e 'foster sister', ḫāl-e 'maternal aunt' and many others, where an originally Arabic suffix has been added to ethnic-Persian roots.

A more pervasive feature of New Persian, which would prove influential in other languages later on, is what it did to accommodate verbs from Arabic. We have already noted that nouns and adjectives had lost their once complex system of endings: this was one of the changes that mark the demise of Old Persian. Hence it was little problem in New Persian simply to accept Arabic nouns, spoken largely without inflected endings even when used natively. The situation was different for verbs: both Arabic and Persian had fairly complex patterns of endings, to express person and number, as well as changes to the stems (and for Persian, possible use of an auxiliary verb) to express tense, aspect, mood, and voice. The two systems were simply incommensurable, and they never mixed. Instead, Persian adapted Arabic verbs by extending massively a Persian construction for converting nouns to verbs. Essentially, it would take the related verbal noun (Arabic verbs would always have a related noun) and combine it with a short verb. This would usually be with the verb *kardan* 'do', less commonly with some other verb, such as *gaštan* 'turn' or *dāštan* 'have', and in intransitives or passives it could also be with *šudan*, a verb concurrently changing its meaning from 'go' to 'become'. So we have *ta'rif kardan* 'narrate', *fikr kardan* 'think', *farq dāštan* 'differ', *tamām kardan* 'finish', *tamām šudan* 'be finished', *vārid šudan* 'happen, enter'. In effect, this allowed any Arabic word stem to be adopted as a Persian verb.

This profusion of new vocabulary is the main reason why New Persian is viewed as a new language. Certain other changes—e.g., the loss of syllable-final -*g* in words such as *pārsīg* 'Persian', *zangīg* 'negroid', *ḫānag* 'house', *nāmag* 'book', *tigr* 'arrow'—may have happened before this period, but were only definitively registered with the adoption of the new (Arabic) script.

This script—which replaced the old, and often cryptic, Aramaic characters—was in fact an extension of the Arabic alphabet, with new triangles of diacritic dots used to indicate *p* ( پ ), *č* ( ث ), and *ž* ( چ ), and an accent on *k* ( ک ) to indicate *g* ( گ ); at last Persian was to be written clearly and phonetically, without reference to its (now definitively obsolete) fifteen hundred years of coexistence with Aramaic. The script still had some deficiencies as a phonetic representation of Persian, notably the indistinctness of *ē* from *ī* ( ی ), and of *ō* from *ū* ( و ); and these were never to be clarified on the page. But in modern Persian, pronunciation has in fact changed to match the script. The script was not in itself at first distinctive of the new language—as it largely became;* but it does indicate the religious affiliation of speakers. In the early days (eighth–tenth centuries) New Persian was also written by Jews in Hebrew letters, by Christians in Syriac, and Manichaeans in Manichaean, though this all seems to have happened farther east in Afghanistan and Central Asia.[17]

The geographical incidence of the new language—initially strongest in the Persian province of Khorasan, and indeed neighboring countries to the northeast, Khwarazm, Sogd, and Bactria (modern Turkmenistan,

---

* Evidently, the compelled romanization (1928) and then cyrillization (1939) of Persian in Soviet Central Asia (continued in modern Tajikistan) broke this association of Persian language and Arabic script, which had been maintained for almost a millennium.

Uzbekistan, Tajikistan and Afghanistan)—was caused by the interaction of the Arab conquest with the preexisting language situation in Iran.

Ibn al-Muqaffa' himself (the Persian translator and fabulist just mentioned), writing in the mid-eighth century, distinguished five languages (besides Arabic) in Iran: Pahlavī, Darī, Pārsī, Khūzī, and Suryānī. Of these, Khūzī is clearly the remains of Elamite, and Suryānī is Syriac, i.e. Aramaic. As for the remaining three, he says that Pahlavī is the language of Isfahan, Hamadan, Nehavand, and Azerbaijan, effectively of the northwest; Darī of the court (that is what it means, deriving from *dar* 'door', always symbolic of royal locations in Persian) but also of the Sassanian capital city (Ctesiphon, on the Tigris), "though in Khorasan [in the far east] the best Darī is heard in Balkh [in Bactria]"; and Pārsī is the language of Fars (in the southwest), but also of the *mowbed* Zoroastrian priests.

This tripartite division (Pahlavī, Darī, Pārsī) is somewhat confusing since the accepted analysis of historical Persian only distinguished two (similar) main dialects over the preceding millennium: viz, Median (later, Parthian) in the northeast, and Old Persian (later, Pārsīg or Middle Persian) in the southwest. In any case, the two were assumed to have coalesced during the Sassanian period (250–650) at least, if not before. But Gilbert Lazard (1993) has quite convincingly restored the intellectual status quo. Pārsī is understood as traditional Persian, which did indeed derive from Fars and may have continued to be spoken there. Pahlavī had originally meant 'Parthian', and this may be what it means here, since the cities are about right for ancient Media—even if it seems rather late (in the eighth century) to be making such a distinction, and it ended up (in the ninth century and after) just taken as 'ancestral Persian'. Meanwhile, Darī refers in effect to New Persian: despite its title, this is the new, predominantly colloquial, version of the language, coming through in the capital but also out to the east. The term *Pārsī-e-Darī*, literally 'court Persian', but actually 'the Darī kind of Pārsī', is actually used in the tenth century specifically referring to translations into New Persian. (And *Pārsī-e-Darī*, or simply *Darī*, is still the name of the variety of New Persian used to this day in Afghanistan.)

This new "Darī kind of Pārsī" spread immoderately in the first century (650–750) after the Arab conquest of Iran, and the main agents of its spread must have been the *mawāli*, those Iranian 'clients' of the Arab conquerors', who effectively fought their campaigns for them and enjoyed many of the proceeds of conquest. It spread in this era to a vast territory that it had never penetrated during the glory days of the Sassanians, Parthians, or even Achaemenids, even when their empires had included much of it.

The territory was Central Asia, across the river Oxus and away to the borders of Chinese Turkestan, what was known in Arabic as Mawārā al-Nahr 'beyond the river'. In this same century, 650–750, armies of Persian speakers (under Arab generals) were active throughout the area of Transoxiana. The Arab conquest of this area was effected with far greater mayhem and bloodshed than that of Iran and took a century to complete. Khwarazm, Sogd, and Bactria (in the areas of modern Turkmenistan, Uzbekistan, Tajikistan, and Afghanistan) were crushed, their traditional power structures destroyed, and essentially a new Muslim-dominated society was established there. Most of the army stayed on as settlers, often in positions of social dominance.

The penetration of New Persian within these regions will have been various. In them all, Sogdian had been current for most of the previous millennium, a language that extended beyond as far as the merchants of Samarkand could establish their trade links, though these were to the east in China and south in India, rather than to the west in Iran. In this role, Sogdian would soon be thoroughly displaced by New Persian, but this is a matter for chapter 5. For the moment here, we concentrate on how Persian came to displace mother tongues.

In Khwarazm (essentially the system of rivers centered on the Oxus, which flowed north into the Aral Sea), the great scholar al-Bīrūnī (973–1048), who was himself a Khwarazmian, reported that the principal Arab conqueror of Central Asia, Qutaiba ibn Muslim,* was responsible in 712 for the slaughter of all the scholars, with the destruction of their writings and effective obliteration of the Khwarazmian literary tradition.[18] However, as often, such physical destruction did not put an end to actual language transmission. Active use of the language† clearly continued for another seven centuries, and we still have texts from the "late Khwarazmian" period (twelfth century and after), which are written in a distinctive Arabic-derived alphabet. Arabic and New Persian must have coexisted with it for centuries,

---

* The first name is a diminutive (affectionate? contemptuous?) of the Arabic *muqautab* 'hunchback'.

† Khwarazmian is also known as Choresmian; and many spellings intermediate between these two romanizations of the name are also in use.

and final extinction, when it came, around the fourteenth century, probably saw the language replaced by a form of Turkish.[19]

Sogdiana itself, a highly developed polity with its chief urban centers in Bukhara and Samarkand, found its position compromised by the Arab-led aggression. The two cities fell first to Qutaiba ibn Muslim in 712, but joined a rebellion against the Arabs a generation later. They were definitively crushed in 750 by Ziyad ibn Salih, an Arab general who went on to win a victory over the Chinese at Talas in the following year. This battle proved decisive in claiming Central Asia as a part of the Muslim sphere, as it has been ever since. The immediate sequel of events is poorly documented, but the long-term outcome was evidently the replacement of Sogdian as the mother tongue in the area by New Persian. From the evidence of place names it has been argued that the cities had probably lost Sogdian by the tenth century, while it may have lingered in the western rural area (around Bukhara) until the sixteenth.[20]

Bactria (or Tukhāristān, as it was known because of the invaders, led by the Kushāna, who succeeded the Greek rulers here) was in the north of what is now Afghanistan, but to the south of ancient Sogd. It had been Persian-ized relatively early, since the time of the Sassanians (third century AD), and contemporary inscriptions on coinage are heavily influenced by Persian or Parthian vocabulary. Greek characters continued to be used in writing here, whatever the language, until the Arabic script (and Darī) took over.[21]

There is an interesting irony of fate here: in the very century when Arab conquests were laying the foundation for the spread of Arabic language as a new mother tongue through the western zones of the Caliphate, Arabic conquests farther east were leading to the spread not of Arabic but of New Persian. Part of the reason for this may have been a kind of language-genetic assimilation, which has its roots in what people find it easier to learn. Arabic supplanted tongues related to it in the Afro-Asiatic family (Aramaic, Coptic, Berber), but when Iranian languages (Sogdian, Bactrian) were threatened, their Persian cousin spread at their expense.[22]

However, a more straightforward explanation is to posit New Persian on the lips of *mawāli* troops as the lingua-franca of the Arabs' conquering army; and, as Richard Frye suggests,[23] the vulnerability of these various Iranian-language populations to the incoming language may have resulted from the general weakness, in a time of massive social disruption, of com-munity organization among Zoroastrians, although they had formed the majority population in these regions before the Arab conquest. In a situation of conquest, especially when cohesive religious communities are being accorded special rights (as, e.g., the Christians and the Jews were by the Arabs), it is a disadvantage to be a member of a defeated majority.

One particular loan word is eloquent of the changes that were sweeping across Central Asia. The Sassanian Persians had long used the word *Tāzīg*, derived from the Tayy tribe, dominant in Iraq, as their name for Arabs. In New Persian, it naturally became *Tāzī*, but in Sogdian the closest pronunciation was *Tājīk* (with *j* pronounced as in French *bonjour*). In the Sogdian version, this word came to refer to the new masters: they were typically but not necessarily Arabs, yet they were always Muslims. *Tājik* came to connote the language that they would be speaking too; and this was—after some time—universally New Persian. Hence *Tajik* is now the name for a Central Asian speaker of Persian, a language known locally as *tojiki*.

Concurrently with this spread of New Persian out toward the northeast, a kind of blowback was to enhance the prestige of its speakers back in the center of Iran, and indeed into Iraq. The final conquest of Mawārā al-Nahr (Transoxiana) had been effected under the command of one Abū Muslim, whose nom de guerre, meaning 'father of Muslim', cloaks his origins from a *mawāli* family. From 736, based at Merv, he successfully organized the east as a power base for the dissident Abbasid faction laying claim to the Caliphate, in 748 deposing Naṣr bin Sayyār as governor of Khorasan, and finally led the Abbasid forces to their famous victory on the river Zab in 750. Soon afterward, in 754, he was perfidiously murdered by the second Abbasid caliph, Manṣūr. Despite this skulduggery, Persians remained prominent under the new dynasty. Tellingly, the new purpose-built capital had a Persian name, Baghdād 'God-given' (and was only thirty kilometers from Ctesiphon, the previous capital of Sassanian Persia). The new institution of a vizier, appointed to head the caliph's administration, together with a staff to assist him (known by the term *diwān*, another loan from Persian—*dēwān* 'archive'), played into the hands of the literate classes, who tended to be Iranian; not only that, from 770 to 804 they were all members of a single family, the Barmecides (Arabic *Barāmika*), whose patriarch, Khalīl ibn Barmak, hailed from Balkh in Tukharistan, where the family had not long before been hereditary Buddhist priests.* Furthermore, a civil war between two sons of Hārūn ar-Rašīd, which took place in 811–813, resulted in the

---

* Barmak seems to be a version of Sanskrit *pramukha-* or Pāli *parimukham* 'in front, foremost'.

triumph of the heir based in Khorasan, establishing the political fortunes of the Iranian families that managed his campaign, the Banū Sahl (who specialized as viziers) and the Tahirids (as governors of Khorasan).

This did not at first affect the status of Arabic as the language of government since in any case all literate Iranians, as Muslims, would be conversant with it. But a tendency soon arose under the Abbasids for local governors to establish rather independent governments, which only nominally answered to the central authorities in Baghdad. Separate dominions arose, effectively under their own hereditary lords, the Tahirids ruling Khorasan from Nishapur (821–73), the Saffarids ruling Sistan (eastern Iran and modern Afghanistan) from Zaranj (861–1003), the Buyids ruling western Iran (934–1055), the Ziyarids ruling the north-center of Iran (938–1043), and above all, the Samānids ruling over Khorasan and Central Asia (819–999). In the ninth and tenth centuries the movement known as *šuʿūbiyah*\* took root across the Persian-speaking part of the Caliphate. This promoted the self-assertion of the value of Persian as a literary language—though the argument for self-assertion was conducted (perversely enough) in Arabic.

Among these Persian-speaking domains, all but the last retained Arabic as their official language. Only under the Samānids, centered in Bukhara to the east (not long before, a Sogdian-speaking city), was Persian for the first time reestablished as a full-function literary language, including theology, history, and science, as well as fine literature.† Apparently this was not least for the convenience of the emir himself. Of Manṣūr I, who ruled 961–76, it was written, "It is difficult for him to read this book and get its sense in *Tāzī* [i.e. Arabic] and so he wished that they translate it into Persian."[24]

One novel effect of this less stratified society was at least partly due to Islam. In this era Persian nobles were no longer content to have their reading done for them, perhaps recited in another tongue; so they would not accept use of a lingua-franca that was beyond them, even if it was Arabic.

Just as the vast body of Pahlavi literature had been translated into Arabic by the close of the ninth century, so in the two centuries 925 to 1125 "the

---

\* This was Arabic for 'popular', but derived from a specific verse of the Koran, 49.13: *yā ayyuhā an-nāsu innā xalaqnākum min ðakari wa-ʾunaθā wa-jaʿalnākum šuʿūban wa-qabāʾila li-taʿārifū* 'O mankind! Verily we created you from a male and a female, and made you into **nations** [*šuʿūban*] and tribes [*qabāʾila*], that you may know one another'.

† The administration of their bureaucracies, however, continued to work in Arabic, not least as a symbol of allegiance to the central government in Baghdad.

whole syllabus of contemporary learning had found its way into the new medium"—viz New Persian.[25] And likewise at the Samānid court, beginning with the poet Rudaki (858–941), New Persian literature opened the self-conscious tradition that has lasted to the present.

With growing Persian-speaking self-respect, and indeed (within greater Iran) dominance, it became increasingly difficult to equate adherence to Islam with assuming an Arab identity. Arabic's status as the language of holy scripture was never disputed, and it retained its prestige everywhere as a language of learning. Indeed the rate of conversions—and hence familiarity with religious Arabic—is believed to have been much higher during this period, raising the proportion of Muslims within the population from 10 percent in 750 to 80 percent in 1100.[26] But the operative trend should nonetheless be seen as the decline of Arabic as a useful lingua-franca: it was more and more losing this role in a polity where nowadays most people of influence were native speakers of Persian.

Here again, the prestige associations of the lingua-franca—association with a once-conquering race, or indispensability as an attribute of piety— were unable to sustain it. Above all, Arabic had lost its position on practical grounds: it was simply less accessible. Writing in 968–70, Maisari, the author of *Dānešnāmā* 'Book of Science', justified his choice of language to write in: "Our land is Iran, whose people have command of *Pāresī*" (i.e. Persian).[27] Where for technical reasons Arabic was preferred, it would still be employed. So, for example, the Khwarazmian polymath and genius al-Bīrūnī (973–1048) maintained that Persian simply could not give clear, concise expression to complex reasoning; in his view it should be used only for storytelling and epics of ancient kings.[28] Evidently, it must have been harder to write elegantly and rigorously in a language whose scientific vocabulary had not actively been developed for over two centuries. But meanwhile his equal and rival Avicenna (981–1037), who hailed from Bukhara, was writing his own *Dānešnāmā* in Persian, so it was not an open-and-shut case.

To reinforce the point that a concern for practicality was never far from resurgent Persian, one can note authors who remonstrated against Persian authors who were too purist in their vocabulary, at the expense of ease or comprehensibility. Kai Ka'us bin Iskandar, the Ziyarid ruler ca 1080, wrote to advise his son not to write in a Persian *na-xvōš* 'unpleasantly' devoid of Arabic. Another writer was sensitive to the potential irony that lay in purism defended by pragmatism: "The most astonishing thing is that, when they write a book in Persian, they state that they have adopted this language in order that those who do not know Arabic may be able to use the book. Yet they have recourse to words of pure Persian which are more difficult than Arabic. If they employed the terms currently in use, it would be easier to understand them."[29] This was the defense for the lexical compromise that is New Persian, and a stable balance of vocabularies that has now been kept for over a thousand years.

# CHAPTER 4

# When the Writ of Persian Ran

زبان پهلوی هر کو شناسد
خراسان آن بود کز وی خور آسد

*zabān e pahlavī har k'ū šenāsad,*
*xurāsān ān bovad k'az way xvar āsad*

For everyone who knows the Pahlavi language,
Khorasan is the place from which the sun rises.

—Gurgāni (ca 1050), *Vis and Ramin*, 48.2

U P TO THIS POINT (conveniently, the end of the first millennium AD), the Persian language had never been established anywhere as a lingua-franca, despite its widespread use for over twenty-five hundred years. True, it had often achieved currency as a state language, with written forms standardized in various ways through the penetrating influence of actual lingua-francas (notably Aramaic and Arabic), languages that had been instituted to enable communications within an empire. But Persian had been a widespread and expanding mother tongue within Iran, and lingua-franca for no one else. This was about to change.

What changed it was the increasing role in Iranian history of another people, the Turks. These had, like the Iranians in a previous era, a past as tribal nomads on the Eurasian steppes, though for them this past was much more recent. Like the Iranians, they are characterized by their group of closely related languages (quite unrelated to Iranian), but they earlier achieved substantial political unity. In AD 552 they had united in Mongolia, under the legendary Bumyn of the Aršilas clan,[1] then established control along the Silk Route, from northern China through Central Asia to the steppes north of (Sassanian-controlled) Iran. This commercial interest brought them into contact, and de facto alliance, with the Sogdians, the merchants whose route it was, and they enabled the first Turkic literacy, as seen at its outset in the "runic" inscriptions along the Orkhon valley (from the seventh century and later). Over the latter first millennium, the Turks became divided again, and their subdivisions enjoyed varying fortunes, in the east (including Uyghur, Kyrghyz, and Qarluq) in competition with Tang-dynasty China, in the west transmuting into the Khazar empire in the southern Ukraine, with the Volga Bulgars (in the east) and Balkan Bulgars (in the west). By the eleventh century, the Khazars had the Cuman-Qypchaq confederation to their east in western Siberia, with Oghuz to their south (in modern Turkmenistan), whereas farther to the east, various tribes, including the Qarluqs and some Uyghur, had come under the leadership of the "khan-kings of the Turks," who are known to modern historians as the Qarakhanids, after their founder Qara Khan, "the black Khan."[2]

Besides outright warfare, the main mechanism of social contact between Iranians and the Turks was the curious institution of the *ghulām* (plural *ghilmān*), an Arabic word that literally means 'lusty young lad', but came to designate the slave soldier. The idea that a ruler might ensure the personal loyalty of his troops by employing human "blank slates," specifically Turkish slaves, was pioneered by the Arab caliph Mu'tasim (794–842), but his example was widely followed and was taken up with particular gusto by the Samanids over the last two centuries of the first millennium. A pithy verse epitomizes the theory:

> یک بنده مطواع به از سیصد فرزند    *yek bandeh-e miṭwā' bih az sīṣad farzand*
>
> کاین مرگ پدر خواهان و آن عمر خداوند    *k'īn marg-e pedar xvāhān wa ān 'amr-e xudāvand*

One slave obedient is better than three hundred sons;
for the latter wish their father's death, the former their
master's long life.[3]

This may have been so when the slaves were originally trained and appointed. But the effect in the long term was to create communities of Turks at a high level who, enjoying the borrowed authority of the sovereign, could usurp power for themselves. This was the origin of the group known as the Ghaznavids (after Ghazni, the city in Afghanistan, which, after the Samanids had seized it for themselves, was assigned as the center of their province).

In the early centuries of the second millennium, these various Turkic groups, whether slave or free, usurped control of various parts of Iranian territory, sometimes passing through it to establish dominions even beyond the sphere of the Caliphate. So in 999 the Qarakhanids took control of Transoxiana from the Samanids, which they then held for two centuries. This brought the region firmly within the domain of Turkic mother tongue, as it has been ever since, and by the same token gave Persian the status of lingua-franca.

At the same time as this Qarakhanid action, the Ghaznavids took over the center and south of the Samanids' territory. A little later, the Oghuz (also known as Turcomans), and above all a leading group of them called the Seljuqs, hitherto widely used as mercenaries by the Samanids and the Ghaznavids, infiltrated northern Khorasan. At Dandanaqan in 1040, they definitively defeated the Ghaznavids. Khorasan became theirs alone, and the Ghaznavids were compelled henceforth to look south, for new conquests in India. The Seljuqs went on to destroy Buyid control of the east of the Caliphate, taking Baghdad in 1055 (and receiving the caliph's blessing as his liberators), and in 1071, for good measure, defeating the Byzantine Empire at Manzikert, so opening up Anatolia to Turkic colonization over the next few centuries. In 1089, they defeated the Qarakhanids too, but did not dispossess them, holding them rather as their vassals (*muqta'*) for the next fifty years.

It might have been expected that these different ruling dynasties, Ghaznavid, Qarakhanid, and Seljuq, would have brought a new lingua-franca to the Middle East in the eleventh century. They did, after all, speak mutually intelligible forms of Turkic; and this was the beginning of what would turn into almost a millennium of Turkish rule, as witness the Arabic proverb cited by the North African analytic historian Ibn Khaldūn of the fourteenth century:

> *dawlah 'ind al–turk, din 'ind al–'arab wa 'adab 'ind al–furs*
>
> Power (rests) with the Turk, religion with the Arab, and culture with the Persian.

Some analogy exists between these new conquests by martial ex-nomads and the achievements four hundred years before of the Arabs in Iran, and to a lesser extent of the Persian-speaking *mawāli* in Transoxiana, even if those groups were coming from the other direction. But the Arabs had followed up their military successes with the spread of new languages, Arabic as a new, high-status code, and New Persian as a replacement for the Iranian mother tongues of Central Asia. Now, with the Turkic invasions, nothing of the kind occurred. Instead, all these groups adopted the Persian language, and Persian ways, as their idiom for government, and to a large extent for cultural aspiration. The model, then, was far closer to what had happened sixteen hundred years earlier, when Cyrus and his Persians had subverted the Median empire, then conquered the whole space from Sindh to Kush: as Aramaic had been confirmed and extended in its old role by the ancient Persians, now New Persian was accepted and continued by these Turks.

What was the crucial difference that determined that this series of conquerors would not impose their language? Evidently, they did not bring with them a social idea with the revolutionary potential of Islam, and the boundless self-confidence that that clearly gave the Arabs and the *mawāli*. In fact, rather than attempt to establish the cult of their ancestral sky god Tengri, the Turks were all eager to embrace Islam. Their leaders had already been converted: the Ghaznavids by early indoctrination as *ghilmān* within Muslim society; the Seljuq khans freely for their own political reasons; and the Qarakhanids by preemptive proselytizing, as their future khan Satoq Bughra had been converted in his boyhood by the Samanid merchant Naṣr bin Manṣūr on a trade visit to Kashgar.

This religious surrender was probably crucial to their acceptance of Persian, but it was not accompanied by a total linguistic surrender. The Ghaznavids, of course, being few in number and from a community of ex-slaves that had been totally Iranized, were unlikely to promote Turkic literature. They presided over a literary court that wrote exclusively in Persian and Arabic, and their literary stars included the paramount chronicler of Iranian culture, Firdawsī (writer of the national epic *Šāh-nāmeh* 'Book of Kings'), as well as the scientist and ethnographer al-Bīrūnī. But they continued to use Turkic in their own speech.[4] This was to remain typical of the Turkic dynasties that followed, even more so when they were of non-slave origin such as the Seljuqs, since they also changed the ethnic balance of the Muslim lands, introducing large numbers of Turkic tribesmen. (Records exist of the Turkic dialect Qypchaq, spoken by their dynasty of ex-slaves the Mamlūk in Egypt.)[5] Turkic was spoken among the dominant tribe, but the Persian language, and the urban culture that came with it, was accepted as the standard of civilized life, and the mother tongue of the Turks was largely overlooked as a basis for a written literature.

Nonetheless, the Qarakhanids were an exception to this. From their capital in Kashgar they presided over the first two great literary works to be written in Turkic (using Perso-Arabic script), as early as the eleventh century: Yūsuf Balasaǧuni's *Qutadǧu Bilig* 'For Royal Bliss the Wisdom', completed in 1070, which is a wide-ranging exposé of indigenous learning (not excepting its Turkic title), but evidently written by someone who has read his Firdawsī, since it shares the meter of the *Šāh-nāmeh*, and its phraseology is full of Persian borrowings;[6] and Maḥmūd al-Kašǧarī's dictionary, compendium, and comparative dialectal study of Turkic, a world first, completed in 1072 (though entitled—in Arabic—*Dīwānu l-Luǧat al-Turk* 'Archive of the Language of the Turks').* A halting literary tradition was founded here, of which some few other works have survived, including *'Atabatu'l Ḥiqāyiq* 'Threshold of Truths', a collection of verse, and Rabguzī's *Qiṣāṣu'l Anbiyā* 'Tales of the Prophets', completed in 1310.[7] Still, it was only in the fifteenth century, when successors of Tamerlane ruled in Central Asia, and the early Ottomans were establishing themselves in modern Turkey, that Turkic would burst definitively onto the page and begin the literary traditions that have continued to this day.

Meanwhile, in an amazing quasi-racial tour de force, Turkish dynasties not only retained their position of power for most of the second millennium AD, at the expense of Persian and Arab ruling lines, but they expanded the Muslim lands into most of India to the southeast and the Balkans of Europe to the northwest. This they achieved despite the devastating irruptions of Mongols in the thirteenth century (imposing for a time a Mongol-speaking

---

* Despite his name, Kašǧarī was actually working in Baghdad, perhaps aiming to expound the language of the Seljuq rulers to the Persian- and Arabic-speaking elites. He was conscious of how committed Turk was to Persian in his world, since he included the ambivalent Turkic proverb *Tatsız Türk bolmas, başsız börk bolmas* 'Without a Persian a Turk is nothing, like hat without a head'. (fol. 88b, 204a). But another proverb (fol. 204a) is more robustly pro-Turk: *qilič tatiqsa iš yunǧir, er tatiqsa et yunǧir* 'If a sword rusts [*tatiqsa*], its strength rots; if a man turns Persian [*tatiqsa*], his flesh rots'. He made ample use of Perso-Arabic terms, but still considered Turkic to be most eloquent (*afṣaḥ*) when it was unaffected by Persian or city folk (fol. 24). (Ermers 1999, 20)

and Buddhist elite), and then of Tamerlane at the end of the fourteenth, and continual turmoil among the profusion of Turkic-led states that rose and fell for at least the first five centuries.

Sindh had been won for the Caliphate by Arab forces as early as 712 (essentially as part of the first Muslim expansion), but for three centuries they were kept to the Indus valley by the Thar Desert, which lay beyond. No more Muslim incursions occurred until the Ghaznavids, coming from the Hindu Kush, took central north India in 1004–22, establishing their capital in Lahore. Between 1175 and 1192 they were deposed and defeated by a subordinate dynasty, known as the Ghurids, from their base in Ghur, to the west of Ghazni, who were in fact not Turks, but Tajiks (with a family name *Šansabānī*, which seems to be derived (consider the consonants!) from the Pahlavi name *Wišnasb*)—evidently no less enthusiastic for the use of Persian. Anyway, in 1206 the Ghurids conquered Delhi, initiating the Delhi Sultanate, a Muslim empire that would last over three hundred years. (It only fell in 1526—to their fellow Muslims the Mughals.) Successors to the Ghurid dynasty were not Tajiks, anyway, but *Mamlūk* slaves (i.e. 'owned', in Arabic), i.e. another dynasty emerging from *ghilmān*. By 1215 they had expanded Muslim control to the whole of India north of the Vindhya mountains, as far as Bengal (a Persian form of Indic *Vangāla*), and their dynasty endured till 1290. Most of the rest of India was in turn annexed by another group of the Ghurids' favored *ghilmān*, who formed the Khalji dynasty (1290–1320), a name derived from Turkic *qilij* 'sword'. They were in turn followed by three more dynasties over the next two centuries, by which time the Turkic connection had dimmed, and unity proved hard to maintain, but Persian remained the ruling lingua-franca throughout the Muslim domains.

The famously multilingual poet Amir Khusrau of Delhi (1253–1325), living at the Mamlūk court and himself the son of a Tajik officer from Balkh and an Indian Rajput mother, noted that Persian as used in India was standardized, unlike the variability it showed in Khorasan: "There is no other correct style than the style of Transoxiana, which is the same as that of Hindustan. Because the Khorasanis pronounce the word *cheh* 'what?' as [chi], and some read *kujā* 'where?' as [kaju] . . . But the Persian speech prevalent in India, from the bank of the Indus to the coast of the Indian Ocean, is everywhere the same."[8] He was not above making the odd joke about inconveniences of the language barriers in India:

*Zabān-e yār-e man Turki, wa man Turki namidānam,*
*Che khush budi agar budi zabānash dar dahān-e man.*

My lover's tongue is Turkic, and Turkic I do not know;
How glad I'd be if only that one's tongue were in my mouth.*

In the opposite direction, the Ghurids had briefly (from 1201) contended for control of Khorasan too, only to be finally dispossessed here in 1215 by the equally Turkic (by this time) shahs of Khwarazm, a dynasty originally (since 1097) established by the Seljuqs and recently grown mightily in power.

This was the dynasty that faced Chinggis Khan's Mongol holocaust of 1219–21. This deliberate annihilation of the populations of many of the key cities of northern Iran and Central Asia was followed in the next two generations by violent elimination of the last Khwarazm-shah from Iran (1231–41), the last Seljuqs from Anatolia (1242–56), and the last Abbasid caliphs from Baghdad (1256–58). The resulting Mongol Il-Khanate (i.e. subordinate Khanate) ruled Iran from 1258 to 1335. After a brief period of Tibetan Buddhism as the rulers' religion within Iran, in 1295 the Khan Ghazan accepted Sunni Islam and restored the religious status quo.

The Il-Khanate had annexed most of the Seljuq domains in Anatolia after 1243, but after 1335 centralized control began to break down throughout the empire, and a number of Turkic-ruled states sprang up, notably the 'Uthmān (better known in its Italian guise as Ottoman) in the western Anatolia, and the Aq Qoyunlu and Qara Qoyunlu (Turcomans of the White Sheep and the Black) in eastern Anatolia and Iran. Despite major disruption caused by the invasions of Tamerlane (1363–1403), these states survived. By 1475 the Ottomans had taken all Anatolia and the Balkans (later too Palestine, Iraq, and Egypt), while the White Sheep had spread eastward to dispossess the Black and establish control of all Iran.

The Mongols had achieved total military success from Central Asia to Anatolia, and they were naturally not short of prestige or cultural self-esteem. Mongols were ruling at the time from Poland to Vietnam, and even after the parts of the Khanate went their separate ways, a boast of descent

---

* But there is more (or less) going on here, given the clichés of Persian verse: "The 'Turk' is the beloved . . . because . . . the beloved is cruel and so are the martial Turks . . . Turks are also enchantingly beautiful." (Thackston 1994, xi)

from Chinggis Khan would be the ace to play in dynastic politics for many generations. Mongolian inscriptions graced the coinage of the Il-Khanate from the reign of the second Il-Khan, Abaqa, who reigned 1265–82. (Partly, this seems to have been a gesture of union with the Mongol Khanate of Khubilai Khan (1264–94), since later inscriptions even used his special alphabet, 'Phagspa, designed to be language-neutral.) Mongolian was still being used on coinage issued under the Jalayrids, one of the successor dynasties, who ruled in Fars and the Baghdad region from 1339 to 1401.[9]

But Mongolian never displaced Persian as the lingua-franca of culture and administration, any more than Turkic had; nor did it displace Turkic itself as the lingua-franca of the army. The simplest explanation of this is that the Mongols were few, and the vast majority within the armies mobilized by them (and by Tamerlane, who came after) were Turkic-speaking, so these onslaughts, though immeasurably bloodier than anything that had gone before, were linguistically quite analogous to the Turkic conquests of the eleventh and twelfth centuries.*

A contact vernacular between Mongol and Uyghur-Turkic seems to have been the first main medium of communication for the new overlords, probably relying on the routine bilingualism of the scribal classes to feed information and commands through the Persian bureaucracy. One of these bureaucrats, 'Alā' ud-Dīn Joveini, who also became the prime historian for this period, permits himself in 1260 this broadside (in Persian, naturally) against the jumped-up careerists of the age, revealing both what was happening in this time of social revolution, and what the traditional elite thought of it: "Lying and falsifying they take for homilies and sermons, viciousness and slander they term ingenuity and hardihood . . . They recognize in Uyghur speech and script the epitome of excellence and accomplishment."[10]

---

* Mongolian did leave some lasting mark on New Persian, however enriching its everyday vocabulary all over the vast territory in which it was, and would be, spoken. Most prominently the widespread title *āġā* or *āqā* 'Sir, Mr.' (as in *Agha Khan*) is from Mongolian *aqa* 'big brother'; another such is the word *naukar* 'manservant', from *nökör* 'comrade, henchman, marshal'; and the number *toman* '10,000' from *tümän*, applied for the last few centuries in Iran mostly to a sum of money (Yule and Burnell 1886, s.v. *tomaun*), but by the Mongols and the Mughals mostly to a large unit in the army. Martinez 1991 gives list of about a hundred other loans, from which he infers (p. 139) "considerable insight into the societies that shared them, particularly the coarseness and ribaldry of many of the terms, their concern with grooming and appearance . . . and an extraordinary number of [insults]." But then foreign imperialists are seldom short of rich vocabulary with which to put down lesser mortals, and the underlings in turn tend to catch on rather quickly.

At the same time, the Mongols had no militant religious faith to give them a distinctive cultural presence. Despite the new religion that they brought, a mixture of Mahāyāna Buddhism with shamanism under the sky god Tengri, some Mongols (or more notably, the foreign princesses they might marry) were even Christians; in general, they made no serious attempt, even in their early years of control, to dissuade their subjects from Islam. Meanwhile, when it came to establishing administrations, they tended to be learners rather than instructors. The instruction they received was from specialists who were used to operating in Persian, notably the Joveini family, whose most famous member, the historian, has just been quoted. But his grandfather, father, and brother all held the post of *sāḥib-e-dīwān* or minister of finance, bridging the transition from the last Khwarazm-shah to the third Mongol Khan.

1501 brought a wide-ranging changing of the guard, but this just meant that yet more Turkic-speaking dynasties took over in the center and east of the vast zone of Persian culture. The new administrations brought a greater stability to it at last. The Ottomans changed least, carrying on in Anatolia, and the Arab lands to the south, until 1918. In Iran, the Safāvids (speaking Azerbaijani Turkic) came first (1501–1722), followed (after two generations of turmoil) by yet another Turkic dynasty, the Qajars (1781–1925); India meanwhile was taken by the Mughals (1501–1858), led by a princeling descended from both Chinggis Khan and Tamerlane, who with his comrades spoke the Chagatay Turkic of Andijan in the Ferghana Valley. Central Asia alone remained without a centralizing power, ruled by a diverse and changing set of smaller Khanates—though almost every one was Turkic-ruled—until the Russians conquered them all in the latter half of the nineteenth century.

◦◦◦◦

So from the early sixteenth century until the dawn of the modern age, within this apparently eternal *qalamrau-e-zabān-e-fārsī*, a trio of empires (Ottoman, Safāvid/Qajar, Mughal), and a host of smaller states, perpetuated the tradition of Turkic power within lands where, whatever the local language, the lingua-franca of culture and the ruling elite was ever and anon Persian.

This language deal, by which the mother tongue of conquerors coexisted with a lingua-franca derived from their wealthy and cultured subjects, is in some ways reminiscent of what had emerged in western Europe in the fifth century AD, when the Goths and other Germanic tribes (notably Vandals, Franks, and Saxons) overwhelmed the defenses of the Roman Empire, but ultimately accepted its language, Latin. Like this postimperial Latin, Persian used as a lingua-franca under Turkic auspices was to last for about a millennium. We know that the overall story of Latin's survival in medieval Europe had many complications—some elite Romans in the early days attempting to win favor with the new overlords by learning Gothic; long survival of Gothic in the church services of Arian Christianity; one territory (Britain) losing its Latin altogether[11]—and it would be fascinating if we had any knowledge of similar glitches in the Turks' acceptance of Persian. Sadly, only a few records exist of the ups and downs in the languages' relationships.

One came in 1277, when Turkish was briefly proclaimed state language for Anatolia by rebels against the Il-Khanate in the city of Konya, apparently in resentment against imposed foreign (Persian-speaking) financial experts (called in Turkic *māliyetçi* 'wealth men'). But the rebellion was swiftly crushed, and Persian reimposed, by the Mongols.

This was a running sore in the decades of the 1270s and 1280s, when the Il-Khanate was incorporating the Seljuq Sultanate of Anatolia (still called Rūm, in memory of the Roman Empire on whose conquered territory it was built). Persian had been little used in this area, which, after all, had owed its Islamic status (and population) over the last century to Turks and no one else. But after the first irruption of Chinggis Khan in 1218–22, senior Iranians from the northeast had moved into positions of power in the sultanate, causing a first overlay of Persian-speaking officials. Now, two generations later, the opportunity was taken, after an attempted revolt against Mongol authority, to impose a whole new cadre of officials from the east, trained in working (in Persian) with Mongolian masters. The change was described by a contemporary:

> In the caliphate of 'Ali [656–61] the fiscal registers had been transferred from Persian (*pārsī*) and Greek (*rūmī*) to Arabic (*tāzī*), and under the administration of Lord Fakhru'd-din 'Ali [ca 1277–85], they were returned to Persian, lest, on account of his attainments and preparation [this insinuating he was not up to the job, with poor Arabic], anything should elude his review . . .
>
> When they arrived in Anatolia, each one seized his post by the horns. In place of a single governor, two brothers governed; instead of one inspector-general, two officers; in place of one comptroller,

four; instead of one transcriber, eight; for one secretary, ten persons. Moreover, each one brought another in his train . . . So much ink did they expend that the light of day was extinguished at the ministry of finance . . .

Naturally, there was no crime that affairs did not establish with a bracelet of good counsel in the centre of righteousness. [Anything that could go wrong was set up as a model of good practice.] If the official was from Tabaristan, he was without conscience; if from Kerman or Khorasan, he went at the unfortunate public without mercy; if from Ray or Shiraz, he did no work at all.[12]

Not all, then, were impressed at first by the linguistic spread of Persian (with Persian experts) as a working language. But Persian spread, nonetheless.

For almost a millennium, until the mid-nineteenth century, Turkish remained the language of the soldiers and the royal court[13] (to some extent learned by nonnatives in the army, e.g., Kurds), while Persian was used in the chancelleries (*dīwān*) for administration, as well as remaining the preeminent language of science and literature (more and more so, as it won out over Arabic in this respect). The linguistic effect of this has been that the Turkish loanwords that passed into Persian are mostly military, taken from "the fields of government, state, law, army, warfare, armaments and booty"; Turkish was also much used in official titles.[14] Royal courts evidently differed in how much Persian they used. While it was de rigueur in India under the Mughals[15], as it had been before under the Delhi Sultanate, a European visitor to the Safāvids' capital in Esfahan in 1685 commented, "It is almost shameful for a man of any standing not to know Turkish; . . . [the Persian language] so loved abroad is demeaned by the eminent in its own country."[16]

One of the best-documented areas for Persian in use was Mughal India.* From the thirteenth to nineteenth centuries, this was the main area where Persian texts were being written, many of them translated from Sanskrit on the one hand and Arabic on the other.[17] This prominence of Persian in India

---

* It is telling that all but one of the first six (and greatest) Mughal emperors had Persian names: Bābur from *babr* 'tiger'; Humāyun 'auspicious' (related to the *humā* bird of good omen, which never lands); Akbar [Arabic] 'greatest'; Jahān-gir 'world-seize'; Shāh-e Jahān 'king of the world'; Aurang-zēb 'Majesty-adornment', who also used the title 'Alam-gir 'universe-seize', a mixture of Arabic and Persian.

was not unnoticed in Persian's homeland and even inspired a defeatist verse
by the poet 'Ali Quli Salim of Teheran:

نیست در ایران زمین سامان تحصیل کمال

تا نیامد سوی هندستان حنا رنگین نشد

*nīst dar Irān e zamīn sāmān e taḥsīl e kamāl*
*tā nayāmad suyi Hindustān ḥenā rangīn našud*

Absent in Iran's land any means to reach perfection:
Till it came toward India, henna had no colors.

Bābur, the originator of this dynasty, had had reservations about the use
of Persian, which are demonstrated by his decision to write his memoirs in
Turkic, even if it is a Turkic shot through with Persian vocabulary and
snatches of Persian verse. (The title though—as almost all titles in the Islamic world, whatever the language of the text—was in Arabic, *Wāqāʾiʿ*
'Events'.) His impressive (and surviving) oeuvre of both Turkic and Persian
poetry makes it clear that he would have had little difficulty in writing it
directly in Persian, had he so chosen. This was a conscious decision: he
wanted it to be read by those he saw as his peers, the Turko-Mongol elite in
Central Asia, rather than more widely in the Islamic world.[18] Bābur's ac-
quaintance and cultural hero Mīr 'Ali Shēr, usually known as Nawāʾi, had
written a comparative appreciation of Persian and Turkic (*Muḥākamat al-
luġatain* 'Verdict on the Two Languages'), in which he saw Persian "more
refined and profound than Turkic for purpose of thought and science," while
Turkic was "more intelligent, more understandable, and more creative."[19] He
gives his verdict pretty one-sidedly in favor of Turkic, feeling that it can express all sorts of nuances that cannot be touched in native Persian vocabulary.
It seems, then, that typically for a lingua-franca, Persian could be seen by the
native speakers of other languages as rather bland and soulless.*

Nawāʾi, in Herat, remarked that "not one member of the Persian nation,
be he brigand or notable or scholar, can speak Turkish or understand anyone who does."[20] As we now know, this is typical of those whose native

---

* In the same context, Nawāʾi characterized Arabic as "a language of ideas and elo-
quences," while Hindi is "one of exaggerations and corruptions," and, summing up, "the
one honored and sublime, the other utterly corrupt and base."

language has become current as a lingua-franca: "After all, everyone speaks [the language that I speak], don't they?" Amir Khusrau, by contrast, with experience in India, had been impressed by the linguistic versatility of those who—by necessity?—cut their linguistic teeth on Persian not natively, but as an acquired language:

> No Arab, Khorasani, Turk, Indian, nor any other who comes to the Muslim cities of India and spends his whole life in places like Delhi, Multan and Lakhnauti* . . . suffers deterioration in his own language. Assuredly, he speaks according to the standard of his own country. For example, if he is an Arab, he is the master of his own language only, and he cannot lay a proper claim to the language of others; his broken speech is a proof of his foreign origin . . . A Khorasani, Iraqi, Shirazi or a Turk, however intelligent he may be, commits blunders in the Indian language . . . But the Munshis [i.e. professional secretaries] born and brought up in Indian cities and particularly at Delhi, with but little practice, can speak and understand the spoken language . . . they can adopt the style of every country they visit.[21]

It is not clear if this describes an effect of early study of Persian, the literate language par excellence, or if it is a boast about the special linguistic abilities of Indian intellectuals. It is rather reminiscent of those nowadays who recommend learning Latin in order to expedite learning other foreign languages later on. (Or of those four centuries ago who likewise recommended learning Latin, but because it was then the best way to make yourself understood anywhere.)[22]

But part of this universal applicability of Persian studies may have been its associations with a poetic canon that was everywhere seen as setting the classic standard for verse—in whatever language—and also provided inexhaustible fonts of quotable wisdom and shared sensibility. In this era, higher education meant having read—and memorized the best lines, ready to quote, from—at least Firdawsī (935–1025), Niẓāmī (1141–1209), Saʿdi (1200–92), Mawlānī (better known to us as Rūmī) (1207–73), Amir Khusrau (1253–1325), Ḥāfiẓ (1326–89), and Jāmī (1414–92), necessarily in that order, since

---

* Gour in West Bengal, conquered by Muslims in 1198, and thereafter a major center for them.

the tradition of professional poets had always been founded rigorously on knowledge of those that had gone before and so built itself up like a stalagmite. And composition was not just for a tiny elite: Nawā'i had conducted in 1491–92 a survey of contemporary poets just in his own Khorasan: he found 336 of them, 90 percent writing in Persian.[23] The origins of the leading poets just mentioned—respectively Khorasan, Azerbaijan, Fars, Anatolia, India, Fars again, and Samarkand—hence from all four corners of the *qalamrau-e-zabān-e-fārsī*, show how widely this one language was admired.

From that day to this, as the tradition has grown, enthusiasm for Persian poetry, shown by the ability to quote meaningfully from it, has remained a mainstay of conversational savoir faire in Central Asia and Iran; yet the bias of the poets toward expressions of ineffable mysticism protects these retailers of its riches from platitude, if not obscurity:

پارسی گو گرچه تازی خوشتر است
عشق را خود صد زبان دیگر است

*pārsi gu garče tāzī xuštar ast: 'āshq rā xvad ṣad zabān-e-dīgar ast*

Speak Persian even if you'd rather Arabic: love itself has a hundred other tongues. —Rumi

Amir Khusrau's remarks make clear that Persian was useful as a means of communication among people from all over the Islamic world. It provided a basis for direct conversation among the otherwise highly multilingual society of the cities; but it also provided a common written code for correspondence and administration. A Persian-skilled *munšī*, such as those mentioned by Amir Khusrau, would (if he deserved the title) have been skilled in *inšā'*, an Arabic term for 'formation' but also elegant composition according to formulas, the essence of 'business Persian', and manuals for instruction in it were as common across the Persian-language domain as textbooks in *dictamen*, the rhetoric of Latin letter-writing, were at the same time popular in western Europe. Nabi Hadi's *Dictionary of Indo-Persian Literature* lists thirty distinct guides to *inšā'*, mostly made up of model letters. Efficient, or at least rule-governed, correspondence articulated the life of these medieval states and empires; and the clerks of the British East India Company, learning to do business in India in the seventeenth and eighteenth centuries, would have found style guides in use still recognizable from the eleventh. To such Anglo-Indians *moonshee* meant above all 'a native teacher of languages, Arabic, Persian, or Urdu', since that was likely to be the first way that they encountered these literate secretaries.[24]

New Persian, then, was not just a language for the poetry of love and mysticism, as its global reputation would often suggest. It provided the sinews of administration, in a phrase the command, control, and communication, within the states that the Turks had made their own. Besides these civilian functions, it also did service within military life, despite the usual generalization that Turkic was the language of soldiers. Even in Ottoman Turkish much military vocabulary is borrowed from Persian. The highest rank, *paşa*, was a shortening of Persian *padišāh* 'emperor', and lowest (cavalry) rank, *sipahi*,* was derived from Persian *sipāhi* 'soldier' from *sipāh* 'army'. Every unit was under the command of its *kethüda*, from Persian *kat-xuda* 'householder'. The words *piyade* infantry and *süvari* 'cavalry' are both borrowed directly from Persian. Certain crucial institutions that made it all work are Persian borrowings too: *tımar*, the fief of land needed to support one horseman, is from Persian *timār* 'care (of the sick), grooming (of a horse)'; *sipariş* 'commercial order, commission, allotment of pay (to a relative)' is from Persian *sipariš* 'trust, consignment'. After the great disruption caused by the Mongol invasion in the early thirteenth century, Turks adopted small cannon called *zarbu-zan* 'beat-strike', combining Arabic and

---

* This is in the origin of the Indian *sepoy*, which however was an infantryman. An Indian cavalryman was a *sowar*, from Persian *sawār* 'horseman': this also underlies Turkish *süvari*.

In fact, in the Central Asian style, best attested in India, the military was even more defined in Persian. The highest rank in the original system had been *sipāhsālār* 'army-leader', which had meant 'general' under the Delhi Sultanate, but under Akbar and later Mughals became the rank of a provincial governor. Many rank titles have the Persian suffix -*dār*, literally 'holder' (e.g., the general word for a commander in chief is *sardār* 'head-holder'), although the rest of the word is usually a borrowing from Arabic. Thus, in the Mughal army, a *manṣabdār* 'office-holder' was graded by the number of mounted retainers he brought to the army, from ten to ten thousand; e.g., more specifically, *hazāri* (1,000), *deh-hazāri* (10,000). Later, in the army as redefined by the British, among the ranks (given their color bar) assigned for native troops, we find *ṣūbadār* 'province-holder', captain; *risāldār* 'troop-holder', cavalry squadron leader; *jemaʿdār* 'group-holder', lieutenant; *ḥavāldār* 'trust-holder', sergeant; *dafaʿdār* 'thrust-holder', cavalry sergeant.

Persian elements, and matchlock muskets, *tüfe(n)k*, borrowing the Persian word *tufang*, originally the word for a crossbow.

○✕✂○

Besides such effects on the technical terms of empire, Persian, as a lingua-franca, i.e. a useful auxiliary language, also influenced the mother tongues of the people who were making constant use of it. Nawā'i, even when inveighing against use of Persian and in favor of Turkic, uses at least 50 percent Persian vocabulary in his work in Turkic "Verdict on the Two Languages."[25] In the same era (late fifteenth century), the warlord and first Mughal Bābur can write a sentence such as

> *Čūn 'Umar Šayx Mīrzā **buland himmat**lıq ve **uluq dā'iyah**lıq **bādšāh** irdi, **hamīšeh mulkgīr**liq **dağdağah**-sı **bār** irdi*

which translates word for word as

> As Omar Sheikh Mirza high ambitious and great covetous ruler was, always imperialism inclination-his there was

where the Perso-Arabic words (excepting the proper name) have all been marked in bold. Beyond vocabulary, his sentence structure too is heavily Persianized. Turkic has always been a "left-branching" language: adjectives and whole relative clauses precede their head nouns (e.g, the elements ending in *-lıq* do above), whereas Persian structure (like that of English) is the opposite. But Bābur (and all writers in Chagatay Turkic) regularly used Turkic *kim* (who) or indeed the borrowed *ki*, as if it were Persian *keh* (which/what/that), to open all sorts of subordinate clauses that tag along at the end, just as in Persian: *dirlar kim* ... 'they-say that ...', *anı üçün kim* ... 'there-for (it is) that ...'

Likewise, the characteristic *ezāfe* construction of Persian noun-phrases, which appends all dependents to the head noun with a linking *-i-or-e-*, is copied in Chagatay Turkic: ***kisver**-i **körk*** 'land-of-beauty'. All these phenomena were also seen in Ottoman Turkish and have in some cases even hung on into modern Turkish, despite the attempts since 1926 to purify the language of such foreign influences: e.g., the ironically self-designating term *galat-ı meşhur* 'mistake widespread', proverbially preferable to *lûgat-i* *fasih* 'language plain'.[26] And another feature of Persian, verb compounding—which as we saw (pages 84–85) had once made it capable of incorporating vast numbers of Arabic verbs—was now adopted in Turkic. Just as Persian made any noun into a verb by adding *kardan* 'do', so the Turkic languages, whose verbal system was as different from Persian's as Persian's had been from Arabic, could add *qɪlmak/etmek/äylämäk* (Chagatay) or *etmek/eylemek/qɪlmak* (Ottoman) to similar effect, though other verbs are also sometimes preferred. Hence, e.g., expressing 'to forgive', 'to have mercy', 'to pray', Chagatay said *afü qɪlmak*, *raḥm qɪlmak*, *namaz oqumak*, as against Ottoman's *affetmek*, *rahmet eylemek*, *namaz qɪlmak*.

The overall result is a strong family resemblance to Persian of Turkic text, whether in Chagatay or Ottoman Turkish—so much so that in the case of written Ottoman in particular, it could sometimes be unclear whether the text was actually intended to be in Persian or in Turkish. Meanwhile, the spoken languages remained much less touched by this interlingual style; readers with less formal learning could often fail to make sense of what was written nominally in their own language.

Hence in the east and west of the *qalamrau-e-zabān-e-fārsī*, over the second millennium AD, Persian was infused into Turkic, primarily at the higher levels of vocabulary and learned prose. But south of the Himalayas its influence was even more radical, with effects on the sounds available in north-Indian languages, the structure of their words and sentences, as well as masses of vocabulary, until in the extreme case of Urdu—more fully known by its Persian title *zabān-i-urdū-i-muallā* "language of the camp exalted"—it can claim to have been a major element in the creation of a totally new language.

The Islamic influence on north-Indian languages has been marked, apparently permanently, by the spread of Perso-Arabic script, which has been applied (in variant forms) to write the languages from Sindhi in the west to Kashmiri in the north, although significantly it never spread to Bengal. Bengal, despite being converted since the thirteenth century, has retained its own distinctive writing. Furthermore Islam, although it spread widely in India, never spread so densely as to exclude all other faiths; as a result, many languages continued to be written variously, in Perso-Arabic but also in some other script. Panjabi and Kashmiri are two such languages, and another is *Xaṛī Bōlī* "the standing speech" characteristic of the Delhi region, which (in the nineteenth century) came to be seen as having two variants, Urdu (developed under Persian influence) and Hindi (whose writers have increasingly emphasized its roots in Sanskrit). But despite their differences in high-flown vocabulary, they are still pretty much indistinguishable in everyday speech, including the heavy influence from Persian.

The influence of Persian in Indian languages can be discerned where one hears fricative consonants other than *s*, *š*, or *h*, notably *f*, *v*, *z*, *χ* and *γ*; these immediately identify such words as *fikr* 'thought', *vāpas* 'back, in return', *zilzileh* 'earthquake', *χatm* 'end', and *γam* 'sorrow' as loans.* Also the uvular stop *q* is distinctive where it occurs—though in fact this is an Arabic sound that Persian itself never fully accommodated. Persians still confuse it in popular speech with *γ*, while Indians replace it with *k*, so Arabic *qil'a* 'castle' becomes *γila* in Persian but *kilā* in Hindi. (Delhi's 'Red Fort' is the *Lāl Kilā*.)

Above all, Hindi/Urdu contains a vast stock of words borrowed from Persian (and so do the other languages of the northwest). Not just the words for abstractions and technical ideas (which are in any case usually taken from Arabic or Persian, though often, more recently, language planners have replaced them in Hindi with Sanskrit roots), but quite basic vocabulary, such as *ādmī* 'man', *aurat* 'woman',[†] *zamīn* 'earth', *āsmān* 'sky', *daryā* 'sea', *zindagī* 'life', *mawt* 'death', *mausam* 'weather', *subah* 'morning', *roz* 'day', *sāl* 'year', *farš* 'floor', *darvāzā* 'door', *dīvār* 'wall', *daraxt* 'tree', *parde* 'curtain', *bīmār* 'sick', *xuš* 'happy', *zyādā* 'more', *kam* 'less', *har* 'each'. And some Persian word-building prefixes and suffixes have also been absorbed: *-stān* 'place' (in so many country names), *-ī* for derived adjectives (e.g., *pārsī* 'Persian', *torkī* 'Turkish', *čīnī* 'Chinese', *angrezī* 'English', *sūbāī* 'provincial'), *be-* 'devoid of . . .' (e.g., *be'aql* 'witless', *befikr* 'carefree'). All of these are freely applicable to non-Persian roots: hence *beant* 'endless', *bekār* 'unemployed'. To absorb Persian verbs, there is of course the time-honored resource of verb compounding, as common in these languages as in Turkic, and Hindi/Urdu in

---

* Those Indians who still cannot cope with Persian consonants usually approximate them with *p*ʰ, *b*, *j*, *k*ʰ and *g*ʰ, so this set of words would popularly be pronounced *p*ʰ*ikr*, *bāpas*, *jiljileh*, *k*ʰ*atm*, and *gam*. Traditionally the languages of north India had aspirated consonants instead, *p*ʰ/*b*ʰ, *t*ʰ/*d*ʰ, *ṭ*ʰ/*ḍ*ʰ, *č*ʰ/*j*ʰ, *k*ʰ/*g*ʰ—something that must conversely have tried the patience of Persians and Turks in India. But in some cases, their failure has simply been accepted; so the word *p*ʰ*ul* 'fruit', has a variant, *ful*.

† These first two are, by their etymology, especially surprising on the lips of Hindi-speaking Hindus, the former meaning 'son of Adam', the second being the Arabic word for 'imperfection' or 'deficiency', *'awrat*. But to complete the trio, *bačchā* or *bačchī* 'child', is almost identical in pronunciation with the Persian equivalent, *bačeh*.

fact achieves a closer copy of Persian than Turkic ever does here, since the operative verb is chosen for its base meaning, Hindi/Urdu *karnā* 'do' corresponding to *kardan* for transitive verbs, and *honā* 'be, become' to intransitive *šudan*. So not only do we have *māf karnā* 'forgive', *rahm karnā* 'have mercy', *namāz karnā* 'perform [Muslim] prayer', but also *pasand karnā* 'to like', *band karnā* 'to shut', *šurū' karnā* 'begin', all of which have passive or intransitive equivalents with *honā*.[27]

∞∞∞

Looking back at the rise and reign of this millenary language, one can pick out some important points that may generally be valid for this type of institution, the international lingua-franca.

First of all, a lingua-franca can only be recognized as such when it is taken up and used by third parties. Persian, with its closely related dialects, notably Median or Parthian, has continuously been the most widespread mother tongue across Iran since early in the first millennium BC. But that was not sufficient to make it the lingua-franca of the empire that occupied this whole space, the realm of Cyrus the Achaemenian. Persian never became the lingua-franca of the Persian Empire. Instead, two long-established written languages played the key role in imperial communications. The home provinces continued to use Elamite as their written language, and the empire as a whole relied on scribes who encoded all documents in Aramaic, a third-party language, which could be read out in whatever mother tongue was needed, from Greek to Egyptian to Sogdian. When that empire was dissolved and reconstituted by Alexander and his Greek-speaking Macedonians, Greek did achieve an official symbolic status for two centuries, though for practical reasons this was probably not fully at the expense of Aramaic. The clear origin in Aramaic text of official written Persian (or Pahlavi), the language of the Parthian and Sassanian empires that dominated Iran for the next seven centuries, shows that Aramaic never went away. The trading activities of the Sassanians in the Indian Ocean established Persian as a lingua-franca among foreign merchants; once again, it took nonnative speakers to recognize a lingua-franca, but now it was Persian itself cast in that role.

With the Muslim conquest of the Sassanian Empire, Persian the mother tongue was no longer the official language of Iran, displaced now by an Arabic language symbolic of the new power reality. But after ingesting the religious message of the new masters (and transforming the literate version of Persian to conform with it), Persians gradually promoted and spread the official use of their language in its new form throughout the eastern reaches of the Arab Caliphate. The long-term result was that, as the power of the Caliphate declined and was replaced by a plethora of more or less independent Muslim sultanates, Persian expanded as the language of power. The rulers in the new era were almost always of Turkic origin and often continued to speak some form of Turkic, especially with their military colleagues, as Muslim power continued to spread; but the language of their governments—as well as their literatures—was either in Persian or profoundly infused with it. Persian was the lingua-franca of eastern Islamdom for the many centuries, and even, for a time, crossed the religious divide to remain as the commercial and administrative language under the British East India Company.

Predominantly, the spread of the Persian language in the second millennium AD was due to the triumph of arms, largely arms in Turkish hands. This created Persian-using strata of society in Anatolia (under the Seljuqs, and later the Ottomans) extending ultimately across the Bosphorus and into the Balkans, in Central Asia (under the Chingizids and Timurids), and south into Hindustan (under Ghaznavids, Ghurids, Mamlūks, Khaljis, Tughlaqs, and Mughals). Everywhere, then, when Persian spread into new territory, it was brought on the lips and pens of warlike marauders. Nonetheless, nowhere was this military basis for the expansion of the *qalamrau-e-zabān-e-fārsī* prejudicial to Persian's acceptability as a language of culture. Everywhere it went, Persian was seen as a high-level, urbane medium. This was true even for Indians, who (in a modern context) might have been expected to resent the Persian language's stereotype of them as dark and infidel.* Despite their limited take-up of Islam, however, elite Hindus did accept use of the Persian language.

This universal acceptability of Persian contrasted markedly with the reception of Turkic itself, the mother tongue of the conquerors. Turkic persisted as an elite court language for insiders; but despite Nawā'i's early attempts to show that it had an expressive power superior to Persian's, and the admiration, traditional in Persian poetry, for the beauty of the Turks

---

* Consider the Steingass dictionary as it records Persian connotations of the word *hindū*: "an Indian; black; a servant; a slave; a robber; an infidel; a watchman; a mole on the cheek of a mistress . . ."; overlapping, but in no way equivalent to those of *turk*: "a Scythian, barbarian, robber, plunderer, vagabond; (met.) a beautiful boy or girl, the beloved."

themselves,* Turkic speech retained in many quarters an (undeserved) reputation for relative uncouthness. Even in the early twentieth century, the Qajar ruler of Iran, another scion of a Turkic dynasty, could rudely reject presentation of some Turkic poetry from its author, Mo'jaz Shabestari, with the words "I do not know Turkish: what do you think I am? This is Turkish, and what is sprung of Turks you can call Turkish ignorance.† Oh God! it will sap the crown and throne of the Qajar line!"[28]

This long-lasting "cultural cringe" of Turkic before Arabic and Persian may have arisen because Turkic never and nowhere became a lingua-franca widely separated from its native-speaker community. To develop full self-confidence, a language's speakers need to see it taken up beyond its natural domain.

---

* Already Rudaki was writing in the early tenth century:

> *bādeh dahandeh buti, badī' zi xūbān | bačeh xātun e tork wa bačeh e xāqān.*
> *tork e hāzārān be-pāy pīš ṣaff e andar | har yek čun māh e bar du hafteh dirafšān.*

He who proffers the wine is an idol, more lovely than the fair, son of a Turkic dame and sire. Thousands of Turks afoot in the foremost ranks, each shining like a two-week moon. (Cited in Gandjei 1986, 67)

† *Jahālat.* The Qajar uses the Arabic word connoting the state of ignorance that reigned before Muhammad's prophecy.

# CHAPTER 5

# Traders' Languages and the Language for Trade

> He knows every language and knowingly pretends he doesn't:
> a typical Phoenician, know what I mean?
>
> —Roman comment on Phoenicians (third century BC)[1]

> The Suli have gone wherever profit is to be found.
>
> —Chinese comment on Sogdians (AD 1060)[2]

ONE ASPECT OF THE past of English that has clearly contributed to its present status as a global lingua-franca is its historical role as the language of a great trading nation.

Since the first voyage of the East India Company in 1591, there have been Englishmen (later, more generally, Britons) abroad seeking opportunities for profitable trade, and gradually building up a network of trading posts and military bases to support its growth. Naturally they always spoke English among themselves, even as they learned to use other languages for their business contacts—notably Portuguese, Persian, Malay, and Chinese. But as their wealth and power increased—not least through the direct military support of the British state—those around them began to aspire to speak English too, with a view to sharing in the fruits of this success.

This zeal of foreigners to learn the rich men's language was palpable, and in the early nineteenth century the market for it had grown enough to become a new line of business in its own right: commercial teaching of English was on offer in all the centers of power in British India. Protestant missionary zeal to spread the word of God, as well as provident concern by governors to develop a network of bilingual administrative staff, added to the effort to provide education in the language, and the long-term result was to spread English as a language of business and education all round the Indian sub-continent, in a swath across Malaya and the East Indies, and over the China Sea to Hong Kong. Subsequent events, such as the nineteenth-century spread of British colonialism into every continent, and then the rollout across the world, after World War II, of commercial strength built up in the USA, have reinforced the perception of English as owing much of its global success to commerce.

But the British and their kin are only the latest nations to distinguish themselves, and potentially their language, for links with international (and cross-linguistic) trade. By now, the historical record has enough such nations to form a few judgments about the careers and likely destinies of lingua-franca communities grown on this basis, the voluntary exchange of goods for profit. The recording of commercial transactions is accepted as one of the fundamental uses of literacy—even perhaps the original motive for the invention of writing—so in principle one might expect the history of such languages to be well documented. In practice, the records of such languages—which would include Phoenician, Aramaic, Greek, Sabir (the eponymous Lingua Franca of the Mediterranean), Sogdian, Persian, Portuguese, Malay, Nahuatl, Mobile Trade Language, Chinook Jargon, Tupi (*Lingua Geral do Brasil*), Swahili, as well as French and English—if they were ever written down, have only tended to survive if they were noncommercial. These languages, when used to support trade, are decidedly for the here and now.

The concept of a "trade lingua-franca" needs refinement. Many of the languages just listed, although clearly used as media of communication over centuries by merchants, are not known to have spread more generally into surrounding populations. One can distinguish the languages of communities that simply expanded abroad in pursuit of international long-distance trade from those languages where this spread was followed by significant take-up of the language by host populations. Both clearly spread a language. But in the former case, the spread is by migration and infiltration only, as the native speakers of the language follow perceived business opportunities far and wide, creating a diaspora of ethnic communities in foreign parts; in the latter, the language undergoes a further diffusion into the surrounding society and may be used in many cases for communication among third parties. The former kind of spread can be considered "supply-push," as the merchants move outward, bringing their language with them; the latter is "demand-pull," where outsiders are inspired with an active desire to use the language, often as a step to immediate recruitment into its speakers' activities, but ultimately for any reason at all.

Only the latter are fully lingua-francas in the sense of being secondary languages adopted for wider communication beyond the reach of the speakers' mother tongues. But this does not mean that the former kind should be overlooked. They are common in history and have often led to significant cultural diffusion into host languages, even if, in the end, they never "take off" beyond the trading communities who spread them. They often represent the initial stage of lingua-francas that have spread beyond their trading roots and never looked back, such as the Greek of Athens, which morphed into the *koinē* of the ancient eastern Mediterranean, the Portuguese of the seventeenth- and eighteenth-century Indian Ocean, or the Malay that now serves as the official language throughout the modern states established in what was once the East Indies.

The first such supply-push trading language known to us is the Phoenician of the first millennium BC, a language originating in the area of modern Lebanon, and hence similar to Hebrew. The Phoenician cities founded their trading network through selling wood (the famed cedars of Lebanon) to the Egyptians, but they soon developed a reputation for papyrus (from Byblos) and luxury textiles, particularly those dyed with their local murex shellfish. Ezekiel, chapter 27, gives a vivid account of over twenty different places of business for the city of Tyre, the richest of them all, naming characteristic products for each, from Spanish metals through Aegean slaves and bronze and Armenian equines to Syrian textiles. (We know this is not an exhaustive list since Phoenicians were also visiting Britain to obtain tin, Egypt for grain, and Ophir, perhaps in southern Arabia, for gold and precious stones.)[3]

Not later than the eighth century BC the Phoenicians had built up a string of mercantile and mining bases all around the southern shores of the Mediterranean as far as modern Huelva (probably to be identified with ancient Tarshish or Tartessus) in southern Spain, and Lixus and Mogador on the Atlantic coast of modern Morocco. They colonized, or at least set up bases and trading posts, on all the major islands from Cyprus to the Balearics, with a particular emphasis on Sardinia and Sicily, and nearby Carthage on the coast of Africa. These activities continued despite the fall of their mother cities in Lebanon first to the Persians (in the sixth century BC) and later to Alexander (in the fourth).

Carthage was the only colony of the Phoenicians that became an independent city. Its language has become known to the world, through a Roman accent, as Punic; and sadly for its speakers, the longest text surviving
in it is a speech within a Latin play, Plautus' *Poenulus* 'the Punic guy'. In
Africa, various elites appear to have adopted it (notably the famous princes
Syphax and Massinissa, who grappled with Rome in the late third century
BC), although the indigenous people clearly continued to speak Libyan (the
ancestor of modern Berber). The official language of the states to the west of
Carthage along the shore, Massaesylia and Massylia, was Punic, as seen on
boundary stones, and on their coinage.[4] This is the only evidence that Punic
was beginning to move from supply-push to demand-pull as a lingua-franca;
but defeats of Carthage by Rome in 202 and 146 BC decisively shifted the
balance of linguistic power among African elites, from declining Punic to
growing Latin. Punic survived as a mother tongue in Carthage itself and
was probably still surviving at least in the countryside in the time of Bishop
Augustine of Hippo (AD 354–430).

The Phoenicians were routinely literate, and arguably they had abstracted
their radically simplified, alphabetic style of writing from Egyptian hieroglyphs. The Phoenicians had the earliest known, identifiable alphabet. They
later introduced it to Greeks, some of the first people with whom they must
have had dealings in their westward exploration of the Mediterranean. This
contact seems to have happened on the islands of Thera, Melos, and Crete.[5]
No linguistic transfer, or Greek-Phoenician bilingualism, is attested, but it
is clear that the Greeks essentially adopted the Phoenician system (reinter-
preting it to include vowels); indeed, they originally called their alphabet *ta
phoinikēia grammata* 'Phoenician markings'.

Despite this crucial cultural transfer (the Greek alphabet directly or indirectly laid the foundation for all the European scripts that have followed),
and the Phoenicians' ubiquitous presence round the Mediterranean in association with the supply of luxury goods from at least the eighth to the
fourth centuries BC, the Phoenician language never spread to neighboring
communities or became a lingua-franca outside cities and settlements of native speakers. Even Carthage, which had possessions in North Africa and
Spain as well as Sardinia and western Sicily, did not spread its language
to its subjects there, perhaps because (unlike its competitor Rome) it was
dominated by trading interests rather than landholders (who might be, or
inspire, potential settlers).

It is worth considering why Greek was taken up as a lingua-franca while

Phoenician was not, especially since the two languages' arrival in the western Mediterranean is almost simultaneous (with a slight priority to Phoenician) and prima facie so similar. Greek colonists were entering the western Mediterranean from the middle of the eighth to the fifth centuries BC, and like the Phoenicians' bases, the Greek cities remained coastal settlements, mostly without extensive claims on the hinterland. Like the Phoenician colonies too, Greek colonies would have ended up speaking the same dialect as their mother cities.

Whereas the Phoenicians' motives appear to have been focused on mining and trade in goods—in a word, profit—the Greek settlers were more variously driven, looking to farm as well as trade, and always founding independent cities that, despite nostalgic loyalties to their founding communities back in Aegean Greece, were politically self-governing. Greek colonies were revealingly called *apoikiai* 'away-homes'; they were places to live abroad, not just bases for foreign business. Together they were known as *Megalē Hellas*, which can be translated as 'Greater Greece'. To strike an analogy with British overseas activities in the seventeenth and eighteenth centuries, the Phoenicians were like the servants of the East India Company, the Greeks more like the settlers of the Thirteen Colonies in America.

A first clue to Greek's linguistic advantage in the west comes from the differing fate of the Greek colonies that were meanwhile being established in the east, around the Black Sea, then known as *Euxeinos* 'hospitable'.* Almost all of these (which covered its entire coast and have ever since been the sea's principal ports) were founded by a single city of the southern Aegean, Miletus—ninety in number, according to Pliny (*Naturalis Historia* v.112), although no more than twenty can now be located. Despite holding this corner on the Black Sea market (and its significant commercial grip on the other major source of grain, Egypt, through its colony Naucratis, founded in the seventh century BC), Miletus was a relatively small player in Greek politics. Nonetheless, the colonies remained economically important to Greece as a whole, and above all vital to its cultural leader (and main mar-

---

* This word was a euphemistic reversal of *axeinos* 'inhospitable', the Greek attempt to represent a Scythian, or perhaps Persian, name for the sea, related to Old Persian *axšaina* 'turquoise-colored'; Khotan Saka *āṣṣeiṇa-* 'blue', Ossetic *æxsīn* 'dark gray'. (*Encyclopaedia Iranica* (R. Schmitt), s.v. "Black Sea")

ketplace), Athens.* Yet for all their optimistic names such as Olbia 'Prosperity', Nymphaion 'Shrine of Nymphs', Eupatoria 'Noble Sires,' and Dioscurias 'City of the Heavenly Twins', the Greek cities at the mouths of the Dnieper and the Don remained remote outposts of Greek culture, nothing more.

Miletus' Greek was Ionic; it was close to the *koinē dialektos* 'common talk' which would become the universal standard from the third century BC, although this was based most closely on Attic, the speech of Athens. However, except on the southern shore, in Anatolia, which after Alexander's conquests in the 320s BC was to receive continuous Greek immigration, the Greek spoken by merchants did not spread around the Black Sea to become the vernacular. The Roman poet Ovid, who was fluent in Greek, was in AD 8 lamenting being condemned to learn Getic to get by in Tomoi (originally another of Miletus' foundations, on the western coast). Black Sea cities remained a byword for multilingualism, in fact: at much the same time Strabo wrote that in Dioscurias, on the eastern coast, you could hear seventy tribes each speaking a different language "because they lived scattered and unmixed, through stiff necks and wild ways."[6]

The purely commercial activity round the Black Sea did not lead to the development of a lingua-franca community there: despite so much traffic, that sea never became a Greek lake. In this area, the sociolinguistic effects of Greek were similar to those of Phoenician generally—a language of frequent travelers that did not get picked up more widely. Meanwhile at the other end of the Mediterranean, Greek was garnering much more influence.

In the west, Greek colonists had spread round the northern shoreline, leaving the south, and the islands, to their Phoenician competitors. Only Sicily was an exception to this, since Greeks also took over the east and center of this island. The more than forty cities so founded included some

---

* Scythian corn from the Ukraine was, along with imports from Egypt, the staple of Athens' food supply from the sixth century BC on. The city was prepared to use main force to guarantee its access to the Black Sea colonies (as reported in Plutarch, *Pericles* xx, though the expedition's date is obscure). Furthermore, Demosthenes (384–322 BC) reported (*Speeches* xxxv.50) that it was illegal for any Athenian or any resident alien in Attica, or any person under their control, to lend out money on a ship unless it was commissioned to bring grain to Athens. They were also forbidden to bring grain to any harbor but the port of Athens, Peiræus, a measure that would enforce Athens' domination of supply to the rest of Greece.

that were to become among most influential of the Mediterranean—Taranto, Syracuse, Naples, Cumae, Nice, Marseilles—but they were already aggressive contributors to "Greater Greece" shortly after their foundations, which began in the eighth century BC, asserting their presence against quite determined opposition from both Carthage and the Etruscans. Marseilles, founded ca 600, even became a university center for higher Greek studies, a status it would retain well into first few centuries AD.

Already in this contested period, however, the Greeks were seen as the leaders of cultural innovation in this part of the world. The Etruscans, of obscure origins but dominant within northwestern Italy between 750 and 475 BC, had an urban-centered (and maritime) civilization that had been deeply influenced by the Greeks based in the south. Their language is only scantily known—from inscriptions and one ritual document written on an Egyptian mummy's linen winding-sheet—so direct evidence of Greek's influence is hard to come by. The mere fact that Etruscans learned their alphabet from Greeks does not signify linguistic influence; after all, the Greeks had taken as much from the Phoenicians. Nevertheless, in Etruscan, Greek is the evident source of words for drinking equipment: *aska* (from *askos*) 'wineskin flask', *culichna* (from *kulix*) 'handled cup', *qutun* (from *kōthōn*) 'jug', *lecht-umuza* (a diminutive of *lēkuthos*) 'oil bottle'.

The stock of Etruscan vocabulary borrowed into Latin gives richer insight into the prior influence of Greek on Etruscan. It is always clear when a Greek term has come into Latin through Etruscan because of the strange deformations it has undergone: e.g., *formīcae* from *murmēkes* 'ants', *laena* from *khlaina* 'cloak', *persōna* from *prosōpon* 'mask', *fascinum* from *baskanion* 'dildo', *guberna* from *kuberna* 'steering oar', *catamīta* from *Ganumēdēs* 'pretty boy'. (Direct borrowings of Greek into Latin, of which there were many later, show none of this.) Looking at the vocabulary as a whole, one can see that over 25 percent of the Etruscan terms in Latin are from original Greek, and for nautical language the proportion rises to 75 percent. This terminology would have come into Latin around the fifth–fourth centuries BC.[7]

This does not prove that Etruscans had once been widely fluent in Greek (any more than its shows that many Romans had a working knowledge of Etruscan). But it does show that Greek ways enjoyed a high level of cultural prestige among the Etruscans, a point that is reinforced by the overwhelming popularity of Greek mythological themes on the backs of Etruscan ladies' mirrors. By contrast, one finds hardly a single Etruscan loan in Greek, even though the Etruscans were, for over three hundred years of a formative period in Greek history, quite dominant in the zone north of Greater Greece: the contact seems to have been quite one-sided.*

There is evidence too that elite Carthaginians might be educated in Greek. The clearest sign of an existing practice is an attempt to ban it. Circa 409 BC the Carthaginian senate had outlawed the study of Greek at home, to guard against individual contacts with their perceived enemy.[8] Nonetheless, in the third century BC, after reforms instituted by the Spartan general Xanthippus, Carthage's mercenary troops were apparently commanded not in Punic but in Greek. (Alongside Africans, they did include slingers from the Balearic Islands and Celtiberians from northern Spain.) Hannibal himself had studied Greek and wrote books in it; and his old tutor Sosylus of Sparta came along on his campaigns and wrote up their history in the language, together with two more Greeks, Silenus and Chaereas.[9] Inscribing an altar in Italy with his achievements in 205 BC, besides Punic Hannibal used Greek, but certainly not the local—enemy—languages, Latin and Oscan.[10]

After the defeat of Carthage in 202, Rome went on to conquer the Greek empires at the eastern end of the Mediterranean, with the long-term effect that its Roman (i.e. Latin-governed) and Greek zones were amalgamated. Italy received an influx of educated Greeks looking for employment, and Greek was henceforth an intrinsic part of Roman higher learning, almost becoming a second mother tongue for elite Romans.

Aristotle in the fourth century BC had already distinguished four functions for literacy: money making (e.g., contracts and accounting), management, education, and civic life (e.g., laws, treaties, citizen lists, certificates). To these we can add religious expressions (e.g., curses, dedications), commemoration (e.g., epitaphs), and personal contact through letters.[11] Greek and Phoenician were evidently used for all of those, but in Greek's case, this went beyond mother tongue users. The Sibylline books of prophecy, written in Greek hexameters, were the highest source of oracles for the Roman republic, by tradition since the reign of Tarquinius Priscus (early sixth century BC).

Greek had turned into a lingua-franca for the western Mediterranean,

---

* The only barely recognizable loan words from Etruscan into Greek are *antar* 'eagle' (according to Hesychius' dictionary); *tēbenna* 'toga' (whose ending *-enna* looks right, but has no known cognate in Etruscan); and *koleón* 'sword sheath' (cf. Latin *culleus* 'leather bag', which also has the right ending [*-eus*] and is famous among other things for its use in the drowning of parricides, the *poena cullei*, which was supposed to be originally an Etruscan practice; but this may be a general Mediterranean word that predates all the languages: cf. Latin *coleus* or *culiō* 'scrotum').

seen as a key language of wider communication, while Phoenician, the language of the Greeks' trading rivals, apparently never did. Why not? Arguably, the crucial difference between these two, both spread by traders with home markets in the east, was cultural—speakers of Greek had always been much more open, secular, and hence widely attractive. Either that, or Greek speakers' characteristic self-confidence, not to say solipsism, tended to be taken at its own valuation.

Phoenician like Greek must have had a literature, and at the earliest period both would have had pronounced religious overtones. Various hints suggest that this literature, long lost, had a common Semitic heritage with what we know from the Old Testament, but was closer to much older Ugaritic tablet literature (ca thirteenth century BC), which came from just north of the Phoenician homeland. It is paraphrased in a late Greek text, the *Phoenician History* of Philo of Byblos, adapting the work of Sanchuniathon of Beirut. Both the Ugaritic texts and Sanchuniathon refer to the gods El, Hadād, Dagon, Kothar the Smith, and Ashtoreth the Beautiful. Phoenician or Punic religion, with a reputation for sacrificing children in *tophet* furnaces, was not attractive. Greek religious cults—associated, by contrast, with wild festivals such as those of Bacchus—certainly were. One of the earliest surviving Latin texts (186 BC) is a senatorial decree against the spread of bacchanalian celebrations in Italy; and Herodotus recalls how two famous Scythians, Anacharsis and Scyles, ultimately yielded to the charm of Greek cults—even though this ultimately cost them their lives.[12]

In these early centuries neither Greek nor Phoenician was the language of a religion that sought to convert outsiders; but Greece had pioneered the development of religious texts and rituals into epic recitation and drama. Out of myth telling in hymns to the gods came Homer's *Iliad* and *Odyssey*, and Pindar's lyric odes; out of religious pageants, the tragedies of Aeschylus, Sophocles, and Euripides, and the comedies of Aristophanes and Menander, developed step by step. Homer, the language's cardinal poet, had been available as a written text since at least the seventh century BC.[13] After the fifth century, a vast variety of texts were available in Greek language, many of them factual (memorable didactic verse, and history and philosophy in their widest senses), many more fictional, often purely for entertainment (epic, lyric, and dramatic poetry). These inquiring, skeptical, self-confident, humorous, and generally humane works were unprecedented and unparalleled, a cultural development unique in the world, as far as anyone knew at the time. When in the middle of the first century BC King Orodes of Parthia, a native speaker of Pahlavi, received the severed head of the Roman general Crassus, he was attending a performance of Euripides' *Bacchae* at the time. And his host, King Artavazdes of Armenia, had written his own plays in Greek.[14]

So, until Cicero and other Romans self-consciously attempted to build a Latin version in first centuries BC and AD, Greek really had no competitor as a common culture for the Mediterranean world. Greek speakers were that world's only "audience for wise guys."[15] To its status as the medium of Athenian and other Greek cities' trade, Greek had added a reputation as *the* language for science, the arts, and entertainment.

∞≫○

The Sogdians of Central Asia were like the Phoenicians in that they were an alliance of city-states who shared a common language, rather than citizens of a single state or empire.* The principal cities were Bukhara, Samarkand, Panjikent, and Kish (modern Shahr-i-Sabz), but this was just their starting area. Again like the Phoenicians, they established colonies over a long extent in one direction from their homeland. The Phoenicians moved west, by sea; the Sogdians moved east, overland. By the fourth century AD they had expanded eastward to Chach (modern Tashkent), and subsequently they established colonies much farther afield, eastward into Chinese Turkestan and Mongolia.

They were also like the Phoenicians in that claims of their language's lingua-franca status have been rather exaggerated. The idea goes back to a 1912 article of the French orientalist Paul Pelliot, which claimed that Sogdian was "the lingua franca of the Silk Road," subsequently reiterated—but never substantiated—by many other scholars of Central Asia.[16] It is clear that the speakers themselves were widespread, and settlements, whether

---

* Like the Medes and Persians, Sogdians were by origin Iranian nomads who had settled down prehistorically. Their name is a dialectal variant of the quintessential name for Iranian nomads, Scythians, in Greek Σκύθαι: *skutᵇ-ai* or *skūθ-ai*. The name *Sogd* represents *suğδ* or *sğuδ*, evidently a similar root, differing in not much more than voicing some consonants. It originally meant 'shooters', which is a related word, i.e., 'bowmen'. (See Beckwith 2009, 377–80.) Athens in the fifth century BC employed a police force of Scythian slaves and called them τοξόται *toxótai* 'bowmen'.

independent colonies or merchant enclaves within greater (Chinese) cities, are reported from modern Uzbekistan, through Semirechie (Slavic 'seven-river-land', i.e. Kyrgyzstan, southern Kazakhstan) all the way along the Silk Road through Khotan and Gansu to the Chinese capital Chang'an, with outlying colonies northward in the Ordos loop of the Yellow River (in Inner Mongolia), and near Lake Baikal in Siberia.[17] Inscriptions in Sogdian, which often show a link to the Samarkand area, have been found near the newly built highway across the Himalayas between China and modern Pakistan, demonstrating that, in the fourth to sixth centuries AD, Sogdian speakers were, at the very least, responsible for most of the graffiti on this trade route to India and hence were quite likely present in major northern cities of that country.[18] The Sogdian monk known as Kang Senghui, whose surname Kang shows that his family came from Samarkand, and who became a famous translator of Buddhist literature in the Chinese metropolis of Luoyang ca AD 250, had been born in Hanoi, of a family that had been resident (for trade) in India. There is a report too of one Maniakh, a Sogdian merchant, heading a Turkic trade delegation that went round Sassanian Persia to reach Constantinople in AD 567.[19] But only in one period and area (namely, among the Turks in Xinjiang from the seventh to mid-ninth centuries) does Sogdian seem to have been accepted as an elite language by non-Sogdians and so perhaps become a true lingua-franca in our sense.[20]

But apart from spreading their language, Sogdians had a considerable reputation, especially in Chinese sources. One of the earliest is due to the historian Sima Qian (ca 100 BC): "Although the states from Dayuan [Ferghana] west to Anxi [the Parthian Empire] speak rather different languages, their customs are generally similar and their languages mutually intelligible. The men all have deep-set eyes and profuse beards and whiskers. They are skilful at commerce and will haggle over a fraction of a cent."[21]

Later the Chinese pilgrim monk Xuanzang, whose *Records of Western Countries* date to the seventh century AD, writes from personal experience: "The land is called Suli, and the people are called by the same name, the script and the language likewise . . . they are as a rule crafty and deceitful in their conduct and extremely covetous. Both parent and child plan how to get wealth, and the more they get the more they esteem each other; but the poor and the well-to-do are not distinguished; even when immensely rich, they feed and clothe themselves meanly. The strong-bodied cultivate the land; the rest engage in money-getting.[22]

More officially, though perhaps apocryphally, in the ninth century, archives report, "Suli [Sogdian] children have rock sugar put into their mouths at birth, so that when they grow up their talk shall be sweet. Gum is brushed on their palms so that money they receive shall never leave their hands. They learn to trade from the age of five, and on reaching their twelfth year they are sent to do business with a neighbouring state."[23]

Surveys of population records at Turfan in Xinjiang tend to reinforce this last point: past infancy, the sex ratio of resident Sogdians, but only Sogdians, slips from equality to two women for every man. Half the boys were indeed sent off on trade apprenticeships.[24]

In India, the Sogdians were known as the Čulikā, evidently a deformation of their Suli name used in eastern Central Asia; but that word means a cock's crest—and this is rather similar to a typical Sogdian cap—so perhaps this had something to do with its popularity. Indian literature strangely has nothing to say about the Sogdians, except in myth: they form a contingent of the Kuru army in the elemental battle of the *Mahabharata*. By contrast, one of the first texts attributable to the Sogdians—*Ancient Letter* no. 2—places the Indian merchants in company with the Sogdians in the Chinese city of Luoyang when they all suffer a deadly famine, shortly after AD 311.

These comments reflect a historical career that, like that of the Phoenicians, is less well documented than we should like. Sogdians appear first in the historical record as far-flung subjects of the Achaemenians, brought into the Persian Empire by Cyrus, recognized by Darius as purveyors of lapis lazuli and carnelian, and duly represented on the monumental *apadāna* staircase at Persepolis, as archers in tight, crested caps, and offering a scimitar, battle-axes, and a stallion to the king. They are said by Herodotus to have contributed detachments to Xerxes' army ranged against Greece in 480 BC. When they next show up, in 329 BC, it is as redoubtable opponents to Alexander: they succeed in halting his advance into Central Asia, but come to terms with him, as sealed by his marriage to Roxane,* whom he takes back to Babylon. In this period, the Sogdians seem to have impressed more for their military effectiveness and access to precious stones than their commerce. They then disappear from the record.

A Chinese pioneering diplomat, Zhang Qian, came to Central Asia in the late 120s BC, on a mission to gain access to the horses of the Ferghana

---

* Sogdian *ruxšān* 'bright'.

valley. It seems to have been the Sogdians' southern neighbors, the Wusun,* and the Bactrians, who took up the opportunity, but a century later Sogdians were turning up in person at the Chinese court, offering to trade.[25] The Sogdians may then have benefited from their proximity to the Kushana (Guishuang) Empire (first and second centuries AD) to establish links south into India, and across to the east into Khotan. From the third century, Sogdian and Kushana merchants (those Bactrians again, but possibly Indians too) were on a par in negotiations with the Chinese.[26]

Trade terms in Sogdian language bear the marks of their early collaboration or competition with Bactrians and Indians: e.g., *pany*, from Bactrian *pano*, Sanskrit *paṇa* ('penny'=eighty cowrie shells); *mūδya* from Sanskrit *mūlya* 'price'; *prast(ak)* from Sanskrit *prastha* (about a liter); *mēδāmbn* from a Bactrian form of the Greek *médimnos* 'bushel'. On the road, the *čəxr* 'wheel' was from Bactrian *saxro*, Sanskrit *cakra*; *sārth*, the 'caravan' itself, was from Sanskrit *sārtha*, and its leader, or literally 'protector', was *sārtpāw*, Bactrian *sartopao*. The Sogdian word became a general term for a leader; and the leaders of Sogdian colonies were called by the Chinese 薩寶 (now read as *sàbǎo*, but at the time pronounced *satpaw*, with the *sat* of *bodhisattva* and the *puaw* that meant 'treasure'). The ultimate client, the Chinese emperor, generally introduced as the Son of Heaven (天子 *tiānzi*—then *pʰiantsz̧*) was referred to by all these Iranian merchants as *bāγpūr* 'god-son', the same title used for the Kushana emperor.[27]

For the next five centuries (essentially until the Muslim conquest from the west, and its sequel in the An-Lushan Rebellion† of 755 in China), the Sogdians were the dominant caravan merchants of Central Asia. The crucial exchange would have been of valley horses (*čerpāδ*—'quadrupeds')[28] for Chinese silk, but a variety of other luxury goods would have been carried,

---

* This is the modern reading of a Chinese name, 烏孫, literally 'crow children'. But Beckwith 2009, 376, argues that its fifth-century pronunciation *ɔ-swən* represents Sanskrit *Aświn* 'horseman'. This fits their known role in history; archaeology suggests they were Europoid in appearance; and they were also described by the linguist Yan Shigu (581–645) in his comment on the Chinese chronicle *Han shu* (96b: 3901) as "barbarians who have green eyes and red hair, like macaques"; so they may well have been some kind of Indo-Aryans.

† Its leader, An-Lushan—who among many other achievements had seduced the emperor's favorite concubine, Yang Guifei—was half-Sogdian, with a name interpretable as '*Ruxšān* from Bukhara'.

among them musk, slaves, gold, precious stones, silverware, amber, rock candy, and rhubarb.

It has been calculated that in 712 an adult slave was valued for sale in Samarkand at 200 dirhams, and a bolt of raw silk at 28. The markup for covering the Silk Road, the trip from Dunhuang to Samarkand, was about 100 percent, and the price paid in China for the same bolt would have been 14.3 dirhams.[29] Horses were traded in the opposite direction. Toward the end of the same century a horse in China could fetch 40 bolts, or about 572 dirhams.[30] We may infer that a *čerpāδ* would have been purchased in Samarkand for half the price, viz 286 dirhams, rather more than the value of a slave.

Besides expertise with horseflesh, Sogdians became renowned for their knowledge of languages. This may have been one advantage gained from their early travels as apprentices round the traders' triangle of Sogdiana, India, and China. A Sogdian, growing up in a colony somewhere on the network of Silk Road routes, might find himself first bilingual in his father's and mother's languages, and perhaps also another language of the surrounding country. Once apprenticed he might find himself at an early age somewhere else in Central Asia—always rich in languages—or even visiting the far west in Persia. One example is provided by An-Lushan himself (703–57), son of a Sogdian father and a Turkic mother, who moved from Turkestan to the northeast of China when he was thirteen. His first work was as a military interpreter, skilled in six languages besides Chinese. Another example is Kang Senghui (222–80), that same name just mentioned, whose Buddhist name was Sanghavarman ('redoubt of the Church'). He became a monk at ten when his parents died, but spent his career in southern China, translating Buddhist sutras into Chinese with royal patronage, and particularly noted for his teaching of how to chant in Sanskrit, songs that were still being sung three centuries later.[31]

The Sogdians used this cosmopolitan tradition to permanent effect by producing many of the translations of sacred texts that supported the spread of Buddhism, Nestorian Christianity, and Manichaeism in this period. The Sogdians have been described as "like cultural bees, cross-pollinating ideas and traditions from one civilization to another."[32] So, after an unexplained period (late second century AD) of pioneer translators from Parthia, which is not a place where Buddhism has ever flourished, there came a series of Sogdian-surnamed translators to China (Kang Senghui (222–80), Kang Sengyuan (267–330), Kang Falang (310–420), Zhi-yi (ca 380), Shi Huiming

(427–97), all working to translate Buddhist texts from Indic languages into Chinese. The latest were some of the greatest, and apparently still of non-Chinese extraction: both Fazang (643–712) and Bukung Amoghavajra "unquenchable thunderbolt" (705–74) had a Sogdian mother and an Indian father.*

As for the other religions that had spread before the advent of Islam, a Sogdian named Adam assisted in translating the Nestorian Christian monument in Chang'an into Chinese (781). The original texts of Nestorian Christianity and Manichaeism were in the Syriac dialect of Aramaic, a very foreign language for Central Asia in the early first millennium AD. Nevertheless, only a moderate proportion of texts were translated into Sogdian, and even fewer into Chinese.[33]

Although it might be thought that this scholarly fraternity were independent of the mercantile Sogdians, their succession ended in the late eighth century, just as Sogdian traders were yielding to, or being absorbed into, the ranks of Muslim Persians. The intellectual overlay provided by Sogdian linguists came by courtesy of a Sogdian business community and could not apparently survive without it.

Sogdians were linguistic intermediaries, enabling the spread of others' cultures, but there is little trace of wider use of their own language. Perhaps the translations of Buddhist classics from Chinese into Sogdian, undertaken in Turfan and Dunhuang in the eighth and ninth centuries, can be seen as evidence of an attempt to use Sogdian as a language of wider communication, but this is unlikely: they were probably for the use of devout monolinguals who knew no Chinese. Although written in three different alphabets, depending largely on the religion of the writer (Buddhist, Manichaean, or Christian),[34] most texts in Sogdian seem to have been written exclusively by and for Sogdians themselves.

The one major exception to this is among the nomadic Turks, whose early Central Asian empire is known as the Qaghanate (552–744), and also likely among their successors the Uyghurs (763–840). These empires of Turkic speakers adopted their writing systems from the Sogdians, so the cultural influence is evident. It is also true that Sogdian is the language of the western Qaghanate's coinage, from the sixth and seventh centuries.

---

* All these dates are derived from Chinese sources, according to Walter 2006, 64–66.

But this alone would mean relatively little: when the idea of coined money is introduced for the first time, it often continues to use quite slavishly the model of its foreign source. If the majority are illiterate, the choice of language for the currency is fairly academic.*

More tellingly, a couple of royal obituary inscriptions for qaghans (i.e. khans) have been discovered that are likewise in Sogdian alone. These are at Bugut in Mongolia (from 581) and at Yili or Ili in Xinjiang (from 599). Much later, in the old Uyghur capital of Qarabalghasun 'Black City' or Ordu Baliq 'Army City'—also in modern Mongolia—a trilingual inscription was set up describing the qaghan Alp-Tegin (808–21), written in Uyghur, Chinese, and Sogdian in parallel.[35] All these monuments strongly suggest that the Sogdians' language was involved at the highest level, and for official purposes, in these societies of Turkic speakers. Sogdians were prominent in the Turks' affairs, and the Chinese neighbors evidently resented it. "The Turks [tu-jue] are by nature honest and simple, and one could sow discord among them," wrote a Chinese minister, Pei Ju, to his emperor, in the early seventh century. "But many Sogdians [hu] live among them, all highly cruel and canny, to instruct and guide them."[36]

∞∞∞

Neighboring languages' borrowings of Sogdian words were rather few. E.g., Chinese days of the week were at first (courtesy of that redoubtable Bukung Amoghavajra) taken over phonetically from Sogdian names of the sun, moon, and planets (themselves largely derived from Iranian deities);[37] but these were soon largely replaced with equivalent Chinese terms (where the planets are associated with what were called phases or elements). And it should not be inferred that these were necessarily crucial to daily life: for the following eleven centuries the Chinese terms were only for astrological purposes. The Chinese seem to have gone about their business perfectly well without days of the week.

---

* A joyous example of this "coiner's conservatism" is a *mancus* (4.25-gram golden coin) struck by King Offa of Mercia (in England) in the late eighth century, which on the obverse combines the central legend OFFA REX with the Islamic *šahāda* 'There is no God but Allah . . .', in Arabic, round the rim, and an Arabic inscription on the reverse. It is all copied off a 774 dinar of Manṣūr in the contemporary Abbasid Caliphate. (British Museum, http://tinyurl.com/mobmuz, Blunt 1961)

| DAY | SUNDAY 'SUN' | MONDAY 'MOON' | TUESDAY 'MARS' |
|---|---|---|---|
| SOGDIAN | *mīðre, mīš* | *māx* | *unxān* |
| IRANIAN GOD | Mithra/ The Sun | The Moon | Vr̥traǧna/ Bahram |
| LATE MIDDLE CHINESE (8TH CENT.) | 密或, 蜜 mit.xɦušk, mjit | 莫 mak | 云漢 yn.xaǹ |
| MODERN CHINESE | 日 rì | 月 yuè | 火 huǒ |
| CHINESE PHASE | 'sun' | 'moon' | 'fire' |

It might be countered that Chinese is traditionally resistant to borrowing words from other languages. But the other surrounding languages too that ended up inheriting the Sogdian speaker populations have retained little trace of the half millennium or more in which Sogdian speakers moved among them. The Persians did borrow from Sogdian, and perhaps across a wide spectrum, although relatively few loanwords are now recognized. Henning identified some forty, apologizing that he could not discern any particular domains, and it is indeed difficult: disappointment, trouble, nib, topsy-turvy, mountaintop, plain, frog (two words), owl, ornament, stoning, tooth decay, winepress . . . All human life seems to be here. Given the Sogdians' mercantile reputation, it is surprising not to see more words for more serious, gainful activities, but there is only *alfagdan* 'earn', from *ðβaxš*. Having fifteen hundred years of their own civilization to look back on when they supplanted the Sogdians on their principal trade routes, perhaps the Persians had little to learn in arts of expression from their northeastern neighbors.[38]

But de la Vaissière has noted among them a cluster of words for sensory indulgence (*rēž* 'desire' and also *āruǧde* 'greedy' are identical in the two languages; *rabūxe* 'lust' is from Sogdian *arpūx*; *balād* 'depraved' from *paðātē*; *ēfude* 'frivolous' from *āyaβðē* 'adulterous'). These certainly correspond with some of the few graphic scenes that have survived of Sogdians at play. This Sogdian maxim, found written on the rim of a storage jar, adds to the atmosphere:

| WEDNESDAY 'MERCURY' | THURSDAY 'JUPITER' | FRIDAY 'VENUS' | SATURDAY 'SATURN' |
|---|---|---|---|
| *tīr* | *urmazt* | *nāxid* | *kēwān* |
| Tištrya | Ahura-mazda | Anāhitā | (Keyvān) |
| 咥 | 温没斯 | 那頡 | 雞緩 |
| tʰiat | ʔyń.mut.sẓ | na`.xʰjiat | kjiaj.xʰuań |
| 水 | 木 | 金 | 土 |
| shuǐ | mù | jīn | tǔ |
| 'water' | 'wood' | 'gold' | 'earth' |

*āδē xō ēči γišēp nē-šmār xēp[θ] γəznu-wān nē kē-sī: ərt marti xwār!*

No loss is felt by anyone not watching his own wealth: so, mortal, drink![39]

The Turkic languages had a dozen or so loans, most filtered through from the Sogdians' neighbors the Uyghurs. The Uyghurs of southern Siberia were close to the Sogdians and seem to have adopted Manichaeism as their state religion from 763 to 840 (uniquely in the history of the world) on Sogdian recommendation. But they accepted relatively few of the Sogdians' words: *acun* 'Buddhist incarnation' < *ažun* 'life'; *akşam* < *əxšəp* 'evening'; *borç* < *purč* 'debt'; *dindar* 'faithful acolyte' < *δīnδār* 'having religion'; *hatun*, *kadın* 'lady' < *xwatin* 'queen'; *kent* < *kanθ* 'town'; *kılavuz* 'guide' < *kuδa-βuz* lit. 'sensing where'; *nom* 'Buddhist law' < *nūm* 'rule' (from Greek *nomos*); *put* 'idol' < *put* 'Buddha'; *uçmağ* < *uštəmāx* 'heaven'; *tamu* 'hell' < *tam* 'darkness'.*

Despite the acknowledged role of Sogdian as an elite medium in the early Turkic societies of Siberia, one conjectures that it was largely the Sogdians who learned the foreigners' language in order to communicate.

---

* Other words are vaguely related to Sogdian words, but have probably been borrowed much earlier, from other Iranian languages; e.g., *pay* ~ Sogdian *βāg* 'share', *sarı* 'yellow' ~ Sogdian *zern* 'gold'.

*Sogdian banquet, on funeral couch of a sārtpāw (community leader) in China, sixth century AD. (Credit: Shumei Culture Foundation at Miho Museum)*

By contrast with Sogdian, its linguistic cousin Persian, which was to replace it as the language of merchants along the Silk Road, had a significant overlay of general cultural prestige. Persian did become a full-function lingua-franca, a medium of communication for vast numbers who had grown up with some other mother tongue. As such it has played a role in medieval and modern Central Asia somewhat more analogous to Greek in the ancient Mediterranean, even though the Mongols for a long time attempted to limit wider knowledge of foreign languages in their Chinese domains.

Persian's first extension as a language of trade had been far away from Central Asia, when it established itself as a lingua-franca in the Persian Gulf and Indian Ocean. Here its use extended from Siraf, Oman, and Hormuz in the Persian Gulf, via entrepôts in Sri Lanka, as far as Canton across the China Sea; it also extended in the reverse direction, southward along the African coast to Zanzibar.* Overseas presence of Persian merchants, in Oman, and then in Africa and India, had been promoted by Sassanian kings since Ardashir I (r. 225–41).[40] By the fifth to ninth centuries AD the typical

---

* The Persian interest in the Indian Ocean is marked by the two place-names *Zanzibar* and *Malabar*, on the opposing coasts of Africa and India. In Pahlavi, *zangīg* means 'black man' and *bār* 'coast' or 'bank' (*māla-* coming from a local word for 'highland', also seen in *Malaya*). The first term is already mentioned in Greek guise by Ptolemy, iv.7.4, (*Zingis akra*) in the second century AD.

merchant on the Indian Ocean was a Persian, or else a Radhanite Jew (named possibly from Persian *rāh-dān* "way-knower").* Abu Zayd al-Hasan, who visited later in the ninth century, reported that in Huang Chao's sack of Canton in 878, 120,000 Muslims, Jews, Christians, and Zoroastrian Persians had been the massacred. For the Tang poet Li Shangyin (813–58), the phrase *poor Persian* (*qióng bōsī* 窮波斯) was an incongruity, comparable to *illiterate teacher* or *pious butcher*. Chinese fiction of the era painted the stock Persian as wealthy yet generous, devoted to outlandish wonders such as precious stones (and knowledgeable of how to value them), possibly also an adept in sorcery.[41]

Use of Persian as a trade language round the Indian Ocean lasted at least until the fourteenth century, although by then the actual trade had long been dominated by Arabs.[42] This was not a literary or even perhaps very much a written language, and direct records of Persian as a lingua-franca for commerce are scarce. Perhaps arguably the case for Persian as the Indian Ocean's maritime lingua-franca is no stronger than that for Sogdian as a lingua-franca of the Silk Road: in both cases, Paul Pelliot was the first to suggest it, and despite his immense learning on Central Asia, he offered no substantive evidence of the language on the lips of foreigners.[43]

Nonetheless, traces of maritime Persian are in loanwords that remained in Arabic, the language of the next wide-ranging voyagers of these seas. These center on terms useful for navigation, such as wind directions (called *xann*, from Middle Persian *xān(ag)* 'house'), stars, and constellations, whose risings and settings (like the monsoons) medieval Arabs still measured from the Persian New Year (*nauruz* 'new day', often deformed in Arabic to *nīruz*). One word for a boat was *būṣī*, derived from Persian *būzī*.[44] The usual word for a rutter, a pilot's guidebook to sea routes (the earliest known instances going back to the turn of the eleventh-twelfth centuries) is *rāhmānaj*, a corruption of *rāh-nāmag* 'road book'[45] In the Indian Ocean, the Arabic word *nāxaðā* 'sea captain' derived from Persian *nāv-xoðā* 'ship lord'; likewise harbormasters in that area were known as *šāhbandar*, i.e. *šāh-e-bandar* 'king of the harbor'. And a ship's pilot was *daidabān* (*al-marakāb* 'of the

---

* Ibn Khordādhbeh, a Persian who as director of posts and police for Jibal province in western Iran wrote *Kitāb al-Masālik wal-Mamālik* 'The Book of Roads and Kingdoms' ca 870, reported, "These merchants speak Arabic, Persian, Roman, Frank, Spanish, and Slav languages" (cited in Adler 1987, 2). Here *Roman* means Byzantine Greek, and *Frank* probably the Romance-based Lingua Franca of the eastern Mediterranean.

ships') from Persian *didvān* 'lookout'. (These last three words were still going strong a millennium later, as *nacoder*, *shabunder*, and *didwan* in Anglo-Indian jargon, *necodá* and *xabandar* in Portuguese.)[46]

In Central Asia, from the eighth century, Persian-speaking "Tajiks" began to supplant Sogdians as the dominant merchant community, bringing their language too right across the continent. One or two references note merchants from the west turning up in the Far East in the eighth century,[47] but the steps of their general commercial progress are not documented. The merchants would have been reinforced in the eighth century by a large number of émigré Persians looking for new homes and livelihoods beyond the reach of the Muslims. Still, the variety of names that they were called tells a story of its own.

First, the word *Tajik* itself, originally a Sogdian term for an incoming Muslim, began to add overtones. For example, in the Sanskrit classic Somadeva's *Ocean of the Streams of Story* (written 1063–81) a party of innocent Indian travelers to "the north" is waylaid and then traded as chattels by *Tājika* merchants. The word spread by association to their characteristic stock-in-trade, coming also to designate an excellent breed of horse. With mercantile literacy came a patina of culture: *Tājaka* was also applied to astronomical treatises translated from Arabic or Persian. So much for the Indian reputation; for the Turks, Persian literacy in itself was endlessly impressive. Their first recorded use of the word is in Mahmud al-Kashgari's *Compendium of the Language of the Turks* in 1072.

> *Tejikler bitigde bitimiş muni | Bitigde yok erse kim okkay anı?*
>
> The Tajiks in a book set down this. In a book if it were not,
>    who would have mentioned it?

The Chinese came to refer to the whole Arab empire—which naturally impinged on them from its eastern end—as *ta dʒeĭək*, writing it, perhaps in the light of experience, as 大食 'great food', though a thousand years later the word is now pronounced more like *dàshí*.[48]

The Turks were responsible for two other words for Tajiks used widely across Asia: *Sart* and *Tat*. Each grew out of reference to a contingent fact about Persian speakers into a general quasi-racial term.

The ultimate origin of *Sart* is doubtful: it seems to be either a dialectal pronunciation of Soğd or a shortening of the Sanskrit *sārthavāha* or Sogdian *sārtpāw* 'caravaneer'. Either way, it could be a nice irony, the Persians being identified with the Sogdian caravan merchants that they were replacing, and quite comparable with the origin of *Tajik* itself—an Arab from the Tayy tribe, which was best known to the Persians. *Sart*'s first recorded use is in the Turkic text the *Qutadğu Bilig* (1070), where it already refers not to merchants but to settled populations (specifically, locally in Kashgar), whom the Turks of that age might have expected to be Persian speakers, in contrast with the free-ranging Turks. By the fifteenth century, when Mīr ʿAlī Shēr Nawāʾ was robustly comparing the value of Persian and Turkish as literary languages, he happily used *Sart* as a strict synonym for 'Persian', so he could speak explicitly of *Sart tili* 'the Sart language'.

As for *Tat*, it always seems to have been a convenient term for Turks to refer to many significant peoples that were not Turkic (much in the same way as the *Wall* root has been used round Europe for non-Germans, Welsh, Walloon, and Wallachian). *Tat* was known to have been used at different times to designate Crimean Goths, Greeks, and sedentary peoples generally, but its primary reference came to be the Persians within the Turkic domains. Hence unlike *Tajik* and *Sart* it had nothing to do with any reputation of Persians as merchants. (*Tat* is nowadays specialized to refer to special groups with Iranian languages in the west of the Caspian Sea.)[49]

The Chinese had less ability or interest in distinguishing any different groups of Iranians who came to them in the guise of merchants. All—including Sogdians and Persians—were lumped together as *hú* 胡, which originally referred to an ox's dewlap and hence was a convenient slur on foreigners' flowing beards. The term had originally been applied to the Huns, the people who, through their mounted attacks, had inspired the Chinese yearning for "heavenly horses," which lay at the root of the whole Silk Road trade. Many Chinese imports have been given names that include this root: *hú táo* 'walnuts', *hú jiāo* 'pepper', *hú luó bo* 'carrots'—not forgetting that double Dutch can still be called *hú shuō* 'Hun talk', and *hú lái* 'to come the Hun' is to mess things up. This word, probably influenced by the word for the Turkic people of the area, Uyghur, may have been the source of another word that was much more explicitly for Muslims, *huí* 回. *Huí jiào* is the Muslim faith, and doubled, the *huíhuí* are China's Muslim minority to this day, lumping together descendants of resident Persians, Uyghurs, and many others. But *huíhuí wén* 回回文 'Muslim text' in Khubilai Khan's empire (1271–94) usually meant nothing less than Persian itself, though few beside the speakers would have been able to distinguish that from Arabic, or any other language written in the script.*[50]

Persian merchants coming through Central Asia did not purvey a variety of religions as the Sogdians had. Some of the earliest, still retreating from the Arab conquest of Persia, did bring Zoroastrianism; but in the long term, they brought Islam or nothing. Yet unlike the Sogdians, they ultimately had some effect in propagating the language to their associates and contacts in foreign markets. Early evidence is sparse. A Pahlavi/Chinese bilingual epitaph of a Persian general's wife in Chang'an is dated as early as 874—"Māhnūš wife of Farroxzād"—and the earliest Persian literary text discovered in the Far East, "some mediocre strophes with Chinese annotations," is dated to 1217.[51]

Some sense that Persian might have potential as a convenient global interlingua is revealed by the Mongol Khan Güyük's choice in 1246 to use it for a reply to a letter that had reached him from Pope Innocent IV.[52] But familiarity with mercantile Persian was reinforced in the thirteenth century by the Mongol conquests: the Mongols' practice was to round up craftsmen from conquered cities in Central Asia and deport them east, e.g., to work on the new capital at Qara Qorum, but also for settlement in many parts of China. The Persian historian Joveini, who visited the capital in the 1250s, wrote that Mongolian courtiers were "served by every type of scribe, scribes for Persian, Uyghur, Chinese, Tibetan, Tangut, etc., so that to whatever locale a decree is to be written, it is issued in the language and script of that people."[†] By the time of Marco Polo's visits (in 1264–91) Persian was "spoken by many of the conscripted artisans and soldiers from Central Asia, merchants and all the educated nobility and imams." As a result, it made sense for Persian to be included as one official language by Khubilai Khan's Yuan

---

* To show the level of confusion here, the first Chinese reference to *huíhuí* refers to a king of Khwarazm surrendering to the Chinese at Samarkand in 1124 (Dillon 1999, 13). Neither *hú* nor *huí* ended up as a favored term for foreign merchant: they had long been given the courtesy title *fānkè* 'foreign guest', replaced in the modern era by *fānshāng*, which means, rather optimistically, 'feudatory trader', as if the foreigners were under Chinese control.

† Another visitor in the same period, the Franciscan friar from Flanders William of Rubruck, only mentions four scripts in use in the administration: "They (i.e., the Cathayans) write with a brush such as painters paint with, and they make in one figure the several letters containing a whole word. The Tebet write as we do, and have characters quite like ours. The Tanguts write from right to left like the Arabs, but they repeat the lines running upwards; the Iugur, as previously said (write) up and down."

dynasty, and so used (in parallel with other languages) on some of the coins, metal passports (*paizah*), and copper weights issued by that government.[53]

From William of Rubruck's description, we recognize Chinese characters, unchanged between the second century BC and the twentieth century AD; Tibetan (which had originated from the Brahmi alphabet used by Indian Buddhists); a distinct system of characters used for Tangut (from a north-Asian kingdom subdued by Chinggis Khan)—although William of Rubruck apparently confused it with Persian; and Uyghur (which had been developed for the Uyghurs by their Sogdian merchant consultants, using Sogdian cursive written vertically. This last had been adopted for writing Mongolian and is used in Chinese Inner Mongolia to this day). Khubilai Khan was also to introduce a new 'Phagspa script, intended to replace them all, but it did not survive in use.

It would be misleading, however, to say that Persian was a true lingua-franca under Mongol rule, although a college (1289) and later an institute (1314) were established for its study. Indeed the concept of a "free language" seems to have been something the rulers wished to avoid, especially for written communication. Although high promotion remained available to foreigners with multilingual skills, Chinese subjects were forbidden in 1337 to study either Mongolian or *sèmùrén* 色目人 'miscellaneous' written languages—anything but Chinese itself. Multilingual literacy remained a potential danger to the body politic.[54]

In the wider world, Persian persisted for a millennium (approximately the tenth to nineteenth centuries) as a kind of accessible bridge for outsiders to access Oriental languages. This was a pedagogical use that went far beyond its status as the lingua-franca of the lands conquered by Turks in western Asia (as related in chapter 4).

All round the Black Sea, Persian was the second language. So it appears as intermediary between Latin/Romance and Cuman (i.e. Qypchaq Turkic) in the *Codex Cumanicus*, an interpreters' manual for merchants. This had been compiled in the 1290s by Venetians or Genoese, but fifty years later was reused by Franciscan missionaries. (For foreigners' convenience, the Persian here is written in the Roman alphabet.) In fourteenth-century Azerbaijan, or perhaps Iran, Ibn Muhanna compiled an Arabic-Persian-Turkic-Mongolian vocabulary. At Aden on the Red Sea, hailed by the Arab historian Al-Muqaddasi (ca 985) as the entryway to China, King Al-Malik Al-Afḍal (1363–77) compiled a set of glossaries, known as the Rasulid Hexaglot, with equivalences among Arabic, Persian, Turkic, Greek,

*Mongolian* paizah '*badge of office' discovered near Beijing, with inscription in Persian and Mongolian (in two scripts—'Phagspa and Uyghur). There is a Chinese inscription on the reverse.*[55] *(Credit: By permission of Harrassowitz (Wiesbaden), reproduced from Nicholas N. Poppe,* The Mongolian Documents in Hp'agspa Script *[1957])*

Armenian, and Mongol. At much the same time but in the opposite linguistic direction, in India, Badr al-Din Ibrahim produced the *Farhang i Zafân-gûyâ va Jahân-pûyâ* 'The Dictionary of Speaking Language and Covering the World,' with Persian, Arabic, Turkic, Aramaic, and "Rūmī" (a smattering mix of Greek, Latin, and Syriac). Meanwhile, the Ming dynasty (1368–1644), which took over China from the Mongols, always included Persian in the two agencies for translation and interpreting respectively that it maintained, among seven (later ten) other foreign languages.[56]

The sixteenth and seventeenth centuries saw the increasing presence across the Indian Ocean of adventurous and competitive Europeans, people determined to open up markets, but with no background in any Asian language. Portuguese established itself first, in the major ports and then along the coast, as a sort of "beginner's lingua-franca" between Europeans and Asians. The availability of such a preexisting comfort language was useful to the incoming Europeans, but all early traders tended to make heavy use of native partners in business who became bilingual long before they did—hence the term for them, *dobash*, an anglicization of Hindi *dubhāśiya* 'bilingual'.

Only in the early seventeenth century did Persian begin to be studied in Europe, but then a trio of Persian grammars were published: by Ludwijk de Dieu (Leiden, 1639), John Greaves (London, 1649), and Ignatius of Jesus (Rome, 1661), the last followed up with a *Dictionarium Latino-Persicum*. In England in 1669 Edmund Castell produced a *Heptaglotton*, which added Persian to a multidictionary covering six Semitic languages. (This contributed to the discovery that it was an Indo-European, not a Semitic, language itself.) And in Vienna in 1680–87 Franciszek Meniński published a monumental grammar-dictionary, *Thesaurus linguarum orientalium*, opening up the grammars of Turkish, Arabic, and Persian.

To develop business in India beyond the coasts, one had to negotiate and communicate with the established powers on their own terms. This necessitated the use of Persian, and this was still the principal language for trade in western and southern Asia when in 1771 William Jones published his famous practical grammar of the Persian language. He remarks in its preface, "There is scarce a country in Asia or Africa, from the source of the Nile to the wall of China, in which a man who understands Arabic, Persian and Turkish may not travel with satisfaction, or transact the most important affairs with advantage and security."* The book went through nine editions to 1828 (together with French and German translations) and was followed by many other practical guides for English-speaking learners, notably *The Persian Moonshee* by Francis Gladwell (1801).

○✄○

---

* If this does not seem a particularly telling recommendation for a grammar specifically of Persian, it immediately follows a passage where Jones points out that Persian is in any case shot through with Arabic, while "Turkish contains ten Arabic or Persian words to one originally Scythian, by which it has been so refined that the modern kings of Persia were fond of speaking it in their courts."

Traders' languages benefit by the good things that merchants have to offer; through the positive power of association this may boost recruitment of learners, not least through the opportunities that may be created for lucrative employment. Not all the positive associations are exclusively for their stock-in-trade, however. Greek merchants were definitely proffering a lifestyle too to the ancient Mediterranean, much as English-language business does today to the rest of the world. As we have seen, even beyond what they achieved with the distribution of silk and heavenly horses, the Sogdians are famous now for having spread the good news of various approaches to salvation that were on offer in Central Asia before the spread of Islam: Mahayana Buddhism, Nestorian Christianity, Mazdaism, and Manichaeism.

But not all such hopes of enlightenment and social renewal have come in with commercial enterprise, whether as unseen stowaways, or extravalue promotions. Many missionaries traveled for no other reason than to propagate their various gospels. They too might spread their languages. As James Elroy Flecker put it in the mouths of his pilgrims: "We travel not for trafficking alone; By hotter winds our fiery hearts are fanned."[57] Next we must consider the direct effects of religious missions on the rise of lingua-francas.

❦

# CHAPTER 6

# God's Own Language

Wider still and wider shall thy bounds be set.
God, who made thee mighty, make thee mightier yet.

—from the hymn "Land of Hope and Glory"
A. C. Benson, 1902

*jina-vacana-yuttaṃ hi.*

[The rules of Pali grammar are]
applicable to the discourses of the Buddha.

—Kaccāyana, *Pali Grammar*, 1.6.1
(seventh or eighth century AD)

A MOTIVE FOR THE spread of English that is not often emphasized is its role as a medium for propagating the Christian gospel. But from the eighteenth century until the twentieth, English was often first heard by foreigners on the lips of missionaries, who arrived shortly after the traders and the soldiers and spread out more widely among the population, away from the cities, ports, forts, and cantonments, and into the villages of Asia, Africa, and the Pacific islands.

Early in its introduction to India, English was known to many as "the Christian tongue."[1] But the first years of British mercantile involvement in India did not allow much purchase to missionary concerns, which were seen as a threat, or at least a disturbance, to Anglo-Indian relations, specifically in trade. Missionaries were banned from British settlements throughout the eighteenth century, so that a determined pioneer preacher such as William

Carey (who arrived undercover in 1793) could only set up his school in Serampore, which was in 1800 a Danish possession.

Still, some sympathetic Christians were among the most influential of British merchants. Best known today is Charles Grant, who as a director with twenty-five years' service to the East India Company had published in 1792 *Observations on the State of Society among the Asian Subjects of Great Britain, particularly with respect to Morals and the Means of Improving it*, in which he proposed introducing English as the medium of instruction, and its adoption as the official language of company and government. Christianity, delivered through English, would be the remedy for Hinduism and what he saw as its risible superstitions. (In 1789 he had smuggled in five missionaries, in the guise of chaplains to the Company's servants.) Over 1805–9 he was continuously either chairman or deputy chairman of the board. Nonetheless, despite parliamentary agitation in behalf of missionaries by William Wilberforce and others, not until 1813 were the Company's restrictions on their access to India lifted. The charter of the East India Company was then renewed to include promotion of "useful knowledge and moral improvements," and this was interpreted as giving all assistance to Christian missions. Evangelicals went on holding one or other of the Company's top two positions until 1830.[2] The spirit in which the "useful knowledge" was offered is pithily expressed in a couple of verses of a popular hymn by Reginald Heber (1783–1826), who ended his career as bishop of Calcutta:

> From Greenland's icy mountains, from India's coral strand;
> Where Afric's sunny fountains roll down their golden sand:
> From many an ancient river, from many a palmy plain,
> They call us to deliver their land from error's chain.
>
> What though the spicy breezes blow soft o'er Ceylon's isle;
> Though every prospect pleases, and only man is vile?
> In vain with lavish kindness the gifts of God are strown;
> The heathen in his blindness bows down to wood and stone.

Between 1815 and 1840 Christian schools and colleges were set up by a variety of (Protestant) missionary societies all over the Company's Indian domains. To the Company's relief, they were accepted without significant hostility, and indeed with widespread enthusiasm by elite Indians and opinion formers such as Ram Mohan Roy, who seemed to judge (more perceptively than the British) that the students could take what they wanted from modern European learning, including competence in English, without undermining their own religions.

This missionary advance into India, which came trailing clouds of English lessons, was one result of a totally new development at the end of the eighteenth century. Evangelical Christianity enjoyed a massive revival in English-speaking society, and suddenly missionary societies began to spring up, for "conversion of the heathen" all over the world. William Carey had been one of the earliest in this trend; while still in England he had formed the Baptist Missionary Society in 1792. In 1795, the (nondenominational) London Missionary Society was founded, in 1796 the Scottish and Glasgow Missionary Society, and in 1799 the (Anglican) Church Missionary Society. The year 1804 saw the foundation of the British and Foreign Bible Society, and 1813 of the Wesleyan Missionary Society. A parallel growth of societies occurred on the other side of the Atlantic: the Missionary Society of Connecticut (1798), the New York Missionary Society (1800), Massachusetts Baptist Missionary Society (1802), the American Board of Commissioners for Foreign Missions (1810).

These English-speaking (and English-teaching) missionaries would be sent all over the world in the nineteenth century. Consider this self-description of early activities by the London Missionary Society alone:

> Mission activity started in the South Seas, with the first overseas mission to Tahiti in 1796. Missionary work expanded into North America and South Africa. Early mission activities also centred in areas of eastern and southern Europe including Russia, Greece and Malta. There was even an LMS "mission to Jews" in London. However, during the 19th century, the main fields of mission activity for the LMS were China, South East Asia, India, the Pacific, Madagascar, Central Africa, Southern Africa, Australia and the Caribbean (including British Guiana, now Guyana).[3]

Wherever the missions went, they established schools, and English was always on the curriculum, although local languages might be used as well, especially if they were already in literate use. Besides the motive of de facto European control in India (conceived as too good an opportunity for Christians to waste), the motive in Africa was above all to preempt the activities of slavers: Evangelicals felt all too keenly a guilt for Britain's recent profit from the "Triangular Trade" over the seventeenth and eighteenth centuries. An early focus of missionary zeal was Sierra Leone in West Africa, a place of refuge for freed slaves since 1767 that was finally established as a British crown colony in 1807, the year that the slave trade was abolished.* In 1815–16 the Wesleyan Missionary Society and the Church Missionary Society arrived, and by 1840 they had twenty-eight schools (with some six thousand regular pupils), twice as many schools as those established by the colony's government. All the same, an Inspector's Report of 1841 criticized the mission schools for an excessive bias to religion in their teaching of English, "reading and writing in the school being done wholly out of the Bible."[4]

Mission schools also led the way in Hong Kong, at the opposite end of the British Empire in the Old World. Here, from foundation in 1842 to 1859, they controlled the colony's education, but were, if anything, too successful in the English side of the curriculum: all their pupils preferred to apply their new skills in the commercial world, and not one wished to be ordained. Hong Kong provided an interesting object lesson in how a commercial lingua-franca might eclipse a religious one, even if they were the same language. "Native converts would never enter the Church on $25 a month if they could get $50 as clerks or interpreters," an Inspector reported, noting that Catholic schools (which taught Latin instead of English) were free of this distraction from their higher intent.[5]

It is estimated[6] that by 1900 thirty-five hundred English missionaries were working abroad in various parts of the "empire on which the sun never set." What of their effectiveness? Historical comparisons set the bar rather high. Roman Catholic missionaries in northern and central Europe in the late first millennium AD, like Spanish and Portuguese missions in sixteenth/seventeenth-century Latin America, had ultimately achieved almost total saturation of vast populations. The "good news" was decisively spread. By contrast, the penetration of Protestant Christianity into the Evangelicals' great target nations in Asia does not appear a particularly rich harvest: 1.2 percent in China, 0.7 percent in India, 0.8 percent in Sri Lanka, and 2.1 percent in Malaysia.

But other parts of the world tell a different story. Even in countries with

---

* It had previously (1795–99) had as governor Zachary Macaulay, the father of Thomas Babington Macaulay, whose famous *Minute on Indian Education* of 1835 was a turning point for the English language in India.

ultimately few white settlers, Protestant religion has stayed and flourished. In Papua New Guinea, the proportion of worshippers is 61.8 percent, and in sub-Saharan Africa generally, direct impact has been serious. There, Christians (and mostly Protestants) are now in the majority in almost every country where English functions as lingua-franca.[7] It is ultimately impossible to disentangle the long-term effects of the religious missionary pioneers from the later workings of the European colonial enterprise more generally; for example, schools that were originally mission foundations were often later incorporated as national institutions. Nonetheless, there are already more practicing Christians in Africa than on any other continent, and on current rates of growth, by the coming decade Africa will overtake Europe as the continent with most self-identifying Christians.[8] This is some kind of a harvest for all that Evangelical planting.

If those missionaries had had a directly linguistic as well as a spiritual purpose, it might have been considered to have been even more fulfilled: the English they taught in their schools has spread out as a lingua-franca, not just in the African and Pacific colonies but worldwide, beyond even the bounds of the British Empire (and the Anglican Communion). But they had no such purpose. Rather, a commitment to worship in the vernacular is as old as the Church of England* and has never been challenged by Protestants. One part of their missionary work was always to learn and, hence ultimately, to propagate the local languages; many of the British and American missionaries wrote grammars and dictionaries of languages hitherto unknown to them, just to give their converts more direct—and English-free—access to translate the Holy Scriptures. Although most of them had a strong nostalgic affection for the ever more antiquated English of the King James Bible and the *Book of Common Prayer*, expression of the faith in English—let alone sixteenth-century English—has never been seen as in any way intrinsic to Protestant Christianity. So the English-language teaching that went

---

\* As witness this passage from Thomas Cranmer's first *Book of Common Prayer* of 1549:

> *And in these all our dooynges wee condemne no other nacions, nor prescribe anye thyng, but to oure owne people onelye. For we thinke it conveniente that every countreye should use such ceremonies, as thei shal thynke beste to the settyng foorth of goddes honor, and glorye: and to the reducyng of the people to a moste perfecte and Godly living, without errour or supersticion: and that they shoulde putte awaye other thynges, which from time to time they perceive to be most abused, as in mennes ordinaunces it often chaunceth diverselye in diverse countreyes.*

along with the missionary work can only have been viewed as a practical help to give access to Christian knowledge that happened to be available in English.

⬦⬦⬦

English was not the first missionary language to face a rending fate when practicality (and the administrative priorities of church and state) began to tell against spreading the faith in any language natural to the convert. It is all very well to allow a profusion of tongues and reach all manner of people in their own terms. But what then guarantees that the faith put to them will be the same? This problem was already afflicting disciples in the first generation to be taught by the Buddha, but the solution he proposed for it is less than clear.

The story goes that two monks were affronted: they could see that members of the community, coming from different parts of India (and perhaps from different classes too), were expressing the words of Buddha in their own dialects, hence potentially distorting their meaning. However, this kind of problem in India had a traditional solution—a language that was supposed to be above local variation, namely Sanskrit. The monks therefore proposed to the Buddha that they translate the Buddha's words into Sanskrit, putting them into verse (called *chandas*) for good measure. But the Buddha demurred and added, *anujānāmi bhikkhave sakāya niruttiyā buddhavacanaṃ pariyāpuṇituṃ*.[9]

The proper interpretation of this fairly simple sentence has never been agreed and will never be because of the heartrending dilemma just considered. The Buddha had clearly picked up the phrase used by the monks to mean "in their own dialects"—*sakāya niruttiyā*—and stated, "I authorize the monks to learn the Buddha-words *sakāya niruttiyā*." But does this mean "each in their own dialect"? Or rather "in my own dialect"? Clearly the Buddha was rejecting the Sanskrit option, probably because of its then association with the Brahmanical religion from which he was attempting to distance his teaching, or ( just possibly) because it might have been less accessible to the uneducated. But was he saying that monks could learn (and hence propagate) his teaching in any language they spoke? Or was he rather hinting that a language good enough for the Buddha should be good enough for them? It may be significant that all the languages in question were related north-Indian "Prakrits," all close to Sanskrit, and indeed to one another.*

Nowadays modern Westerners naturally feel that the Buddha would have wanted his disciples to focus on the message of enlightenment, not its medium—still less on prejudices about the local origins of different bands of disciples tied up in loyalty to one dialect or another. But the Buddha did clearly reject Sanskrit so was not blind to the social significance of language choice, even if only in others' minds. The eminent commentator known as Buddhaghosa 'voice of the Buddha', who lived in the fifth century AD, perhaps a millennium after the Buddha himself, commented specifically on this line, "Here, 'own dialect' means Magadhi speech as spoken by the Buddha."[10]

The subsequent linguistic history of the Buddhist *sangha* 'community' or 'church' has made the whole question even more fraught. The Buddha had come from Kosala (modern Awadh) in the Himalayan foothills (where the language would have been Awadhi, a predecessor of modern Hindi), but passed his preaching life in the area of modern Patna and Bodh Gaya, where the local language was indeed Magadhi. We know something of this language: it was similar to modern Bengali in that the *s* sound is replaced by a hushing *ś*, and the *r* by *l*. But the language that became established for Buddhist discourse was something else, the lingua-franca now called Pali, in which all the documents of the Buddhist canon, the famed *Tipiṭaka* 'three baskets', have been preserved.† Although southern commentators thought it was Magadhi—especially in Buddhism's early stronghold of Sri Lanka, where everyone spoke Sinhala—it is phonetically unlike it. It appears to be a compromise mixture of dialects, related to, but mostly less highly inflected than Sanskrit.‡ It might have evolved among a mixed

---

* *Prākṛti* means 'nature' while *saṃskṛta* means 'elaborated', which is a fair indication of the difference between these styles of Indian speech, all called *ārya* 'noble' in their own tongue, but 梵語 (pronounced *buamh ŋiá*) 'Brahman talk' by Chinese pilgrims of the age.

† Originally a Sanskrit word *pāli* 'line' came to refer to lines of text; *pālibhāsā* is then originally 'language of the text'. Hence Pali, like Avestan and Vedic, is a holy language that derives its name from the canon of texts preserved in it (*pāli, avesta, vēda*). As such, the name has no local resonance.

‡ So-called *Ardha-Magadhi* 'half-Magadhi', the language of the Jain scriptures (contemporary with, and from neighboring district to, the Buddha), is like Pali in keeping the distinctions of *s* against *ś*, and *r* against *l*. Perhaps Mahavira, the founder of Jainism, found a similar solution to a similar communication problem.

community in the generations after the Buddha's death, or even be the Buddha's approach to talking intelligibly for an audience known to speak many different Prakrits. In the event, this lingua-franca is neither Magadhi nor a Babel of different dialects, but, in a sense, a new Prakrit.

A further complication comes from the way that the Buddha's doctrine was transmitted, by precise oral recitation and memorization. This has gone on throughout the tradition, but was particularly significant in the early years, before the doctrine was written down anywhere. Precise memorization requires a fixed language; if none is yet established, the practice will tend to fix whatever style of language is first used. And a prestige text that is widely known and respected will tend to project its influence onto the general linguistic background in which it arose. This is prima facie evidence, therefore, that Pali, as received, represents quite well the language that was current among the Buddha and his disciples. Likewise, the Arabic preserved in the Koran shows signs of a dialect that had lost the glottal stop *hamza*, and most case-endings; and the variety of grammatical inflexions in the *Iliad* and *Odyssey* suggests that Homer was bringing together materials he knew from several dialects.

After the Buddha's death the *sangha* grew in north India for some centuries, expanding in the third century BC to Sri Lanka. But the *Tipiṭaka* canon, although established formally over a series of three councils up to the reign of King Ashoka (274–232 BC), was not written down until the turn of the millennium. There has always been in India a suspicion of literacy used for intellectual pursuits, and conservative elements in the *sangha* must have retarded its introduction. The writing down is known first not in the original Buddhist heartland, but in Anuradhapura, then capital of Sri Lanka, where Sinhala itself had already been used in inscriptions for some two hundred years. Pali thus became a language for literature, as well as recitation. But both because of the oral bias and the content of the texts, Pali would undoubtedly have been used throughout for dialogue and discussion, as well as religious discourse: the canon had long contained a variety of texts, including original words, interpretations, and commentaries on them, as well as a mass of 550 popular verse and story combinations known as the *Jātaka*, which were in content more like *A Thousand and One Nights* than improving literature (although they were officially interpreted as tales of the Buddha's earlier births and given appropriate commentary). There were also historical chronicles of Sri Lanka (which among much else give a date for the introduction of writing), and open letters to spiritual friends or kings.

Whatever its origin in the linguistic stocks of northern India, Pali seems to have existed for over a millennium as a lingua-franca of Buddhism, or more specifically of the southern, Theravada, movement within Buddhism. Little or no evidence exists of its use outside Sri Lanka until it crops up in inscriptions in Southeast Asia, a millennium later, precisely the places abroad where the Theravada school was taken up.

But Buddhism had also been spreading throughout this period, northward into Central Asia and China, rather than across the Bay of Bengal. Crucially, it had been accepted by the Maurya emperor Ashoka, who presumably fostered missionary activity, as he most certainly set up monumental inscriptions with Buddhist content all over his domain from modern Andhra Pradesh in the south to Orissa in the east and southern Afghanistan in the northwest. His inscriptions (the earliest documents in Indic languages that are known, written in the original Brahmi alphabet) are almost all in that very Magadhi Prakrit that so many wrongly believed to have been the basis of Pali, although as it happens the inscriptions in the west (in Girnar and Bombay-Sopara) are in a Prakrit that could well be Pali itself. Yet another Prakrit is also seen in Ashoka's inscriptions in the northwest, a dialect that is usually known as Gandhari and is written in another alphabet, Kharoshthi (a script long since derived from Aramaic, since this area had originally been in the Achaemenian Empire).[11]

Fifty years after Ashoka's death his empire had dissolved, and although successor empires came and went in the next four centuries, they were built by non-Indians coming from the north, Greeks, Scythians, Parthians, and Huns. In general, nomadic-horde armies who conquered Buddhist realms ended up accepting Buddhism themselves. The most durable of these conquerors were the Kushana, easterners from the borders of China who spread out from Bactria in the first century AD to control Gandhara and much of northern India and sustained their rule for a good two centuries. Besides Bactrian, Gandhari became used much more widely, as an administrative language in Khotan and much of the Tarim Basin (modern Xinjiang), an area to be widely colonized later by Sogdians. The Kushana were sufficiently enthusiastic about Buddhism to have the Buddha (with legend BOΔΔO) in effigy on their coinage; and in the second and third centuries Buddhist texts in Gandhari were used as originals for the first translations into Chinese.

Presumably these northern missionaries were often working in the local vernacular languages. Even so, many had by now overcome—or

*Kushana coin from Gandhara, featuring the Buddha, 1st–2nd centuries AD.*
*(Credit: Professor Bente Kiilerich, University of Bergen, Norway)*

forgotten—the Buddha's strictures against Sanskrit, since that is the language of the key Mahayana texts that were emerging at this period, works such as *Prajñāpāramitā Sūtra* 'Perfection of Wisdom', written in the first century BC or AD. But the Sanskrit used in these Buddhist texts is in many ways nonclassical and seems to have been written by adding artificial classicizing touches to one or more Prakrits.

Indian Buddhists in the south seem to have been in a lingua-franca culture, adopting Pali for their religious communion, whereas those in the north were in a translation culture, using texts and rituals that had been directly customized into their own languages. Essentially, the two possible interpretations of *sakāya niruttiyā* have been realized, one party employing the Buddha's own language, the other everybody's own languages.

To an extent, one can match these two linguistic tendencies with the major sects within Buddhism, since the Pali-speaking southerners ended up following the Theravada doctrines—more closely based on the tradition of

Gautama Śākyamuni,* the historic character known as the Buddha 'the one who awoke'—whereas the northerners, who relied on local vernaculars (or Sanskrit), developed Buddhism in the direction of Mahayana, generalizing the concept and appearance of Buddhas (and bodhisattvas) until they were difficult to distinguish from deities, and being much more innovative in their doctrines.†

Naturally, exceptions occur to this overneat tie-up of geography, doctrine, and linguistic philosophy. In the north, the kind of early Buddhism that was spread in Gandhari, for example, is comparable to Theravada and probably predates the rise of Mahayana in the late first century AD. Conversely, in the south, for much of the first millennium AD, Buddhism as practiced in Sri Lanka was split between competing monasteries that followed Theravada and Mahayana traditions. In the wider world, Buddhism as a proselytizing religion was almost always Mahayana, even in Southeast Asia. Later, in the second millennium AD, Buddhism was in many parts of Southeast Asia reformed on a Theravada model, with introduction of Pali, both derived from Sri Lanka.

Outwardly, the linguistic differences between these tendencies can be minimized: after all, the Prakrits (including Pali) are similar as forms of speech, and long, complex technical terms, compounded from standard Aryan roots, dominated the written texts in similar ways. But the implication of these linguistic policies showed up more clearly when Buddhism began to spread outside *Āryāvarta*, the area where Aryan Prakrits were spoken. Texts discovered in Central Asia, when not in Sanskrit or Gandhari, are found to contain very similar Buddhist content, but translated into local languages. The languages here are radically different from Aryan Prakrits, including Bactrian, Sogdian, and Khotanese (all Iranian languages); also as one goes farther east, Tokharian, Uyghur Turkic, and indeed Chinese. Much later on, in the seventh century AD, Tibetan would be added to this list. The northern tradition was serving a highly diverse and multilingual society, without use of any lingua-franca for the religious community.

By contrast, as it spread to the south, Buddhism early encountered linguistic environments that were non-Aryan, notably the Dravidian languages. Ashoka was concerned to cover the known world with the love of *dhamma*

---

* A name for the Buddha, "sage of the Śakya tribe."

† Appropriately, the term *Theravāda* 'Senior Doctrine' is in fact Pali (in Sanskrit *sthāviravāda*), whereas *Mahāyāna* 'Great Vehicle' is Sanskrit.

'the law' and on his own testimony sent medical experts and herbs throughout the subcontinent. The zones of the Telugu and Kannada languages (modern Andhra and Karnataka)[12] were already within his empire, but Buddhism was also well received farther south, in places that he calls Čola, Pāndya, and Satiyaputa; Keralaputa; and Tambapanni. These seem to map respectively onto the areas for Chola, Pandya, Atiyaman i.e. Villupuram (all Tamil language); Kerala (Malayalam language); and Tamraparni i.e. Sri Lanka (Sinhala language).[13] The last of these was apparently proselytized by members of Ashoka's own family, Mahinda (his brother or son) and Sanghamitta (his daughter). Sanskrit had already penetrated these areas together with Brahmanical Hinduism, so the advent of Buddhist monks speaking Pali would not have come as a total shock.

In this environment, Pali's aspect changed gradually, from the vernacular of the incoming monks, to a lingua-franca specifically associated with Buddhism. (Since monks and nuns kept celibate throughout, the transmission to later generations would have occurred exclusively through recruitment to the monasteries.) The vernacular languages continued to be spoken around them, and indeed to borrow words from them, often for concepts alien to local life, such as technology or imports: e.g., Tamil *eṭṭi* (and Malayalam *eṭṭiyān*) from Pali *seṭṭhi* 'merchant'; common Dravidian *ēṇi* 'ladder' from Pali *seṇi*; Tamil and Malayalam *iñci* 'ginger' from Pali *siṇgī.*\*

After a couple of centuries, and probably because of a panic that the oral tradition might fail in a time of social and political turmoil, its raison d'être, the Pali canon of the Tipiṭaka was set down in writing, initially with an accompanying commentary in Sinhala. According to tradition, this happened in 89–77 BC. Much later, in the fifth century AD, under the presiding genius of Buddhaghosa, a full Pali commentary was written out, and the Theravada school became totally self-sufficient in the language. Thereafter, it acquired all the accessories of a serious language (on a par with Sanskrit, or indeed Tamil); above all, it was formalized with a grammar. The first was produced by Kaccayana, probably in the seventh or eighth centuries, whose

---

\*   These clearly came from Pali, not Sanskrit: cf their Sanskrit forms *śreṣṭhī, śreṇi, śṛṅgavera.*

   In Sri Lanka the loans into Sinhala are harder to identify, since this was a language originally almost identical to Pali, its original speakers having probably migrated from the Aryavarta in the fifth century BC. But (not being a learned language defined by use in the Tipiṭaka) Sinhala has been free to change. We can, however, compare Sinhala *tena* 'place' with Pali *ṭhāna*, Sinhala *mega* 'path' with Pali *magga*, and Sinhala *eta* 'bone' in *eta-sekilla* 'skeleton' with Pali *aṭṭhi*. (Sanskrit equivalents *sthāna, mārga, aṣṭhi*).

knowledge of Sanskrit grammar is, as it were, guaranteed by the fact that his name is a Pali version of another famous grammarian, Katyāyana, a commentator on the ultimate Sanskrit authority, Pāṇini himself. Something of the style can be felt in the first three (of its 673) rules.

> *attho akkharasaññāto*
>
> meaning character-known
> Meaning comes from knowledge of characters.
>
> *akkharāpādayo ekacattālīsam*
>
> characters-A-beginning one-forty
> There are forty-one characters, beginning with *A*.*
>
> *tatthodantā sarā aṭṭha*
>
> thence-o-ending vowels eight
> Among them the first eight, ending with *O*, are vowels.

In the twelfth century, Aggavamsa wrote the *Saddanīti* 'word-art' (1154); a dictionary, the *Abhidānappadīpika* 'the lamp of nouns', was compiled; and one Sangharakkhita wrote the first work of literary criticism, *Subodhālaṃkāra* 'the ornament of good learning'.[14]

While this literary aura grew about Pali, the impressionable were enhancing its virtues in another direction, seeing it as a religious medium in its own right, available to be used in charms and imprecations to get magical results, e.g. as a cure for snakebite or to exorcize ghosts. Such practices, known as *paritta*, are documented from the middle of the seventh century but may be much older.[15]

Buddhism appeared well established in southern India, but the religious balance was not constant. The fall of the Sātavāhana dynasty (royal Buddhists, who had originally been vassals of Ashoka) at the end of the first century AD led to a fragmentation of power in the south. For a time, Buddhism was particularly patronized by queens, and in the late third century the Ikšvāku dynasty in eastern Andhra maintained strong links with the

---

* The word *akkhara* (Sanskrit *akṣara*, literally 'imperishable') refers either to a written symbol or the speech sound that it represents. Compare the changing sense of Latin *elementum*, which originally meant just a letter of the alphabet.

Sinhala monasteries. The Pallavas, a dynasty from the north (conceivably identical with Iranian *Pahlava*), then came to power and put greater influence in Brahman hands; from 350 the land grants inscribed on copper plates, which document the reigns, are all in Sanskrit. Nevertheless, Buddhism maintained its popularity, spreading southward into Chola, Chera, and Pandya, supported perhaps through military activities of the Buddhist king Accutavikkanta (a Pali name—'untoppled conqueror'), and, according to some, introducing a new melancholy tone into previously happy-go-lucky Tamil literature.[16] These were fruiting years for Buddhism, the period of Buddhaghosa's expansion of the Pali canon, but also of a revolution in logic and epistemology, led by Dignāga (ca 480–540), a scholar who hailed from Kanchi in Andhra territory and went to study (naturally in Pali) in Sri Lanka. It is significant that he ultimately chose to go north to spend his mature years at the monastery at Nalanda (near Bodh Gaya in Magadha), where he would write and debate in Sanskrit.

In the following three centuries (ca 600–900) Buddhism (and Jainism too)—apparently for the first time—was subjected to a militant Hindu revival, backed by new work by sages such as Kumārila Bhaṭṭa* (ca 700) and Ādi Śankara (ca 800), who countered Buddhism on an intellectual level. The result was a long-term decline in Buddhism, especially in the Tamil country, although Buddhist communities survived here and there.[17] The link between Buddhism and use of Pali was broken on the mainland. The wars in south India among Pallavas, Pandyas, and Cholas spilled over into Sri Lanka, culminating in the sack of its ancient capital, Anuradhapura, ca 993. When the island was reunited a century later, one effect was the expulsion of Mahayana (1160), leaving the Theravada sect alone and supreme. Sri Lanka's Buddhist community began to feel itself isolated, with result that Buddhism there (and Pali) came to feel more and more like a national or a local possession.

While south-Indian Buddhism (and Pali within it) were tracing this

---

* It is revealing that one of Kumārila's arguments against Buddhism centered on Pali itself: "The scriptures of Buddhists and Jains are composed in overwhelmingly incorrect language, words of languages of Magadha or the South, or even their dialects. Since they are therefore false compositions they cannot possibly be true knowledge. When texts are composed of words that are [grammatically] false, how can they possibly communicate meaning that is true? And how could they be eternal if we find in them degenerate forms? By contrast, the very form itself of the Veda proves its authority to be independent and absolute." (*Tantravārttika* on *Pūrva Mīmāṃsā Sūtra* 1.3.12, p. 164, lines 8–15, largely as translated by Pollock 2006, 55–56)

parabolic development over the first millennium AD, Indian culture, language, and religion were reaching and gradually establishing themselves in the varied lands of Indochina. This came about largely through the contacts created by Indian merchants and adventurers, emanating from all the ports from Gujarat to Bengal. Sri Lanka too would have played a part in this, especially from the fourth to seventh centuries.[18] Cosmas Indicopleustes, a sixth-century traveler from Alexandria in Egypt, recorded, "Since its position is central, the island is a great resort of ships from all parts of India and from Persia and Ethiopia and in like manner it despatches many of its own to foreign ports. And from the inner countries *Tzinitza* [viz China] and other markets, it receives silk, aloes, cloves, sandalwood, and other products."[19] Thereby he identified the sources of these trades as (respectively) China, Sumatra, the Moluccas, and Timor. These regions on the way to China came to be known in India as *Suvarṇabhūmi*, the 'Golden Land' and *Suvarṇadvīpa*, the 'Golden Islands'.

Linguistically, however, this had only led to the spread of Sanskrit, not Pali. During the first millennium Sanskrit was widely learned and appreciated, for official and prestige uses (e.g., inscriptions for public buildings) and a badge of cultural attainment for members of the elite (including for example, at the close of the twelfth century, the noted Sanskrit poetesses Queen Indradevi of Cambodia and her sister, both Buddhists).[20] It has naturally remained as a source of loans into the extremely varied local languages. Knowledge of Buddhism was conveyed as part of the general diffusion of the culture, but what was generally taken up at first was the Mahayana variety, possibly because it was more comparable to a form of polytheism, and hence more immediately popular with foreigners.

The first Pali inscriptions in Cambodia are as old as the Sanskrit ones, dating to the seventh century AD, and there is evidence (from stone inscriptions) for loans from Pali into the Khmer language there since the thirteenth century at the latest. Inscriptions mix overwhelming use of Pali vocabulary, and resounding phrases such as *lokuttara dhamma* 'world-transcending law', with Khmer syntax and function words (in a way rather reminiscent of Ottoman Turkic's use of Arabic and Persian).[21] But this first penetration of Buddhism, coming within a transplanted Hindu context, apparently had few implications for widespread use of Pali.

Yet subsequent acceptance of Theravada Buddhism most certainly did. Knowledge of this sect and its views had long been available and played a role as a kind of "ultra-ist" option for Buddhists, an outward symbol of authenticity. Notably, on a number of occasions when Pali was explicitly taken up, it was seen as of major symbolic importance, betokening a conscious change in the kind of Buddhism that would henceforth be the king's, or the state's, religion.

When Anawrahta united Myanmar under the kingdom of Pagan ca 1050, he supposedly decorated his court with the cultural glories of the defeated Mon court at Thaton, which, by (implausible) legend, was believed to be the hometown of Buddhaghosa himself, reputed as the purest of the pure when it came to maintaining the Theravada tradition. The gaining of a decent copy of the Tipiṭaka in Pali is traditionally given as the leading motive for Anawrahta's conquest. But this legend is open to question, and the truth seems to betoken an even greater devotion to, and active support of, authenticity in the Pali language. For Anawrahta went on to assist the Buddhist Vijayabahu I to regain the throne of Sri Lanka in 1067, restoring Pali after fifty years of Hindu domination; and subsequently he sent a deputation of Myanmar's best scholars to help in reconstructing the monastic rules, and the text of the Tipiṭaka. In return, Myanmar directly received a copy of Pali scriptures from the place of their very origin. Too late for Anawrahta: it seems that he died a Mahayanist, but his son Sawlu became Myanmar's first Theravadin king.[22]

A later king of Sri Lanka, Vijayabāhu II (1186–87), is on record as writing in Pali to a king of Myanmar, Narapatisithu, showing the language in use as a straight lingua-franca among Theravadin powers. Such examples are rare, however, and it seems likely that even this letter would have been on religious matters.[23]

Choice of language in itself has been taken to send a clear message about one's spiritual intent. When in Cambodia, sometime after 1327, the king Jayavarman Parameśvara converted to Theravada, the tradition of inscriptions in Sanskrit came to an abrupt end. There are no more inscriptions for over a century, but the inference is that Pali had supplanted Sanskrit as the court's literary language.[24] When inscriptions resume, in the fifteenth century, the Khmer used is full of (misspelled) Pali loans, with Pali predominant over Sanskrit, a pattern that has largely continued till the present day. Not until recently has Theravada Buddhism been questioned as the moral backbone of Cambodian society.[25]

Pali and its scriptures still play a lively role in the Buddhist states of Sri Lanka, Myanmar, Thailand, Laos, and Cambodia. When the first interna-

tional conference of Theravada Buddhist universities was convened in
March 2007, they defined Theravada as "Buddhism based on the Pali can-
ons." All these countries continue to teach Pali in their school and university systems.

It is not used as a language for ready conversation, and some say that, in
Thailand at least, Pali expertise does not extend nowadays much further than
word-by-word interpretation of canonical texts. Yet paradoxically enough, it
does tend to be the spoken (or chanted) word that unifies the language across
all these countries—paradoxical, because each has traditionally written Pali
distinctively (usually in the script also used for its own language).

For example, those first three rules of Kaccāyana

*attho akkharasaññāto*
*akkharāpādayo ekacattālīsam*
*tatthodantā sarā aṭṭha*

would be written in Sri Lanka as:

අපො අක්බරසඤ්ඤතො॥

අක්බරාපාදයො එකවත්තාලීස॥

තපොාදන්තා සරා අටඨ॥

in Cambodia as :

អត្ថោ អក្ខរសញ្ញាតោ॥
អក្ខរាបាទយោ ឯកចត្តាលីសំ॥
តត្ថោទន្តា សរា អដ្ឋ॥

and in Myanmar as:

အတ္ထော အက္ခရသညာတော॥

အက္ခရာပါဒယော ကေစတ္တာလီသံ॥

တတ္ထောဒန္တာသရာ အဋ္ဌ॥

while many further variants are in use, not necessarily determined by the country of location, in all the countries of Southeast Asia and over into China's Yunnan province.

These all represent the same language, up to a point. But in fact, when read out by natives of the different countries, they would sound totally distinct: the pronunciation of the Pali words differs markedly in the traditional accent associated with each ambient language. Sinhala, Khmer, Burmese, Lao, and Thai have very different sound systems, not all of them tolerant of the consonant and vowel distinctions made in Pali. So the simple evocation *buddham saraṇam gacčhāmi* "I turn for refuge to the Buddha" comes out fairly straight in Sri Lanka, but as more like *budhā tayanā gissami* in Myanmar, as *puntam taranam gōčāmi* in Cambodia, and as *pudam salanam kačāmi* in Thailand or Laos.

It could even be claimed that only in a virtual, or mathematical, sense is Pali still one language, since it is only the systematic correspondence among all these alphabets and phonetic styles (or Kaccāyana's set of rules) that defines it. Still, that sense is very real. And there is only one canon of Pali literature, regardless of the alphabet (and pronunciation style) used.[26]

For Sri Lanka, the link to the language is rather more personal. The statement of scope and focus of the syllabus at the Pali University of Sri Lanka (founded in 1981) includes the passage:

> The Arahant Mahinda brought the Tipiṭaka, the language of which was Pâḷi, to Śri Lanka. The subject matter of the Tipiṭaka is called Buddhism. Therefore, Buddhism and Pâḷi are inseparably linked together. It was Śri Lanka which preserved and fostered Pâḷi and Buddhism. The Pâḷi Tipiṭaka was committed to writing in Śri Lanka. The Pâḷi commentaries and sub commentaries were also written in Śri Lanka. The primary exegetical works on the Vinaya and the Abhidhamma were composed by the Śri Lankan scholars from time to time. Śri Lanka pioneered the Pâḷi grammatical tradition by introducing the First Grammars on the language of Pâḷi. Taking all this and many more into consideration, the Buddhist and Pâḷi University of Śri Lanka was established to rejuvenate the Theravâda Tradition by promoting Pâḷi and Buddhism in its past glory.

So besides the religious nexus of this language with Buddhism, Sri Lanka also claims a special national link with Pali, although it has never been more than a learned language there.

Pali is a language that was employed by the Buddha and his successor monks as a reasonable alternative to Sanskrit, to reach a wide audience directly and comprehensibly. It was soon fixed, as its sayings were committed to memory, but was not originally claimed—unlike its great competitor and aunt Sanskrit—to be particularly pure, eternal, or incorruptible as a language. But after a millennium as the language of scripture, unchanged and unchanging, it was felt to have a value in its own right, the pervasive symbol of Theravada, the only Buddhist tradition left standing in Sri Lanka after the disruptions of the tenth and eleventh centuries. In the next millennium, it was sustained in use among speakers of a variety of different and mostly unrelated languages throughout Southeast Asia, as well as in its homeland to the south of India. All of them saw it as a key feature of their faith's identity, and indeed its use in worship as the touchstone of religious orthodoxy.

꘎꘎꘎

English then was a lingua-franca propagated with a religion, but one that turned out to be, in many places, ultimately more popular than the religion that it was being used to spread. Pali, by contrast, was a lingua-franca that acquired a holy status by association with the religion's scriptures. This change of status is comparable to what happened to Latin over a thousand years in the Roman Catholic Church in Europe.

Latin came only gradually to a position where it could be adopted as the official language for western Christianity. This happened between the second and fourth centuries AD. Prima facie, it would have seemed doubly unlikely as a linguistic development. The first disciples of Christ had largely been speakers of Aramaic, but in Christianity's spread westward across the Roman Empire (first to the urbanized areas around Rome and in North Africa), the main agents had actually been speakers of Greek. In this it had been no different from many other cults that benefited from the good communications round the Mediterranean. These included the sects worshipping such figures as Mithras, Sabazius, and Isis, and indeed Judaism itself. All had prospered and grown within the single "circle of lands" created by Rome's spreading (and apparently stable) conquests and its network of roads and shipways.

However, as Christianity was a cult that appealed above all to poorer and less privileged people, there was a clear advantage to making it available in the vernacular languages of potential converts. In the early centuries AD this meant Latin. Since the second century BC, Latin had spread, as the language of Roman soldiers, tax gatherers, and traders, round the coasts of the western Mediterranean. After ten generations, by the second century AD, it had gone beyond a status as lingua-franca and was established as a mother tongue in most of the provinces of western Europe, as well as in the provinces round Carthage in North Africa. In these areas too—except perhaps in the cosmopolitan city of Rome itself—Greek was not so widely used as a lingua-franca as it remained all round the eastern Mediterranean, so there was a clear premium on adopting the local language.

The steps needed for a new language to become the vehicle of a missionary religion are particularly clear in the adoption of Latin. First, it had to be adopted in scriptural and pastoral texts. Translations of these began to become available in the second century. Then it had to be used in the Church's administration. From the mid-third century, we can see that bishops were indeed corresponding in Latin. Finally it had to be adopted in the liturgy, the acts that defined Christian worship. This began from the papacy of Damasus I (366–84). Each change took about a century (three to four generations) to bed down, but each would have involved active change by a much greater band of Christians: the first, just a few bilingual translators; the second, the Church's hierarchy (not a large group in the third century, just a few hundred people); and finally, the whole congregation, by then a few million souls, probably one in ten of the population.

One can compare Latin's progress to that of Pali as a vehicle for Buddhism. The translation of the scriptures corresponds to the writing down of the Tipiṭaka in 89–77 BC, though here the transition was not from one written language to another, but from the joint oral authority of a living tradition to one that was fixed in writing. The adoption of Latin by the clergy, making Latin the single medium in which Christian doctrine would henceforth be developed, corresponds to Buddhaghosa's substitution of Pali for Sinhala the commentary tradition in the fifth century AD; and the translation of the liturgy can perhaps be compared to the spreading use of Pali by lay believers as a *paritta* language for direct communication with the spirit world, through incantations and prayers.

Both Pali and Latin later expanded their use as religious lingua-francas when their respective faiths, Theravada Buddhism and Roman Catholicism, were propagated to far distant countries where they had no connection to anyone's vernacular. In the case of Pali this happened when Theravada was adopted on behalf of a nation (at various times, but usually as a top-down government decision) in Myanmar, Thailand, Laos, and Cambodia. In the case of Latin, the situation was not far different, although—at least as the stories were told—the initiative usually lay with the missionaries rather than the converted rulers.

Nevertheless, when Roman Catholic missionaries, such as St. Augustine in England (597), St. Boniface in Germany (727), and St. Ansgar in Scandinavia (ca 850), were attempting to win converts in northern Europe, they always went straight to the top, attempting first of all to persuade a king (or his queen), in the well-founded belief that, if successful, this would soon win the whole kingdom for the faith. (In the case of Norway, subject to contention for the throne between 960 and 1014, the crusading "missionary" was often a would-be king himself, using his own mailed fist to impose the Roman faith along with his own rule.) The conversion of eastern Europe, including Bohemia (983), Poland (1000), and Hungary (1001), was more an achievement of the foreign policy of the Holy Roman Empire (i.e. the high-minded expansion of Saxony by its three successive emperors Otto I, II, and III) than the individual initiative of any pathbreaking priests. Teutonic Knights seeking territorial conquest (though acting with a papal license) were likewise responsible for securing the Baltic states for Roman Christianity (1226–42). The only conversion conducted by democratic means was that of Iceland (in 1000), though it was a Norwegian dependency at the time.

Whatever the means of conversion, acceptance of the Roman Catholic faith was always accompanied by imposition of the Latin liturgy, even though in almost every case the language was totally unknown to worshippers at the outset. An early period of resistance occurred in a few cases, as when the Moravian king Svątopluk attempted to retain the vernacular service previously devised for his people by Greek Orthodox missionaries, despite a simultaneous concordat with Rome. In 880 he was advised by the pope, "In all the churches of your land the Gospel must be read in Latin because of its greater dignity, and afterward it should be announced to those who do not understand Latin words in the Slav language, as seems to be done in some churches . . . If you and your judges wish . . . we recommend that you celebrate the rites of the Mass in Latin." But five years later the next pope was already angling to diminish even this use of Slavic.[27]

The "greater dignity" that Pope John VIII claimed to discern in Latin (and one can doubt whether he was sufficiently acquainted with Slavic to conduct a fair comparison!) could only have derived from some sense of Latin's majesty as a language, and that in turn had a lot to do with its long-term associations with the political glory of Rome and its long-lasting and wide-ranging power. At the turn of the millennium, when episcopal Latin was being installed as far east as Poland and Hungary, this memory of ancient greatness still illuminated the Church and its chosen language. Latin also supported the administration, and indeed all educated life, in every state in western Europe. This was equally true in the neighboring Holy Roman Empire, even though here most people had some dialect of German (*lingua theodisca*) as their mother tongue, and it was not much more than two centuries since St. Boniface had begun the effort to evangelize them. Latin had not spread among the common people, but it was now everywhere the language of officialdom, not least because in this age the officials were themselves churchmen, the ubiquitous *clerici*, who (as etymology shows) were the recognized experts in clerical work. The association, and indeed the exclusive bond, of Latin with authority, learning and holiness, was due to continue throughout western Europe for at least another five hundred years.[*]

This is the main reason why the Roman Catholic Church's spread of Latin was so effective and so pervasive in the medieval kingdoms of eastern Europe. The acceptance may seem puzzling from our standpoint after the nineteenth and twentieth centuries, since subsequently most of these same kingdoms have become nation-states, each flaunting its own (non-Latin) language. After all, these same national tongues had already been spoken in the tenth century. But then, Latin had been the vehicle of civilization in its widest sense, vanguarded by its use in spreading the Word of God. Over the preceding five hundred years, Latin's prestige had soared, in defiance of the intervening political collapse of the empire in the west, when an orderly hierarchy of Roman offices had been replaced by a slew of independent Germanic kingdoms and lordships. From being, in the third century, the language more convenient for the common people than the traditional use of Christian Greek, Latin had become, by the eleventh, the language symbolic of their common, Christian, way of life and governance.

⊙⊰⊷⊙

---

[*] In Hungary and Poland, government through Latin proved indispensable and would resist all attempts at reform in favor of the vernacular until the early nineteenth century.

The irony of this can appreciated by comparing Latin's career, as the banner language for latter-day Christianity in the west, with Aramaic, that religion's original language. This had been the common language of Christ and his immediate disciples, living in the northern Palestinian regions of Galilee and Samaria, although Hebrew would probably also have been audible farther south, in Jerusalem and Judaea.

Northern Palestine had acquired Aramaic as its lingua-franca (and soon its mother tongue) through having forcibly been incorporated in 721 BC into the Assyrian Empire, with many or most of the indigenous population being deported to distant territories, and others (primarily Aramaic speakers) settled in Palestine.[28] This effectively cleared the area of Hebrew. Later, in 589 BC, the remaining Hebrew-speaking state, centered at Jerusalem, was also dispossessed and scattered, principally to Babylon, even if some Hebrew continued in southern Palestine (i.e. the land of Judah).[29] Although Cyrus, the Persian successor to the Assyrians and Babylonians, permitted these Jews to return to Palestine in 538 BC (after only two generations away), this brief but thorough churning of the Jewish population had effectively disrupted the vernacular transmission of Hebrew. Aramaic was to remain the mother tongue of most in Palestine, both during the two centuries of Persian rule, and after Alexander's and Pompey's conquests, which followed (in 333 and 67 BC).

To see what had changed here, let us compare a text in the two languages, say Isaiah's prophecy (7:14) of the virgin birth. In Hebrew this appears as:

|  |  |  |
|---|---|---|
| לָכֵן יִתֵּן | lāxēn yitēn | Therefore gives |
| אֲדֹנָי הוּא | 'ăðōnāy hū' | Lord himself |
| לָכֶם אוֹת הִנֵּה | lāxim 'ōθ: hinnē' | to-you sign: Lo, |
| הָעַלְמָה הָרָה | hā-'almāh hārāh | the-virgin conceives |
| וְיֹלֶדֶת בֵּן | wə-yōlěðěθ ben | and-bears son, |
| וְקָרָאת שְׁמוֹ | wə-qārā'θ šəmō | and-she-calls name |
| עִמָּנוּ אֵל: | 'immanu'el | Immanuel. |

This was picked up, essentially word for word, in the Aramaic translation of the Christian New Testament (at Matthew 1:23):

| | | |
|---|---|---|
| ܗܐ | dəhā | Lo |
| ܒܬܘܠܬܐ | bətultā | virgin |
| ܬܒܛܢ | tebṭan | she-conceives |
| ܘܬܐܠܕ ܒܪܐ | wə-têlad bərā | and-she-bears son |
| ܘܢܩܪܘܢ | wə-neqrōn | and-they-call |
| ܫܡܗ | šmeh | name |
| ܥܡܢܘܐܝܠ | ʿamanuw'il | Emmanuel, |
| ܕܡܬܬܪܓܡ | dəmettargam | interpreted |
| ܥܡܢ ܐܠܗܢ | ʿaman 'alāhan | "with God" |

Recall that Hebrew and Aramaic, as Semitic languages, have words whose basic meaning is largely determined by their skeleton of consonants. Thus *wə* is 'and', *wld* 'give birth', *qr* 'call', *šm* 'name'. Comparing the romanized versions, one can see that for the same text, even if the consonants (marked in bold) show many shared roots, most of the words are completely unrelated, and much of the rest (notably the surrounding vowels) also differs phonetically.*

These two illustrative texts are far from contemporary: the Hebrew was written around the eighth century BC, whereas the Aramaic was written well over a millennium later. Nevertheless, both are in literary forms that persisted throughout that period, so it is not unreasonable to use them as specimens of quasi-eternal differences between the languages. Hebrew and Aramaic, though related, were evidently widely divergent languages, no more similar than English and German.

The two conquests by western powers had no further effect on the vernacular of the region, though the former of them did result in Greek's installation as the lingua-franca for elite use. Roman government after Pompey made no impact on any aspect of the language dispensation among locals, except that the garrisons were commanded in Latin. Hence the situation created by Alexander, of a Greek-speaking elite (including most of the gov-

---

* Here each row is written strictly word for word in original script, romanization, and English translation, but the scripts (originally related, despite appearances) are written right to left.

ernment) lording it over an Aramaic-speaking populace, would continue for a thousand years, until the Arab conquest in the mid-seventh century AD. (This last seismic shift would displace both of them in favor of Arabic, which has been in use ever since.) During this period, since Aramaic had lost the high-level uses that had required a common standard across most of western Asia, spoken Aramaic began to split into a variety of distinct dialects.

Aramaic, then, though once a lingua-franca par excellence in the Babylonian and later the Persian empires, was for the early Christians of Palestine under Roman rule a vernacular language, their mother tongue. It was written alphabetically (as it had been for a good thousand years), although in an environment where writing was current in at least three other languages (Hebrew, Greek, and Latin). Of these, Greek seemed by far the most useful and cosmopolitan at the time in the eastern Mediterranean. (It also lacked the stain of association with the Romans, which comes across starkly in the New Testament writings.)[30] So it was no surprise that the Christians who produced a literature for the new religion and propagated it round the Roman Empire, particularly to the west, should have chosen to do it all in Greek.

Meanwhile, the forms of the language spoken by the Christian disciples— Samaritan and Galilean Aramaic—never became a vehicle for the wider spread of the religion. Yet another Aramaic-speaking community was not far away, which, as if by coincidence, did become highly influential in the eastward spread of Christianity. This was Edessa (now Urfa), to the northeast of Palestine, the capital of its own territory, known as Osroëne. The dialect of Aramaic spoken here (not very different from the old literary standard) was known as Syriac. Independent of both Greek and Roman power from 132 BC to AD 244 (when it was absorbed into the Roman Empire), the city seems to have become host to a significant Christian community in the midsecond century AD, but taken no part in the predominant Greek-language tradition. Instead, there was much translation of Christian materials from Greek into Syriac. To start with, the Church relied on its own special compilation of the (Greek) Gospels, Tatian's second-century *Diatessaron* (Greek for 'Across the Four'). This was used together with translations of the Acts of the Apostles and Paul's letters. The full New Testament, in a translation known as the *Pšíttâ* (a word meaning 'simple, common, straight'), did not become available until the late fourth century.

Syriac was another language that began its connection with a faith as the popular, vernacular speech of its believers, but then became a religious lingua-franca that would spread with it. So it came to connote the religious community in the minds of speakers of quite different tongues. Syriac's destiny would take it across Asia, ultimately to Malabar on the western coast of India and in the east to Beijing and the shores of the Yellow Sea. But it was also used by many communities of Christians who remained in western Asia, including the Jacobites of Syria, who sent missions south into Arabia. There is some indication that by the fourth or fifth centuries AD it was no longer a vernacular even in the west, or at least there was a sense that standards were slipping, since the texts then began to be "pointed" explicitly to mark the vowel sound, which suggests that speakers no longer knew them implicitly.[31]

In Iran there had been Christians since the Arsacid dynasty (which ended in AD 224); they continued to grow in numbers throughout the Sassanian dynasty that followed, surviving periodic persecutions inspired by the Zoroastrians, though both religions were just as concerned to resist the competing faith of the Manichaeans, which was a kind of intermediate between them.* In the mid-fourth century, the Roman emperor Constantine's official recognition of Christianity, with Athanasian creed, had some long-term effect in tending to drive Christian dissenters eastward. After 431 the Syriac-speaking Christians were themselves split doctrinally (by the Nestorian schism, on the precise relation between the human and divine aspects of Christ). The Persian kings actually intervened to provide refuge for the Nestorians after 462 and, in 489, when the whole community of Edessa was expelled by the Roman emperor, accommodated them in neighboring Nisibis (modern Nusaybin, now in southeastern Turkey). Thereafter, the Christians in Persia were predominantly of the Nestorian persuasion. The faith spread not least through the activities of merchants, *tāgrā*, who (like their Sogdian contemporaries!) could also be thought of as dealers in salvation. A

---

* The Manichaean faith was highly multilingual, and unique in its approach to languages. Its original sacred books were written by the prophet Mani (ca AD 210–76) in Syriac, his native language, but its first spread was in Iran, and his final work, the *Šābuhragān*, was written in (middle) Persian specifically for its king, Shapur I. The subsequent rapid spread of the faith, into the far east (to Central Asia and China) and far west (to Egypt, Rome, Gaul, and even Britain) in the following two centuries, caused the sacred books' translation into Persian, Pahlavi, Sogdian, Uyghur, and Chinese in the east, and Greek, Coptic, and Latin in the west. Although like Christianity it was first expressed in Aramaic, Manichaeism never adopted a single associated lingua-franca in its millennium of active life. But a distinct version of the Aramaic alphabet, supposedly invented by Mani, was used for religious documents in some very different languages, Syriac, Persian, Pahlavi, Sogdian, and Uyghur.

Syriac hymn of the fourth century goes "Travel well-girt like merchants, that we may gain the world."[32] By the mid-seventh century, just before the Arab Muslim invasion from the west, they seem to have gained considerable penetration, and the perceptive scholar al-Biruni, although writing in another age (the eleventh century), could write, "The majority of the inhabitants of Syria, Iraq, and Khurasan are Nestorians."[33]

Syriac—at first enjoying some natural advantages in its associations because it was a dialect of the Imperial Aramaic that had once been Persia's lingua-franca and was still written in a script not too dissimilar—became the language of Christianity in the east. Its prestige in the Persian world and beyond made it able to build on the transmission of scripts for literacy that had previously come to Persia's eastern neighbors through Imperial Aramaic. Among those previously illiterate, the Nestorians were now particularly successful among Turkic and Mongol nomads: major tribes among them received their script from missionaries ca 550, in 781–82, and in 1007.[34]

Many may have spoken Persian or other languages at home, but for their worship they continued to use Syriac. By 650 Central Asia east of the Oxus had over twenty Christian bishoprics.[35] They used literal Sogdian translations from Syriac original texts. In 781 a stela was put up by Chinese Christians in the capital Chang'an, in Chinese and Syriac, to commemorate their faith's first arrival 150 years before. (The faith was to last there perhaps another 150.) When in 1503 Portuguese adventurers discovered Christians in India, estimating their number at thirty thousand, their liturgy was still in Syriac, even though the Christians' vernacular was Malayalam.[36] Once again, a language originally used by missionaries for vernacular preaching had remained associated with the faith as a sacred lingua-franca.

∞≈∞

The languages reviewed in this chapter, Pali (with Sanskrit in the background), Latin, and Aramaic, have parallel careers: each of them, although originally chosen as a vernacular medium to propagate a proselytizing faith to a wide audience, achieved a close association with that faith and became in effect its sacred language. In this they were unlike missionary English, as it once careered through India, Africa, and the Pacific and is now making inroads (associated with U.S. Evangelicalism) into Central and South America. English has kept its secular status despite always being a lingua-franca that was mostly taught quite artificially in mission schools.

Although English has largely survived wherever it was taught, as has (to a lesser extent) the accompanying Protestant Christianity—often the very Church of England—the language has never become closely associated with the faith, but left this field open for local vernaculars.

To explain why it has followed this different route, it is not enough to plead that English has always happened to be the premier secular lingua-franca of its era and has hence not been able to accept a close association with a newly preached religion, for, by the same logic, Latin, as the universal elite language for European civilization from 500 to 1500, should have been unavailable to adopt a sacred guise in the Catholic Church. Yet it did, with no apparent contradiction or even tension. Something else must have been keeping English away from developing a special association with Christianity, even though it has been—for well over two centuries—employed to propagate it.

The probable reason has something to do with Protestantism itself, the characteristic form of Christianity that arose in the sixteenth century in Europe. The Protestant movement arose as a reaction against the excesses of the Roman Catholic Church, but unlike its rejected mother church, it has no single strong leader and has never been able to enforce unity among its followers. They, since the original break with Rome, have split into a large number of different churches. Since all Protestants emphasize the role of written scripture as the key to right doctrine and hold that it is best interpreted by individual conscience (rather than the authority of priests), their churches have always encouraged access to scripture in vernacular languages, since Jacques Lefèvre d'Étaples first translated the Bible into French in 1530. Other landmarks have been Martin Luther's translation into German (1534), Myles Coverdale's into English (1535), Oddur Gottskálksson's into Icelandic (1540), Jurij Dalmatin's into Slovenian (1584), and William Morgan's into Welsh (1588).

Catholic missionaries dominated the worldwide propagation of Christianity in the first three centuries of European imperialism; for them, the central language of the Church remained Latin, although vernacular worship was also encouraged.* But when Protestant missionaries did begin their

---

* They invented documentary linguistics, with production of grammar, dictionary, and texts—typically prayers, catechisms, and confessionals—as preparation for this activity. They did not translate the Gospels or the rest of the Christian scriptures directly into indigenous languages, however. Nonetheless, most missionaries preferred to associate with indigenous people in their own languages, rather than Spanish or Portuguese, although the safety of preaching doctrine in these languages was disputed.          *cont.*

work, they soon set about giving each new target community a firm vernacular basis for its worship by translating large parts of the scriptures. An isolated trailblazer was the translation of the Bible into Massachusett in 1663 (though the language did not survive long afterward); next, the New Testament was turned into Greenlandic Inuktitut in 1744–66. Worldwide, the effort was made by Protestant missionaries of varying denominations not to create Christian communities in the missionaries' languages, but to reach each population in its own language. By 2008 according to the United Bible Society, the Bible had been translated into 451 languages, with parts of scripture available in 2,479 overall, about 40 percent of the world's known language total.

Despite this, as was described at the beginning of this chapter, British missionary activity did in practice involve a lot of use of English. It was delivered as part of a colonial, cultural package that was as effective, in general lifestyle, in propagating the language as it was in propagating the Christian faith. Yet English has nowhere established itself as the language of the new Christian communities so created. In the face of the ancient tendency for a vernacular language long associated with a religion to become seen as a necessary part of it, a sacred language in effect, English has been offered no part in this mysticism. Protestant conscience, in league with nationalist reaction, has in this case triumphed over nostalgic associations, and indeed anglophone aspirations.

This deep-seated support of Protestant Christians for vernaculars is worth bearing in mind as one force that will contribute to a possible global shift away from universal lingua-francas in the modern world. In the first sign of a reaction against the use of a foreign lingua-franca in their spiritual life, modern Protestant Christians in Africa, Asia, and the Americas, have voted with their tongues for the use of their own mother tongues.

---

Catholicism had priority in mission work because the Catholic powers of southern Europe (Spain, Portugal, and to a lesser extent France) led the advance of imperialism. Most early settlements from Protestant countries, when they came (from the seventeenth century on), were little interested in mission work, seeking rather to establish communities of faithful citizens from Europe.

In any case, they were not party to the Catholic quid pro quo whereby conversion of the heathen was demanded by the pope to balance the prima facie injustice of conquering them and taking their land.

# PART III

# A RANGE OF OUTCOMES

. . . the store
Of Aboriginal and Roman lore,
And Christian monuments, that now must burn
To senseless ashes. Mark! how all things swerve
From their known course, or vanish like a dream;
Another language spreads from coast to coast;
Only perchance some melancholy Stream
And some indignant Hills old names preserve,
When laws, and creeds, and peoples all are lost!

—William Wordsworth
"Monastery of Old Bangor," 1821

# CHAPTER 7

# Regenerations

> It seems to me that Your Majesty should order that all the Indians
> learn the Mexican language, for in every village today there are many
> Indians who know it and learn it easily, and a very great number who
> confess in that language. It is an extremely elegant language, as elegant
> as any in the world. A grammar and dictionary of it have been written,
> and many parts of the Holy Scriptures have been translated into it; and
> collections of sermons have been made, and some friars are very great
> linguists in it.
>
> —Fray Rodrigo de la Cruz, in Mexico,
> to Emperor Charles V, letter of May (March?) 4 1550[1]

AN IMPORTANT CLUE TO a lingua-franca's end lies in its beginning. A lingua-franca, as we have seen, grows through recruitment; hence, when people learn lingua-francas, it is for some purpose. New overlords may have imposed themselves on the would-be speakers' community, so that they want to learn it to advance themselves—or are compelled to learn it to survive. A new market may have opened up in which the new speakers wish to trade. Potential learners may become aware that learning is being developed in a new medium, and so they may present themselves for education in it. In the extreme case, religious salvation may be on offer. In all these cases, which will often tend to overlap, lingua-francas are learned instrumentally, as means to some material, intellectual, or spiritual end. But what happens to a language so learned—and perpetuated—when the circumstances change, when goals that it served are no longer accessible or are attainable by other means? How much loyalty will its speech community feel to it? Conservatives may yet send their children to school to learn the old medium, which they may remember as having served them well, even been the making of their careers. But will the children themselves care— once they have an option—to spend time and effort learning a language with the stench of superannuation on it?

A language that, for whatever reason, is no longer judged "cool" by the rising generation is in dire risk of extinction. This has become a truism of present-day campaigns in favor of endangered languages, which are usually focused on small mother tongue language communities. But it is even more true of lingua-francas, which unlike mother tongues cannot rely on being transmitted naturally, without premeditation, from one generation to the next. If a rising generation can turn away from a family's traditional speech,* how much more easily will they abandon a language that they are being asked to learn specially if it seems to be for reasons that no longer make sense? The language itself will come to seem old-fashioned, along with the culture that surrounds it. As a result, a lingua-franca's continued existence depends on the successful renewal of the marketing campaign, implicit or explicit, that has supported its rise to currency.

All the same, one cannot always be sure that an obsolescent purpose will translate into a dying lingua-franca. Lingua-francas may guarantee their futures in two ways. One is for the lingua-franca to develop into a fully fledged vernacular, that is to say, a mother tongue that is transmitted naturally. With a proper speech community to speak it and pass it on to their children, its purposeful origins become irrelevant to its survival. The other is harder to achieve, but not uncommon when the lingua-franca is the language of a long-lived and wide-ranging empire. This is for the language to find itself another raison d'être.

The former of these ways of preservation is common. It is the root of most examples of language shift, where one language comes to replace one or many others, and by the same token (but when the focus is on the language in danger of being replaced), it is the cause of most language endangerment. Essentially, a lingua-franca comes to supplant a previous mother tongue, becoming the new language that the community speaks to its children.

Examples are many, from every age. It is happening, for example, in the present generation all over Siberia, as the ancient languages of the steppe, taiga, and tundra are supplanted by Russian. As a researcher writes:

---

* Admittedly, this usually happens with the collusion, witting or unwitting, of their parents.

> Language loss in indigenous minority communities of the area was speeded up during the last two or three decades by the arrival of television in all corners of the taiga and tundra . . . Once we asked a young . . . Selkup . . . why the young generation abandons Selkup and shifts to Russian. The young man pointed to the TV set in the corner of the only room in his house and replied, "It's because of that box!" . . . A series of sociolinguistic surveys carried out in the late 1990s showed that most parents want their children to speak the language of their ancestors. At the same time the language actually spoken with children, even in most mono-ethnic families, is Russian . . . parents want their children to feel at ease at school.[2]

It happened widely in the Spanish colonies of America in the generations after the issue of the *Real Cédula* 'Royal Decree' of April 16, 1770, with its explicit purpose: "in order that at once may be achieved the extinction of the different languages used in the said domains, and the sole use of Castilian . . ."[3] Castilian Spanish, which had been the lingua-franca of the ruling class and the cities for the previous two centuries, henceforth became the mother tongue of the vast majority of the population, and knowledge of the indigenous languages, unrespected by church or government and starved of any further recognition in education, obligingly withered away except in remote villages. Mestizos, the "New Race" that the Spanish Empire prided itself on creating, would henceforth be overwhelmingly speakers of Spanish only.

It had evidently happened long before, in the middle centuries of the first millennium AD all over England and the Lothians of Scotland, and a few centuries later in Cumbria and Wales, as more and more of a once British-speaking population came to accept that their full lives, from cradle to grave, would be lived in the language of the overbearing English, first their neighbors, then their overlords.

The process was not certain and in practice could take a long time. In Cornwall, as one example, though the first Anglo-Saxons had arrived in the seventh century, five hundred years later most still spoke Cornish only. In the Prayer Book Rebellion of 1549, the Cornishmen's petition, in rejecting the introduction of English into their worship, pleaded, "And so we the Cornishmen (whereof some of us understand no English) utterly refuse this new English."

They were given short shrift by the English establishment of Henry VIII (who also dissolved the principal seat of Cornish learning at Glasney College). Life was now to be lived in English. And so it was: by 1602, a chronicle states that the Cornish language was "driven into the uttermost skirts of the shire." Still, enough native Cornish speakers remained to serve as code talkers for the Royalists during the Civil War (1642–45). On a tour of Cornwall in 1662, John Ray noticed that, even in the far west, "few of the children could speak Cornish, so that the language is like, in a short time, to be quite lost." In fact, the last vernacular speakers of Cornish (through continuous oral tradition) probably lived in the eighteenth century, a good millennium after the first encounter with English.[4]

This process, through which a lingua-franca becomes accepted as a mother tongue, is also responsible for the birth of many new languages, when a pidgin, a partial or combined version of a language developed by adults for communication between language groups, is passed on to children as the only language they know and so becomes a creole. This process created Bislama and Tok Pisin, now official languages in their own right (as well as widely spoken vernaculars) in Vanuatu and Papua New Guinea.

When the sources are major languages that are widely known in their original forms, these creoles get little popular respect and are seen as somehow inferior alternatives to a properly learned language. This has happened a great deal on the margins of the great European colonial empires of the seventeenth to twentieth centuries. Languages such as Gullah in the southeastern USA, Haitian Creole French, Papiamentu (from Spanish or Portuguese in the southern Caribbean), spoken by marginal communities of uneducated people long treated as second-class, have been dismissed as no-account languages. But these attitudes do not survive in the long term. It is a respectable view* that the major modern Indo-European languages themselves (including, as a scattering of representative examples, German, Italian, Greek, Russian, Persian, Armenian, and Bengali) all owe their variety, which must go back at least three thousand years, to a common language that was repeatedly creolized in this way, through introduction to different populations all over Europe and the southwestern half of Asia. Languages certainly change left to their own devices in isolation from fellow speakers; but

---

* Explicitly argued in Beckwith 2009, 369–74.

they change much faster when those who speak them have picked them up from others who spoke them imperfectly.

Regardless of such substrate influence, one occasion when this propagating of lingua-franca into mother tongue has widely and permanently applied has been the creation of the Romance languages in Europe. These are spoken now in areas where languages such as Tartessian and Celtiberian (in Spain), Aquitanian, Gaulish, and Ligurian (in France), and Getic and Thracian (in Rumania) were once spoken, but where Latin was introduced as the language of the imposed Roman government and propagated by veteran-soldier immigrants, traders, and possibly missionaries. We know the origin, an imposed lingua-franca, and we know the outcome was a variety of local vernaculars derived from it, with no known remnants (except for Basque, and perhaps Breton) of the previous mother tongues, which those same communities had used from time immemorial.

The process has happened so often that it tends to be overlooked as a distinct process of development at all, but a fundamental change in linguistic status is involved here: within a community, the language is changing from one spread by recruitment to one passed on within families. Once this has happened, the incoming language (in these cases, Russian, Spanish, English, or some creole) effectively "gains tenure." Its survival here no longer depends on its perceived utility; instead, it has become the default medium of social contact, which will be transmitted down the generations until either the community is totally disrupted and dispersed, or some other lingua-franca comes to supplant it as a new mother tongue for the community.

∞≈∞

A harder trick for a lingua-franca to pull off is to change what it is seen as good for: to regroup and, as it were, to reposition its brand. Nevertheless, this has happened and so given a new, and different, lease of life to an old language.

The Persian language, as we have seen, had already been a widespread mother tongue in Iran for well over a thousand years when it was taken up—evidently as an army language—by the *mawāli* 'clients' of the caliph's Arab Muslim forces in the seventh century AD. As such, it was spread over a wide area to the northeast of Iran too, as the language of the conquerors, who became known (not to Arabs but Central Asians) as *Tājik*s.

This language, as a new lingua-franca, written in Arabic script with a heavy admixture of loans from Arabic, gained prestige as the court and literary language of the Samanid dynasty centered on Bukhara. The language then proved itself far more durable than any specific dynasty and was taken up, transformed into a language of the court, rather than of the army and mosque, by all the many Turkic factions that followed, from Ghaznavids and Seljuqs ultimately to Mughals and Qajars, imposing themselves as rulers of different parts of western and southern Asia between the eleventh and the nineteenth centuries. Endued with the iridescent form that so many court poets conceived and embellished for it—resplendent but non-assertive—it seemed unique and indispensable as the attribute of true culture. The classic poet Firdawsī was prescient (as with hindsight, classic poets always tend to be):

بسی رنج بردم در این سال سی

عجم زنده کردم بدین پارسی

*basī ranj bardam dar īn sāl-e sī*
*'ajam zinde kardam bedīn pāresī*

Much pain I bore in these thirty years passing:
Gentile I brought to life in this my Persian.

Appropriately enough, his work, which had first been commissioned by Persian-speaking Samanids, was actually delivered to the Turkic-speaking (but Persian-respecting) Ghaznavid Sultan Mahmud, the first in a vast and varied pageant of Turkic rulers. The Turks' acceptance of Persian, in preference to their own language, ensured its long life.

Another example of a classical language that changed its role—and hence its user community—is the great lingua-franca of most of India, Sanskrit.

Sanskrit was originally conceived, and indeed standardized (*saṃskṛta* 'composed'), as a perfect language for the expression of Hindu devotion. The great tradition to regiment and perfect knowledge of Sanskrit reached its zenith in Panini's *Aṣṭādhyāyī* 'Eight Lessons' of the fifth century BC, but this is too pure a document actually to say what its value is. The great continuer of the tradition was the commentator Patanjali, in the second century

BC. For his day, in the *Mahābhāṣya* 'Great Commentary', he claimed there were five reasons for studying Sanskrit grammar, and three of these were religious in motivation (the others being language learning and textual interpretation). Over the first millennium BC, Sanskrit was above all a lingua-franca with a sacred calling.

This changed, or rather was expanded, at the beginning of the first millennium AD. Sanskrit became the principal vehicle for secular poetry, what is known as *kāvya*. The first great poem is the *Rāmāyaṇa*, an adventure narrative—admittedly of the sacred hero Rama—and the first named poet is Vālmīki. There is even a tradition (recorded in the poem—i.2.14) of the first couplet of verse, whose spontaneous meter was to infuse the whole epic (and indeed all Sanskrit epics to follow, since it defined the *śloka* meter):

> *mā niṣāda pratiṣṭām tvam agamaḥ śāśvatīḥ samāḥ*
> *yat krauñca-mithunād ekam avadhīḥ kāma-mohitam*
>
> may-not, O Nishada, peace-of-mind you-reach for eternal
> years,
> because from-a-crane-couple one you-killed who-was-
> distraught-with-love!
>
> — v — v | v — — v | v v — — | v — v —
> — — v v | v — — v | v v — — | v — v —

This sentiment is not religious at all, but an outpouring of passion in the face of a pathetically slaughtered animal, a male crane transfixed by an arrow while in the throes of mating. This is pinpointed as the moment when Sanskrit changed its tone.

Sanskrit went on in the first millennium to become the vehicle for a vast secular literature, in prose and verse. Its heroic poets and authors were now no longer only ascetics and sages who wrote on philosophy, grammar, and religion, but urbane men-about-town, writing sophisticated love poetry and romantic dramas, history books and wide-ranging collections of fables, or analytic treatises on sex, statecraft, and medicine. Sanskrit also, in the same period, came to replace the current vernacular languages in all inscriptions. Until then all secular inscriptions—even the most ancient ones known, placed by the Buddhist emperor Ashoka for the moral betterment of his subjects—had been in language much closer to the spoken style of the day, but henceforward they would all be dignified in the "perfected" language.

∞⋙∞

A more complicated example of this kind of change is what happened to Latin. In fact, it happened not once but twice, as Latin morphed in the first millennium AD from the language of the Roman Empire to the language of the Catholic Church, then again in the second millennium to the language of ancient (and superior) learning in schools and universities. Christianity's original language, as that of most eastern sects that spread within the Roman Empire, had been Greek. But the Catholic Church, centered on Rome, switched to Latin in the second to fourth centuries AD to give itself the advantage of accessibility in the then vernacular language. Sacred texts were translated in the second century; church administrative correspondence began to be in Latin in the third; and in the papacy of Damasus I (366–84) the final step was taken of converting the liturgy itself. In three centuries, Latin had switched from being the language of pagans to being at the full service of Christians—and soon came to be expected on official Christian lips. In 358 Bishop Athanasius could attack the emperor's choice for bishop of Milan as "an intruder rather than a Christian . . . as yet even ignorant of the Latin language, and unskilful in everything except impiety."[5]

Not long after, Latin's new Christian association would prove crucial for its very survival; without this new religious identity, Latin would have faced a dubious future when the empire's western half was overrun and reorganized in the fifth century. Goths and Vandals, prominent among the new military rulers, were attached to the Arian sect of Christianity and worshipped in their own vernaculars, notably Gothic. As centralized (Roman) administration and communications broke down, to be replaced by smaller-scale Germanic lordships, Latin itself gradually developed into a set of local dialects, each of which became unintelligible farther afield. Britain, remote and inaccessible in the north, had hosted only a weak Christian presence under the Roman Empire; now it lost its Latin altogether, along with its Christianity.

But as the persistent language of Christian worship in the west, Latin was maintained by the institutions of the Church. As the respected language of liturgy, with a massive core that was recited (and listened to) according to given forms rather than spoken spontaneously, it actually changed far less than the vernacular speech of congregations. Latin learning too was maintained in the monasteries, although with a small participant population. As Gregory of Tours, famous for his ropy Latin, wrote ca 575, "The rhetorician philosophizing is understood by few, the plain man talking by many."[6]

This elite language of the Church became, independently of the various vernaculars spoken around Europe (and whether or not the local language was derived from Latin), the leading medium of literacy in western Europe, especially after a common standard for Latin pronunciation was defined and propagated by Alcuin of York, the head of Charlemagne's Palace School at Aachen in the late eighth century. Subsequently, intrepid Germanic missionaries and conquerors spread Roman Christianity (and with it Latin, as the language of all intellectual life) all round northern and central Europe (as far as Norway, Iceland, and Hungary), and somewhat later, the remaining countries bordering the Baltic Sea. The Church supported not only the survival of Latin as western Europe's lingua-franca, but also its spread into northern and eastern Europe where the Roman Empire had never had any foothold at all.

The Church continued its dominant role in the intellectual life of Europe throughout the first millennium AD, and on into the fourteenth century. Only then, in the first awakenings of the Renaissance in northern Italy, did a more secular approach begin to gain favor. But although this did change the climate of conscience and research, leading ultimately to a more independent spirit of inquiry (and among much else, the religious Reformation in the north of Europe), it did not threaten the perceived value of Latin as an established, and well-developed, lingua-franca for the discussion of high-level issues. Instead, innovative thinkers such as Petrarch went back to the Latin classics of the ancient world to seek inspiration, and critics such as Lorenzo Valla sought out textual evidence of how best to express ideas in the classical language. Although still actively deployed in the Roman Church and all its works, Latin no longer exclusively Roman, but had become the language rather of a European "republic of letters." Copernicus, Erasmus, Kepler, Galileo, Newton, and Descartes all published most of their key works in Latin. For the last time (as it turned out), Latin had found a new and influential community to serve as lingua-franca.

# CHAPTER 8

# Ruin and Relegation

| | |
|---|---|
| *Beorht wæron burgræced, burnsele monige,* | Bright borough-buildings, bath-halls many, |
| *heah hordgestreon, heresweg micel,* | high the treasure hoards, hubbub was mighty, |
| *meodoheall monig mondreama full,* | mead-halls many, man-dreams aplenty, |
| *oþþæt þæt onwende wyrd seo swiþe.* | until it was upturned by Destiny doughty. |

—"The Ruin," an eighth-century lament, probably
for Bath's vanished Roman glories

P ERSIAN, SANSKRIT, AND LATIN had all become, in their different subcontinental societies, standardized written languages with massive literatures and succeeded, over many centuries, in transcending the particular circumstances from which they had first arisen and expanded. Each established itself as having an intrinsic value and was seen as a valuable institution in its own right. They were considered worthy to be preserved and transmitted to future generations, quite independently of whether they survived anywhere as vernacular languages.

Yet the modern reader notes that none of these languages is still a lively lingua-franca in the early twenty-first century.* Something ultimately went very wrong for all of them, at least by the standards of their traditional uses.

---

* Persian is very much alive as a mother tongue—all over Iran, and in pockets over much of the old *qalamrau-e-zabān-e-fārsī* in Central Asia. Sanskrit and Latin are not forgotten, but their roles as lingua-francas are arcane and severely restricted.

What is the fate of a lingua-franca that neither succeeds in becoming a mother tongue nor finds a new community that sees its value for wider communication?

The answer, of course, is extinction. This is the only possible outcome for a lingua-franca when the community whose interactions it has served becomes inoperative. But the breakdown can come about in different ways, just as the community served can have formed itself for quite different purposes. It is tempting to classify these different manners of breakdown as the three R's of lingua-franca death: Ruin, Relegation, and Resignation. **Ruin**, defined* as 'complete loss of means, solvency, position,' refers to the downfall of an economic network; **Relegation** 'exile, assignment to an inferior position' is a political act, summarily ending an official status; and **Resignation** 'giving up a position, patient submission' is the most diffuse of the three, a social trend that undermines and demeans the position of a previously respected elite. Each can unseat a previously ruling lingua-franca, and each has many examples—among them, the latter careers of most languages described so far in this book.

〇⚭〇

Ruin would, at first sight, seem the natural termination for a lingua-franca that had been spread as the language of a commercial network. In practice, the life and death of languages is not so neat: he who lives by the market does not necessarily die by it. Some languages first spread by trade have been stopped—as lingua-francas at least—by Relegation action (e.g., Punic, suddenly, through Roman aggression in 146 BC); and others by Resignation (e.g., Sogdian, in the long term, in its Central Asian colonies). These exceptional cases will be described below. But it is worthwhile, first, to consider some more straightforward examples of the process to see the final stage in the life cycle of a trade lingua-franca.

The most evident examples of languages ruined by the decline and closure of the market opportunities that spread them are the pidgins, languages that are prima facie associated with trade contacts between groups previously alien to each other. Since pidgins are the creatures of particular market opportunities, they cease to be spoken when the market moves on and

---

* All these definitions are derived (admittedly selectively) from the Third College Edition of *Webster's New World Dictionary*.

the opportunities no longer exist—unless, of course, the pidgins have made the leap to become creoles, by acquiring native speakers of their own. Thus, many recorded pidgins no longer exist: they were phenomena of different eras of economic contact. These include the old trade jargons from all over the world: Sabir, the original Lingua Franca of the southern and eastern Mediterranean (fourteenth to nineteenth centuries); Russenorsk, used in the Norwegian Arctic for Russian-Norwegian trade (from the eighteenth century till 1923); the Mobile trade language Yamá, spoken in the U.S. southeast (from the eighteenth century till the great Indian removal of 1830–35); Chinese Pidgin English on the southern coasts of China (from the seventeenth to nineteenth centuries);* the Chinook jargon Wawa in the Pacific Northwest (until the early twentieth century); and Hiri Motu, spoken from time immemorial until recently among the Motu and their neighbors in the southeast of New Guinea.

Many other pidgins came about as a result of one-sided relationships that were built up in the three-hundred-year spree of European imperialism, as businessmen became aware of populations and crops outside Europe and learned to exploit the one to maximize profit in production of the other. Often in the early years this was through nakedly slave-based economies, but later the balance swung to indentured-labor contracts. Both are now in the past, and with them went a few of the pidgins they created, e.g., in the Pacific, Samoan Plantation Pidgin and Broome Pearling Lugger Pidgin. But since the relationships created had some irreversible human effects (few slaves or indentured laborers could return), most of the pidgins developed in later generations into creoles and have not died out. Hence Sranan in Suriname, Krio in Sierra Leone, Kamtok in Cameroon, and Tok Pisin and Bislama in the Pacific are still working as common languages. Sometimes groups of fugitives escaped and set up their own communities with these languages (e.g., Palenquero, Saramaccan, in the Caribbean, Pitcairn in the Pacific). Sometimes too the contact languages between immigrants and indigenous populations have stuck; this has produced, for example, Kriol, a form of English used by Aboriginals in Australia.

It was different when the first generation of immigrants faced a tempo-

---

* This is an interesting case in that trade between Britain and China has never ceased. But Chinese came to feel that the pidgin language was demeaning to them and dropped it in favor of well-formed English; this change could thus be interpreted rather as a case of lingua-franca death caused by (social) Resignation rather than (economic) Ruin.

rary linguistic melting pot, which would disappear when their children successfully learned the local language. Cocoliche in Argentina, created by uneducated Italians of various dialects coming together in common ignorance of Spanish, was not passed on down the generations: effectively, the basis for this language was ruined as the next generation assimilated to the wider linguistic environment.

Not all the trade languages that faced this kind of long-term ruin were newly reconstituted languages, i.e. pidgins or creoles, although the economic and linguistic changes do seem to have run faster in these cases. Essentially the same phenomenon has happened to eliminate Portuguese as a lingua-franca from the seaboard of the Indian Ocean. Spread by Portuguese enterprise after Vasco da Gama opened the route to the Indies in 1498, the language was learned by many coastal residents who had dealings with the Portuguese mariners (and missionaries) and had become a conveniently accessible lingua-franca for international visitors for three centuries. In the mid-seventeenth century, for example, the Buddhist kings of Ceylon and Arakan (in north Burma) were using it for their negotiations with the Dutch United East India Company (VOC). In 1786, the eminent French oriental scholar and adventurer Abraham Hyacinthe Anquetil du Perron could still write: "Merchants of the Hindus, Moors, Arabs, Persians, Parsees, Jews and Armenians who do business with the European factories, as well as black men who wish to work as interpreters, are obliged to speak this language; it serves also as a medium of communication among the European nations settled in India."[1]

In this same period, the British East India Company was stocked with two hundred Portuguese dictionaries and posted a Portuguese linguist in every one of its agencies.[2] Yet concrete Portuguese trading interests, which had introduced the language, had already been reduced to insignificance for over a century. Between 1605 and 1662 the Dutch had taken over the vast majority of Portuguese possessions in the East Indies, Malaya, Ceylon, and south India (with the exceptions of Macao in China, Timor in the East Indies, and the enclaves of Goa, Daman, and Diu in India). Inevitably, though it took almost two centuries, the value of Portuguese as a lingua-franca gradually died away too. New European interests, above all Great Britain, were inserting themselves and their languages into practical trade and politics, while Portuguese as spoken round the Indian Ocean came to be mostly limited to the creoles of Christian converts.

But not all lingua-francas that spread through development of commerce are allowed to survive until those links are abandoned, and the cultural memories and habits, which may support the language for a time, finally disappear. Effectively, trade lingua-francas can succumb to main force—to Relegation—before they are ruined. Punic, the Carthaginian offshoot of Phoenician, gives an example of what happens to an established lingua-franca when a greater power wishes to annihilate it.

Phoenician had died out at home in the first century BC, replaced as a mother tongue by the neighbors' closely related Aramaic. This was clearly an example of one mother tongue spreading to replace another, since the encroaching lingua-francas were quite different. In this period Canaan had been subdued and occupied first by Greek speakers (with Alexander in 332 BC), then by Romans (with Pompey in 63 BC). There was no clean break with the regime of the Persian Empire when the Greeks took over, but Greek administration (and perhaps trading interests) led to loss of Phoenician cities' distinctive identities, allowing population flows that evidently caused leveling in favor of the dominant regional vernacular, Aramaic.* Meanwhile Greek spread, as it did throughout the Levant, as the language of the ruling classes and administration. When the Romans took over, little changed, except that a few centers attracted large-scale Roman colonization, hence elite use of Latin. Among the (erstwhile) Phoenician cities, Berytus (Beirut) was settled in 19 BC with two legions' veterans and later became a great center of Roman legal expertise.

Punic was the same language as Phoenician, but named in Latin, the language of its mightiest neighbor. There is little evidence of its long-term survival where it must have been used in Phoenician commercial (and mining) outposts round the western Mediterranean, except in central North Africa (the original "Africa") and also in the colony of Sardinia. A formal inscription in Punic has been discovered at Bitia, on the south coast of Sardinia, no older than the mid-second century AD, four hundred years after Roman conquest of the island and supposed abolition of all things Carthaginian.[3] The fact is that Sardinia was always treated with contempt by the Romans, and local languages in this part of the empire may have passed beneath their notice.

But things were different in the African metropolis. Here Cato's famous

---

* Philon of Byblos, in his *Phoenician History*, claimed to be translating an ancient source, Sanchuniathon, in the mid-second century AD.

destructive doctrine, KARTHAGO DELENDA EST, was applied with full rigor. In Africa, literacy in Punic largely died out in the generation after Rome's intended final destruction of Carthage in 146 BC. The last known stone tablets inscribed in the language there are precisely from that late second century BC. The Roman senate evidently expected the tradition to cease since it distributed the accumulated wealth of Carthaginian libraries to the Punic-speaking allies, "the princes of Africa" as Pliny calls them (*Naturalis Historiae* xviii.22–23), picking out the works of just one author, Mago the agronomist, for translation into Latin.*

Still, the vernacular use of the language persisted. It is attested by mixed Latin-Punic graffiti left four and a half centuries later by Roman soldiers at Bu Ngem, on the southern limit of the empire, and in other places. Even six hundred years later, St. Augustine (who had the African bishopric of Hippo) was writing that Punic was still understood in the country districts of Numidia; he would even prefer candidates for the ministry on the strength of their (evidently useful) skill in the language.[4] Some maintain that the language never died at all, but with an infusion of Arabic (when the Muslims arrived in the eighth century) has been transmuted into Darija, the vernacular of "Arabic" used to this day in the west of North Africa.[5]

These are impressive survivals, but they both show that the last gasp, or afterlife, of a language comes through its use as a mother tongue. The evidence for Punic as an official, public language dries up after Rome's elimination of Carthage as an independent power.

Removal of a lingua-franca is usually a less physically brutal process than the sack of Carthage (which had the termination of Punic as only one implication). Nevertheless since languages—especially national languages—are salient symbols of political powers, they are often deliberate targets after a major military conquest of one empire by another.†

Hence in the period 697–700, as his empire reached its maximum extent,

---

* Nonetheless, the Roman historian Sallust, writing his *War with Jugurtha* just a century later (41–40 BC), claims (xvii.7) to have been able to consult a translation of "Punic books" attributed to King Hiempsal (of Numidia). But these would have been written at most a generation after the sack of Carthage.

† Aramaic escaped serious consequences after the Persians unseated the Babylonians; indeed it was de facto accepted as a new medium for the transaction of business in the new Achaemenian Empire that the Persians were building. But it is hard to imagine that Akkadian, the ancestral language of Mesopotamia, would so easily have been enlisted to the Persian cause if it had still been the empire's medium of business.

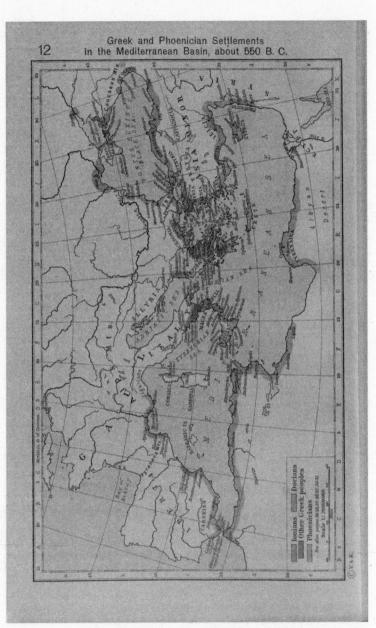

Greek and Phoenician Settlements
in the Mediterranean Basin, about 550 B. C.

12

*(Credit: University of Texas at Austin, Perry-Castañeda Library Map Collection)*

the caliph in Damascus, ʿAbd al-Malik, took action to substitute Arabic for all the previous languages of administration inherited by the Caliphate. This meant replacement of previous administrative systems written in Greek (in Syria and Egypt), Pahlavi (in Iraq and Persia), Sogdian (in Transoxiana), Latin (in the Maghreb and Spain), and to a smaller extent other languages, including Aramaic, Coptic, and Bactrian.

Since clerical classes could, at a pinch, be flexible in their choice of language—and tended to use the family as an appointments system—it does not often seem to have meant the removal of the secretaries themselves. They liked to think, and with some justice, that they had the whip hand. As one exultant new Arabist (ʿAbd al-Ḥamīd ibn Yahya al-Kātib),* secretary to the last Umayyad caliph, wrote in the mid-eighth century, "God . . . made you secretaries in the most distinguished positions . . . By your counsel God fits government to the people, and the land prospers. The king cannot do without you. You are therefore, for kings, the ears with which they hear, the eyes with which they see, the tongues with which they speak, the hands with which they strike."[6] (And—by implication—let's keep it that way!)

ʿAbd al-Malik's Greek adviser Joannes Damascenus, when informed of the new ban on use of Greek in administration, had found a portentous way to pass on the news to his colleagues: "You had better seek another profession to earn your living: your present employment has been withdrawn by God."[7] In practice, the language conversion was not immediate, and it can be followed in the papyrus trail of Egypt. All documents remained in Greek until the 740s,[8] a good century after the Muslim conquest (in 640), so ʿAbd al-Malik's decree must have had little real effect for a full generation. But bilingualism gradually set in, even if Arabic only totally replaced Greek in the late eighth century, after 150 years of Islam, and a century after the command had first gone out. Likewise (as we have seen, page 81) in Khorasan, the actual conversion of accounts from Pahlavi to Arabic only took place in 742, under the famed governor Naṣr bin Sayyār.

North Africa in the seventh century had undergone at least two disorienting changes under the late Roman Empire. The Vandals (speaking a close relative of Gothic, and using it to worship according to the Arian sect of Christianity) had ruled from 439 to 533; then the Byzantine Empire had

---

* I.e., 'son of Yahya the secretary'. He came of a Persian family, having learned Arabic as a second language. But he is reputed as the first great prose stylist in Arabic.

reasserted "Roman" rule from 533 to 696. (Part of the settlement after the Byzantine victory by Belisarius was that all Vandals should be deported from the country; so one language not to survive the war would have been Vandal.) The linguistic situation in North Africa would have been complicated during this era, since the victorious forces would have followed the Greek Orthodox rite, and in 620 the emperor Heraclius actually changed the official language of his empire from Latin to Greek (yielding to that stubborn language that had never lost its hold—as vernacular and as lingua-franca—on the east). This use of Greek would only have affected the highest levels of administration in North Africa, but it did imply that Latin as spoken would more and more have a status comparable to a Romance dialect, except as buttressed by the use of Latin in the Catholic Church. Such vernacular use did indeed continue for at least another six hundred years, since in 1154 a Moroccan geographer reported that most people in the southern Tunisian cities of Monastir, Gafsa, and Gabès spoke some sort of Latin.[9]

But in 696 Tunisia, followed by the rest of the northern seaboard of Africa, had been taken by the Arabs. The thrust continued westward and only ended in 711, by which time Iberia too was largely under Arab-speaking control.

In North Africa, the Arab government was centered on the new southern foundation of Kairouan (*al-Qayrawān* 'the caravan'), a military camp where nothing but Arabic had ever been the norm. It is not clear if a preexisting "Roman" (but perhaps Greek-using) administration had to be displaced in Tunisia, but Arabic was immediately the high-status lingua-franca here, with Berber and vernacular Latin (and probably remnants of Punic too) the mother tongues spoken on the street and in the country. The Catholic Church in North Africa did not survive the Arab conquest for more than a century, and with it went any memory there of Latin as a high-status lingua-franca, which might have competed with Arabic.

In Iberia (then known as al-Andalūs) Arabic likewise succeeded to a confused linguistic state. This previously quiet part of the Roman Empire, being the final cul-de-sac of intruders' westward advance, had been invaded from the north by a succession of highly exotic central-Eurasian tribes (Suevi, Vandals, Alans, Visigoths), with alien languages and an Arian creed. This took up much of the fifth century. Then (just like North Africa), it was invaded from the sea by the resurgent (eastern) Roman Empire. This happened in 554. These Byzantines, however, did not succeed (as they had in North Africa) in totally overthrowing the incumbent Visigoths; in fact, they were little by little pushed back out of Spain until they lost the last foothold in 631. Nevertheless, in the midst of this, the Visigothic king Reccared had moved his people in 587 to general acceptance of the Catholic faith (and hence acceptance of the primacy of Latin as their language).

When the Arabs, led by Tariq bin Ziyād, entered Iberia and defeated the Visigoths in 711, it was immediately integrated into the Umayyad Caliphate, directed from Damascus, and received governors appointed from there. Although the first coins struck (in 712–14) bore Latin legends, the next issue (716–17) was bilingual, and after 720 they were exclusively in Arabic.[10] The capital was immediately moved from Toledo to Cordoba, and Arabization began. Although al-Andalūs was to become relatively independent of the Caliphate, since it essentially repudiated the Abbasids' overthrow of the Umayyads in 750 and in 756 accepted an Umayyad prince to found a Caliphate in Cordoba in opposition to the one in Baghdad, there was never any suggestion of reinstating Latin as the official language. As vernaculars, people spoke an Andalusi dialect of Arabic, or Berber (like the vast majority of the invading army), or the local Romance (known to the Arabs as 'ajamiyya—using the same word for foreigners, 'ajam 'lispers', as favored in Iran). As in North Africa, Catholic Christianity was tolerated here, but it did not thrive, especially given that mixed marriages with Muslims would produce Muslim children, and that non-Muslims needed to pay an extra tax, the jizyā. Overall, official Latin was as effectively relegated by the Arab conquest and reorganization of Iberia in 711 as Greek in the Levant, or Pahlavi in Khorasan, all at much the same time.

In understanding this Relegation of a lingua-franca, it is important to keep it distinct from other government actions taken to suppress a vernacular language, whether by forcible replacement or by deliberate neglect. Imperial powers may well act to discourage, and discontinue, the use of mother tongues by certain subject populations. This is much more usual than the disempowerment of an incumbent lingua-franca and is the classic practice of active language endangerment.

This is what the English government of Henry VIII tried to do to Welsh when it passed the Laws in Wales Act of 1535, aiming "utterly to extirpe alle and singular the sinister usages and customs differing from the laws of this Realm," although the concrete provisions only forbade the use of the language in the courts, and its speakers from appointment to any public office in the realm. (The humiliating use of the "Welsh (k)not," hung round the shoulders to discourage use of the language by schoolchildren, had to wait until the nineteenth century.) At the same time, as against Irish, Henry urged "every inhabitant . . . [of Galway to] indever theym selfe to speke Englyshe . . . and specially that you, and every one of you, do put forth your childe to scole, to lerne to speke Englyshe." The new French government after the Revolution tried to do this to Breton and all other French "patois" in 1793, when it declared war on all *"idiomes anciens, welches, gascons, celtiques, wisigoths, phocéens ou orientaux"* and required that French alone should be the language of schools in France: "In this way the local jargons, the patois of six million Frenchmen who do not speak the national language, will insensibly disappear, for, as I cannot too often repeat, it is more important than people think to extirpate this diversity of rude idioms which prolong the childhood of reason and the old age of prejudice."[11]

◌⋝◌

Relegation of an established lingua-franca is an altogether more formal and clean-cut procedure than deterring use of an undesired mother tongue. Although (as we have seen with Punic) it can happen to a language that owes its original growth to trade, it is only possible if the language has become an official language of government. The government, for whatever reason, passes into new hands, and the new powers choose to discontinue the old lingua-franca and impose a new one. Removal, then, is all about the exercise of authority and comes about when a lingua-franca's links with political dominance have been cut.

For the Persian language, which had owed its global spread to the conquests of Turkic dynasts, the end came by this route, but multiply so. The traditional power of the now ancient Turks (still expressed in Persian to symbolize their refinement) was overwhelmed by completely alien powers coming from unknown parts of the world.

In India after the Mughals, the power of Relegation was in the end exercised by the British. Persian had remained as the language of court and administration in India throughout the period of Mughal power since 1536, as it had over the preceding centuries since the first forays of the Ghaznavids down from the Hindu Kush in 1004. The Mughal domains were, however, progressively reduced throughout the eighteenth century till at last they were no more than the environs of Delhi. Such withdrawals had begun the decline of Persian, since the main force expanding to fill the areas lost to the Mughals was the Maratha Empire, which (being Hindu) did not give any special status to—or indeed use—Persian.*

But at the same time, the power of the British East India Company was being expanded from their bases (presidencies) in Bombay, Madras, and Calcutta, all established in the seventeenth century. The first area to be taken under British control was Bengal after the battles of Plassey (*Palāśi*, 1757) and Buxar (*Baksar*, 1764)—a great swath that included modern Bihar and Orissa as well as both West and East Bengal. The next to be controlled were the so-called Northern Circars (named from Persian *sarkār* 'court, government'), territories on the coast of the Bay of Bengal wrested from the French in 1759, then ceded by both the Mughal emperor (1765) and nizam of Hyderabad (1768). The third expansion was to large areas of the south (modern Karnataka, Tamil Nadu, and Kerala), which had been controlled by Tipu, the sultan of Mysore (conquered and killed in 1799). Since all these areas had had Muslim governments, their administrations had been conducted in Persian. This continued under British control. The language had long been familiar from its use in the commercial business of the Company, since its first contacts with India in 1611–12, though in practice, admittedly, mostly through the mediation of some bilingual agent, the *banyan* or *dobash*.

The Persian language, then, was no stranger to these future masters of India. Some Indian Muslims who visited England between 1767 and 1800 earned pocket money by giving impromptu lessons in it.[12] William Jones had produced his popular grammar of it in 1771 (page 139) and so filled a need. Warren Hastings, governor-general from 1773 to 1785, was of the opinion that "the Persian language ought to be studied to perfection, and is requisite to all civil servants of the company, and it may also prove of equal use to the Military Officers of all the Presidencies." He went on to pay 57,745 rupees (later charged to the Company) to establish a madrassa for Indians in Calcutta in 1781. This was the first school paid for with Company money; Fort William College, which taught Persian to British officers, was founded there in 1800. Many of those officers became enthusiasts for the language, and in general these British traders, administrators, and soldiers went along with the traditional opinions that they encountered, contrasting

---

* Some Maratha coinage is inscribed in Persian, like the Mughal issues it replaced. But this proves little about its actual use in administration; the coinage is in any case often also issued in the name of Mughal kings.

the "elegance" of Persian with the "uncouth rudeness" of local vernaculars (more likely to be judgments on typical speakers than the languages themselves)—and often using both in their work.[13]

However, as British power continued to expand in the nineteenth century, often into areas (such as the Maratha domains) where Persian had not been widely used, it became clearer that while vernaculars were inseparable from popular life, Persian was obsolescent; in fact, it was associated with the power structures that they, the British, were replacing. It was also strongly associated with Muslims. This had appealed to the British in the early years, when they saw the Muslims (after several centuries of tradition) as India's natural "officer class." But later, the British viewed this religious-influenced linguistic division as an unsatisfactory basis for a new class of rulers. Instead, they more and more promoted "Hindustani" (i.e. Hindi/Urdu) as the vernacular language largely used in the army, but were not averse to admixture of Persian vocabulary and phraseology, and hence some of the pleasantly cultured overtones of Persian itself. Perversely, Persian's associations with traditional power long made it hard to withdraw it from the school syllabus. One teacher wrote as late as 1866, "The chief reason why our vernacular schools are so unpopular is, because so little Persian is taught in the lower classes."[14] Eight centuries of elite status were hard to set aside, in parents' and in pupils' minds.

Nevertheless, British rule in India would not in general be led by local opinion, except as caution required. A parliamentary committee of 1832 inquired whether replacement of Persian would cause a revolt, but was reassured it would not, provided it did not threaten too many people's employment.[15] Coming now under influence from Evangelical Christians, the Company was sensitive to its responsibilities, and increasingly self-confident of what Britain had to offer in contrast to the message of Indian tradition. Justice should be comprehensible to those being judged, and not only to the elite. Muslims should not see themselves as privileged citizens. So in 1832 in the Presidencies of Bombay and Madras, and in 1837 in Bengal (this difference marking the different levels of investment in Persian in the different regions), the language of Indian courts (and government) was changed—to the relevant vernacular at the local level, and at higher levels to English. Persian was thereby removed, essentially at a stroke, from the exercise of Indian governance, after eight centuries of unchallenged mastery.

As hinted, Persian by no means immediately lost its role in Indian educa-

tion. Schools are notoriously conservative institutions, and among the refined classes of Muslim society too nostalgic demand for Persian continued.
Only in the early twentieth century, four generations later, was Persian removed from the syllabus of most schools in north India. For white sahibs
too the language lingered. John Beames recalled how, when embarking on
a career in the Indian Civil Service in 1858 and destined for the North-West
Provinces, he had had first to pass an exam in Persian as well as in Hindi.[16]
Even in 1872 the government was offering its officers a bounty of 1,200 rupees for a qualification in Persian, contrasted with the 750 rupees offered for
Urdu. But the British in this era were comfortable with an education based
on an alien language (as their own would have been, back at the dear old
school). And like the contemporary use of classical allusions in English, use
of Persian was seen as the icing on the cake, the "top-dressing" that made
the difference between plain Urdu and *inšā'* (stylish composition); luxury, of
course, always has a higher price tag.[17]

Ultimately, economic differentials conspired with political realities: by
1872, English secretarial skills were commanding ten times the salary of
those in Persian.* The Punjabi cultural society Anjuman-e-Panjāb, formerly
a stickler for Persian, then petitioned the director of public instruction that
more time should be given to English at the expense of Persian. In 1883, the
National Muhammadan Association of Calcutta asked for "measures . . . to
facilitate the study of English by Muhammadans."[18] Even a cultural icon
such as Mirza Ghalib (1797–1869), a great poet in both languages who lived
mostly in Delhi, always wrote to his Indian friends in Urdu, even if he used

---

* The predicament of Persian teachers facing the end of their world in this era is reminiscent of Greek teachers of the Roman Empire, in the late fourth century AD, one of
whom wrote:

> You know how the present age has transferred to others [the Latin teachers] the
> rewards for our language studies, and reversed the ranking of respect to our
> disadvantage, presenting them as giving access to all good things, while sug-
> gesting that we only offer mumbo-jumbo and a formation for hard grind and
> poverty. That is why there are all those frequent sailings, voyages with only one
> destination, Rome, and the cheers of young people off to fulfill their dreams: of
> high office, power, marriage, palace life, conversations with the emperor. (Liba-
> nius, *Speeches* 43.4)

It is interesting to recall that within a century the pendulum had swung back from
Latin, and this time it stuck in favor of Greek for the next millennium. The fortune of a
lingua-franca is a fickle thing.

Persian when writing to the British chief secretary.[19] With the decline of Persian-language education over the rest of the century, this lingua-franca's days were numbered. SIC TRANSIT GLORIA MUNDI.

❦

On the other side of the Hindu Kush, in 1837, in the Emirate of Bukhara, the same Persian language could likewise look back on many, many centuries of genteel dominion, having been the language of government, commerce, and higher culture since the spread of the "Tajiks" in the seventh century. From the twelfth century, however, this area had been more closely linked with peoples to its north, hence guarding the southern flank of a succession of Mongol and Turkic dynasties of Muslim faith (Chingizids, Timurids, Chagatayids, Uzbeks, and Shaybanids); and Persian here had been in diglossia (as a lingua-franca and prestige literary language), i.e. sharing the linguistic work with the various forms of Turkic that they spoke, as well as the common Turkic literary language, Chagatay. By the seventeenth century, Bukhara had become the acknowledged center of the region, and the capital of an emirate (broadly covering modern Uzbekistan and Tajikistan), but was flanked on either side by more outwardly Turkic states, the Khanates of Khiva and Khoqand—in the areas that had previously been known as Khwarazm and Qara-Khitai (now Turkmenistan and southeastern Kazakhstan). The three constantly intrigued and skirmished among themselves, but shared a disregard for the wider world, and the technical advances that were giving that world far greater power to invade them, and also radically new interests in their region's economic potential. These areas all had a literate tradition still based on Persian as always, maintaining a sense of common culture with the greater Islamic world, although the parallel use of Chagatay gave a distinctive character to Central Asia as such.*

The power that was to take possession of them all was Russia, which steadily expanded its territory, largely through settlement, across the steppes of what is now Kazakhstan in the century from 1760. Military campaigns

---

* Although Uzbek and Tajik are very different languages, showing their respective Turkic and Iranian origins, they have converged over the centuries of bilingualism. Their repertoires of speech sounds, for example, are now almost identical. Uzbek has lost vowel harmony, elsewhere a general characteristic of Turkic languages, whereas Tajik syntax has in many cases been changed to mirror Uzbek. For example, in questions, it has adopted the interrogative particle *mi*, as in the common phrase *Mumkin mi?* "Is it permitted?"

were fought in the 1820s and 1840s to suppress the armed resistance of Ka-
zakh hordes, the main obstacle to Russia's control of the steppes. This stage
of combined settlement and military invasion ended with the storming of
Tashkent in 1865. A rapid series of military campaigns in the following decade to 1876 gained control of all the significant centers of population in
Central Asia too (although Bukhara and Khiva were left under their rulers,
as protectorates with reduced territories). The last areas of resistance were
crushed with the bloody battle of Göktepe in 1881, and the conquest of Merv
in 1884. Any last problems with this unilateral advance of Russia's borders,
caused by British concern about their full extent (and notably their impact on
the buffer state of Afghanistan), were resolved diplomatically in 1895.

The whole area of Central Asia, outside the two protectorates, was now
reconstituted as the Governorate-General of Turkestan (Туркестанское
Генерал-Губернаторство). This advent of Russian language, and Cyrillic script—itself a remote trace of Russia's long-past conversion by Greek
Orthodox missionaries—indicates that something very different indeed was
now at large in Central Asia, which had for fifteen hundred years only
known Iranian, Turkic, and Mongolian languages, and the descendants of
scripts Sogdian, Indic, Arabic, or Chinese. It also symbolizes the flow of
Slavic immigrants from the northwest, which was to permanently change
the demographics of the region. The proportion of Europeans in the area
grew rapidly and massively, from 20 percent to 1887, to 40 percent in 1911,
and 47 percent in 1939, after which it stabilized.[20] It would be governed
from Tashkent, medieval Chach, a previously obscure center that had never
before aspired to equal the fabled cities of Merv, Bukhara, or Samarkand.

This sudden appropriation of every state in the region, followed by a new
flow of immigration, was very different from the changes mediated by the
British in India over the previous century. The British had initially inveigled
themselves into political and financial control of Bengal, and to domination
of princely states such as Hyderabad. Military force had certainly been used
in many other areas, but British government in India had established itself
through a series of coerced deals with existing authorities. It remained concerned to avoid any changes that would needlessly disturb Indian sensibili-
ties, not least because they would be harmful to trade, and also because the
British were conscious that their hold on Indian loyalties was precarious.
They had continued to use traditional languages on the precautionary principle, and indeed beyond necessity. When a British captain had written in 1863
what now seems eerily farsighted, "If sufficient encouragement be afforded,

English will soon take the place that formerly belonged to Persian . . . It is my belief that English will become in time, what Persian never has been, the commercial language of the country," the lieutenant governor slapped him down, reasserting the need to keep the examinations in Persian.[21] The British might be moving India forward by their own lights, but they needed to conciliate the vast majority of the native population to the new, reformed structures they were evolving. The removal of Persian was part of this, but in the British manner, outward radicalism was eschewed.

By contrast, the forceful imposition of Russian power in Central Asia was in no sense a negotiation or a conciliation. Nevertheless, as far as Central Asian society and its languages were concerned, it was nonintrusive: there was no interference in the prime linguistic fields of religion, education, administration, or the courts. Russians established their own quarter of Tashkent. The motive for this neglect was not benign. For example, Governor-General von Kaufman's stated philosophy toward the schools was "That means—ignoring them. Without any sort of government protection, freed of all supervision and direction, deprived of all means of compelling parents to send children to it, the Moslem school is in an entirely new position under Russian dominion, unfavourable for it, but extremely advantageous for us."[22]

Nonetheless, under the governorate-general, the main adverse influences were not on the lingua-francas, Persian and Chagatay, but on the vernacular languages—because of the steady turnover of population, in response to Russian immigration and settlement; forced reorganization of agriculture to cotton monoculture (especially in the Ferghana valley), thus decreasing the availability of staple food crops; and uprisings, military suppression, and massacre, starvation, or resulting flight by many (up to 17 percent)[23] of the native people, whom (alone in the Russians' empire) the Russians termed *inorodcy* 'aliens'.

Although little Russian education was in effect offered to the native population, some reform movements did begin. Most important was the *usūl-i-jadīd* 'new method', also called the Jadidists, which emanated from other Muslim parts of Russia (Tatarstan and the Crimea). Their main explicit concern was to introduce more modern school methods, e.g., desks, blackboards, and maps, and the use of printed books from Muslim cities outside the empire. Modernizing tendencies, even such apparently innocuous ones, were suspect to the Russian authorities, who feared any hint of cross-border Muslim or Turkic sentiment and were happier if the traditional cultures maintained their backward-looking, hence powerless, ways.

A notable figure was Abdurrauf Fitrat (1886–1938), from Bukhara, a young man trained in Istanbul, who wrote his classic tract *Munāzarah* (Arabic for 'Dispute') in Persian, before distinguishing himself as a promoter of literature in Chagatay. Another such was the poet and novelist Sadriddin Ayni (1878–1954), author of Tajik's first novel, *Dokhunda* 'The Mountain Villager': like Fitrat, he was bilingual in Uzbek and Tajik (as the local versions of Chagatay and Persian were reidentified in the Soviet era). Such Central Asians, at ease in both their traditional lingua-francas and Russian, ultimately were the cultural leaders toward their new status under the Soviets.

The role of Persian (like Chagatay) had been under no threat in Russian Turkestan; it could continue its traditional role as a learned lingua-franca, though with a low profile, used by people without political influence. Its undoing came with the Russian Revolution. This might well have led to the exit of the Central Asian provinces from the Union (and hence a continuation—perhaps even promotion—of Persian), but did not. The years of turmoil between 1917 and 1924 benefited no one directly, but did end up preserving Moscow's control of the area. Russian priorities had been changed by the Revolution, and when peace returned, a radically new attempt would be made to articulate the new Soviet republics—now identified as Kazakhstan, Turkmenistan, Uzbekistan, Tajikistan and Kyrgyzstan. Significantly, the borders were assigned on the basis of languages that were presumed, or at least asserted, to be distinct.

The early attempt to work toward communism was in some ways idealistic, aiming to bring the different peoples of the old Russian Empire, now the Soviet Union, into a common progressive socialism. This involved the active spread of literacy, and on any reckoning this was a great triumph of Soviet policy, probably in fact its greatest human achievement. It occurred all over the Union, but especially in the states of Central Asia. There, literacy rates soared, from figures that had been under 10 percent in the Tsarist Empire, with great variation among regions and languages, to double by 1926. Roman script was introduced to replace Perso-Arabic script for all Turkic languages in 1926, with Tajik itself following by 1928, and this of course set the new literates back almost to zero. Yet by 1939, rates were well over 60 percent everywhere, even in the remotest and most backward areas. A further disruption occurred at the end of the 1930s when a new alphabet reform did away with most Roman scripts and replaced them with Cyrillic—i.e. Russian. Nevertheless, by 1959 literacy throughout the Union was close to 100 percent.

But rolling out a written language—especially if this is combined, as it was here, with the imposition of a new alphabet (Roman till 1939, then Cyrillic)—requires standardization. Textbooks are mass-produced products, as all literature has been since the introduction of printing, and spellings have to be fixed. Once languages are written down, small differences become prominent; more differences may be added as quirks of a spelling system. In the Soviet case, these were emphasized as the characteristic features of different languages, and hence of different nations. Given the turmoil of tribal rivalries in medieval Turkic history, there was some reason to distinguish different nations, e.g., Kazakh-Kyrgyz, as against Turkmen; the Irano-Turkic cultural mélange of Tajik and Uzbek, which dominated the center of Central Asia, made up a third proto-"language." But more important, the Soviet government had every political reason to discourage any perception of common Turkic identity.

This identification of territories by language, which occurred in the early 1920s, was alien to the ancestral customs of the Middle East, which had always been more inclined to use religious affiliation as the identifier of distinct communities. It did conform with the doctrines of nationalism, which had swept through much of Europe in the nineteenth century, and were to be projected onto the rest of the world in the twentieth. Such doctrines naturally discounted a lingua-franca that was employed over a multi-ethnic region, as Persian had been since the Turks took it up in the eleventh century. However, not all features of Soviet policy were consistent with this: even if ethnolinguistic self-determination was approved in principle, the overriding imperative was for Russian to remain the first official language in every constituent republic or district of the Union.

Persian, then, was the big loser from the new dispensation.* Persian had now to be a national language, or nothing at all; and the Tajik nation was carved out of two areas that had remained of predominantly Iranian speech, the valley of the Zarafshan, which had once been the center of Sogd, and the Pamir mountains to the south. These were pulled together as Tajikistan, but once again some political calculation to prevent a dangerous unity trumped linguistic accuracy: Bukhara and Samarkand, the great urban centers of Persian language were excluded and, on the first cut, in 1925, placed in Uzbekistan. Khojand (not to be confused with Khoqand, farther

---

* Chagatay was a loser too, as far as it transcended the different regional variants of Turkic. Nevertheless, Uzbeks were encouraged to view it as "Old Uzbek," thus giving them the right to appropriate historically the literary canon of the language.

east) was at first likewise made part of Uzbekistan, but then in 1929 was as-signed to Tajikistan—though along with it came much of the Ferghana val-ley, now heavily Uzbek in population and language. In the Pamir region, the vernacular languages were East Iranian, rather than Persian; but at least the universal lingua-franca there is Tojiki—as the local brand of Persian, now universally written in Cyrillic script, has been dubbed for the last century.

This dispensation was an interesting curiosity as long as the Soviet Union survived, since the different areas of vernacular Persian in Central Asia were at least parts of the same, apparently strong and unified, state. When the Union was dissolved in 1991 (for reasons that had little to do with the region, though they included the failed war that was waged during the 1980s in neighboring Afghanistan), the borders suddenly became hard to cross, and separation between different pockets of the Persian-speaking commu-nity may—in the medium term—lead to the kind of fragmentation that we have recognized as a possible long-term threat to a widespread language (page 62). The three distinct states that now recognize Persian as an official language (Iran, Tajikistan, and Afghanistan—where it shares the honors with Pashtu) suffer culturally from being officially and in practice cut off from Bukhara and Samarkand, the original centers of growth for Persian as a prestige lingua-franca.

The fate of Persian, then, has been adverse under both the British and the Russian empires. Both effectively removed it as a lingua-franca, to make way for local vernaculars, though these were simultaneously being promoted as potential official languages in their own right: Hindi/Urdu in India, and various varieties of Turkic in Central Asia. The British did it with an official Relegation of Persian, the Russians by simply disregarding Persian's special role altogether. Although local vernaculars were being preferred, and being developed through education for widespread public use, the unspoken prem-ise in both cases was that the true lingua-franca of the future—for the ruling elite—was the imperial power's own language, English or Russian.

A first thought, in generalizing this, might be that imperial powers do not readily tolerate an alien language as a lingua-franca within their do-mains. But this is better seen as a coincidence than stored up as a conclu-sion. Where the will is there, an alien lingua-franca can indefinitely be maintained. What about Latin's long cohabitation with Greek, after all, in four early centuries of the Roman empire (say, 100 BC to 300 AD), as well as Quechua's somewhat shorter partnership with Aymara under the Incas (1400–1520)? What about the instrumental use of Malay for three hundred years of Dutch rule in Indonesia (1650–1950)? In fact, to accept such a conclusion would even disregard Iran's own happy pragmatism, the exploitation of Aramaic for long-distance imperial communications under the Achaemenians and after (at least 600–300 BC), without a thought for the wider use of their native Persian.

What these two recent cases of the removal of Persian do demonstrate is that an alien ruling government, if it is unsympathetic, does have the power to summarily terminate a lingua-franca, and even one that retains considerable cultural support among its speakers. It can be done at the stroke of a pen because a lingua-franca requires a coordinated structure of official bodies and educational institutions to survive. This vulnerability to executive action, this dependence on continued official support, is one thing that distinguishes a lingua-franca from a mother tongue.

CHAPTER 9

Resignation

Each Morn a thousand Roses brings, you say:
Yes, but where leaves the Rose of Yesterday?
And this first Summer month that brings the Rose
Shall take Jamshyd and Kaikobad away.

Well, let it take them! What have we to do
With Kaikobad the Great, or Kaikhosru?
Let Zal and Rustum bluster as they will,
Or Hatim call to Supper—heed not you.

—Edward Fitzgerald,
*The Ruba'iyat of Omar Khayyám* (4th ed.)

Finally, we can consider situations where the loss of a lingua-franca is due to Resignation. This usually comes about through social reformation, change in society that leads to the disempowerment of a dominant elite of some kind, and with it the lingua-franca that had marked them out. The linguistic decline is not the direct effect of an economic shift or brought about by political enforcement, although either of those forces may have triggered the social transformation that unseats the lingua-franca. Other forces too may trigger the change, such as a military conquest, a technical revolution, or something as diffuse in society as the "reformation" that gripped Europe in the sixteenth century. The essential common feature is that a class of society just fades away, and with it its distinctive means of communication.

This was the kind of change that did away with the Sogdian language, which was spoken for most of the first millennium AD in a diaspora of merchant communities, spreading from its historic roots in Sogd eastward across Central Asia and northern China. Although the Sogdians' Asiatic trading network had been weakened by the catastrophic conquest and occupation of their home base by Muslims in 712–22, then further weakened by the 755–57 rebellion that shook the entire Tang dynasty in China, such a deep-seated fixture as Sogdian enterprise abroad withstood the shaking, for a time. For another century Sogdians continued to be active in military circles in Baghdad, and then also, far to the east, they reached their pinnacle of influence with the Uyghurs.[1] Everywhere they were seen as useful intermediaries for trade with China, and their settlements there remained, especially in the north loop of the Yellow River, the Ordos, where they were so dense that Chinese called the area *hú yuàn* 胡苑 'the Hu Park'.[2]

But with Muslims and then Uyghurs apparently resisting Chinese policies with impunity, China lost confidence and began to be distrustful of foreign influences. In 840, when the Kyrgyz tribes conveniently (for the Chinese) overthrew the vast Uyghur Empire, China's Tang government acted to assert home values. In 843–45, it organized religious persecutions not only against Manichaeans (coreligionists of Uyghurs), but also Christians and Buddhists, a xenophobic purge that only the tradition with the deepest and oldest roots, i.e. Buddhism, seems to have survived. Tellingly, perhaps, of this trio, only Buddhism had roots that went back before Sogdian influence on China.

Somewhat later, in 878, a massive rebellion (led by an obscure figure, Huang Chao) sacked Canton, with slaughter of its foreign trading community. How many Sogdians were among the 120,000 Muslims, Jews, Christians, and Zoroastrians who are said to have been killed is not known, but it would have dealt a massive blow to trade for generations. As noted above, since the seventh-century rise of the Muslim Caliphate in the west, the Sogdians had in any case been losing ground as traders to the Persians. The Sogdians were constrained to lower their profile and, by the tenth century, were ceasing to be a distinctive community abroad; this is when we find the last evidence for use of their language outside Sogd.

The power structures of the Tang (618–906), the Chinese dynasty that had had most to do with the Sogdians over the centuries, never really recovered after the Huang Chao rebellion, and it collapsed in the following generation. The stance of Chinese diplomacy, and its sense of its own center, also moved east; the western regions, seeming less profitable or perhaps (after a brief respite, from the fall of the Uyghurs) more dangerous, were increasingly ignored. One telling sign of this new orientation is the Chinese government's choice of location. From 907 the capital was no longer in the west (usually Luoyang or Chang'an), but was located in more easterly cities (Kaifeng, Nanjing, or Beijing).[3]

The established communities of expatriate Sogdians do not seem to have been expelled; rather, they were assimilated into Chinese society. Closer to home, in Sogd and its neighboring areas, they merged with Turks. A letter in Turkic for an Uyghur prince from the early eleventh century is a petition about two Sogdian prisoners and refers to something written in Sogdian being accepted as understood. This transaction is believed to relate to the area between Turfan and the Tienshan mountains, beyond the eastern edge of Sogdiana. In the late eleventh century, Mahmud al-Kashgari mentions that at Balasagun, Talas and Isfijab (on its northern extremes, in the territory of modern Kyrgyzstan) people were still bilingual in Sogdian and Turkic.[4] But the language may have lingered on until the seventeenth century in parts of Sogdiana, from Samarkand and the Zarafshan valley to the Ferghana valley farther north. Some evidence suggests that it was still spoken in the sixteenth century in rural areas round Bukhara.[5] The only place where the language (or its close relative) survived until the twentieth century was in the inaccessible valley of the Yaghnob, a southern tributary of the Zarafshan. This is a part of the original homeland of Sogdian, so only the stay-at-home farmers' language ultimately lasted, and that as an unassuming mother tongue, no part of the vast and culturally influential Sogdian diaspora.

✦

Sogdian, then, died away in the late first millennium, along with the special role of Sogdian expatriate communities. Another disappearance that led to the demise of a lingua-franca happened much more suddenly, much more recently, and indeed for the Western world, much closer to hand. This is the eclipse of German as a language for research in the world's scientific community.

In most of Europe Latin had remained the language of academia throughout the eighteenth century, a single *respublica litteraria* for the whole continent. But German was widely used as a lingua-franca among the different central-European polities, and at last in the early nineteenth century German academics began to follow the early example set by France and

England, where scholars had largely gone over to the vernacular in the seventeenth century.* The early nineteenth century was precisely the period of German nationalism, which arose after the dissolution of the Holy Roman Empire in 1806 and culminated in the unification of Germany under Prussia, finally declared in 1871. The prowess of the German universities was such that German speedily became an important language for serious scholars in universities throughout Europe, especially so in the physical and life sciences. Some reckon it to have been preeminent in the nineteenth century, as for example the biologist Theodore Savory: "It was true to say that the language of science was the language of Heidelberg and Göttingen."[6] Up to 1914 German periodicals provided the authoritative abstracting services in biology and medicine, making German the essential interlingua of international research. The Japanese, in particular, tended to choose German as their lingua-franca for science publishing, and articles in Japanese or Russian would often appear with abstracts in German.[7]

Nevertheless, in reality the languages of major European powers still shared the honors of the development of science at the turn of the century. The chart shows that in the last decade of the nineteenth century, published work in the natural sciences was still split pretty evenly between English (35 percent), French (28 percent), and German (23 percent). It also shows that whereas French has since consistently declined, German's share actually grew to be greater than that of English for the first two decades of the twentieth century, before it fell back precipitately thereafter (though never falling quite as low as French).

The initial high (and rising) position of German as a principal language of science was due to the intrinsic excellence of intellectual focus among the German-speaking nations of central Europe in the nineteenth and early twentieth centuries. In 1925, when the Technion, Israel's Institute of Technology, was being founded, it was unsuccessfully urged by the Ezra Society, of Berlin, that its teaching should be given in German, on the then plausible ground that *"es gibt keine Wissenschaft ohne die deutsche Sprache"* (there is no science without German).[8] German-speaking scientists then dominated

---

* Christian Thomasius, a jurist at Leipzig, had dared in 1687 to try lecturing in German, his talk entitled "How One Should Emulate the French Way of Life." But his scandalous precedent was not widely followed for over a century. Among the three academies of science established in Germany in the eighteenth century, Göttingen used Latin, Berlin Latin and then French, while Munich used German from its foundation in 1759. (Kretzenbacher 2004)

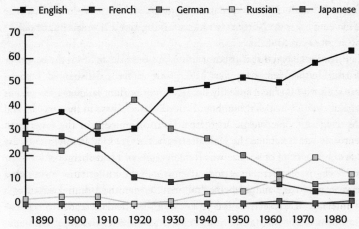

*Language percent shares of publications in the Natural Sciences (1890–1980).*
*(Credit: Based on a chart in* Deutsch als Wissenschaftssprache: die Entwicklung
im 20. Jahrhundert, und die Zukunftsperspektive *by Ulrich Ammon,*
*1999, Berlin: De Gruyter Publishing)*

physics, chemistry, biology, medicine, and psychology as well as mathematics and much of the humanities. In this era Germany was also at the center of innovation in science-based engineering, founding and developing companies such as Siemens, Bosch, Thyssen-Krupp, Bayer, Hoechst, BASF, Mercedes-Benz, and BMW. Unsurprisingly, given the eminence of the German-language universities, it had been common during the nineteenth and early twentieth centuries for scientists from all over the world to go there for their higher training. In the 1930s this practice trailed off; and it never recovered after World War II.[9] In this period, German simply ceased to be a contender as a medium for world science.

This dying fall in its career can be explained in terms of global politics, especially the evolving balance with the English-speaking USA, the other dominant center of innovation in the sciences.* Otto von Bismarck, the

---

* The U.S. population was being increased massively through immigration from Europe, not least the very central-European areas where German was spoken. From 1820 to 1998, of the 65 million immigrants to the USA who came from Europe, 7.2 million were from Germany and some 2.2 million from German-speaking parts of Austria-Hungary, a total comparable with the English-speaking immigrants, 5.2 million from the United Kingdom, and 4.8 million from Ireland, and dwarfing the million or so from France and Belgium.

former German chancellor, remarked portentously in 1898 (in the last year of his long life) that North America's speaking English would be the defining event of his time.

This reversal had three (distantly related) causes. The first was the hangover of anti-German sentiment that had grown in the English- and French-speaking worlds (and especially the USA) at the time of World War I, extending even to the public burning of some libraries' German-language books. This lingering discrimination against German could probably have been overcome had it not been for the catastrophe that hit German politics in the 1930s. This second cause was the Nazi government's persecution of Jews (an enormous proportion of German scientists),[10] who were thus encouraged (at first to salvage their prospects, and soon for very survival) to emigrate and so pursue their academic careers in English. The third cause, which ensured no return to the centrality of German, was the overwhelming economic power of the English-speaking USA. It offered much greater availability of academic employment and research funding than in Germany or Austria (or anywhere else in the world) during the second half of the century.*

The second of these causes was crucial, and also the most sudden, and totally self-inflicted by the German state, which chose to see the Jews, a clearly identified subgroup who had been remarkable for their leadership and distinction among the country's intellectuals, as somehow the cause of German woes. After Hitler came to power in 1933, fully one third of Germany's forty-five hundred active professors were summarily dismissed; most of these victims were Jewish. Crucially, after 1933, three hundred thousand emigrated from Germany, again mostly Jews. Almost 10 percent of these were scientists, academics, or professionals.

Not all of these went to the USA: at least fifty thousand of them went to Palestine, and many too went to the United Kingdom. But their numbers dominated the 528,000 immigrants accepted by the USA in 1931–40. In most of the destinations where they would find academic or professional employment, they would henceforth be working in English, rather than German. The heart also went out of the German scientists left behind. David Hilbert (1862–1943), the doyen of German (and world) mathematics

---

* Academic talents recognized in East Germany would naturally be likely to pursue their studies under the auspices of the other superpower, thus adding not to German- but to Russian-language science. As the chart also shows, Russian made a notable surge after 1940 to become the second language of the natural sciences by the 1960s.

in the early twentieth century, told Bernhard Rust, the Nazi minister of science, education, and national culture, that now, without "Jewish influence," there was really no more mathematics at his university. In a similar anecdote, Otto Hahn, who later won the Nobel Prize for physical chemistry, once told Hitler that the expulsion of the Jews had not so much damaged German science as annihilated it.[11]

These causes—which have more to do with prejudice, fear, and comparative advantage than hardheaded judgments about the validity and energy, or indeed potential profitability, of the research tradition in German—were capable of undoing the world reputation of the German language as an indispensable source of scientific benefits. However true the warning by German Nobel Prize winners that "the majority of important German scientific works are neither translated into English in their entirety nor in the form of comprehensive digests," the pressure to drop the courses that would have made German accessible to foreign students grew steadily, and it became irresistible between the 1960s and 1980s.[12] The survival of a lingua-franca is always a matter of confidence and ideology as much as reasoned calculation. Any benefits its use may proudly offer, however truly and objectively, can be ignored into nonexistence.

Once foreign scientists stopped learning German, a generation of those who were best able to work within it undoubtedly suffered a loss, and many of their insights may have failed to get their due recognition. But afterward the language indeed had little to offer to the global research community, since even German speakers themselves have chosen to accept English as the lingua-franca of the natural sciences. This viewpoint is now beyond debate in Germany and enforced in a highly coercive fashion. Currently, government research funding within Germany is dependent on a procedure known as the *Exzellenzwettbewerb*, the 'competition in excellence'. Within this there is a premium for academic departments to submit their applications in faultless English. Science moves on then, in English, and seemingly without a sense of irony.

German for the sciences is another example where a distinct social set has been dissolved, and with it the appointed use of its lingua-franca. In this case, the social set was the self-selected community of academics and engineers in central Europe, who for the duration of the nineteenth century had been accepted as occupying the pinnacle of the world's intellectual life. Because of adverse political developments in the twentieth century, confidence in the language community's value was shattered, not through any fault in the community itself. German (and Austrian) state militarism alienated a wide range of opinion outside in the powerful French- and English-speaking worlds, while the socially destructive internal policies practiced by the Nazi Party in the 1930s severely weakened and scattered the community itself. A house facing opposition within and without cannot stand, and the German-language academic community, despite a reputation for innovation and successful development that was as good as the best anywhere, duly fell.

∞∞∞

In chapter 4 we considered the establishment of Persian in India, serving as court language for an extended series of Turkic conquerors, led off by Maḥmūd of Ghazni, who lived 971–1030 and first raided India (Peshawar) in 1001. This conquest of a new realm for Persian had an implication for another language, Sanskrit. Sanskrit had a background of at least fifteen hundred years as the common lingua-franca of north India. But now, for the first time after a number of major conquests coming from that northwestern quarter (Śaka, Kushana, Huna) down the centuries (first BC to sixth AD), India was beset by a force sufficiently determined to wish to rule on its own terms. The *turuška* 'Turks' would preserve their own religion, Islam, and their own lingua-franca, Persian. The political primacy of Sanskrit was ended at once, whether native princes recognized it or not. As time wore on, the overall scope for its use shrank under the influence of Persian, the new language whose use was percolating down as more and more Indians were recruited by the ruling princedoms and their military following into the hierarchy of offices that they gradually developed.

With Maḥmūd, as historical luck would have it, traveled one of the most brilliant men ever produced by the Muslim world, Abū Rayḥān Muḥammad ibn Aḥmad Bīrūnī, generally known as al-Biruni. He was born in Khwarazm, and we have already mentioned his testimony (page 87) on the sufferings of that region (and possible decline of its language) in the early Muslim conquests. Al-Biruni lived from 973 to 1048, and in this long life he is said to have written 146 books, essentially covering the whole range of knowledge. One of these was an extended study of India, arguably the world's first work of anthropology, and this has survived in its entirety, made particularly fascinating because of its depth, but also because of its key position in the first generation of Turkic irruptions into India.

The detail of his account, together with the copious recording of technical terms, makes it evident that al-Biruni learned Sanskrit—adding it to his lifetime score of Arabic, Persian, Hebrew, Syriac, and Greek—and studied with Indian masters, earning the nickname *Vidyāsagara* 'ocean of knowledge'. His overall view of the Indians, and the first point in his book, was that "they differ from us in everything which other nations have in common. And here we first mention language . . ." He thought it quite natural that the Indians all accepted a single lingua-franca, though was struck that this was neither Persian nor Arabic. "If you want to conquer this difficulty [i.e. to learn Sanskrit] you will not find it easy, because the language is of an enormous range, both in words and in inflexions, something like Arabic . . . The language is divided into a neglected vernacular one [presumably Old Gujarati] and a classical one [Sanskrit], only in use among the upper and educated classes, which is much cultivated, and subject to the rules of grammatical inflexion and etymology, and to all the niceties of grammar and rhetoric."*[13]

Al-Biruni's second point of "total difference" that distinguished the Indians was religion, "as we believe in nothing in which they believe, and vice versa." He was less struck by their attachment to particular doctrines than by their total rejection of anything alien as impure—*mleccha*.[14] Al-Biruni was in no sense a bigot, but his patron Maḥmūd has gone down in history for his desecration of the Hindu temple at Somanāth (on the coast of Gujarat) in 1026, a deed that was lauded in Turko-Persian chronicles, such as by the poet Farrūkhi Sīstāni, because the idol broken there was identified as the goddess Manat (identified in the Persian spelling of *Somanāth* as Su-manat), a pre-Islamic goddess whose idol Muhammad had explicitly identified,[15] and a deed that was subsequently—in 1842!—made into a cause célèbre by the British Lord Ellenborough, who proposed to retrieve the gates of the temple from Ghazni (and so salvage a little honor from his lackluster invasion of Afghanistan).[16]

This religious difference between invading Muslims and resident Hindus has subsequently become a red-rag issue among historians of India, turning

---

* Al-Biruni expands on the sources of difficulty, mentioning the context dependence of the meaning of words, the use of non-Arabic-Persian sounds, slapdash scribal practices, complex consonant clusters (especially at the beginning of words), and the fact that most literature is made obscure by being in verse. These are all perfectly valid as analysis of Sanskrit, as seen from an academic Arabic perspective.

on whether the fundamental divide between the two religions was recognized at the time or rather became salient as a result of British imperial theorizing in the nineteenth century. It is certainly surprising (pace al-Biruni) how little the Sanskrit references to these invaders focus on their religion, referring to them as *tājika* 'Tajik', *turuška* 'Turk', *mleccha* 'barbarian', *pārasīka* 'Persian', *yavana* (Greek 'Ionian'), *hammīra* 'Amir', and *śaka* 'Scythian'; anything but *musalamāna* 'Muslim', a term that is only used once, after two centuries had passed from the first encounters, in 1246. This is in the Veraval inscription (from the very Somanāth area raided by Maḥmūd), in a Sanskrit that is stuffed with loanwords from Arabic and is a legal appropriation of land to build a mosque in the area, for a merchant sea-captain (*nākhū* 'nacoder') from Hormuz.[17] (Veraval/Somanāth was an established port for the Indian Ocean trade and had long been familiar with Muslim merchants before Maḥmūd arrived overland on a ghazi raid to shatter its temple, and possibly also—combining business with pious bellicosity—to disrupt its competitive trade in Arab horses.)[18] Another Somanath inscription (also written in Sanskrit, from the fourteenth century) is a memorial to one Vohara Farīd, a Muslim who actually died fighting to protect the town from Turks.[19]

All this shows that the use of Sanskrit for practical, nonreligious purposes continued for some centuries after Muslim Turks had begun to establish their sultanates in northern India, and that Islam, at least as practiced among the settled population, was not necessarily seen as totally beyond the pale of traditional Hindu civilization, as expressed in Sanskrit. Indeed Maḥmūd himself, in 1027, had a dirham struck at Lahore with a (heretical?) version of the Muslim *šahāda* in Sanskrit:

> *avyaktam eka muhammada avatāra nṛpati mahamuda*
>
> The Unmanifest (is) one; Muhammad (is its) incarnation;
>    king (is) Mahmud

And at least two later sultans, Ghiyāsuddīn Balban (r. 1266–86) and Alāuddīn Khilji (r. 1295–1315), were made subjects for that formal Sanskrit eulogy poem, called the *praśasti*.[20]

Sanskrit was not lost or forgotten. Yet as the domains of the *turuška* princes expanded, with their Muslim cultural self-confidence, Sanskrit was increasingly contested as the language of high-level discourse in northern and central India. More and more, it had to yield to Arabic and (later) to Persian as the medium for court culture, and administrative pronouncements. This is evident from the record of surviving inscriptions. Sanskrit had two centuries of grace under the first Muslim rulers, but then Arabic inscriptions begin, at Delhi, in the last decade of the twelfth century, during the interregnum of struggle between Ghaznavids and Ghurids, and continue for a century. Thereafter, with the accession of the Khalji dynasty at the close of the thirteenth century, Persian took over as the language for public inscriptions. Arabic still coexisted with Persian in administrative records, until the Mughal takeover in the sixteenth century; then Arabic drops out.[21] As so often, language change lags behind political change (especially in the written sphere), but in the end the language of the court prevails. By the sixteenth century, Sanskrit was once again firmly felt to be, in essence, a language for Hindu devotional uses, a restricted status that it had not known since the first century AD.

Akbar was the great secularizer of Persian (and hence, in effect, underminer of Sanskrit). During his reign (1556-1605) and at his command, Hindu legends were translated into Persian (as was the Bible). Hindus had started learning Persian under Sikander Lodhi (1489–1517), he being a Muslim notorious for his intolerance of Hindu faith. But it was in Akbar's reign that it became possible for them then to go on to use it as functionaries of the state. Todar Mal, an upper-caste Hindu was one such, who progressed to become Akbar's minister of finance from 1560 to 1586 and actually discontinued all accounting in Hindi, in favor of a Persian-only rule.* Nevertheless, Persian remained restricted to the power elite; in this, it has been compared to the later use of English in nineteenth-century India.[22]

As Persian rose, Sanskrit's breadth of use contracted, and its pundits had to reconcile themselves to a kingdom that was less and less of this world. At the same time, Sanskrit was losing other functions as the vernacular languages in the far-flung Sanskrit realm were also increasing in prestige. All over India, in the first half of the second millennium, vernacular languages were more and more accepted as the media for written literature, constricting another of Sanskrit's functions. This process began in the south (as well

---

* Hindus writing in Persian even accepted some of its Islamic stylistic tics, beginning with an Arabic flourish, *b-ismi-llah* 'in the name of God', and perhaps a religious verse, a *ḥamd* or a *na'at*, praising God or the Prophet. Hinduism was, of course, always more relaxed than Islam about others' gods.

as in distant Java and Tibet), where the major indigenous languages (Kannada, Tamil, Malayalam, Telugu, Javanese, Tibetan) were quite unrelated to Sanskrit (as well as more likely to be spoken in areas under non-Muslim rule).* But by the thirteenth century the process had been taken up even in the Sanskrit heartland of north India.

The reason for this rise of the vernaculars is a matter for speculation,[23] but was clearly widespread. Early on, vernacular compositions were classed as "song," essentially oral, musical, informal (e.g., most anciently, when set down as *gīta-vinoda* 'song-entertainment' in King Someśvara III's royal [Sanskrit] encyclopedia, the *Mānasollāsa*, of 1131, from Karnataka in southern India). In some places (especially in northern India), the presence of the Muslim elite themselves may have hastened it, whether through Sufi missionaries' innovative use of vernaculars in their preaching, or through the creatively playful compositions of court poets of the Delhi Sultanate.

Whatever the several origins, the rise of the vernaculars, like the development of a Persianate bureaucracy, clearly involved the cultural demotion of the Sanskrit-using class par excellence, the caste of Brahmans. Legends grew up in the sixteenth and seventeenth centuries that expressed this in tales of Brahmans' attempts to foil the circulation of works by particularly successful vernacular poets (e.g., Tukarām and Eknāth, who wrote in Marathi; Nanddās in Braj Hindi; Kṛṣṇadāsa in Bengali). In these, the Brahmans threw the offending texts into their local river (Indrayani, Ganga, Yamuna, Ganga again) to destroy them, but the works miraculously resurfaced unharmed. In an ironic Telugu reversal, the high-caste poet Srinathudu, famed for his sensuality, was in punishment cursed that his epic work (in Telugu, the *Palnāṭi-vira-bhāgavatamu* 'Exploits of the Heroes of Palnāḍu') would fall into the hands of untouchables. He tried throwing it into the river to escape such a dread outcome, but the book was annoyingly retrieved by low-caste men. Ouch.[24]

The origin of vernacularism is widely and traditionally understood in India as having been a kind of revolt against the ancient dominance of the Brahman elite in religion, and in society at large.[25] Sir George Grierson,

---

* There is an interesting parallel here with what happened at about the same time in Europe. There too languages without a direct relation to Latin (principally, English, Welsh, Gaelic, High German, Saxon) all initiated vernacular literary traditions before the Romance languages. This may have been because speakers of those Romance "dialects" felt that Latin remained just the right, traditional—if increasingly distant—way to write them down. See Pollock 2006, 391–92.

the great surveyor of Indian languages, memorably said of Sanskrit, "This sacred language, jealously preserved by the Brahmans in their schools, had all the prestige that religion and learning could give it."[26]

A reading of Patanjali, a grammarian in the second century BC, suggests that, in his day, full competence in Sanskrit was restricted to Brahman males.[27] Sanskrit snobbery does indeed go back a long way, even if for long periods in the first millennium AD it may have been mitigated in an open-minded cosmopolis.[28] The idea of a revolt against this snobbery fits snugly with the idea of Sanskrit's decline as one more instance of a lingua-franca lost to Resignation.

More recently, it has been contended that the clear association of Sanskrit with Brahman possessiveness is a result of the switch to vernaculars rather than a provocation for it, a kind of defensive drawing-in, entirely comparable with the way that the Roman Catholic Church became distinctively associated with Latin after the language was abandoned by a wider republic of letters in Europe.[29] But the two approaches are in fact quite compatible, especially if one accepts the likely dynamics of reaction (by Brahmans) in the face of social change. To neutralize the parallel with the Church's role in the decline of Latin—just as the Brahmans had their early association with Sanskrit—the Catholic Church had (in the second half of the first millennium AD) played a vital role in the spread of Latin across Europe, giving the prime motive for using it until it became useful for secular communication.*

Whatever the precise order of events (which probably differed in the many different language areas), Brahman power declined along with the use of Sanskrit. Language shift (such as the decline in use of a lingua-franca) is a kind of social change and in such events, the power relations between elites are susceptible to change. Sanskrit had failed to charm the ruling elites when they became Muslim and simultaneously lost ground all

---

* Pollock (2006, 423ff) takes issue with the traditional view in a further way, arguing that the switch to the vernacular was led by the existing ruling class and was not somehow an effervescence of popular sentiment (identified with *bhakti* devotional religious cults). But in the north of India, the real ruling class used Persian, not Sanskrit, even if they also experimented with literary composition in Indian vernaculars. So Sanskrit could have faced vernacular pressure on two fronts, from amateur poets in the ruling class, and *bhakti* devotionalists in the masses. It is irrelevant to my point who initiated the change: whoever or whatever led to the new roles for vernacular languages, Sanskrit's role was diminished, and there would inevitably have been social losers by this, most of them Brahmans.

over its domain because people's mother tongues increasingly replaced Sanskrit in its formal and written uses. So Sanskrit went down, resigning before two kinds of rivals: competing lingua-francas, invading from the north (Arabic, and above all Persian); and encroaching mother tongues, being promoted from the lower orders.

∞≈∞

Latin's later history is complex. It had survived the fragmentation of the vernaculars of western Europe, which occurred in the second half of the first millennium AD, and which gave recognition to the different regional varieties of spoken "vulgar" Latin as distinct languages. Gradually they had come to be used as written languages too, inevitably more accessible to their speakers than traditional Latin. To remain an unchanged written code while its "daughters" changed from generation to generation on the lips of their speakers, Latin relied on transmission through the school system; its grammar, codified first by Donatus (in the mid-fourth century) and then more fully by Priscian (at the close of the fifth), lasted and caused the Latin that was written (and to a large extent spoken) for the next thousand years to be a passable equivalent of the educated style of language known to Cicero in the first century BC. This language was not only learned at school: it was then actively used for almost all serious writing and recording undertaken in western and central Europe over the millennium and a half from AD 1. The only exceptions to its monopoly of written materials were popular writing, which increasingly asserted itself in the tenth and eleventh centuries as "romance" (from *rōmānicē* 'in the language of the Roman Empire'), including love poetry and heroic tales of battle and adventure; and later commerce, in which from the thirteenth century traders—first Italians and then their associates and competitors far and wide—used their own vernaculars to draft contracts and to keep records and accounts. For the rest of the written world, a vast area of activity, Latin continued to reign supreme: Christian liturgy and hymns, clerical administration, law, history, academic disputations and scientific treatises, magic and mysticism, architecture and engineering, encyclopedias. The fact, too, that just one language was so privileged kept Europe as a single academic community.

Nevertheless, even this well-seated language, with eighty generations of unquestioned tradition behind it, could be overthrown or, rather, subverted.

Between 1600 and 1800, Latin simply went away, although the conditions that seemed to have fostered it over preceding aeons had not; indeed, if anything, they seemed to have grown stronger.

Since the Renaissance emanating from Italy in the fifteenth century, Latin grammar was better understood and more explicitly rooted in focused study of the ancient authors who had natively used it (e.g., undertaken by Lorenzo Valla in Italy, and Joseph Scaliger in Paris). The Germans' development of the printing press, which within a generation had spread all round Europe, meant that communications in Latin were easier than ever, and furthermore that the texts on which the whole educational edifice was based were much more effectively standardized by mass production. The whole of Latin literature that had survived from the classical era was soon in print, and now that texts could be duplicated without error, textual criticism could become systematic, best editions could be reconstructed through comparing the various available manuscripts, and the results agreed as standard. In addition, with books becoming cheap, scholars might now be expected to purchase their own copies, and classes could learn from textbooks. Many of the early bestsellers were indeed Latin textbooks. Furthermore, since users of Latin made up the only language community that could be assumed to be 100 percent literate (always having learned the language at school), and since they were distributed throughout Europe except in the Orthodox zone (of east and southeast), Latin would seemingly offer the best language in which to print books, and to produce them in the longest print-runs.

Nonetheless, over the next two centuries Latin wasted and died. Various reasons are proposed for this curious death.

A technical explanation has been given in terms of the economics of the new "print capitalism": on this theory, the markets for vernacular literature simply squeezed out those for Latin books and pamphlets. Vernacular publishing fed a demand created by increasing bourgeois education and had supply costs inevitably lower than for Latin literature, since the different language communities were concentrated in particular cities and regions—indeed nations—rather than spread as a thin elite across the whole of Europe. Increasingly the discourses of Europe were taking place through the new mass-produced print medium, and in this the vernacular languages (especially the large vernaculars, such as French, English, and, a little later, German) had an advantage. Latin was at a disadvantage because it had no substantial domestic market.[30]

But although the bottom lines of publishers' balance sheets* no doubt had their cumulative effect on the availability and relative accessibility of Latin texts, the fundamental motives for the decline in demand for Latin were less technical. The rising nations of Europe in the seventeenth century, above all France in the west, but to a lesser extent Britain too, had early decided to let all their business be conducted in their own vernaculars. In France, this began officially with the Ordinance of Villers-Cotterêts in 1539, requiring all French government documents henceforth to be in French, but French intellectual work was also published exclusively in French from the seventeenth century on. After Descartes (1596–1650) in France, and Thomas Hobbes (1588–1679) in England, Latin was no longer the language of the highest intellectual debates in western Europe. There was a sense that the French, and even the newly assertive British, saw their own capitals, their own political institutions, as their world centers, replacing any ancient nostalgic acceptance of Rome.†

At just this time, European mariners—first Portuguese and Spanish, then French, Dutch, English, and Danish—discovered the vast potential of the world beyond Europe's coastal waters. European settlements sprang up in the illiterate and sparsely populated lands of the Americas, as well as in the highly developed markets of the Indian Ocean, and China beyond. All the captains of these expeditions, as educated men, knew Latin, and the first accounts of their discoveries, by such writers as Peter Martyr, were circulated round Europe in that language. Although the different European nations were in competition to set up these settlements and trading posts, the Catholics among them were explicitly charged by their pope to win souls for Christ on these expeditions, something that would have been unthinkable for them without use of the Latin language, especially if a native priesthood was to be established and educated in the new lands.

Nevertheless, just when Latin—the textually based language par excellence—had finally got its classical texts firmly defined and economically distributed and seemed poised to travel with European venturers as they spread their interests, their faith, and soon their control round the wider

---

\* Actually, in medieval and early modern accounting these were the top lines—literally, in Latin, *summae*—which accounts for the English words *sum* and *summary*.

† There was no similar move in the established great power of the era, Spain. True to this country's engrained conservatism, Spanish universities continued to teach exclusively in Latin until 1813.

world, it began to lose its preemptive dominance. Educated discourse began to be acceptable in vernacular languages, first in the leading powers of the west, France and then England, then in the powers of central Europe, such as the Netherlands, Germany, and Italy, and finally in the peripheral powers of the east and north, such as Austria, Hungary, Poland, and Sweden. The book markets that had sprung up all over the Continent switched during sixteenth and seventeenth centuries from Latin to the various vernaculars. Even in the New World, the printing presses were producing texts in the indigenous languages, which the Spanish missionaries had just succeeded in analyzing and reducing to (Roman) script.

The elite were less and less traditionally educated clerics, and more and more urban bourgeoisie who had had a more practical and vernacular education. As people educated without Latin came to assume greater influence (and the influence of the greatest Latin-using power, the Roman Catholic Church, declined), there was simply less call for skill in Latin. The international contacts that were facilitated by use of Latin as a common language were naturally diminished. But this was less crucial in a new society where separate nation-states dominated in their own interests. The "founder effect," which had transmitted Latin through a good millennium, or forty generations, when it was not close to the vernacular for much of Europe's population, had been undone.

The political and academic self-centeredness in the emerging powers was probably the key fact, but it coincided with a boost of reading in vernacular languages, originally of the Bible and Prayer Book, a surge that had begun in the sixteenth century with the Reformation in northern Europe. The prestige of European powers was rising, even more so as the powers with coasts on the Atlantic began to win themselves empires in faraway continents. Spain, the first great colonial power, was an exception in that it made an effort to project Latin learning (along with the Catholic faith) among its new subjects. But in general it came to be accepted that these empires were not the creatures of Christian Europe as a whole, but of the individual, secular states, each with its own—national—language. The conquests of the sixteenth to nineteenth centuries were achieved not by representatives of Europe's traditional Latin-speaking elite, the courtiers and clerics, but by adventurers, soldiers, and merchants who represented individual Great Powers.

Although they took little or no part in this opening up of the world to European enterprise, the states with less populous (or less politically influential) vernaculars, in central and northern Europe (e.g., Hungarian, Polish,

Swedish) were ultimately forced to follow the example set by the western powers and communicate internationally in some vernacular language. In their case, though, it would always be someone else's mother tongue. Even so, the large realms of Austria-Hungary and Poland-Lithuania were still reliant on Latin not just for cultural communication but even for civil administration until the nineteenth century. Prussia, having annexed much of Poland in 1772, still found Latin indispensable for government there in 1798. In Hungary, the Austrian government failed in its 1790 attempt to replace Latin with German.[31] Intellectually these countries could clearly have made a more effective contribution to the councils of Europe if those councils had continued to be in Latin rather than in other, more partial vernaculars— initially, usually French. The Swedish chancellor Axel Oxenstierna is on record as refusing in 1653 to use French, since he felt its use to be an undeserved honor to the French nation; he found Latin "more honourable and more copious." His protests were in vain, of course.[32]

This decline of Latin, like the retreat of Sanskrit before the advance of courtly Persian in India, is a classic example of the loss of a lingua-franca through the diminishing influence of the elite that had spoken it. But in this case the motive was social and intellectual, rather than the long-term effect of an alien invasion. No one ever abolished Latin in early modern Europe; even in 1687 Sir Isaac Newton still thought it advisable to have his *Principia* published in it. But he was the last major British scientist or philosopher to do so. In a time of great political and intellectual change, Latin had remained firmly associated with tradition and the past. Although its use fell away at different speeds in different places, and in different subjects (German mathematicians such as Gauss, for example, were still using Latin until the mid-nineteenth century), it nowhere survived to develop, or even transmit, the radical new ideas that transformed all the natural and life sciences in the seventeenth to nineteenth centuries.

The decline of Latin coincided, not exactly by chance, with the rise of French. French spread as the fashionable language to use among the elites of Europe in the seventeenth century, current in polite society everywhere in Europe, but especially toward the east—in Sweden, Poland, and Russia. The French literary culture responded by producing its classics of the stage, in the works of the trio Pierre Corneille (1606–84), Jean Racine (1639–99), and

Molière (1622–73). French was also popular in more intellectual circles; tellingly, the great mathematician and philosopher Gottfried Leibniz (1646–1716), although a German and largely resident in German courts, wrote all his major works in French. Its standard was explicitly regulated as from 1635 by L'Académie française, founded on the authority of none other than Cardinal Richelieu at the highest level of the French government, but with a motto that was suitably immodest, if in fact sadly unattainable: *À l'immortalité.*

Richelieu's France even succeeded in imposing French as the accepted language of diplomacy among its northerly neighbors; later, its spread encompassed the east too, beginning with Denmark (1691) and the Holy Roman Empire—viz Germany—(1712), and later spreading to Russia and the Ottoman Empire (1774). French, by now familiar everywhere in upper-class education, had become the de facto standard lingua-franca for European elites, even among France's political adversaries. This status persisted at least until the second decade of the twentieth century.

The decline of French from this height was perceived suddenly, and for its enthusiasts, rather painfully. Its underlying cause was the global advance of English-speaking powers at the expense of French prestige, which had been over 150 years in the making. Although the crux came with the loss of the Seven Years' War between France and Britain (1756–63), for most of the following century and a half the relative advance of English-speaking powers was most evident in Asia and the Americas, far away from Europe. As a result, its first evident symptom did not emerge until the Treaty of Versailles in 1919, when the Allied victors from World War I, who included France, agreed on terms to impose on the defeated Central Powers. For the first time since the Treaty of Rastatt in 1712, in apparent deference to the limited linguistic abilities of the two Anglo-Saxon leaders (Woodrow Wilson of the USA and David Lloyd George of the United Kingdom), an international treaty was agreed with a text other than in French, namely with an additional English version—a small thing seemingly, but in fact a significant crossover point.

As the chart on page 22 shows, the position of French as a second language in European schools declined from 1920 on, crossing English (on its way up) around 1937, and continuing to lose share to it until the present. The actual use of French in Europe has, with a lag, largely followed the pattern of French teaching. Its three-hundred-year-old status in Europe as the principal lingua-franca since the fall of Latin has yielded to English over the twentieth century. Although France has endeavored to maintain a high profile in cultural affairs, particularly in the fields of design and information technology, it has not been able to equal the global influence and scale of investment of the USA (as the leading English-speaking society), especially given France's lackluster performance in World War II. And the USA—with four times its population, and eight times its GDP—is not its sole competitor as a language leader. There are also the United Kingdom and the principal English-language dominions, Canada, South Africa, Australia, and New Zealand, and even India (though English is not its first language). Each of them is a dominant power in its region, making it hard for France to compete on its own throughout the world.

Nevertheless, in this wider world outside Europe, French has been able to hold its own in its traditional spheres of influence, surviving as a prestige lingua-franca in most of the French ex-colonies (particularly in Africa, and in Quebec within Canada), and having also its guaranteed status as a working language in many of the United Nations institutions. In practice, it is still more widely used by third parties than the languages of powers with much larger populations, Russian, Chinese, and Arabic. Although reduced from what it once aspired to be (namely the world's preferred language of wider communication)—because the elites who spoke it in Europe converted to English—French is still significant as a second language globally and not yet ready to be numbered among the lost lingua-francas whose decline has been anatomized in this chapter.

# PART IV

# WHO'S IN CHARGE HERE?

Oh, East is East, and West is West, and never the twain shall meet,
Till Earth and Sky stand presently at God's great Judgment Seat;
But there is neither East nor West, border, nor breed, nor birth,
When two strong men stand face to face, though they
come from the ends of the earth!

—Rudyard Kipling
"The Ballad of East and West," 1889

# CHAPTER 10

# Big Beasts

*Ici repose un géant endormi; laissez le dormir,*
*car quand il s'éveillera, il étonnera le monde.*

Here rests a sleeping giant; when it awakes,
it will astound the world.

—Attributed to Napoléon Bonaparte,
gesturing at a map of China, 1803

THE HISTORIES OF OTHER lingua-francas and their paths of development to the modern world suggest some possible futures awaiting the major languages of our time.

One point that has plainly emerged is that the prospects of a lingua-franca, whether still spreading or firmly established, are crucially dependent on the competition it faces. Robust capacity for linguistic survival is not the same as effective military resistance, accumulated capital from trade, or indeed religious fidelity.

The prior spread of Greek was what prevented Rome from projecting Latin equally round the eastern shores of the Mediterranean as around the west; for even when Rome was at its peak, its military clout turned out to be powerless to counter Greek's cultural prestige. Nevertheless Greek lost its dominance when the invading power was Muslim: little by little after the eighth century, the combined forces of Arabic, Persian, and Turkish replaced it throughout its former Asian expansion. Yet meanwhile in the west, Latin itself was able to continue for over fifteen hundred years, amid vast social and political disruptions, as the common language of Europe's church, state, and learning, only to be unseated by new, self-confident powers in the seventeenth century. Effective opposition to Latin, when it came,

came from within Europe—caused by innovating powers such as France and England—rather than from invaders beyond.

Arabic, despite its uncontested role in Muslim liturgy, and its early enforcement as a language for administration by the conquering Caliphate, fell back before Persian as a secular lingua-franca for the Islamic world. The Turks who then overmastered that world—and already had a common language of their own—still accepted, and reinforced, the linguistic fait accompli of Persian. Yet a millennium later, faced with new, quite alien European Christian elites who had arrived as if from another planet, Persian's use as a lingua-franca was at length abandoned—without much of struggle—before the onslaught of English and Russian. So in this case, the effective opposition did come from without.

These stories are difficult to understand in terms of any coherent pattern of language dynamics. But they do show that the life and death of lingua-francas are not autonomous nor entirely self-determined. Widespread currency of a language beyond its mother tongue area can be stable for centuries and will persist until other powers intrude to upset the balance or indeed impose their own language as a replacement.

So in an era when there is a certain complacency about the global role of English, we must assess the other great languages that currently have potential as global lingua-francas. What forces are driving their expansions or buttressing their positions? What weaknesses do they have that limit their long-term potential?

A survey of the world's most widely spoken languages at present produces a list largely equivalent to the world's languages with greatest mother tongue populations. Here is a table that shows for the twenty-five languages with greatest speaker numbers how many of those are mother tongue speakers, and how many are lingua-franca speakers.

They are all major languages, the world's top twenty-five by population, but as an innovation they are ranked here by the relative dominance of their population of lingua-franca speakers.* This turns out to be a useful indicator of languages' significance on the world stage. Many major regional languages in vast states, such as Telugu, Shanghainese (Wu), Cantonese (Yue),

---

* These figures are largely derived from the overall (first-language) and L2 figures from the latest *Ethnologue* (Lewis 2009), supplemented—admittedly optimistically—with home non-native-speaker populations (e.g., for non-mother-tongue speakers of Persian in Iran, and of Turkish in Turkey) where they are routinely educated in it.

| RANK | LANGUAGE | MOTHER TONGUE SPEAKERS (MILLIONS) | LINGUA-FRANCA SPEAKERS (MILLIONS) | PROPORTION (LF/TOTAL) | TOTAL SPEAKERS (MILLIONS) |
|---|---|---|---|---|---|
| 1 | Swahili | 1 | 39 | 98% | 40 |
| 2 | Malay | 55 | 147 | 73% | 202 |
| 3 | English | 331 | 812 | 71% | 1143 |
| 4 | Persian | 36 | 73 | 67% | 109 |
| 5 | Urdu | 61 | 93 | 60% | 154 |
| 6 | Russian | 144 | 110 | 43% | 254 |
| 7 | French | 68 | 50 | 42% | 118 |
| 8 | Arabic | 206 | 140 | 40% | 346 |
| 9 | Hindi | 182 | 120 | 40% | 302 |
| 10 | Hausa | 25 | 15 | 38% | 40 |
| 11 | Italian | 43 | 23 | 35% | 66 |
| 12 | Turkish | 51 | 20 | 28% | 71 |
| 13 | Bengali | 181 | 69 | 28% | 250 |
| 14 | German | 90 | 28 | 24% | 118 |
| 15 | Mandarin Chinese | 873 | 178 | 17% | 1051 |
| 16 | Spanish | 329 | 60 | 15% | 389 |
| 17 | Tamil | 66 | 8 | 11% | 74 |
| 18 | Portuguese | 178 | 15 | 8% | 193 |
| 19 | Telugu | 70 | 5 | 7% | 75 |
| 20 | Japanese | 125 | 1 | 1% | 126 |
| 21 | Javanese | 85 | 0 | 0% | 85 |
| 22 | Shanghainese | 77 | 0 | 0% | 77 |
| 23 | Vietnamese | 69 | 0 | 0% | 69 |
| 24 | Korean | 66 | 0 | 0% | 66 |
| 25 | Cantonese | 56 | 0 | 0% | 56 |

Javanese, are at the bottom of the table, along with the national languages of large, predominantly monolingual states: Japanese, Vietnamese, Korean. These are all fundamentally local languages since, for all the vastness of their populations, their use is concentrated among those who have acquired them as mother tongues. The chart also shows that the official languages of multilingual states, although many are not among the largest in their absolute populations, do massive work as effective bridge languages, even in their own countries: Swahili, Malay, Persian, Urdu (even when evaluated as a separate language from Hindi), and Turkish.

At a second level, it shows interesting exceptions to the generalizations we have just formulated: Bengali and Tamil in India, Hausa in Nigeria, are established enough as languages of culture to be learned, deliberately and nonnatively, by significant numbers. The lingua-franca status of Bengali reflects its official status across a wide area, both in Bangladesh and in India (West Bengal and Tripura), where only two in three are in fact native speakers of it. Tamil has this property to a lesser extent, being spoken as a contact language widely in southern India outside Tamil Nadu. Its speakers outside India (in Sri Lanka and countries of Southeast Asia) naturally have it as a mother tongue. Hausa too is widely spoken in other cities of West Africa outside its heartland in northern Nigeria and southern Niger (e.g., Ibadan and Lagos in southern Nigeria, and Accra in Ghana) and can be considered a useful practical lingua-franca across North Africa. It is in fact spoken (though as a native language) as far away to the east as in the Blue Nile region of the Sudan.

Another interesting feature of this listing is that it maps readily onto the different causes of the spread of the lingua-francas. This correlation may be partly coincidental, but it is interesting nonetheless.

The top two, Swahili and Malay, are of obscure origin, and correspondingly their mother tongue populations fade into the shadows. They are above all lingua-francas created through trade links and travel networks. (This is certainly true of Malay, even though the fundamental statistical reason for its predominantly lingua-franca status in this list is the fact that Indonesia adopted it in 1945 as its official language when only a fairly tiny minority used it as their principal language.)

Passing over English for the moment, the next six languages, Persian, Urdu, Russian, French, Arabic, and Hindi, which have lingua-franca proportions from 67 to 40 percent, are all lingua-francas that owe their status to military conquests and empire-building. Persian, Urdu, and Hindi might be thought somewhat out of place here, since they are all now predominantly indigenous languages of their territories, Iran and northern India, and do not extend far beyond them. But Persian did indeed owe its previous lingua-franca spread across Central Asia and India to armies—just not to its own armies. Likewise Urdu, even if it is today seen as indigenous where it is spoken, historically derives its particular status and attributes (as predominantly a lingua-franca for South Asian Muslims) from its role in the Mughal, and then the British, armed forces.* Hindi has identical origins, but its speakers and apologists have chosen to distance themselves from them, emphasizing instead the indigenous origins of the language in the vernaculars of northern India.

The next group, including Hausa, Italian, Turkish, Bengali, German, Mandarin, Spanish, Tamil, Portuguese, and Telugu, is rather mixed. But these are all languages that have now become lingua-francas only as an afterthought. Their historical origins are mixed, and certainly in the earliest period, for Turkish, Spanish, and Portuguese, they were founded on at least as much imperialistic violence as any in the previous group. But the actual root of the language spreads here was through settlement, not a new administration with a new language spread by military conquest as such.

For Hausa, Bengali, Tamil, and Telugu, use as a lingua-franca has come as people have perceived the wide spread of the speaker communities, through natural growth and gradual settlement. Turkish established itself in Anatolia through infiltration and colonization by Turks of areas that the Byzantine Empire could no longer control militarily after the battle of Manzikert in 1071, not through the establishment of a Turkish-speaking empire. German likewise penetrated central and eastern Europe through spread of farmers, even if the way was opened up by crusading Teutonic Knights in the thirteenth century. The northern dialect of Chinese (later to be standardized as Mandarin) was spread round China in the first millennium AD through the gradual diffusion of farmers from the north, though in the southeast this was creolized into a profusion of different dialects; more recently, in the twentieth century, the language has been seeded directly into Xinjiang and Tibet through deliberate opening up of these territories to Han Chinese (i.e. Mandarin-speaking) immigration, and making Mandarin the language of instruction in schools.

Spanish evidently first went round central and southern America as

---

* The careers of Persian and Urdu are rather reminiscent of that of Greek, another language that once upon a time, and originally by main force, claimed a vast Asian territory as its domain, but is now reduced to its starting point. Greek is now rather small for a national language, with only 13 million speakers; and it has nothing like the 8.5 million lingua-franca users that it would require to fulfill this statistical pattern.

brought by conquistadores; but it was not effectively spread as the sole lingua-franca of the Spanish Empire until the Spanish king's *Real Cédula* of 1770 withdrew support from the various (indigenous) *lenguas generales*, languages that had until then been used for much administration, and certainly most contact with the indigenous population. This resulted in a universal shift to the use of standard Spanish, not only by the government and urban classes, but by the rural masses too.

Italian is the language of a European nation that did not exist as a political unit until 1861, although the spoken and literary standard had been emerging since the sixteenth century, heavily influenced by the high prestige of Renaissance works written in Tuscan dialect, primarily those of Dante Alighieri. In the sixteenth century, it was the most widely studied foreign language in Europe after Latin and French. It then achieved particular prominence, which lasted till the onset of the twentieth century, as the first language of opera and classical music. Standard Italian has emerged through some process of negotiation, but is familiarly characterized as *lingua toscana in bocca romana* 'the Tuscan language with a Roman accent'. It is said that at the foundation of the Italian state, only one in forty could speak standard Italian; and the majority of lingua-franca speakers to this day are Italians whose mother tongue is another dialect. Besides Italy, the language is also a mother tongue in the city-states of the Vatican, San Marino, and in southern Switzerland, especially Ticino province. Despite some messy imperialism in the early twentieth century that led for a time to Italian settlements in various states of northeastern Africa, Italian is not now a major lingua-franca outside Europe.

In the Portuguese possessions, from the sixteenth until beginning of the eighteenth century, the only area where the Portuguese language spread beyond the colonists themselves was in the Indian Ocean, as a result of successful conversions to Christianity, and the language's adoption as a trade jargon. This, then, would belong with Swahili and Malay as a trade-created lingua-franca, if it had not largely died away by the early nineteenth century. Africa and Brazil saw some take-up of Portuguese creoles, mostly among slaves. But the spread of Portuguese to Brazil—by now far the most populous speech community that it has—only began in earnest in the late seventeenth century, when discoveries of gold and precious metals, and the opening up of the interior to economic development, caused mass migration from Portugal itself. Once it was known that there were fortunes to be made in Brazil, European settlement, and hence the spread of Portuguese, took off.

In general, then, these world languages with less than 40 percent lingua-franca use are languages that have grown through gradual immigration, a process which acts mainly to create larger mother tongue communities rather than lingua-francas, although inevitably in a multilingual environment some bilingualism and recruitment of speakers of other languages will occur.

In this quantitative survey of potential world languages in the twenty-first century, languages spread by religious proselytism—modern analogues of Pali, Latin, or Aramaic—are conspicuous by their absence. This has been a contributing motive to spread, especially of the Romance (in practice, Catholic) languages: Spanish in the Americas in the sixteenth to eighteenth centuries, Portuguese in the Indian Ocean in the sixteenth and seventeenth centuries, and French in Indochina, Africa, and the Pacific in the nineteenth. But its effects are here swamped by the other forces that drove the expansion of these now vast languages.

English's position in this list of current linguistic big beasts remains easily preeminent, even if it does not quite take the palm for lingua-franca predominance. Worldwide, it is almost as lingua-franca-heavy (over 70 percent) as Malay is, a language whose mother tongue community is one sixth the size of that of English. But its lingua-franca speakers have been multiplying so fast that, for total numbers of speakers, English is now as big as the greatest (viz Mandarin Chinese). And so it should be: it has been spread in every which way—not only as a settlers' mother tongue in North America, Australia, South Africa, and New Zealand, but notably also as a vehicle of imperial administration in Asia, a medium for miners and missionaries in Africa, and a jargon for the workforces of slavers and profiteers across the Caribbean and the Pacific. Like the great prestige languages of the past—Greek, Sanskrit, Persian, Latin, Chinese, French—it has been, and is being, eagerly embraced by foreigners who see it as the path of access to grave learning, great wealth, and gracious living.

Its only weakness—if such it is—is its comparative youth: English has been on the path to its present eminence over only two and a half centuries, while Chinese has been there—unchallenged in its (admittedly smaller) known world—for two and a half millennia. Remember too the previously towering aspirations of Egyptian (3000 BC–500 BC), Greek and Sanskrit (300 BC–AD 1200), Latin (100 BC–AD 1600), and Persian (AD 1000–1800). English may be just at the beginning of its period of dominance. But equally, it has yet to prove that it will stay the course. In principle its dominance might end prematurely, as it did for Quechua, when the newly established

Inca Empire was suddenly devastated by a handful of Spanish conquista-dores, or for Tangut, the language of "The Great State of White and High" in what is now northwest China, brought down when its leaders proved in-sufficiently loyal to Chinggis Khan.

So much then for the current speaker balances of the world's major languages, and the effects of history on them. What of the effects of geo-graphy?

In considering worldwide English in chapter 2, we noted its description in terms of three "circles," but ended up understanding this as a means, rather, to view the language's penetration into every continent through the prism of the very different proportions of mother tongue and lingua-franca users in various countries. Looking at the position of other major languages' territories on the world map (see the frontispiece), we see few that even faintly echo this truly global distribution of English. The only languages with com-parably spacious and far-flung territories are Portuguese and French, both spoken in Europe, the Americas, and Africa; but as the table just showed us, these languages have global speaker communities which are respectively 16 and 10 percent of those of English. Furthermore, the English-speaking world (with 71% lingua-franca speakers) is almost twice as much colored by lingua-franca use as French (with 40%); and it leaves far behind Portuguese (with 8%).

The main impression made by the other major languages when observed geographically (as in the frontispiece) is how regional they are—as if they were still living in the ancient or medieval worlds. Although these lan-guages have numbers of speakers that each take up a significant share of the world's population, they all function on a continental, not a global, scale. The biggest of all, Mandarin Chinese, is one of the most concentrated, neatly filling up the southeastern quadrant of Asia; but so are such lesser giants as Spanish, Arabic, Hindi-Urdu, and Russian. Indeed, Swahili and Malay, the languages that, in terms of total speaker community, are even more lingua-franca oriented than English, are geographically rather compact, centered as they are on eastern Africa and the archipelago of Southeast Asia.

Since the era of global empire-building seems now to have come to an end, there are few direct ways for these languages, vast as they may be, ever to infiltrate other parts of the world so densely as to establish themselves as use-ful lingua-francas beyond their existing regions. For this to happen, there would have to be either large-scale migration, e.g., of families seeking secu-rity or a better life, or perhaps commercial travel of massive proportions.

But something on the lines of the former has in fact been happening since the latter half of the twentieth century: a reverse flow of populations from the colonies of European empires to their metropolitan countries in Europe. This has applied not just to the major western empires of France and Great Britain, but also to smaller (or older) colonial powers such as the Netherlands and Spain, and even (since the collapse of the Soviet Union in 1991) from the states of Central Asia to Russia.

Moreover, this is not just an effect of the twilight of Empire. Similar trends have affected powers that did not have relevant ex-imperial territories: these notably include the mass immigration of Turks into Germany (long characterized as *Gastarbeiter* 'guest-workers', though large numbers have eventually taken up residence), and of Latin Americans into the USA (much of the latter clandestine—hence the term *mojados* 'wetbacks', suggesting informal crossing of the Rio Grande). Most recently (especially in the last decade) additional flows of "asylum seekers" have left the war-troubled countries of the Balkans, Middle East, Africa, and South Asia for quieter and richer lands, usually in Europe or North America.

The scale of this immigration in the late twentieth century came as a surprise to policy-makers in the recipient countries. It had not been foreseen by any of these powers a century earlier, at the time when the empires were being taken by force and actively colonized. In that period the trend had been the reverse, with metropolitan emigrants (especially Britons in the temperate UK colonies, and Frenchmen in Algeria) seeking to take up opportunities to make their fortunes abroad and settle permanently there, as in previous centuries Spaniards had done in Latin America, and Portuguese in Brazil; the future was then seen as "more of the same." But the colonial enterprise in Asia failed to recover after World War II; and in the 1960s most European governments recognized what Harold Macmillan called "the wind of change" as inescapable in Africa.* Henceforth, foreign control of any but tiny colonies anywhere in the world was unsustainable. But people all over the world had been forming (or imagining) social links with the metropolitan countries. Emigration was a rational response by enterprising, or desperate, citizens of countries in what was now called the Third World when they faced hardship at home and (through colonial education, war service, or just the spread of mass media) knew of better economic conditions

---

* It was not recognized by the government of Portugal until 1975, hence the wars that convulsed Angola and Mozambique from 1961.

elsewhere. Naturally, where possible, they chose places that claimed to be their "mother" countries.

These migrations have often created mother tongue communities of foreign-language speakers in the receiving countries, in their capital cities, and also in other, usually urban, localities. So Arabic (usually in North African dialects) is strong in France and the Netherlands; Turkish in Germany, the Netherlands, and Britain but also in Russia; Malay in the Netherlands; Hindi-Urdu and Bengali in Britain; Cantonese in Britain and the Netherlands; Persian in Russia (as Tajik), but also in Germany and the Netherlands (though outnumbered there six- to eightfold by Kurdish). These new transplanted communities are dwarfed in scale by the foreign-language immigrants to the USA, where the Chicano Spanish community now has over 28 million speakers (bigger than any of the language's native-speaker groups but in Mexico, and roughly equal to that of Spain itself), and even the Vietnamese have 1.9 million.

For convenience and fascination, there is a table of the foreign-language strengths of those same twenty-five languages on pages 236–37, as estimated by *Ethnologue* (Lewis 2009). These are the largest groups; empty boxes show small or nonexistent communities of the language in the country.

These groups, although significant in world terms as language communities in their own right—currently the median size for a language community in the world as a whole is just sixty-five hundred—do not directly raise the profile of these languages as lingua-francas in the host countries. Since the languages are being used as mother tongues, often in communities where the majority language is rarely spoken, these potentially global languages are socially on a par with small "native dialects" and hence seen as of no practical or economic use to the rest of society. There is beginning to be a sense that these communities are potential assets through their links to their original nations, if these are conceived as allies, or (more usually at present) as export markets; but as yet, little use is made of these pockets of language expertise to reach out to their relatives abroad, let alone to use them as learning centers to train second-language learners. They are seen, even by many in government, as markers of minorities whose loyalty to the host nations may be in doubt.

Although these groups act as reservoirs of multilinguality in many of the richest states of the world, states that are otherwise rather notorious for monolingual cultures, they do not, in themselves, increase lingua-franca use—i.e. active multilingualism. But in the future, there might be a different mechanism, especially if there are major shifts in the economic center of gravity of the world: diasporas of businessfolk (from China, say, or India, Brazil, or the Arab Emirates) might perhaps then act as vectors to seed lingua-francas, just as the Sogdians and then Persians once did across Central Asia, or the overseas Chinese in Southeast Asia in the second millennium AD. An exchange of economic investment for exploitation of primary resources might make such armies of commercial agents acceptable (this is already happening with the Chinese in sub-Saharan Africa). But, as witness the limited long-term linguistic penetration of the Phoenicians or Sogdians (chapter 5), even long-term relationships of this kind can fail to seed a lingua-franca permanently.

It is significant that the most evident prospect for the building of new lingua-franca links should be in Africa. Such innovation is likely to occur where there is scope for new links to be established, i.e. where the current situation is relatively fluid and open to development. Continents that host apparently developed and stable political systems, capable of self-defense, such as Europe, Australia, or North America, are not promising in this regard. Radically new lingua-franca spread is favored more by radical change, though the change needs to be constructive of new societies, or new relationships. The abundance of disruptive change that comes in wartime situations as such does not give rise to new language orders; so, for example, the continuing frictions in Palestine, Afghanistan, Kashmir, Sri Lanka, and the Congo have not led to the spread of languages or their wider use, though terror can lead to the departure of smaller language communities altogether—as witness the damage that the continuing Iraq insurgency is doing to Aramaic.

Language spread, and specifically, the wider use of a lingua-franca, may follow on successful military campaigns, of course, when population restructuring takes place, often by government fiat. This was frequent in the early days of the Assyrian and the Roman empires, when mass colonization, often accompanied with deportation, was usually seen after major new conquests. In the same way, Malay is effectively being spread at the moment by government settlement programs round Indonesia, and Mandarin Chinese by the increasing penetration of Xinjiang by Han Chinese. Mother tongue speakers may be the ones who move, but soon the receiving population will find that there is effective pressure for them to acquire the incomers' language as a lingua-franca. A similar phenomenon was seen in the early twentieth century when Russian settlers from the west increased the average

## Numbers of Immigrant Speakers in Some Major States

| LANGUAGE | L-F SPEAKERS IN WORLD (MILLIONS) | UK | FRANCE | GERMANY |
|---|---|---|---|---|
| | | (THOUSANDS) | | |
| ENGLISH | 812 | na | | |
| MANDARIN | 178 | 12 | | |
| MALAY | 147 | | | |
| ARABIC | 140 | 35 | 1,000 | |
| HINDI | 120 | 0 | | |
| RUSSIAN | 110 | | | 360 |
| URDU | 93 | 400 | | |
| PERSIAN | 73 | 75 | | 90 |
| BENGALI | 69 | 400 | | |
| SPANISH | 60 | | | 134 |
| FRENCH | 50 | | na | |
| SWAHILI | 39 | | | |
| GERMAN | 28 | | | na |
| ITALIAN | 23 | 200 | 1,000 | 548 |
| TURKISH | 20 | 60 | 135 | 2,000 |
| PORTUGUESE | 15 | 17 | | 78 |
| HAUSA | 15 | yes | | |
| TAMIL | 8 | yes | | |
| TELUGU | 5 | | | |
| JAPANESE | 1 | 12 | | |
| JAVANESE | 0 | | | |
| SHANGHAINESE | 0 | | | |
| VIETNAMESE | 0 | | | |
| KOREAN | 0 | | | |
| CANTONESE | 0 | 300 | | |

| NL | SPAIN | RUSSIA | CANADA | USA |
|---|---|---|---|---|
| (THOUSANDS) | | | (THOUSANDS) | |
| | | | na | na |
| | | yes | 208 | 175 |
| 300 | | | 83 | 11 |
| 30 | 200 | | 20+ | 3,000 |
| | | | 227 | 317 |
| | | na | 157 | 706 |
| | | | 139 | 263 |
| 5 | 25 | 120 | 112 | 312 |
| | | | 35 | 129 |
| | na | | 611 | 28,100 |
| | | | na | 1,640 |
| | | | 25 | 37 |
| | | 597 | 636 | 1,380 |
| | | | 681 | 1,010 |
| 192 | | 92 | 33 | 74 |
| | | | 265 | 564 |
| | | | - | - |
| 7 | | | 112 | 84 |
| | | | 5 | 86 |
| | | | 65 | 478 |
| | | | - | 0 |
| | | | - | 2 |
| 16 | | 26 | 166 | 1,900 |
| | | 149 | 85 | 894 |
| 70 | 20 | | 399 | 260 |

level of Russian competence in Kazakhstan and Central Asia, even as the language was increasingly taught in school to a rising generation of non-Russian speakers.

Africa, denied the ability to control its own politics in the nineteenth and twentieth centuries, has also seen new settling languages disappear even faster than they have arrived. In a number of cases the incipient lingua-franca spread of some of these languages has faced insuperable obstacles, particularly through deliberate Relegation.

German, for example, had been introduced as a command language of empire to many territories in Africa. From the Berlin Congress of 1884–85, which attempted to regulate the "scramble for Africa," Germany claimed Togoland (modern Togo and the Volta region of Ghana) and Cameroon in the west, Southwest Africa (modern Namibia) in the south, German East Africa (Tanganyika, with Rwanda and Burundi) in the east, all of which it held until World War I. This amounted to 10 million subjects in Africa, comparable with 33 million then at home in Europe (and the 93 million estimated for Africa as a whole).[1] German colonies were distinctive in these thirty years for their dedication to education, with not only primary but also secondary and vocational courses being established; a widespread network of mission schools was also set up independently of the government. Fittingly, the word for 'school' in Swahili is *shule*, a loan not from English, but from German *Schule*.* But after the first few experimental years, German itself was not taught in this German system; instead, Swahili was adopted as the common language in the schools, just as it was used as the basic language of local administration.[2] In this, Germany's policy was like that of Great Britain, and so in principle it might ultimately have led on to a wider role for German as an elite lingua-franca, on the assumption that the territories would have progressed toward independence later in the twentieth century. But after Germany's global defeat by the Allied Powers in 1918, a generation before this could happen, these colonies passed under the sovereignty of France, Great Britain, and Belgium; and with this any prospects for German as a lingua-franca in Africa disappeared.

Italian was projected into East Africa by a series of military campaigns (Eritrea and Somalia in 1885, the Greek Dodecanese and Libya in 1911, and

---

* Otherwise, Swahili loans from German are remarkably few: perhaps just *kemia* and *fizikia* (from *Chemie*, *Physik*) 'chemistry, physics', *stimu* (from *Strom*) 'electricity', and *hela* (from *Häller*) 'money', originally the coin introduced in 1904 as one hundredth of a *Rupie*.

Ethiopia in 1936). So, strangely enough, something like the original Lingua Franca had returned to North Africa and the Greek Islands shortly after its demise in the nineteenth century, though now what came was fully fledged, grammatical Italian. A significant immigration came from Italy into Africa. African colonization was then seen as a significant opportunity for European states to extend their effective territories (as well as their sense of national glory). According to the 1931 census, almost six thousand Italians were in Eritrea and Somalia, and by 1938, some one hundred thousand in Libya, mostly in the cities of Tripoli and Benghazi, on Italy's new *quarta sponda* 'fourth shore', representing some 12 percent of the population. The aspiration was that, by the 1960s, there could be half a million of them. Even Ethiopia attracted as many as three hundred thousand during its five years of Italian administration, though a third of these were troops.

In World War II, however, all of these territories became stakes in an international gamble, which Italy lost. Italy attempted assaults on British-occupied Egypt, as well as Kenya and British Somaliland, but these preemptive strikes proved futile; by 1943 all the Italian colonies had been overrun by British military retaliation. Italian rule in Africa was terminated everywhere, and Italians there began to return home, although outside Ethiopia, many of those with significant fixed assets remained, at least until the 1970s. Over twenty thousand were left to be summarily expelled from Libya by Colonel Qadhafi in 1970. (Somalia had remained under Italian administration until 1960.) There had been time for perhaps two generations of Africans to begin learning Italian as a lingua-franca; but then it was gone.[3]

But some other colonial European languages have proved far more persistent in Africa.

Westward along the Mediterranean coast, in Algeria, the French-ruled colony that had been instituted by invasion in 1830 and infused with 109,000 European (mostly French) settlers by 1848, had survived all the political turmoil of the nineteenth and twentieth centuries (including World War II). The immigrant-derived population had risen to over a million by the 1950s, but this was still no more than 10 percent of the total. When constitutional measures were proposed in 1947 to give those 10 percent effective parity of representation with the non-European 90 percent, the result was a civil war. This raged until 1962, when the new French president, de Gaulle, opted to lance the wound by giving Algeria total independence. The vast bulk of the million or so French-speaking population—with up to four generations' background in Africa—were then repatriated to France.

This almost total removal of French people from Algeria (with the remaining members, mostly in the oldest generation, dying off heavily in the decade 1986–96, so as to decline from 52,000 to 8,300) was not enough to eliminate lingua-franca use of French itself. It is estimated (though without concrete census data) that today, almost two generations after their departure, half of all Algerians—say, 16 million people—still speak French as a second language.* This would mean that French is stronger in Algeria than in Canada (where in 2001 the francophone population was counted at 6.7 million). The difference of survival between French and Italian has to be attributed primarily to the longer period that the language was spoken—essentially for four generations, rather than barely two. But there is probably also a "halo effect" affecting French in Algeria. It is surrounded by countries that preserve a special role for French: Morocco and Tunisia—both French protectorates till 1956—continue to use it culturally and commercially; and in all the countries on Algeria's southern borders, Mauritania, Mali, and Niger, which were till 1960 part of French West Africa (*Afrique occidentale française*), there is general lingua-franca use of French.

French then is widely known and used throughout northern and central Africa, and this extends as far as the southern reaches of Congo. The coastal states of western and eastern Africa, by contrast, tend to be reliant on English.[†] Southern African countries, though, from Zambia southward, are once again English-dominant, with the exception of the ex-Portuguese colonies of Angola and Mozambique. All these cases essentially continue the dominant language policy from the colonial era and hence are examples of what we have called Regeneration: the old colonial lingua-francas have been granted a new role in a new age.

We shall see, in chapter 12, that South Africa itself (together with Namibia) is a highly complex case, where Afrikaans, fairly recently derived from Dutch, but well placed as the overwhelming majority language of the Coloreds in the Western Cape, had become established as a high-level lingua-

---

* www.tlfq.ulaval.ca/AXL/AFRIQUE/algerie-1demo.htm. These figures remain extremely controversial, though plausible to many with knowledge of the country. A high figure for French is not desired by the Algerian government. There are no official figures, but, for example, the *Ethnologue* (Lewis 2009) attributes only 111,000 speakers to French.

† The state of Cameroon (originally a German colony) is distinctive in having both French and English now as official languages, and a mixture of the two, known as Frananglais, has become a kind of pidginized lingua-franca here. Guinea-Bissau has retained Portuguese.

franca in the second half of the twentieth century, but is now, since the establishment of majority rule in 1992, yielding its lingua-franca role to English, which is seen by policy-setters among black Africans as both usefully cosmopolitan and not so compromised as Afrikaans by association with white domination under apartheid. English appears to be regenerating nicely here; but Afrikaans is still poised on the edge of Resignation, which, if it happens fast enough, can seem like Relegation.

❀

Given today's global linguistic regionalism, where there is relatively little immediate scope for different "big beasts" among the world's languages to spread their use into other major regions, many of these languages are nonetheless being promoted for appreciation by foreigners, in a conscious effort at cultural diplomacy. But will this have any real effect? Since all the language dynamics that have been reviewed in this book have been achieved unconsciously—as a side effect of the spread of empires, markets, or religions, or through the adoption of language policies by governments within their own territories—it is interesting to assess how significant this new kind of policy is likely to be, as a conscious, but quite noncoercive, stance of central government.

Present-day political powers do value the status of their languages. This they have done so since the first widespread recognition of national languages, all across Europe, during the sixteenth century (a movement of "grammatization" led off by Antonio de Nebrija's dedication of his pioneering grammar of Spanish to Queen Isabella in 1492). Languages in this period, however, were not widely enough spoken outside their national borders to justify government diplomatic effort on their behalf, as symbols of national prestige. The only possible exception would have been French, but this needed little official support to power its progress around the cultured courts of Europe. The Académie française was founded in 1635, marking the French state's interest in the fait accompli of French-language prestige: the academy's official role was to watch over the language, supposedly to ensure that its virtues came to no (self-inflicted) harm. The French state's committed enthusiasm to the condition of its national language—being at the time the most widely spoken and respected in Europe—was naturally influential, and in the following century the principal continental courts all attempted to follow suit, with language academies of their own. The focus, however, was always on good style within each language: no state wished to be let down by want of linguistic elegance.

The desire to pursue "cultural diplomacy" by means of language came much later, only in the late nineteenth century. The idea was not to purify the chosen tongue, but to win ever more enthusiastic users for it, ideally from all over the world. This is what is called in French *rayonnement*, literally 'radiation'. The emphasis now was not on language substance, the actual words as spoken and written, but on language use. The associations that made the language attractive were therefore central, including its literature and media output, the scientific work done in it, its social and philosophical traditions, and even nonlinguistic arts and sports.

Once again, the French led the way. An unofficial cultural foundation, the Alliance française, established in 1883, pioneered this new attitude to languages, based on the thought that they could be effectively sponsored. It drew its inspiration from the success of the Alliance israélite universelle, an ad hoc committee that had since 1860 been spreading education among Mediterranean Jews. Specifically the AIU had taught French, very much the language of the future in the mid-nineteenth century, as well as using it as their medium, with teacher training as well as direct instruction. The French schools of the Alliance française likewise met with high demand and immediate success. By the turn of the century, they already had 250 schools on four continents and, in 1902, triumphantly broke into the North American market.[4] A century later it has 1,071 schools and operates in 133 countries worldwide.

The AF was not a department of the French state and has never become one, though it is seen as a national asset. Other such organizations were to be established for all the major European languages in the next century, though first by a long way was the Società Dante Alighieri for Italian (1889). Comparable institutions were to be set up for German (Deutsche Akademie, 1925), Portuguese (1928), Danish (1940), Swedish (1945), and Czech (1949).

For English, the effort began in 1918 as a somewhat self-congratulatory private charity (the English Speaking Union), which emphasized the benefits of global solidarity among English-speaking nations. The British government became involved in cultural diplomacy in 1934, when it set up the British Committee for Relations with Other Countries, which in 1940—in the darkest days of World War II—was transformed into the British Council, now famed worldwide, principally for its English teaching and its libraries.

It currently has 233 branches, active in 107 countries. Its mission is not explicitly to promote the English language and its works, but "to build mutually beneficial cultural and educational relationships between the United Kingdom and other countries, and increase appreciation of the United Kingdom's creative ideas and achievements." Unlike its great rival the AF, it has always been funded by central government, specifically the British Foreign Office, although it is intended to maintain its independence and hence its credibility.*

The vast political change in Europe, especially since World War II, has had a pronounced effect on the goals embraced by cultural diplomacy. As a result, many of the foundations have had to be reconceived and even refounded. The Deutsche Akademie, which had become a Nazi institution, was replaced by the blameless Goethe-Institut in 1951; the Portuguese effort was refounded as the Instituto Camões in 1992, after recovery from the 1976 fall of Salazar's *Estado Novo* and the loss of the African colonies; likewise the Spanish Instituto Cervantes began in 1991, in the new era of democracy post-Franco, which had begun in 1978; and the Greek Hellenic Foundation for Culture was established in 1992, democracy having been firmly reestablished after the colonels' autocracy ended in 1974. The end of the Cold War in 1989 led to a spate of new foundations, notably for Estonian (1989); for Polish (Institut Adama Mickiewicza, 2000); for Finnish (Cultural and Academic Institutes—Suomen kulttuuri- ja tiedeinstituutit, 2005); and even, through a multinational initiative led by Andorra, for Catalan (Fundació Ramon Llull, 2008).

One thing that stands out in this list is how dominated it is by Europe, and hence European languages. There have been no institutions for Arabic, Hindi, Urdu, Malay, or Swahili, for example, despite their political and lingua-franca importance. Nor have any of the major nonindigenous users of European languages, such the USA, Canada, Mexico, or Brazil, seen value in getting into this game on behalf of their majority languages, surprising when one considers that the sheer scale of some of these states, once founded as European colonies, dwarfs the absolute size of their countries of origin.†

---

* In this, it is rather like the World Service of BBC, which is similarly funded.
† Colombia is a lonely exception here, having set up the Instituto Caro y Cuervo in 1942 (named after two noted linguists, one of whom actually attained the presidency of the country). Until the 1990s, however, its work was resolutely focused on Castilian Spanish, making it almost more devoted to the metropolitan form of the language than Spain itself.

Nations that have such languages may attempt to practice cultural diplomacy (as witness the defunct United States Information Agency, which functioned 1953–99), but if they do, they will focus on their own politics, arts, and society; they will not expect to gain sympathizers just by propagating their own language.

For Arabic, such outside pressure as exists to motivate people to learn it comes from Islamic organizations rather than Arab states, and most of the actual teaching offered comes from neither, but rather from private companies in cities within the Arabic-speaking zone. When an Arab state takes to cultural diplomacy, it establishes a service in the language, rather than a cultural organization or a network of schools. So Qatar established the news channel Al-Jazeera; and so Egypt, the largest Arabic-speaking state, has recently (November 16, 2009) applied for the first non-Roman-script domain name, مصر or .mṣr in Arabic (i.e. the three consonants of Egypt's own name), which it plans to use to host Arabic-language traffic.

The club did remain solidly European until the 1970s. But in 1972 Japan, responding to its then unique role as a "fully developed Asian nation," set up the Japan Foundation (国際交流基金 Kokusai Kōryū Kikin—literally the 'international exchange fund'). It was as if it wanted to acquire every last attribute of its honorary European status, something that it had been working toward ever since the opening of Japan to the world in the 1870s. Although the foundation is now active in twenty countries, it cannot be said to have markedly raised world competence in Japanese.

In 1987, an act of the government created by the Iranian revolution of 1979 formed the Council for Spread of Persian Language and Literature, targeted at foreign learners.[5] Since then, over sixty Iranian cultural centers have been set up round the world, known as *xāna-e-farhang* 'house of culture'. The council is a creature of the Supreme Council of the Cultural Revolution (which had stopped the university system in 1980, then purged and restarted it on an Islamized basis.) Hence the resulting measures were not restricted to disinterested love of the Persian language and the literature expressed in it, but place it in an explicit political context.*

---

* Iran has also recently taken to reinforcing links with countries that share its language by seeking to develop a common satellite TV system with Afghanistan and Tajikistan. But it's doubtful if the mere use of a common language can provide a sufficient bridge among three such different governments. (Farangis Najibullah 2008, "Iran pushes cross-border

Recently, and at a vastly higher level of investment, the People's Republic of China has decided to put Mandarin Chinese and its associated culture on the map. In a remarkable burst of focused growth, a global network of Confucius Institutes (孔子学院 *kǒngzǐ xuéyuàn*)—already 396 institutes in 87 countries—has come into existence since November 21, 2004. From a zero base, the Chinese effort has already in five years become the second biggest in the world, still well behind the Alliance française (with 1,071 schools in 133 countries, grown over 126 years) but ahead of the other two previous front-runners, the British Council (233 schools in 107 countries, over 69 years) and the Goethe-Institut (175 schools in 92 countries, over 58 years). This Chinese enterprise is the best evidence of how seriously the value of cultural diplomacy is still taken in the twenty-first century, especially for a nation undertaking a 'peaceful rise' (和平崛起 *hépíng juéqǐ*) and wanting to manage the global implications for public relations that this will have. The suddenness and intensity of the institutes' rise, however, taken together with their clear—if not explicit—association with Chinese foreign policy, is frightening off some potential colleagues. E.g., in October 2009, the Indian government rejected an offer of a greater presence of the institutes in Indian schools, beyond the two already set up in Jawaharlal Nehru University and the Vellore Institute of Technology.[6]

But our roll call of institutions for other languages makes plain that the attractions of cultural diplomacy are felt not just by dominant, or aspiring dominant, powers who want to see their language used as a lingua-franca in a wider world. An institution for cultural diplomacy may now be a kind of token of sincere dedication to a mother tongue, though if so the distinction between a language as a mother tongue and as a lingua-franca seems to have been lost from view.

The institutions' policy goals are various. First of all, they may aim to promote knowledge of their languages abroad. To this end most of them, though not all, organize courses of language teaching. Secondly, they may aim (such as the British English-Speaking Union, Portuguese Instituto Camões, and Iranian *xāna-e-farhang*) to foster a spirit of cooperation between different

---

TV project," Radio Free Europe, www.rferl.org/content/article/1079698.html.) At the same time, it is quite possible for a political or ideological opponent to launch an alternative system, as the BBC has done with its Persian TV channel, launched on January 14, 2009. The value in linguistic diplomacy, if any, must transcend political doctrines.

nations where their language is spoken natively or officially;* they may try
to reinforce links between the mother country and a diaspora of its citizens
abroad; later on, they may expand to bring in nations that simply use the language as a lingua-franca. Thirdly, they may undertake campaigns to spread
use of their languages within their home countries, often combining this
with a concern for purity of the language as used. This last brings them back
onto the traditional ground of the national language academies.

The desire for this kind of cultural comfort is still felt as much by those
hoping to reverse a perceived decline as by those with an access of energy as
they see their nation (and hence its language) grasping new opportunities.
The Alliance française had such a rearguard motive, which is now seen
again in Russia's decision in 2007 to supplement its RosZarubezhCentr
(Russian Abroad Center), which had existed in some form since 1925 and
had achieved representation in sixty-three countries, with a new grant-
giving foundation entitled Russkiy Mir (Russian World/Peace), jointly
under its Foreign and Education ministries. This is explicitly, in President
Putin's words, "to promote the Russian language, which is Russia's national
heritage and a significant aspect of Russian and world culture, and to support Russian language teaching programs abroad."

However, the new fund seems more targeted at the second major goal
listed above and so aims not so much to advance the spread of Russian as a
lingua-franca learned worldwide as to reinforce loyalty to it in what Russia
calls its Near Abroad, that is to say the nations that were once part of the
Soviet Union or its Warsaw Pact allies. All these had used Russian as their
practical lingua-franca until the collapse in 1989–92, which left many free to
choose their own linguistic associates. The new fund now aims to sponsor
and reinforce language and cultural activities in the states that retain an
enthusiasm for Russian, notably Belarus, Tajikistan, and Armenia, but including Russia itself, while giving a cold shoulder to perceived renegades,
such as the Baltic States, Georgia, and Ukraine, as well as (to a lesser extent) Kazakhstan, Kyrgyzstan, and Azerbaijan. The more positive countries
are also those that send large contingents of guest workers to Russia, which
may make their motives a little impure, if still highly acceptable in Moscow.

As a clear example of language policy as a political weathercock, it is

---

* It is more rational, but requires greater ambition and expense, to approach this kind
of aim not through language teaching and libraries, but an explicit political association,
such as Britain's Commonwealth, or France's Francophonie.

notable that in Uzbekistan, official enthusiasm for Russian has waned and waxed since 1991, in line with the direction of its foreign policy. First, over the 1990s, as Russians steadily emigrated (their numbers decreasing from 6.1 to 2.6 percent), and a transition from Cyrillic to Roman script was attempted for Uzbek,* the number of schools with instruction in Russian fell by a third. Russian's status as an official language was withdrawn in 1995 and, around the turn of the millennium, book-burning of Russian-language titles was quite frequent. Essentially, the rising generation in the 1990s stopped being taught Russian. But around 2003, Uzbek's policy stance toward the Western powers changed, then went into full reversal after the repressive measure taken at Andijan in May 2005, followed by the closing of the U.S. air base at Karshi-Khanabad in November of the same year. Since then, Russian has come back into official favor, and economic collaborations that require use of Russian are on the increase, boosting this lingua-franca explicitly through recruitment pressure. It has not been so easy, however, to restore general competence in it among the young, even if there is now broad parity between the use of Russian and of English as languages in Uzbek universities.[7]

❧

The inconstant attitude of Uzbekistan to Russian draws attention to one weakness in the strategy of deriving political advantage for a nation from international use of a language deemed "national." It takes a generation or more for any language to be acquired (or lost) by a new community, while political allegiances, especially since the twentieth century, may be much faster moving.

But there are many more weaknesses. Although national programs of linguistic cultural diplomacy can provide the means for outsiders to learn your language, no evidence suggests that they actually provide a motive to spread it beyond what would have happened anyway with those who have an eye on gaining recruitment through it. Nor is there evidence that, when the language is learned, the new speakers will—for that reason—be more

---

* I.e., from the alphabet used for Russian to that for English. Begun in 1996 in the schools, the change was originally mandated to be completed by 2000, but with two deferments since, to 2005 and now to 2010. Mass media for adults are still largely distributed in Cyrillic script.

supportive of the powers whose citizens speak it natively. Cultural diplomacy through language has only been conceived of relatively recently; but since it has been practiced, first for French, then for a variety of European languages, and since 1972 for some powerful Asian ones, no language has clearly grown its community as a result.

Real lingua-franca spread, as seen in the pages of history, seems to have been made of sterner stuff.

# CHAPTER 11

# The Jungle Is Neutral

*Ma foi! sur l'avenir bien fou qui se fiera:*
*Tel qui rit vendredi, dimanche pleurera.*

My word, on our mad future who'll rely?
Who laughs on Friday, Sunday will see cry.

—Jean Racine, *Les Plaideurs*

O UR QUICK REVIEW OF the big beasts among languages that now stalk the world has shown no immediately threatening contenders to the preeminence of English as a global lingua-franca. The other languages with large speaker populations and wide territorial spreads, even the largest of them, were revealed as regional forces, with little evident prospect of branching out to a global influence in present, or foreseeable, political and economic circumstances. If any have scope for expansion, it is likely to be in the relatively inchoate situation of Africa, where new commercial alliances can be envisaged, especially with China, that might have linguistic consequences; just as in this continent, in the last century, a number of European languages have been summarily eliminated, while others have almost as suddenly come to prosper.

This assessment is based on the ground rules discernible for lingua-franca spread in the last few millennia. But although there are common threads in human society, and in language dynamics as part of that, there is also the fact that human beings gradually, and sometimes very speedily, devise new technical environments that condition their social development. The invention and take-up of logographic writing systems (Sumerian cuneiform, Egyptian hieroglyphs, Chinese characters, Mayan glyphs) made possible the logistics of large-scale agricultural empires; the radical simplification that came with alphabetic scripts disrupted ancient social hierarchies and produced the more open and mercantile societies of the Phoenicians, Greeks, Sogdians, and Arabs; printing overthrew the grip of the Roman church (and Latin) on the cities of Europe; oceangoing ships (directed with magnetic compasses and exactly drawn portolan charts) allowed European ways of war and agriculture to spread beyond the bounds of a single continent, and with them have spread European languages, whether as mother tongues of settlers or as lingua-francas of cosmopolitan powers.

Technical change did not slow in the twentieth century, at the beginning of which the pattern of current lingua-franca use was set, with English in the driver's seat. Some of this change has directly affected the use of lingua-francas or is soon likely to do so. In this chapter, we consider how new developments might disrupt the existing division of the world into linguistic spheres of influence. Will the emerging technological environment offer new options for particular languages' survival and utility, or will it reinforce the status quo? Could it favor some specific languages, or some classes of languages, while prejudicing the chances of others?

This assessment comes in two parts: an enumeration of technologies that could affect the world's language balance, and then a means of assessing their impact. The first is a straightforward statement of what there is or will clearly soon be. The second is more a matter of judgment and needs us to give a qualitative estimate of long-term reaction, worldwide, to innovations. Will leadership and control remain with the cultures and language communities that are the source of the innovations, or will they be more widely spread and hence perhaps more neutral, linguistically, in their effects?

❧

Communications technology, from wired telegraph and telephone through broadcast radio and TV to satellites, networked computers, and mobile phones, is now ubiquitous in the world and familiar to all readers of this book. Arguably it may already have fulfilled any potential it had for linguistic influence.

In this new world, when a common language is being used by author and addressee, only communications in a written medium are in any way language-dependent. The acoustic and auditory media of phone, radio, and television work just as well—and without need for any extra research or development to enable them—in any language. Only the scripts of the world, in their varying degrees of complexity from Roman and Korean to *devanāgari* and Japanese, force electronic media to discriminate among languages and make different provision for each, thus opening the possibility that some languages might be better served than others.

In the nineteenth- to mid-twentieth-century stage of electronic communications, then, the only medium where there was a technical advantage in using one language rather than another was the one that relied on the written form of a language, namely telegraphy. The original idea had come from the Americans Samuel Morse and Alfred Vail in 1844, who naturally encoded messages in English. Americans, in fact, long refused to adopt the so-called continental code, a simplified extension originated for German in 1848 and made the international standard at the International Telegraphy Congress in Paris in 1865.* However, the original Morse code developed for English held no particular technical advantage over the derivatives that were later defined for non-Roman scripts, e.g., Russian, Greek, Hebrew, Arabic, and Persian, which was gratuitously distinct from Arabic, not just an extension of it. There were also Morse codes for Japanese kana syllabary (in this context, usually known as *wabun* 'Japanese text'), and for Korean Hangul (though this is coded indirectly through the SKATS, Standard Korean Alphabet Transliteration System).

Really, the technical constraints on use of any language were more administrative than linguistic. Since Thailand had its own independent monarchy, telegraphy in Thai became available in 1875, whereas Morse for Hindi seems only to have been defined in the 1950s, after Indian independence from British rule.[1] In principle, alphabetic scripts had a decided advantage for coding over Chinese characters (which, according to a system devised by a Dane, Hans Schellerup, in 1869, had to be precoded as strings of four numbers apiece, which must then be sent number by number and regrouped into characters by the receiver). But in practice, Morse codes were developed for scripts as governments or regulatory authorities perceived the need; and any difficulties or complications that might arise were overcome in the quest for instantaneous text transfer over arbitrary distances.

---

* It adds coverage of accented letters, including those distinctive for the artificial lingua-franca Esperanto, as well as the Icelandic symbols ð and þ. It is inexact in that it only shows that a letter has a diacritic, not which one.

Over the following century and a half (say, 1850–2000) more and more reasons were found to encode alphabets or characters for use with a machine.* These included the growing use of typewriters (and hence standardized keyboards) to mechanize the drafting of texts of all sorts (spreading from 1873, standardized by 1910, and remaining in use until the late 1980s); telegraphy, and specifically continuous teleprinting, which took advantage of an International Telegraph Alphabet (originally the Baudot code, patented in 1875) to operate automatically without the intervention of human Morse operators; and after the 1940s, the exponential growth of digital computing, with its text-processing and electronic-mail applications, which since the 1980s have encompassed and essentially replaced manual typesetting, document-drafting, teleprinting, and general correspondence. Computer programming provided the motivation for ASCII, American Standard Code for Information Interchange, the latest, and perhaps last, in a series of attempts to standardize the binary coding of the Roman alphabet, which was finalized in 1968, although not universally accepted, even in the USA, until the late 1980s (mainly because IBM, for most of the period the biggest computer company, programmed its machines with the EBCDIC code, designed originally for card-punch computer programs).

All these different systems were designed with only the Roman alphabet in mind (as well as European numerals and a few other symbols) without the slightest supplement even for the extra forms with accents used in western-European languages; in that respect, these encodings were less adequate even than "continental" Morse. The reason for this lack was fairly evident: the center of innovation was by this time decidedly within the USA; and the USA's favored language (English), in its use of the Roman alphabet, rather uniquely made almost no use of accents.†

But non-English users too had a use for these standards, or rather for the digital processes that employ them. As a result, in the last three decades of the twentieth century a profusion of new standards were set up by various

---

* When intended for electronic transmission, these were all (like Morse) binary encodings, replacing the few dozen distinct symbols that had appealed to alphabet designers since the eighth century BC with contrasting sequences of "on" and "off," the simplest distinguishable states of an electric circuit.

† One might be more charitable to the Americans, perhaps, and attribute the meanness with extra characters to engineering minimalism. Émile Baudot (1845–1903) had been a Frenchman, after all, and even his code had lacked any accented letters.

bodies for various languages, each of them usually incorporating the ASCII standard at its core, but extending it off in innumerable incompatible directions. Some are completely independent national standards (GB in China, JIS in Japan), sometimes named in a spirit of cooperation, e.g., ArmSCII (Armenian), CCCII (Chinese), ISCII (Indian Brahmi-derived scripts), PASCII (Perso-Arabic derived scripts in India), TSCII (Tamil), VISCII (Vietnamese), and YUSCII (Yugoslav). Some have been dignified with international standards in their own right. But many have also been systems customized for particular companies' hardware or operating systems (e.g., EUC for Unix, a series of three-number codes for Microsoft-DOS, and at least twenty-two named by language or region for Apple Macintosh). Most languages, and especially such large and important ones as Japanese, Russian, Chinese, Persian, Urdu, and Korean, ended up with multiple systems in use.

None of this made computing impossible, but it made it much more complicated to get systems to work, let alone interact with one another's texts. Since all these standards are drawing on the same set of possible digital codes (just the possible set of strings of os and 1s), they will overlap and conflict with one another. They do not make it possible—at least without special auxiliary systems—for a digital document to contain multilingual text and be processed or shown without confusion. In the software world, compatibility requires some level of central planning, and the independent development of character codes had not received it.

Had not, but now it has. It is something of a relief that since 1987 another group of computer engineers have been working to undo the restricted parochialism of the ASCII standard. The Unicode consortium in California, based on the work of Joseph Becker, seeks to replace ASCII with Unicode, a far-extended family of fonts on a vast planned architecture, which will have room—and a determinate place—for all the current language scripts of the present, as well as all known scripts from the past. Their first draft standard was published in 1991, and Unicode 5.0 was issued in 2007. ASCII remains as a minimal subset of characters at its heart, but in principle, it is now no more difficult to produce an electronic version of text in any of the world's twenty-five major languages than it is in English.

The problem in principle is solved, but difficulties of practice, and of politics, remain. The practical difficulties are now focused on the degree of support offered by producers of text-processing software. Will they provide users with the necessary means to input all these characters conveniently, so that they receive their designated codes in computer memory; to display them on screen and work with them in editors; and to print them out in fitting form?

There is also the vast problem of transition. This is a practical problem which shades into politics. Should the body of digital text stored with other codes be simply abandoned, or will means be found to convert it into the new standard? If so, this will cost money and effort—a cost that will fall on those non-English users, and not on the English-using originators and developers of these would-be "universal" standard codes (nor indeed on any of the English-using computing public).

Some might choose to retain one or more old incompatible standards, especially if their own market looks capable of growing to outbalance the American one, or even of the whole of the rest of the world. Competitors such as China or India have strong central governments who can set standards if they wish and also have this kind of growth potential. Regardless of priority or convenience, perhaps they will not accept that the coding standards for their languages be set by a committee of Californians.

◌◦◌

So much for the coding support for individual languages in their written forms. From it we can infer that, although the main innovation in this field has occurred in the English-speaking world (specifically the USA), there is no fundamental reason why any of the major lingua-francas of the world should be disadvantaged in the long term by being shut out of information-technology development. Evidently, the spread of computer software developments continues at present to run in a single direction, viz from the USA to the rest of the world, and this gives English an advantage currently in this important part of the modern world economy. It remains, as it has done for the last fifty years, the language of "early adopters" in information technology. Nevertheless, other languages speedily follow and adapt the new developments, so English only retains its advantage by going on as the language of trailblazers. Should the progress slow its pace or stop, or another language area become the center of innovation (as Japan looked as if it might in the 1980s), the present advantage may not be permanent, any more than the United Kingdom has gained a permanent advantage in transport or communications from being the first country with a railway network, or with a television broadcasting system.

In this context, it is worth paying special attention to software that translates or interprets between languages. This is a less fundamental field in information technology than character coding, but it has particular significance for the survival of lingua-francas.

When author and addressee are using different languages, whether in a spoken or a written interaction, the situation requires electronic systems that are designed for specific languages and that relate to structures in them much deeper than their superficial appearance on the page. For written language, some form of translation must be arranged, looking beyond the patterns of the script to the words, phrases, sentences, and whole discourses that constitute the languages, and devising conversion from one code to another. If spoken language is required, all the complexity of translation will have to interface, at either end, with the extra complexity of acoustic analysis and speech synthesis, each of which will inevitably require subtle calibration to fit the particular languages involved. Furthermore, compared with written translation, there will be much greater requirements for the real-time speed of the various conversions, if the system is to be of practical use. At the present, none of the above aspects is a fully solved problem, even for languages familiar to the engineers doing the research and development; and the greater the complexity required of the system (and the exoticism of the language), the further it is from even being presentable as a usable system.

The application of computer technology to machine translation (MT) owed its first surge of development to the competition between the USA and the Soviet Union of the 1950s and '60s, taking in the early Cold War and the space race. It was then adopted and extended by other significant scientific and technical powers of those days, seen for a time (in the 1980s and early 1990s) as an important enabling technology by governments such as those of Japan and the European Union. As the principles of the technology became better understood, a drive began to create a meta-system that might generate new MT systems on the fly, as and when English speakers needed access to any other "low-density language." This history might in itself suggest that MT is only interesting for, or in practice applicable to, the greatest of major languages—Russian, Japanese, the state languages of western Europe, Chinese, and above all to English. These languages have certainly carried off the early laurels for research and exploration, and limited success, in the field.

But founder effects—defined as the continuing dominance of those who have pioneered a move, even as others join in and make their own contributions to it—do not necessarily persist in eras of furious technical or political change. For example, English has indeed continued as the language of foreign colonists who came to dominate North America, even though the native tongues of the majority of later immigrants were different, mostly Slavic or Germanic. By contrast, Portuguese did not sustain its early (sixteenth-to-eighteenth-century) role as the lingua-franca of trade and diplomacy round the Indian Ocean. The collapse of Portuguese mercantile control in the seventeenth century did not linguistically benefit the Dutch who subverted it, but it did leave the field clear for the later growth of English. No simple rule decrees the long-term triumph of those who first take up a technical option, or a dominant position in a new world order.

Founder effects, also known as the force of tradition, are stronger where either there is little cost in sustaining the past pattern (contrast the continuing expense in time and effort to induct new generations in Latin, effectively an artificial language), or the tradition is not at variance with some other new pressure (as Latin was in effect a barrier to entry for less educated bourgeois people). Hence notoriously, wheel gauges have remained at four feet eight and a half inches, originating as the axle length of chariots and carts, from the Roman Empire and its road ruts right on through medieval carriage-work, and as the current U.S. standard railroad gauge. What motive was there to change as one style of wheeled transport succeeded another? One could also note that Renaissance typographers of the fifteenth and sixteenth centuries, choosing the character styles for printing fonts, simply took over the styles (Gothic, roman, and italic) that were then in vogue in manuscript hands. They have been sustained ever since—though Gothic, the least readable, has lost much ground—since there is no more of the particular dynamic in manual pen movement that had previously driven the changes since the capitals of the Classical age. Even more notoriously, the perverse QWERTY pattern of the English keyboard, invented in 1872, has survived a century of mechanical typing and the first thirty years or so of digital text entry. It is likely to continue to survive unless and until it comes to represent a barrier to entry to some sector of the population of would-be typists and writers, which—hitherto disenfranchised, is yet rising in influence.

This kind of situation is precisely what can be expected to provide at least opposition, and perhaps effective Relegation, to English as a global lingua-franca. What about the vast section of the world's population for whom the need to learn English is still a burdensome chore that they would prefer to avoid?

This all provides some kind of answer to the question "What does it take to unseat an established lingua-franca?" In essence, the answer is that the context needs to change so that what was an advantage comes to be seen as a net liability. This we have seen instantiated in the ruin of pidgin languages, and of Portuguese round the Indian Ocean. We have also seen it in the Relegation of erstwhile colonial languages, of Russian in the Turkic states of Central Asia, of Persian in India, and of English in Malaysia, Sri Lanka, and Tanzania. We have even seen it where former dominant languages just wasted away when their speaker communities lost their separate raison d'être: Sogdians in tenth-century Asia, Brahmin litterateurs in fifteenth-century India, German-Jewish intellectuals in the mid-twentieth century.

But by stepping back a little, we can observe that this possibility, of latecomer dominance, is as applicable to the mastery and use of machine-translation technology as it is to the general survival and role of individual languages within the world system. If the two applications are put together, it may even be that the late-coming use of MT technology will give access to other languages, for large or small communities, and so give new life chances to their own languages.

Two questions are key to exploring these prospects. Can the wider application of MT provide what is required to unseat an established lingua-franca, putting a stop to its continued transmission down the generations? Specifically, can the availability of MT cause such a change to the surrounding context for international communication that use of English will be undercut?

Prima facie, this looks unlikely. It has been an unchanging truism of MT, almost from the beginning of its fifty-year history, that its results have been disappointing. The hope that inspired, and for a long time funded, MT was that it could provide a cheap, fast, and high-quality substitute for human translators or interpreters, so that in effect the language barrier would go away. This has not happened, though the reasons for this disappointment are not clear and distinct.

The snares of relying on a translation—even a good one produced by bi-lingual human beings—were dramatized most memorably for me by the Danzin report, which in 1990 evaluated the success of the European Union's twelve-year-long EUROTRA project to produce a multilingual MT system among the (then nine) official languages of the Union.[2] Attending a session of the management committee that oversaw EUROTRA, I was perplexed to note there seemed to be a radical misunderstanding between two sets of delegates. Both sets accepted that the project had not delivered the functioning system that had been the goal of the project; but was the report as a whole supportive or dismissive of EUROTRA's work? Did it suggest that more work should be undertaken, or the whole project abandoned as a failure? Broadly, the delegates split along language lines, the Romance-language speakers taking the report as more positive.

As it happened, the report had been written in French, but many of the committee had only read the English translation. On a crucial summary page, I discovered that the report had characterized the project's work as *insuffisant*, whereas the English version had translated this as 'inadequate'.

Arguably, no mistake had been made by the translator, in truth-conditional meaning, or even in style. When quality rather than quantity is being judged, it is much more natural in English to use *inadequate* than *insufficient*. But what a difference in connotation! What is called insufficient naturally needs to be supplemented, but what is termed inadequate is usually being roundly condemned. The underlying difference, probably, lies in the English-speaking habit of referring to inadequacies, rather than insufficiencies, betokening a more ruthless, less tolerant attitude to life's little infelicities. There could hardly be a clearer example of the treacherous nature of translation, even by the linguistically informed for the (supposedly) politically astute.

But what of MT itself? Have its results been insufficient or inadequate? It is hard to give a final decision, although it is fairly plain that development to give access to the full range of the world's literate languages is still very much insufficient; and perhaps more important, one concept that underlay most of the early work was basically inadequate.

This concept has survived a major change in the technical approach of MT development. The original rule-based models of MT that dominated research until the 1990s were essentially attempts to automate the "grammar-translation" approach to language learning. The syntactic rules of the various languages could be represented and programmed, and translation equivalents could be stipulated for lexical items, and for the semantic content of the various constructions. Proper names required access to vast encyclopedias and gazetteers, seemingly never complete. The systems got larger and larger, and more cumbersome, harder to direct effectively. By contrast, a different response that became popular in the 1990s was to increase the role of machine intelligence, allowing inference engines to derive their own rules from exposure to vast amounts of translation equivalence data. This was computer equivalent of the "natural" method of language learning, essentially waiting for competence to arise unconsciously from massive exposure to language data. Perhaps the problems of performance here would ultimately yield as computers got exponentially faster and cheaper.

Yet under both approaches, systems still lacked any general models that could represent the meaning of texts in the writer's or the reader's understanding, as they flitted from text to text or context to context. Without receiving preprogrammed guidance on the geometry of the various worlds of modern westernized homes, schools, and offices, a system could not easily select the correct sense for *pen* ('writing instrument', as against 'enclosure') in "The pen is in the box" as against "The box is in the pen." Nor was there any general means of selecting appropriate equivalents when language was used metaphorically. If it is ridiculous—because irrelevant to the context—to see references to good vodka and meat of dubious quality when encountering "The spirit is willing, but the flesh is weak" in an essay on government policy, how come in an environmental work "the rape of the countryside" does not refer to oilseed rape, a crop ubiquitous in the fields of modern England? Human reason, and even more human rhetoric, is inclined to be inscrutable. In practice, it seemed to be impossible to divorce the syntactic part of language processing from modeling the meaning of particular texts.

This is all true and sets some limits on the value of machines as all-purpose interpreters of the sense of human communication. The limits do tend to recede as more and more sophisticated systems are developed, and since human intelligence—like machine intelligence—ultimately arises from finding ways to make unbounded use of a finite (if vast) set of experience, we may in the end produce systems that are as ready for new stimuli, and old clichés, as any educated reader.

But the reason for the chronic dissatisfaction with MT's performance is naïveté on the human side about languages, and how they may be partially understood; indeed how most understanding may be partial. (This naïveté is especially strong among monolingual Anglophones, one may add.) MT has always been approached from a monolingual point of view, as a tool that is supposed to eliminate language barriers—i.e. as a means of converting all the alien codes into some readily understandable home language. This is the true inadequacy in our traditional approach to MT. It is comparable to the lingua-franca solution to multilingualism: let us find a common means—be it Latin, be it English, be it Esperanto—in which all the languages' texts' meanings can be represented. But a lingua-franca is a practical solution in terms of a single language. MT has failed to do anything comparable, at least consistently, or reliably, or at a standard at which the user familiar with English (or whatever target language is being attempted) is well satisfied.

Yet even in the forms currently available over the Internet, MT (and many other ad hoc devices) already provides a vast number of tools to access and penetrate texts in unknown languages. It is debatable whether this is truly translation, and in many cases the help is only accessible to those with a partial knowledge of the source language. But it does mean that, increasingly, partial understanding is becoming available of texts that would in the past have been totally closed books.

Meanwhile, the actual users of machine translation were devising their own pis allers, i.e. make-do approaches to handling what was available. The technology has begun to come into its own as a support system for human translators, allowing them to evade drudgery of repetitive translation and dictionary lookup. The field of application has also been transformed by the vast quantities of foreign-language text that are now available across the Internet. Automatic systems are proving useful aids to Web surfers looking for relevant content in foreign disguise, rather than for clean translations of specific documents.

That the technology is already being used serendipitously (rather than developed) by informal and linguistically informed users is a first sign, I believe, of the actual future that awaits MT, and it is not an inglorious one.

Another personal anecdote may illuminate the situation that is emerging. I was surprised to read on the U.S. paperback jacket of *Empires of the Word* that I have "a working knowledge of 26 different languages." This is harder to disprove than you might think. I cannot know precisely which languages are intended here, but it is true that I have derived useful, and true, information from at least that many languages while working on that book and others. I cannot "speak Chinese," but I was able to provide a phonetic transcription of texts from Confucius' *Analects*. Using other materials from the Internet I could gloss passages of Akkadian cuneiform and Egyptian hieroglyphs, locate relevant text in Sumerian, Persian, and Portuguese, apply dialect changes to and parse Mexican Nahuatl and Palestinian Aramaic. In none of these languages can I boast any sort of fluency. But my point is this: if you embrace the presence of foreign languages and are interested enough to try to come to grips with them, more and more you will find the wherewithal to do so available to you (usually free of charge) on the Internet.

The set of language tools of which MT is a leading member are not available as a seamless suite that enables English users to look through the obscuring dark glass of foreign languages to their crystal-pure meaning beneath, even if, here and there, Web page translation may in some cases be good enough to give this illusion. They are not, and cannot be, the realization of the monolingual dream of MT. But they are very much better than nothing, and—coupled with the right attitude to the point and value of foreign languages—they may be crucial aids to interlingual communication.

✕✦✕

It is possible to look ahead into the dynamically improving, and enriching, world of interlingual electronic media. Just as the print revolution—and various other social revolutions associated with urbanization—changed the ground rules of communication among Europeans in the sixteenth century, so modern electronic technology, if it follows its current path, is set to change the ancient need for a single lingua-franca for all who wish to participate directly in the main international conversation. In brief, if electronics can remove the requirement for a human intermediary to interpret or translate, the frustrations of the language barrier may be overcome without any universal shared medium beyond compatible software. Recorded speeches and printed texts will become virtual media, accessible through whatever language the listener or speaker prefers.

Ultimately, and perhaps before too long—say by the middle of the twenty-first century—everyone will be able to express an opinion in his or her own language, whether in speech or in writing, and the world will understand.

This may seem a hopelessly utopian dream, but increasingly progress in all forms of language technology depends on automatic processing of what are now called language resources. In essence these resources are nothing other than large quantities of text (text corpora) or recorded speech (speech databases) in some form that is systematic and well documented enough to be tractable for digital analysis. From these files, it is possible to derive indices, glossaries, and thesauri, which can be the basis for dictionaries; it is also possible to derive statistical models of the languages, and (if they are multi-lingual files as, e.g., the official dossiers of the Canadian Parliament, the European Union, or some agency of the United Nations) models of equiva-lences among languages. These models are calculations of the conditional probability of sequences of sounds, or sequences of words, on the basis of past performance in all those recorded files. They are the first steps toward calculating automatically the fundamental grammar of the languages. They are still highly imperfect, but they continue (gradually) to improve as the size of the data sets grows; and they use methods that are applicable, in principle, to any human language.

This work has been done first, over the last couple of decades, for English, French, Chinese, Japanese, Russian, and their like—in short, for the lan-guages that were the focus of chapter 10. So naturally, these languages have a head start when it comes to applying this quantitative knowledge. But in-creasingly, smaller national languages, and even minority languages within states, are being processed with the same algorithms. As I remarked in 1998, "The old quip attributed to [Max] Weinreich, that a language is a dialect with an army and a navy, is being replaced in these progressive days: a language is a dialect with a dictionary, grammar, parser, and a multi-million-word corpus of texts—and they'd better all be computer tractable. When you've got all of those, get yourself a speech database, and your language will be poised to compete on terms of equality in the new Information Society."[3]

Currently, there is also a global effort to document endangered languages, though when a language has only just been given an alphabet and is being recorded perhaps by a single linguist over a couple of years, one cannot ex-pect coverage comparable to what a fully literate community will produce of its own accord. Nevertheless, all language coverage is in principle building up comparable digital resources; and these models can serve as the basis for the full range of language-technology applications set out in the accompany-ing table. It shows in the first two columns the basic fields of language tech-nology, and for each of them the foundational tools and materials that have to be built up to support the analysis of any language; then in the successive columns to the right, it shows what these can be used to create, in text pro-duction and publishing, in interactive mechanisms that enable speakers to use their languages online, and in interlingual devices that enable outsiders to gain access to those online language activities in other people's languages.

These applications will therefore be available to any of the world's lan-guages, regardless of how late they may have come to documentation or

| APPLICATIONS FOR LANGUAGE TECHNOLOGY | FOUNDATIONS OF TECHNOLOGY | PRODUCTION AND PUBLISHING | IMPROVE ACCESS FOR INSIDERS | IMPROVE ACCESS FOR OUTSIDERS |
|---|---|---|---|---|
| Speech | Speech databases; recognition; generation | Dictation, vocalization | Voice control, alarms | Interpreting |
| Text Documents | Coding standards; localization | Word processing | Text retrieval, summarization | Multilingual document search |
| Reference Materials | Morph analysers; parsers; corpora | Spell-checkers; gram-checkers | Multimedia, document libraries | Machine(-aided) translation |
| Networking Support | Interchange standards; protocols | World Wide Web | E-mail, discussion lists | Electronic networks, World Wide Web |
| Instruction | Dictionaries (computer tractable) | Literacy | Classroom materials | Computer-aided language-learning |

*Note: The full range of language technology applications. (Credit: Nicholas Ostler)*

recording—even if this is, for most of the world's seven thousand or so languages, only a distant prospect. But here the future is easy to predict, as something possible in principle, and not really debatable; the problem only lies in knowing when it will come to fulfillment.

The long-term tendency is for information-technology developments to lessen the inaccessibility of the world's languages, to break down language barriers, but without abolishing the languages that cause them. One long-term implication of this is that information technology is undercutting the necessity to have a lingua-franca at all. Even as more and more people in this generation strive to learn English, to gain direct access to current world culture (and more important, to be recruited into jobs that have global scope), technical developments mean that mutual accessibility among all mother tongues is gradually becoming a realistic prospect.

The online communities that use languages other than English have grown meteorically in the first decade of the twenty-first century. From 2000 to 2009, the fastest-growing languages on the Net (in numbers of

users) were Arabic (twentyfold), Chinese (twelvefold), Portuguese (nine-
fold), Spanish (sevenfold), and French (sixfold). All these exceeded English,
which trebled its number of users. But on average, the world's smaller languages are all growing faster than the bigger ones: the top ten languages grew
their user base 4.6 times in the decade, whereas all the others (though still
only amounting to a twelfth of the world total) grew sixfold. The main story
of growth in the Internet, then, is of linguistic diversity, not concentration.
English still (in 2009) has as many users as the next two languages combined
(Chinese and Spanish), but it now makes up just over a quarter of the online
community, a proportion that is falling every year.[4]

The mutual accessibility of these languages, what might be called their
interoperability, is rising meteorically too, given the ballooning quantity of
online text available to feed into those language models. When it began, in
2001, Google Language Tools provided machine translation for six languages, and all translation was into or out of English, except for one other
pair, which was between French and German. Tellingly, it was as if this
"early" system had been designed in the nineteenth century, since these languages were all from western Europe: English, French, German, Spanish,
Italian, and Portuguese. These were the traditional "modern languages" that
"well-educated" Europeans and North Americans could conceive of studying. This Euro-centric situation continued for the next four years, until 2005,
when Chinese, Japanese, and Korean were added. In a sense, Asia—or the
Pacific Ocean—had arrived. All the new languages were still translated only
to or from English. Two years later, two more languages were added (Arabic
and Russian), and by November the same year (2007) yet two more (Dutch
and Greek). But the doctrine of English as the only colanguage was maintained: essentially, you could translate to and from any of twelve foreign
languages now—as long as your source or target was English.*

It was only in 2008 that truly multilingual translation initiated. The sluice
gates have been opened, in two respects. First, the number of languages began to go up exponentially (to twenty-three in late 2008, then up to fifty-
one in 2009);† but second, the primacy of English as the universal colanguage

---

* From early 2007, a new service also translated between variants of Chinese, but this just
meant swapping traditional characters with the simplified characters used since the
1956–64 reforms in the People's Republic.

† The ten added in 2008 were Bulgarian, Croatian, Czech, Dutch, Finnish, Hindi, Norwegian, Polish, Romanian, and Swedish; the additional twenty-eight in 2009: Afrikaans, Albanian, Belarusian, Catalan, Estonian, Filipino, Galician, Hebrew, Hungarian,

was eliminated.[5] Whatever the workings internally (English is likely seeing a fair amount of electronic service as an interlingua within the system), the user now simply sets his or her source and target from the set of available languages and can currently choose from 2,550 directed language-pairs. As of 2010, the languages on offer are still only 40 percent of the 129 that the Google interface offers for localization.* This is more like the standard we can expect for multilingual access in the future, but Google's two major competitors in this field, Yahoo's Babel Fish, and Microsoft's Bing Translator, only offer twelve and nineteen languages respectively; and while Bing Translator allows any pair of languages as source and target, Babel Fish still only allows French or English as a colanguage. This kind of Euro-centrism will probably not last much longer.

❧

The last two centuries' technological revolution in worldwide transmission of language begs to be compared with the previous revolution of the fifteenth to seventeenth centuries. Locomotives, automobiles, and aircraft correspond to oceangoing caravels; telecommunications and computing correspond to the printing press and the publishing industry; and multilingual language technologies correspond to the grammatization of Europe's national languages, which saw each of them monumentalized with its own grammar and dictionary. One could add, but less exactly, that English, the world's current lingua-franca, corresponds to Latin, the long-established European lingua-franca, which seemed to have everything going for it in the sixteenth century, when the whole world was opening up to European enterprise.

It would seem that just as the early communications revolution of the sixteenth century appeared at first to be cementing Latin's preeminence, so the generalized contacts of the twentieth century seemed to make English (even more than the other major languages of the era) fixed in its position as the predominant lingua-franca and poised to become the world's universal language. The language was in the right place at the right time.

---

Icelandic, Indonesian, Irish, Latvian, Lithuanian, Macedonian, Malay, Maltese, Persian, Serbian, Slovak, Slovenian, Swahili, Thai, Turkish, Ukrainian, Vietnamese, Welsh, Yiddish.

* Note that three of these (Bork, bork, bork!—Elmer Fudd—Hacker) are jokes, and two (Esperanto, Klingon) are artificial languages of different levels of seriousness.

But in the seventeenth century, Latin's position fell away, and the new media turned out to benefit other languages—above all the new national languages of Europe—even more than Latin. In the modern world, although the position of English has strengthened for the past two centuries, the balance among the world's languages is far from stable. Economic trends are likely to raise up powers with very different linguistic interests, and postcolonial scores too may yet need to be settled. Ruin, Relegation, and even Resignation may yet become part of the fate of the English language. Although the linguistic field that is left to be contested in this post-imperial age is not huge, the struggle for influence between lingua-francas is by no means yet resolved.

But the trends that could prefer mother tongues over lingua-francas may prove the most important in the long run. In a world where digital technology is cheap and ubiquitous, evidence suggests that no single language will inherit the mantle of global lingua-franca. More likely, nation shall speak unto nation each in its own language, relying on the global network to make its national messages understood.

# CHAPTER 12

# Under an English Sun, the Shadows Lengthen

"In German and English I've learnt to count down.
And I'm learning Chinese," says Wernher von Braun.

—Tom Lehrer, "Wernher von Braun"

THE CURRENT STATUS OF English is unprecedented. Simultaneously, it has a preeminent global role in science, commerce, politics, finance, tourism, sport, and even screen entertainment and popular music. With no challenger comparable to it, it seems almost untouchable; even in China, the only country with a language that has more native speakers, every schoolchild now studies English. And India, set to overtake China in population by 2050, is already trading on an expertise in English inherited from the British Empire and studiously preserved and fostered ever since.

After our selective tour of world history, and then of more recent developments in global communications and language technology, the final question remains, what does all this accumulated hindsight tell us about the future of English as a world language? To put us in mind of what we know of the historical backgound, let us recapitulate a little.

English, undeniably the world's dominant language at present, still has evident limitations. Its use has created social problems in some countries that have caused it to be rejected, even as it has provided a compromise solution for communication in others. Despite its worldwide distribution, used independently in too many regions for all to remain in regular contact, it is unlikely to split into a family of languages, at least if it retains its value as a global medium.

The globalization of English has come about through a variety of historical processes, and all of them have left distinctive marks. Languages spoken across vast extents are first of all created and maintained by large polities—empires—and the spread of English is no exception. But as seen in the highly various history of Iran, an empire's choice of language has mostly been pragmatic; only rather recently has nationalism inspired states to care about the identity of the language their people speak. The spread of a language has at times been due more to the choice of a series of powerful outsiders than its own native speakers.

Besides being an essential support for empires, languages have also been spread by long-distance commerce. Traders may travel the world and so cause global use of their home languages, but they have not necessarily caused others to pick them up for their own use. Religious communities too have spread their home languages, as they gained converts; but not all missionary religions create a durable link with their accompanying language. Indeed the Protestant missionaries who used English to preach have been rather distinctive in encouraging converts to go using their own vernaculars.

In the long view, it is clear that lingua-francas, the kind of languages whose survival depends on their widespread utility, can easily outlive their usefulness. To avoid this fate, they must either be applied to a new purpose, or (more durably) get accepted as mother tongues, probably replacing some other vernacular. But since they are often visibly associated with a foreign power, they may suffer deliberate abolition when those in government want to make a clean break with the past.

This much, then, was a brief summary of our observations on the life histories of lingua-francas. Applying them to the present situation, we have noted that potential competitor languages to English are distinguished mostly in that their associated economies—and hence potentially their political and military strengths—are outpacing those of the powers that natively speak English. Prima facie, this makes the long-term position of English look precarious. Will use of English be acceptable in a world economically dominated by powers who feel proud to have achieved parity, and more, with the English speakers?

Precarious it may be, but the position is still perhaps tenable. These languages are all far more regionally restricted than English in their areas of use. On the assumption that successful imperialism is no longer possible, it is difficult to see even globally dominant new economic powers spreading their languages as Britain and the USA were able to do over the past three centuries, especially since this coincided with the first spread of instant electronic communications round the planet.

Nonetheless, the continued global use of English is not secure. On the supply side, English may have cornered the market in potential global lingua-francas, so that it is hard now to envisage the entry of a direct competitor. But the demand for lingua-francas is changing, in two ways adverse to English. First, new developments in language technology are sapping the need for any common lingua-franca to support international communications. More and more, automatic tools are going to become capable of bridging the gap between any languages. At the same time, linguistic nationalism (and regionalism) are gaining in strength. Despite its global popularity as a lingua-franca, English is not gaining wider acceptance as a mother tongue; languages are strongly maintained at the national and regional level. As na-tions find ways to communicate globally without bothering with a foreign lingua-franca, they could well take advantage of them.

This is the background against which one can speculate on the kind of future actually awaiting English. Evidently, the situation is currently fluid, and the relative status of English with other languages will for some time continue to change. Here, however, we are trying to identify possible steady states that define the end of these processes, as far as currently foreseeable.

Two polar opposites define the extremes of what is possible. International English might grow to become Worldspeak, as a single, fully global lingua-franca might be called, available as a universal auxiliary (or indeed primary) language to every educated adult. Or it might retreat as other powers advance, losing its global users and status until it is confined to the lands where it is still spoken as a mother tongue. A third, intermediate, option would see English retained as a world language, but developing on a separate standard from that used by native speakers.

The Worldspeak outcome assumes that the sociolinguistic developments that have benefited English over the past two hundred years, and especially since World War II, continue apace, and that newly rising powers will accept the world's lingua-franca status quo as they come to prominence. In 2050 or 2100, Chinese politicians and businesspeople—as they receive fawning deputations from the USA and Europe requesting rollovers of loans, special access to Chinese-centered economic zones, agreement to climate talks, global disarmament negotiations, and joint peacekeeping forces—may still happily indulge the nostalgia of their Western suppliants by speaking to them in English, which they have learned at school, practiced at university, and applied throughout their adult lives. Everyone, it seems, will be expected to be bilingual except for the Anglo-Saxons. American music videos, comedy shows, romantic movies, may dominate networked entertainment worldwide indefinitely, while the burgeoning products of Bollywood and Korean "shoot 'em up" game studios are invariably released with English dialogue to capture the global youth market. This youth market, particularly influential—because vast—in the Brazilian and Middle Eastern parts of the world, may still think that the global English-language culture is cooler than its own parochial products, dominated as they are by Catholic and Islamic conservatism and repressed by a string of military governments.

Well, it could happen at a pinch. But it seems predicated on a belief that an unprecedented, and strangely cringing, deference will be assumed by newly dominant countries—and indeed majority speech communities—and that this attitude will continue indefinitely, even as the pioneering glories of the English-speaking nations recede into the past. The assumption is that English will just be too entrenched, its continued use too convenient, for it ever to be let go.

This assumption we have found reason to doubt. If the majority powers of the future, memorably termed in a Goldman Sachs report[1] the BRIC—Brazil, Russia, India, China—were accepting English as their mother tongue, there might be some truth in this. Such developments have been known in the past, with colonized populations taking up a world language as their own. There is, after all, no going back from Spanish for the vast mestizo population of Central and South America, nor is there any retreat from Russian across Siberia, nor escape from English in Jamaica or Hawaii.

But the BRIC are not. At best, they and their neighbors are teaching their children to cope with English as a second language, a lingua-franca. Long after the anglophone powers' economic and military dominance around the world has faded, and the initiative for the world's political and economic decisions has passed to others, the BRIC or whatever other nations are then dominant will retain a prior loyalty to their own national languages. This will be their default code, the medium in which they feel most at ease, and in which their elites can stay in touch with the vast masses of their populations.

All these powers have a single dominant official language that is close to the top of the table of languages considered in chapter 10: Portuguese, Russian, Hindi-Urdu, Chinese. Although—short of successful aggressive and invasive wars—it is hard to see these languages being generally used outside their current confines, they may develop their own spheres of wider currency. Non-English powers with global clout may inspire respect for the use of their languages, much as the reputations and potency of Britain and the USA were positive for the worldwide spread of English in recent eras. When this happens, the softness of third countries' loyalty to English could well become apparent.

As Chinese folk wisdom teaches (never forgotten by Mao's revolutionaries), the government is a ship, but the people is the sea. Simply to maintain their political base, future non-English-mother-tongue powers will have to emphasize the role of their own national languages as a means of wider communication.

Does this mean that English must ultimately lose its role as a global lingua-franca? Will the rising economic, and then political, strength of the non-English-mother-tongue powers inevitably drive out the convenience-based use of English round the world? Will the Anglophones finally be forced to swallow their pride in their English and approach them in their own languages, as the early traders of the East India Company once learned Persian to beg favors of the Mughals? Certainly this much could happen without the total withdrawal of English round the world. Any language that remains the mother tongue of large populations, as English inevitably would, will hang on to some international uses. But in a world dominated by powers that use Chinese, Portuguese, Russian, or Arabic, it is certainly feasible that English might withdraw to its home territories (far-flung as those might be) and be of use to foreigners only if they wish to communicate with its mother tongue speakers.

Consider, by way of comparison, what has happened to Greek, the main administrative and commercial lingua-franca of the eastern Mediterranean and western Asia from the time of Alexander to the rise of Islam (say, for the millennium from 300 BC to AD 700). It was, however, progressively constrained by the growing influence of various mother tongue languages (Pahlavi from the east in the first century BC, Arabic from the south in the seventh century AD, and finally Turkish from the northeast from the twelfth) until it was effectively confined to its own home peninsula and archipelago, what we now know as Greece and Cyprus. Although Greek had been diminishing in its areas (both as mother tongue and lingua-franca) for over two millennia, the last major loss was the remaining Greek-speaking population of Turkey, amounting to 1.5 million, expelled in the "Asia Minor disaster" in 1922 after Greece had failed in an aggressive campaign to take the western part of Anatolia. Greek now has a population of 11 million at home, and perhaps 2 million more in diaspora worldwide.² Its use as a lingua-franca has long been negligible, but five hundred years ago Greek had, for example, served as a diplomatic language for Ottoman contacts with Orthodox powers, as well as with Venice.³

This extreme outcome, though evidently possible in the very long run, seems an unlikely future viewed from current levels of Anglo-Saxon eminence in military power, economic influence, and cultural prestige—not to mention current levels of investment in learning English all round the world. But strong historic associations with British imperialism and U.S. hegemony may yet be felt as a millstone round the neck of English at some future point, when these great powers' relative influence has undergone decline. Rather than be totally rejected and thrown back on its homelands, English is more likely, in the near term, to suffer that intermediate fate which we could call Wimbledonization.

This term means becoming an institution that is dominated by foreigners, while continuing to bring some prestige and profit to its source country. It was used in financial circles to characterize the effect of the liberalizing "Big Bang" of October 27, 1986, in the United Kingdom. As at the great tennis championship, the City of London seemed to attract all the best players and profited from their presence, although little or no ownership remained English.*

If so, it will not be the first international language to come to this. During the eighteenth and nineteenth centuries, when Latin was in its last stage as a European lingua-franca, use of the language became particularly associated with the countries that had been the last to adopt it officially (albeit a millennium earlier), namely those of northern and eastern Europe. Whereas England and France had ceased all official government use of Latin by the sixteenth century, it continued in Poland and Hungary until the early decades of the nineteenth. German administrators of Poland found it unfortunately indispensable in 1798 "because . . . all the educated strata speak Latin." In Hungary, in 1790, the Austro-Hungarian emperor's attempt to abolish use of Latin (in favor of German) had to be rescinded "until further

---

* The term seems to have originated in Japan (as ウィンブルドン化 *winburudon-ka*) and is also widely used in Chinese (温布尔登化 *wēnbùĕrdēng-huà*). Equivalents are less familiar in European languages, though *Wimbledonisierung* (German) and *Wimbledonización* (Spanish) are well-known to Google. In general, the metaphor does not seem to have penetrated far beyond the original, financial application.

notice" because it was still the only neutral language among the different populations that spoke Hungarian, German, Czech, Rumanian, and Croatian.[4] Already in the seventeenth century French had replaced Latin as the diplomatic lingua-franca between France and most of its neighbors, and even the Holy Roman Empire, i.e. Germany, finally yielded to this practice with the Treaty of Rastatt in 1712; but elsewhere, especially in the north and east of Europe, treaties went on being negotiated and written in Latin till the late eighteenth century: e.g., between Sweden and England (1720); France and Poland (Versailles, 1735); Sweden and the Ottoman Empire (1737); Denmark and the Ottoman Empire (1756). Further east, even the Treaty of Nerchinsk, which in 1689 settled the eastern border between Russia and China, had its official text in Latin, beside translations into Russian and Manchu. (Chinese Mandarins had relied on linguistic and legal advice from Catholic Jesuit missionaries.)[5] And in 1829 Latin was still the language of choice for a letter "to whom it may concern" which the British left in a copper cylinder, marking their claim to the Isle of Deception in the South Shetlands off Antarctica, to the south of Argentina.[6]

In Scandinavia especially Latin was long retained for international communication, well in keeping with this outburst by Axel Oxenstierna, the Swedish chancellor in 1653: "Though he could, yet would not speak French, saying he knew no reason why that nation should be so much honoured more than others as to have their language used by strangers; but he thought the Latin more honourable and more copious, and fitter to be used, because the Romans had been masters of so great a part of the world, and yet at present that language was not peculiar to any people."[7]

This fondness for Latin in academic Scandinavia has had a long-term effect in making botany a Latin-using science, in which the official descriptions are written in Latin to this day, based on the binomial system of classification and description laid out by Carl Linnaeus, a Swede, in his *Philosophia Botanica* (1751).* In Norwegian literature, the excessive concentration on Latin in education was a major theme of Alexander Kielland's novel *Poison* (1883), its pathetic hero famously dying of exhaustion with the empty words *mensa rotunda* on his lips. Academic publishing in Latin continued into the early twentieth century. The tradition continues in some of the strangest places: since 1989 Finland has maintained a tradition of broadcast

---

* Contrast England, where the last major scientific work to appear in Latin, Newton's *Principia*, came out in 1687.

news reports in Latin, and when it has held the rotating presidency of the European Union (in the latter halves of 1999 and 2006), it has extended these to report on Europe as a whole, in the *Conspectus rerum Latinus*. This led to a call in August 2006 by the *Osservatore Romano*, the daily newspaper of the Vatican City, for Latin to be promoted as a working language of the European Union. But nothing seems to have come of this, not even a strengthened link between Latin's historic heartland in Rome and its Wimbledonized European periphery.

The Wimbledonization of English is already better known as International English, and its opposition to the "native-speaker ideal" is a major theme of modern debate in the theory of EFL, i.e. English taught as a foreign language. According to our figures in chapter 10, lingua-franca speakers of English outnumber mother tongue speakers by more than two to one. Many who are charged with teaching the next generation of lingua-franca speakers, or who discuss the status of different registers and dialects of English, believe that the outsiders, being in the majority, should now be accepted as the norm-setters for the language as it is taught. International English is proposed as a language in its own right, used daily for communication among nonnative speakers as well as with natives, with a de facto norm created by the people who use it.

In practice, this doctrine is hard to propagate since most learners naturally look to the native speaker as an intrinsic source of authority, to be taken at his or her own valuation. Only native speakers (though not all of them) feel they have nothing to prove in their use of the language because it is essentially defined by their speech and writing.* Everywhere in the English-teaching world discrimination continues in favor of employing native speakers where possible as teachers and models, even though young and inexperienced native speakers may well be much less knowledgeable about the language, and even in some cases less fluent in it, than foreign lifetime

---

* This pragmatism about where languages really come from applies even to the most artificial language of all, classical Sanskrit. In Patanjali's theory of the ultimate basis of Sanskrit, it was defined for all learners by the rules of Panini's grammar, but given its real-world value because that definition conforms with the natural speech of the *śiṣṭāḥ*, the educated classes, who grew up naturally speaking correctly in the Āryāvarta region, central India. Without their example, there would be no reason to follow the rules of grammar. (Deshpande 1993, 18–19, 80) Likewise, natives and nonnatives feel International English loses its sense without a native-speaker norm to inspire it and "show it the way."

teachers who have learned English as a second language but are very conscious of what it was that they learned. The theorists of International English now characterize this kind of discrimination as "the long shadow of native-speakerism."[8]

This attempt by EFL teachers to cut free of the native-speaker ideal for their stock-in-trade, the English language, is understandable. It removes a constraint on supply in the training of teachers, hence on growth in their industry; and it has the apparent social advantage of appearing more open and democratic: there is no right of birth to the best English. However, this apparently egalitarian spirit does not address two social facts that may ultimately be the undoing of International English. First, English-speaking is the mark of an exclusive elite in every society where it exists, outside the countries where English is natively spoken.* Second, the link of English with its dominant homelands cannot be forgotten: a settled role for English would be a standing affront to local nationalism.

Perhaps the elitism is not the fault of English, but of the situations where it flourishes as a lingua-franca: in the words of one English-teaching theorist, "It is not English that creates the elites: the elites absorb and appropriate English."[9] Still, those elites have achieved (or received) their positions in succession to British or U.S. colonialism. However it has come about, an association with social exclusiveness is a poor strategy for long-term survival: it creates resentment among the majority, and specifically the people who are looking for social change. The association has been particularly unfortunate in its consequences in the last couple of centuries, where many such linguistic elites have been dispossessed (and their acquired languages discontinued or discouraged) by Relegation or Resignation: French in the capitals of easterly Europe and the Mediterranean coast, and (much later) in North Africa and Vietnam; Swedish in Finland; Italian in Libya, Ethiopia, and Eritrea; Japanese in Taiwan and Korea; Russian in eastern Europe and Central Asia.

---

* The phrase *English-speaking elite* currently yields 143,000 hits on Google. Looking at the 12,500 instances from the latest decade (2000–2009), half of them refer to India or Pakistan (about fifty-fifty), and 12 percent to Singapore. Evidently this phrase is part of common-sense understanding of their societies. But the rest, three eighths of the total, are fairly evenly split (at 2–3 percent) among Canada, Europe, South Africa, Nepal, Sri Lanka, Malaysia, the Philippines, and China, with singletons for Nigeria, Hong Kong, Honduras, and Australia (contrasting this elite with Aboriginals). These are precisely the parts of the world where International English prevails.

The English-speaking elites must hope that their future fortunes are more like those of the Spanish- and Portuguese-speaking elites of Central and South America, who have held on to their positions (and their languages) triumphantly for two centuries after their countries' independence from European powers. But, crucially, in all those "Latin" countries, the vast majority of the populations had already become mother tongue speakers of Spanish or Portuguese when independence was achieved. This has emphatically *not* happened in any of the British or American ex-colonies; nor is it likely to in other places where International English is rife for political and economic reasons, notably Europe and Southeast Asia.

International English, i.e. English as a lingua-franca, has been or is being regenerated in one sense, changing its status in many of these countries from the language of imperial administration to the language of national or supranational unity. *Supranational* because this even applies to English as an official or working language of international government organizations, such as the Association of Southeast Asian Nations (ASEAN—English only), the North Atlantic Treaty Organization (NATO—with French), the Organization of American States (OAS—with French, Spanish, and Portuguese), the African Union (AU—with French, Spanish, Portuguese, Arabic, and Swahili), and the European Union (EU—where English mostly shares the work with French, but still tends to predominate in actual use).

The utility of English, therefore, as a practical language of wider communication is not in doubt under current conditions. But as a lingua-franca, it is a creature of those conditions, which have summoned it up and still sustain it. Such conditions are variable, and so English remains vulnerable to the various paths of decline described in Part III of this book. Hence, the key fact about the future of International English is that, wherever it is used, it is not regenerating in the other, more durable way, namely into a mother tongue. As Graddol, a major theorist of modern global English, points out,[10] what has spread round the world since the 1950s is not English so much as bilingualism with English; and English as a Second Language (quite justly, given the values that tend to come with it) lives on sufferance: it is only as good as its last deal.

Part of the reason for this apparent failure of International English to penetrate as a mother tongue may be time: it is just too recent as an incomer to be accepted for family use. Who knows how many generations it took for Aramaic to put down roots as a native language after the Assyrian Empire had seeded it across the length and breadth of its domains through the arbitrary deportations of population? This all happened, nonetheless, in the centuries of the early first millennium BC. How long did it take for Gaulish and Iberian locals to learn to talk like the Roman settlers in their midst and so lay down the linguistic foundations for the medieval languages of France and Spain? The existence of French and Spanish (and absence of Gaulish, Aquitanian, Celtiberian, and Tartessian) are indisputable evidence that sooner or later they did.

But spreading an international language in the current age does come across a major problem largely unknown to the ancient world: nationalism. Governments and their peoples want the apparent economic, and possibly political and social, benefits of access to the global market; but they (and particularly their governments) do not want to lose their identity, and hence legitimate title to control of their own domains, in so doing. Where a national language exists, it will not readily be given up.

Consider the case of the Netherlands, a friendly power to all the principal English-speaking polities, with no anti-Anglo-Saxon ax to grind. Here, since World War II, English has been taught at all levels of school, and command of it has become nearly universal in the middle class. The Dutch mass media have long included English-language TV and films undubbed and unsubtitled, without attracting any complaint. But when in 1990 Jo Ritzen, minister of education, proposed making English the sole official language of instruction at Dutch universities, the measure was rejected by the Dutch parliament, naturally on grounds of national sentiment. It has not returned, though Dutch bilingualism has become even more pervasive. Yet if everyone concerned is fluent and literate in English, why maintain the needless cost of academic book production with short production runs, in a language that simply sets a bound on communication? (The Netherlands also hosts many of the leading publishers of academic books in English.) As a mercantile nation, why not jump boldly into the global market in university instruction in English, taking advantage of the country's hard-won bilingualism in the most profitable second language? These are the kind of arguments that undermine the status and prospects of smaller languages all over the globe and, in extreme cases, threaten the languages' very existence. But when the potential victim is a national language, the proverbial "dialect with an army and a navy,"[11] such arguments tend to be resisted.

Thus, English as a global language is inevitably going to remain insecure, living as a widely distributed lingua-franca, on terms of "easy familiarity" with people all over the world, but because of powerful national loyalties countries will never accept this as their mother tongue. Everywhere outside its mother tongue countries, English will be like a friend of the family, but never a family member. We have seen that this makes it vulnerable to lingua-franca Relegation, where an acceptable substitute is to hand—and even (as in the case of Sri Lanka) where there is none, but a dominant and impatient group wants to deny it status and so demote its perceived elite users. In some cases where it is deeply established, this Relegation has been so long delayed (notably in India, where the original constitution had even set 1965 as a date for its removal as an official language) that it seems to have effectively been abandoned as a political project. Yet even in such countries, the social pressures that come from the spread of education and increasing equality are upsetting the balance that has historically allowed English to be seen as the solution.

It will be strange if India stays loyal to English once any serious trickle-down of its new and growing wealth occurs. Already, if it pursues seriously its declared objective to boost enrollment in higher education by 2015 (from 10 to 15 percent of the age cohort), this will put pressure on the traditional assumption that higher education must be in English.[12] Politically, it seems unlikely that Indian society would relegate English deliberately, much as many in the Hindi-speaking north would like to do so; but it may decide to promote the development of the scheduled languages (i.e. all the other ones with official status) while English marks time. An issue here must be resolved, even if the outcome is not clear in advance. Perhaps, like Latin America in the nineteenth century, India will hold on to the language of its former colonists and content itself with paying lip-service to *indigenismo*, its heroic native roots. But regional languages are entrenched in the government of India as they never were in Latin America. More likely, as in early modern Europe, it will be the elite lingua-franca that has to yield. The bonds that tie India to English are far weaker than those of tradition and sentiment that once tied the several countries of Europe to their Latin. Ultimately, this may lead to some kind of Resignation from the use of English by the elite.

Another, more complex case of English as a local lingua-franca competing with complex linguistic nationalisms is South Africa.

Within countries or organizations, the situation of English is often bound up with the struggle for influence among different mother tongues and may profit from it. We have seen many cases, especially in Africa and Asia, where opting to use it has seemed a convenient way to maintain neutrality among the rival claims of different local groups. Perhaps the same can be said for the choice to use English for international discourse in ASEAN or the African Union. But sometimes English is the mother tongue of one or more of the contending groups, yet it is still accepted as a lingua-franca.* This is the case in South Africa. How can this be?

In South Africa, English is definitely used as a neutral language in the country as a whole, which has since 1996 had eleven official languages. Its reputation may have been helped by the fact that, with 3.7 million speakers in South Africa, it is less significant as a local mother tongue, hence as a sectional community language, than Afrikaans is (with 4.7 million). But both languages have over 10 million second-language speakers there; so objectively, one might expect these two languages brought and developed by white colonists to be on a par. Yet English has, rather curiously, become seen as a symbol of the victory of liberalism and equal rights over the apartheid system, which remains associated with the Afrikaans language, even though most of its speakers are not white but miscellaneous members of the "Cape Colored" community.

This stems from some historical facts of the struggle for equality. Under apartheid, both English and Afrikaans had been official languages of the state, but the government was dominated by Afrikaans speakers. Meanwhile, most of the leaders of the opposition, though native speakers of various Bantu languages, had been educated in English (many at Fort Hare College in the Eastern Cape) and had English as their common language.

---

* A striking, if long-forgotten, example of a set of power groups adopting the language of one of them as its diplomatic lingua-franca is seen in the Near East of the fourteenth century BC, in the "Amarna correspondence": 382 letters between the king of Egypt and all the great powers of the period, from Asia Minor to the Persian Gulf: kings of Babylon, Mitanni, Arzawa, Alashiya, the Hittites, the Hurrians, Ugarit, as well as the leaders of various Phoenician and Palestinian cities, many of them clearly Egyptian vassals. Yet they are written not in Egyptian, but in Akkadian, the language of Assyria and Babylon.

Neither Assyria nor Babylon was by any means politically dominant at this point, both being under foreign control. Rather, Akkadian as a lingua-franca seems to have been the beneficiary of the founder effect: all these powers (but Egypt) had derived their literacy from the tradition developed in Mesopotamia. Akkadian had been the language of every scribe's school days, as they learned how to apply its system to their own languages. So, conveniently, it was taken up for international correspondence.

The English-language press too tended to be more liberal than that published in Afrikaans.* English, by association, came to be felt as more progressive than its fellow colonial language Afrikaans.

In the 1994 negotiations over the constitution and the choice of official languages, white Afrikaners insisted that Afrikaans must keep official status, so blocking what would probably have been the African National Congress's first choice (motivated by a rather dubious pragmatism), namely simply to drop Afrikaans and use English alone. Therefore, all the other languages that had been associated with apartheid "homelands" had their claims reinstated, and the result was a "rainbow" of eleven languages, consisting of four mutually intelligible Nguni languages (Zulu, Xhosa, Swati, Ndebele), three more closely related Sotho languages (Pedi, Sotho, and Tswana), and two more, yet still distantly related, Bantu languages, Venda and Tsonga as well as Afrikaans and English.†

Nevertheless, despite this nominal equality of all, and a continuing hubbub of dissatisfaction at what is being done for all the other languages, use of English has in practice predominated ever since, especially in the public and official realms of Parliament, the courts, local government, and the army and police forces. The Afrikaans speakers feel the changed regime the most since only they had been used to seeing their own language used in these domains. English is also expanding its coverage to a large extent in higher education, as English courses are demanded even at the relatively few colleges that were traditionally only for Afrikaans speakers, which squeezes out the

---

* Nelson Mandela had as a mother tongue Xhosa, practiced law in English, but became notorious for his consummate command of Afrikaans, which he urged his comrades to study, on the "know the enemy" principle: "To wage war, Mr. Mandela told his fellow inmate, Mac Maharaj, 'you must understand the mind of the opposing commander. You can never outmanoeuvre him unless you understand him, and you can't understand him unless you understand his literature and his language.'" (Waldmeir 1998, ch. 1)

The *Rand Daily Mail*, *Sunday Express*, and the *Daily Dispatch* were English-language newspapers with a liberal agenda. When the *Rand Daily Mail* and *Sunday Express* were closed down in 1985, they were replaced by another English-language title, the *Weekly Mail*. *Die Volksblad*, *Die Burger*, and *Transvaler* were Afrikaans papers that aligned with the National Party and took a government line.

† The oldest, arguably indigenous, languages of the country, of the Khoi, Nama, and San families, were not given this status because their speaker numbers are so low. But the same constitution set up a Pan–South African Languages Board (PANSALB), with instructions to promote these along with the official languages, as well as the majority of immigrant-community languages, religious languages, and sign language. On paper, and in aspiration, this constitution has something for almost everyone.

highest level of Afrikaans discourse, a hard-won achievement of the twentieth century. By comparison with that 1990 Ritzen proposal in the Netherlands, proponents of Afrikaans are finding that without an "army and navy" of its own, its position is hard to defend.

This is the current situation, but it only reflects the outcome of the first fifteen years under the new constitution, not yet even a generation. Still, the trend is clearly against Afrikaans, which has suffered Relegation under this new dispensation; its use as a lingua-franca has taken a heavy blow, and as a mother tongue too it appears to be in rapid decline. Speaker populations from 1996 to 2006 show a drop in speakers from 5.81 to 4.74 million, or 18.4 percent. All the other languages, however, are increasing, and English, which registers a 6.1 percent increase in the period, pales against the average growth recorded for the Bantu languages (all the rest) of 11.3 percent. Afrikaans is still the third most populous language (after Zulu and Xhosa), but at these rates it will be overtaken by the next two Bantu languages (Sotho and Pedi), and indeed English itself, in the coming decade.

More to the point, though, as a proportion of the population, mother tongue speakers of ex-colonial languages (Afrikaans and English) as a group are declining (by 19.1 percent) even faster than the absolute percentage decline in mother tongue Afrikaans on its own (18.4 percent), and Bantu proportions are almost stable.

South African English, then, although still flourishing as a lingua-franca, is not gaining ground as a mother tongue; in fact it is losing its relative position. The pattern of the world is repeated, on a smaller scale, even in this country where it might have been thought that the balance was swinging in favor of English. South Africa is not losing its language diversity, at least among all these official languages, which cover some 90 percent of the total population. When technology is sophisticated enough to make the utility of English as a lingua-franca irrelevant, there will be little to stop its simply being abandoned.

∞∞∞

But if not English, what next?

In the medium term, probably by the middle of this century, and possibly earlier, as discussed in chapter 11, a global lingua-franca will no longer he needed. Language technology will take care of interpreting and translation, and foreign-language learning will be become an unnecessary chore, except for specialists and enthusiasts. Active communication with speakers of other

### South African Official Languages (as Mother Tongues), 1996–2006

| LANGUAGE | 1996 | 2006 | 2006/1996 (%) | CHANGE (%) |
|---|---|---|---|---|
| AFRIKAANS | 5,811,547 | 4,740,000 | 81.6 | -18.4 |
| ENGLISH | 3,457,467 | 3,670,000 | 106.1 | 6.1 |
| NDEBELE | 586,961 | 640,000 | 109.0 | 9.0 |
| PEDI | 3,695,846 | 4,090,000 | 110.7 | 10.7 |
| SOTHO | 3,104,197 | 4,240,000 | 136.6 | 36.6 |
| SWATI | 1,010,000 | *1,133,428* | *112.2* | *12.2* |
| TSONGA | 1,756,105 | 1,940,000 | 110.5 | 10.5 |
| TSWANA | 3,301,774 | 3,410,000 | 103.3 | 3.3 |
| VENDA | 876,409 | 980,000 | 111.8 | 11.8 |
| XHOSA | 7,196,118 | 7,790,000 | 108.3 | 8.3 |
| ZULU | 9,200,144 | 9,980,000 | 108.5 | 8.5 |
| TOTAL | 39,996,568 | 42,613,428 | 106.5 | 6.5 |
| TOTAL NON-AFRIKAANS | 33,175,021 | 36,740,000 | 110.7 | 10.7 |
| TOTAL BANTU | 30,727,554 | 34,203,428 | 111.3 | 11.3 |
| TOTAL POPULATION | 42,718,530 | 47,939,000 | 112.2 | 12.2 |
| BANTU LANGUAGES | 71.93% | 71.35% | 99.2 | -0.8 |
| "EX-COLONIAL" LANGUAGES | 21.70% | 17.54% | 80.9 | -19.1 |

*Sources: 1996: South African census; 2006: estimates in Lewis 2009.*

*Note: 2006 figure for Swati (absent in Lewis 2009) has been estimated neutrally using average growth of population for South Africa as a whole.*

languages will no more require a special skill than is currently needed to read a foreign text in translation, or to follow the subtitles of a foreign-language video.

This will not happen immediately, but the importance of English is likely to be downgraded anyway as the relative political and economic power of non-English-using states increases. It is often assumed that power politics and the global competition among great states will naturally be reflected linguistically. Hence if English is doomed to pass with the predominance of the USA, then it must, it is presumed, be followed by some other common language. The choice falls most obviously on Chinese, since this is already the world language with most mother tongue speakers, and on current trends the Chinese economy is growing to be the largest in the world.

As the international importance of the Chinese language grows, and as the Chinese become richer and more widely influential, their concern to participate in the world on terms set by Anglo-Saxons will diminish. There is already evidence of this highly predictable change. Although the 2008 Pew Global Attitudes Survey in China reported, "Most Chinese (77 percent) agree that 'children need to learn English to succeed in the world to-day,'" it continued that this was ". . . down substantially from 2002, when 92 percent agreed with this view." The trend in opinion may well be more significant than the current belief held by a majority.

Chinese, like all the great languages of the modern world excepting English and French, remains very much a localized language in eastern and southeastern Asia, even if it is set to be the language of the world's dominant economic power, and with a truly vast number of speakers to boot. It may well increase its currency in some parts of the world (notably Africa), but the current political structure of the world system makes it unlikely that Chinese will get the chance to seed itself as the common language in new communities around the world that might use it as a lingua-franca. The age of colonial empires is unlikely to be repeated in an era of (rapidly) globalized communications and (gradually) equalizing education; and yet colonialism is the only mechanism hitherto shown capable of creating the basis for global lingua-francas.

In such a world, when the dominion of English had come to its end, what would be the new world language order? No evidence at present suggests that any one language will step up to replace English as an aspirant universal lingua-franca. All of these newly grown economic powers would be emphasizing their own importance, and hence right to express themselves directly and naturally in their own mother tongues. Others with less developed economic clout, but no less sense of their historical identity, such as the Arabic- and Persian-speaking worlds, will be striving to make their own views and voices heard—and language technologies will be making it easier for them to do just that, without thereby being lost or drowned out in the global marketplace.

Similarly, no single language took the position left vacant by Latin's decline in the seventeenth century. Global use of French did increase more than that of other languages at that time, but this was only in some domains, notably diplomacy; and international French when it spread had a different profile from Latin's old, dusty pomposity, carving out new realms in the culture of the *salon*, with displays of courtly and aristocratic wit, and popular fiction, now for a significant female readership. There had been nothing in Latin like Rousseau's bestselling sentimental novel, *Julie, ou la nouvelle Héloïse*, of 1761, though it was paralleled in other contemporary languages, especially English and German. Likewise we can expect that the new linguistic lions of the twenty-first and twenty-second centuries will find different ranges to conquer from those familiar from the fading era of English dominance.

In a world not dominated by a single "global" language, multilinguality will be much more prominent, and awareness of other languages will be routine.

First, for example, material originated in a single favorite language will no longer be expected to somehow have priority over all others. (Recall the current gross imbalance in the markets for published translations, with the English-language market translating virtually nothing of other languages' output, while those other languages have publishing industries heavily stocked with translations from English.)

Second will be the increasing worldwide expectation, no longer just in the English-speaking world, that making statements in one's own language is sufficient to reach the world. Initially this will only hold if the language is one of the "big beasts" of chapter 10, but increasingly the size and importance of the language will be irrelevant. (This already holds for opinion formers with supranational or global status since they can rely on an army of interpreters and translators who will flash their statements round the world; as soon as it is in English, it is globally accessible.\* But in the near future,

---

\* Osāma bin Lāden and Ayman az̧-Z̧awāhirī, who issue audio and video recordings as spokesmen for al-Qaʻida, are evident cases in point. But at present, it is surprisingly

global communications, incorporating elements of language technology, will make this a routine possibility for everyone.)

A third point is that more and more, people will encounter pockets of other language users in their own countries, some of them communities of immigrants, some of them indigenous groups who are a minority in their home state. In either case, their distinctive languages will be retained by many because they wish to keep a historic linguistic connection, and indeed the social traditions of their societies. Increasingly, given technical advances, this will be no necessary barrier to communication. (Just as it has traditionally been considered a mark of loyalty to one's nation to know the national language, the last few decades have seen an increasing appreciation of the value of a language as a mark of identity for smaller groups, and those far from "home." Combined with the results of twentieth-century-style migration—in which immigrants were suppliants, individually seeking work or political refuge, and in no position simply to throw indigenous inhabitants off their land—this has meant that modern societies have become dotted with migrant communities with links to less developed or less peaceful societies in distant parts of the world.)

Fourth, when new nations are constituted, we can expect them to embrace multilinguality. This has already started. South Africa (constituted in 1994) has eleven official languages, as well as a government organization to protect all the rest; Eritrea (in 1997) made none of its nine recognized languages official; and East Timor (in 2002), besides declaring indigenous Tetum and colonial Portuguese as its official languages, also admitted English and Indonesian Malay as provisional working languages, while recognizing seventeen other local languages.

The world's new linguistic order, brought into being by the breakdown of English-speaking linguistic hegemony and the self-assertion of newly rich powers such as China, India, Brazil, and others, will have sufficient balance to allow no single linguistic bloc to dominate. This will be a reasonably stable state of affairs, since technology will ensure that the communicative power of any of the major languages will essentially be global. English speakers will at first find that they can "get further" with their own language than speakers of other languages, i.e. be understood more widely without the use

---

difficult to think of individuals besides national leaders who can find an audience directly with the world's media without addressing them in English.

of technical aids; but this will largely be a historical hangover. As each major nation discovers that it can guarantee its global markets without use of English, and rely rather on technological support to supplement its own language, it will lose interest and motivation in continuing to invest in learning this traditional lingua-franca of the twentieth and early twenty-first centuries. International English will tend to die out, and English, like modern Greek, will find itself thrown back on heartlands where it is spoken natively.

Cultural diversity, and diverse linguistic loyalties, are ancient and persistent traits of human societies. This is the social order created by mother tongues, where each community has its own language, as if by nature. A wider uniformity of language is, by contrast, hard-won and needs enforcement. That has long seemed to be a price worth paying, since through much of known history a forged unity has been conducive to strength—in aggression or defense, in market organization, and even in religious faith. Strength is attractive, and to achieve such unity, or at least mutual understanding, many have been ready to accept a common lingua-franca.

But a lingua-franca, even the most universal, is a burden. It is only to be borne if necessary for some greater good. If not, then at the first opportunity it will be laid down. One day English too, the last lingua-franca to be of service to a multilingual world, will be laid down. Thereafter everyone will speak and write in whatever language they choose, and the world will understand.

# *Notes*

## Chapter 1: The Edges of English

1. For literal and metaphorical uses of *Latin* in the Romance languages of the twelfth and thirteenth centuries, see Ostler 2007, 177. For the early history of *lingua franca* see Kahane 1976. To judge from the *Oxford English Dictionary* and Google News Timeline, *lingua franca* did not become (in English) a bland, general term for a contact vernacular, and then any language of wider communication, until the mid-nineteenth century.

2. Cicero, *Brutus* xxxvii.140.

3. Pliny the Elder (AD 23–79), *Naturalis Historia* iii.39.

4. Dante Alighieri, *De vulgari eloquentia* i.9.11: *grammatica nihil aliud est quam quaedam inalterabilis locutionis identitas diversibus temporibus atque locis* (ca 1303).

5. Goethe, *Maximen und Reflexionen* 91: *Wer fremde Sprachen nicht kennt, weiß nichts von seiner eigenen.*

6. Combining 2–3 percent in 2008 with 6 percent in 2005, figures expressed diffidently (faute de mieux) in www.wischenbart.com/diversity/report/Diversity_percent20-Report_prel-final_02.pdf and www.wischenbart.com/de/essays__interviews_rw/wischenbart_publishing-diversity_oxford-2005.pdf. The level is not in dispute, even if precise figures are not researched.

7. Wittgenstein, *Tractatus Logico-philosophicus*, v.6: „*Die Grenzen meiner Sprache bedeuten die Grenzen meiner Welt.*" (My translation, substituting *signify* for the C. K. Ogden's *mean*.) The emphasis, both in English and German, is Wittgenstein's. The intent of this maxim is very different in its original context, referring as it does to the relation between the logical status of the subjective world and the expressive power of any language used to describe it, each sharing the same necessary limits. But the trenchancy of Wittgenstein's language is unbeatable.

8. Malay is only used generally in Brunei's education system for the first three years; thereafter, in the rest of the school curriculum, it is used specifically to teach Malay, Islamic, cultural studies, arts, and physical education. At university, only Malay and Islamic studies offer degrees in Malay. All the rest, including all sciences, history, accounting, and technical subjects, are in English. This is from Omar 2007, 358, whence too come the explicit quotes. The statistic for use of (Brunei) Malay is derived from Lewis 2009.

9. Details from Omar 2007, and Omar 2004, 130–31.

10. See Dharmadasa 2007.

11. Most of the details here come from relevant chapters in Simpson 2008, notably Topan 2008.

12. Brooke 2005.

13. This is my inference. In 1975, sixteen years later, only 27 percent of those over forty—i.e., who had been over twenty-four at independence—claimed to understand English. Crystal 2003, 57.

14. Crystal 2003, 57; Goh et al. 1979, 403. English-speaking households apparently increased from 11.6 percent in 1980 to 20.8 percent in 1990, while in the same period Chinese-speaking households were declining from 59.5 percent to 38.2 (Pakir 1993).

15. Thompson 2003, 15–17.

16. Thompson 2003, 20–21. The clergyman was John Devins.

17. Ammon 1996, 249–50. The chart is a synopsis of figures in Fränzel 1939, as given by Ammon.

18. Figures from Eurobarometer 2006.

19. Notably Graddol 2008.

# Chapter 2: How Various in the Future?

1. Kachru 1985, 366–67.

2. Mufwene 2001, 8–9; 2008, 226–34.

3. See Ostler 2007, 159–76, 257–59, for a fuller account of the complicated story of Latin's fission into Occitan, French, Catalan, Castilian, Gallego, Tuscan Italian, Corsican, Sardinian, Rumanian, and many others, less well-known or well recognized.

4. These figures are derived from the list in Masica 1991, Appendix I, where the author insists that these entries represent languages, not dialects (which are also listed, numbering some 250 more). An attempt is made to elucidate the rise of the Indo-Aryan literary languages in place of Sanskrit in Pollock 2006, especially 491–94. It is revealing that so little concrete can be said about it, even though it is the principal topic of this book of 684 pages.

5. See Elimam 1977 and 2004.

6. Suárez 1983, 14–18. The SIL's authoritative catalog of languages, *Ethnologue* (Lewis 2009), currently names not nineteen but twenty-eight languages under Nahuatl, including supposedly extinct "Classical Nahuatl."

7. King 1994, 91–93.

8. Schleicher 1871, 6, as excepted and translated in Lehmann 1967, 92.

9. Sebba 1997, 28.

10. The theory is due to Beckwith 2009, 365–69.

11. Edgerton 1951, 4–6.

12. This aspect of common sense is actually endorsed in sociolinguistics by a tradition known as Communication Accommodation Theory, e.g., Giles et al. 1991.

13. en.wikipedia.org/wiki/List_of_dialects_of_the_English_language; and en.wikipedia.org/wiki/English-based_creole_languages.

14. Hoban 1980, 28–29.

# Part II: Lingua-Francas Past

1. Literally: "A language is a gem, whose value to count | in clarity are people of speech incapable | those which are mean are lethal | ready-to-open-eyes is the anointed one for the incapacitated." Here *masīḥ* is the Arabic equivalent to Hebrew/Greek/English *Messiah*.

# Chapter 3: The Pragmatism of Empire

1. *Novella Constitutio* xv, preface (I.80, von Lingenthal).
2. Guatemala, letter of September 8, 1551. Colección Muñoz, vol. 86, fol. 54v.
3. Strabo xv.2.8: *eisi gar pôs homoglôttoi para mikron*.
4. See McAlpin 1981.
5. Herodotus i.136.
6. *hacā Sakaibiš tayaiy para Sugdam amata yātā ā Kūšā hacā Hidauv amata yātā ā Spardā* (DPh 6–8=DH 5–6).
7. Gershevitch 1979, 114–15.
8. Tavernier 2007, 78.
9. Lemaire and Lozachmeur 1996.
10. Qashqa'i, a southern Oghuz Turkic language, arrived in the early second millennium AD. Khalaj (previously Arghu), another more archaic kind of Turkic, may have arrived much earlier, but is first mentioned in a Central Asian Manichaean text of 759–80 AD. Johansson and Csató 1998, 276–77.
11. Greenfield 1985, 708; Polotsky 1971; Schaeder 1930, 208.
12. Khanlari 1979, 2:37; Frye 1996, 19; Danner 1975, 575–76.
13. The first (phonetic and philosophical) contributions to the grammar of Persian are due to Avicenna, writing two centuries after Sībawaih and al-Khalīl bin Aḥmad, e.g., his *Asbāb ḥudūṭ al-ḥurūf* 'Reasons for the incidence of the letters'. See Windfuhr 1979, 9–11. Conversely, the first Arabic grammar of Persian seems as late as the mid-sixteenth century: *Ṣiḥāḥ al-'Ajam* 'Verities of Persian' (see Ermers 1999, 36).
14. Danner 1975, 576–80.
15. 'Abd al-Ḥamīd, *Kurd 'Ali*, 225, quoted by Danner 1975, 577.
16. Lazard 1989, 287.
17. Lazard 1975, 607.
18. Abū Rayḥān al-Bīrūnī, *The Remaining Signs of Past Centuries*, 35.36.48: "When Qutaibah bin Muslim under the command of Al-Ḥajjāj ibn Yūsuf was sent to Khwarazmia with a military expedition and conquered it for the second time, he swiftly killed whoever wrote the Khwarazmian native language that knew of the Khwarazmian heritage, history, and culture. He then killed all their Zoroastrian priests and burned and wasted their books, until gradually the illiterate only remained, who knew nothing of writing, and hence their history was mostly forgotten."
19. Humbach 1989, 193.
20. Lurje 2003.
21. Sims-Williams 1989, 231.
22. Some more possible examples of this kind of assimilation in language shift can be found at Ostler 2005, 553–56.
23. Frye 1995, 215–17.

24. Bahār, *Sabk-shenāsi*, ii.13f: preface to his Persian translation of Ṭabarī's *Tafsīr*, commentary on the Koran.

25. Lazard 1975, 603; Richter-Bernburg 1979, 57.

26. Bulliet 1994.

27. *Dānešnāmā* ii.182.83.

28. Al-Bīrūnī, *Preface to Ṣaidana*: reported in Richter-Bernburg 1979, 59–60; Lazard 1975, 631.

29. Kai Ka'us bin Eskandar, *Qābusnāme*, ed. R. Levy, 119, lines 14ff, reported in Richter-Bernburg 1979, 58–59; and Šahmardān bin Abi'l-Ḥair in his *Garden of the Astronomers*, ca 1073, quoted from Lazard 1975, 632.

## Chapter 4: When the Writ of Persian Ran

1. Too legendary for his name to be quite clear. Bumyn's name, so attested in the Turkic inscriptions of Orkhon, is actually written 土門 in Chinese, so could be Tumyn. But this latter is the same name as the founder of the Korean Koguryo, and the Xiong-nu. The Greek spelling of his clan is Ἀρσιλας (arsilas), and the Chinese 阿史那, which in the fifth century AD would have been phonetically *'aṣi'na'*. Discussed in detail by Beckwith 2009, 390, 410–12.

2. Clausen 1962, 30. "Khan-kings of the Turks" is a translation of an Arabic title, *al-mulūk al-xaniyya al-atrāk*. This rapid summary of early Turk activities is drawn largely from Golden 1998, 19–24.

3. A verse quoted by Niẓām al-Mulk (1018–92), in his *Siyāsatnāme* "Book of Government" xxvii.

4. Christian 1998, 370.

5. From 1245 to the fifteenth century. Clausen 1962, 48.

6. Dankoff 1983, 1, 10–12, 264–67; Doerfer 1998, 240. The meter is called *mutaqārib* and became the standard for epic.

7. Clausen 1962, 48

8. Borah 1934, 326–27, quoting the preface to Amir Khusrau's *Ghurrat al-Kamāl* "Acme of Perfection," which includes a brief biography of the poet.

9. Cribb et al. 1999, 153.

10. Joveini, *Tārīkh-i jahān-gushā* 'The History of the World Conqueror', i.4–5, quoted by Martinez 1991, 142.

11. These stories are taken up in Ostler 2007, 133–43.

12. Māḥmud Karīm ad-Dīn Aq Sarāyi, *Musāmarat al-akhbār wa musāyarat al-aḥyār* 'Entertainment of Affairs and Adjustment of Confusions', 180f, 299f, based on the selections and partial translations in Martinez 1991.

13. Golden 2000, 2; Doerfer 1998, 240.

14. Doerfer 1998, 240, summarizing his voluminous studies 1963–75.

15. 'Abd al-Ghani 1929, 46.

16. . . . *ita ab exteris diligitur quae in ipsâ patriâ sordet magnatibus.* Engelbert K[a]empfer, who visited Iran in 1685. Quoted in Doerfer 1998, 240.

17. Fragner 1999, 70.

18. Dale 2004, 149.

19. Devereux 1966, 5.

20. Ibid., 6.

21. Borah 1934, 325–26, from preface to Amir Khusrau's *Ghurrat al-Kamāl*.

22. E.g., Marc-Antoine Muret (1526–85): "As for the man who knows Greek and Latin, he will be admired by the majority wherever in the world he arrives." Cited in Ostler 2007, 233.

23. Dale 2004, 251; Thackston 1994, x.

24. Hadi 1995; Yule and Burnell, 1886, s.v. "Moonshee."

25. Devereux 1966, xi.

26. The sentence, from *Bābur-nāma*, f. 5b, is cited in Dale 2004, 153. The word-order examples are likewise derived from Dale 2004, 151, and the general rules given by Eckmann 1966, 204ff. The underlying persistence of Turkic verb-final order is shown by the consistency of Tekin 1968 with Lewis 1967. The general malleability of Chagatay and Ottoman Turkic to Persian is noted at Johanson and Csató 1998, 118; Turkish survivals of Persian *ezāfe* are described by Lewis 1967, 50–52.

27. Besides these evident crossovers from Persian to Urdu and other north-Indian languages in sound structure and vocabulary, some have suggested more subtle and profound influences emanating from Persian. Could Persian's third-person pronoun *u* or *way* 'he/she/it' be the origin of Hindi/Urdu's mysterious *wo* or *wah*, with the same neutrality of meaning? (It is quite unlike any Sanskrit pronouns, but is paralleled by similar terms in languages across the northern plains from Bengal to Afghanistan.) Could the Persian marking of definite direct objects with -*rā* (previously a marker of indirect objects) explain a similar transformation in the use of -*ko* in Hindi/Urdu and -*nuŋ* in Panjabi? Could Persian relative clauses, where the head noun is marked with –*i* and the following clause starts with *keh*, have caused the reinforcement of Hindi/Urdu relatives, marked with *jo*, to pick up a reinforcing *ki*? (These three possibilities are hinted in Masica 1991, respectively p. 225, p. 367, and p. 414.) The evidence is diffuse and difficult to present simply, leaving the answers unclear; and the case is complicated by the fact that all these Indian languages have typically had relative clauses that come before their head nouns, just the opposite of the system in Persian. Still, it is undeniable some Indian relative clauses are to be found following their heads, in different languages and texts from Braj (the *Xaṛī Bōlī* of the sixteenth century) to modern Kashmiri and Hindi/Urdu, and there is little else but Persian influence to explain the loosening of the system. (Masica 1991, 414)

28. Cited in Azeri and Persian by http://www.azargoshnasp.net/recent_history/atoor/responseasgharzadeh/asghrazadehresponse.htm (translation mine).

## Chapter 5: Traders' Languages and the Language for Trade

1. Plautus, *Poenulus* 112–13: *et is omnes linguas scit, sed dissimulat sciens | se scire: poenus plane est. quid verbis opust?*

2. *Xin tang Shu* 新唐書 'New Tang History,' 221B.1.a.

3. Bible, 1 Kings 10:11.

4. Lancel 1997, 357–58; Cribb et al. 1999, 227.

5. Daniels and Bright 1996, 262.

6. Ovid, *Tristia* v.10.35–42; Strabo, *Geography* xi.16.

7. Among the 189 Etruscan loans in Latin listed in Ostler 2007, 323–25, 51 are clearly of Greek origin; 6 of the 8 nautical terms are Greek.

8. Justin, *Epitome of the Philippic Histories of T. Pompeius Trogus* xx.5.12–13.

9. Polybius, iii.20.5; Diodorus Siculus, xxvi.4; Cornelius Nepos, *Hannibal* xiii.3. The language used by the mercenaries is not crystal clear: but Polybius remarks (i.32.7) that the Spartan Xanthippus "began the giving of commands according to rules." In the great mutiny (241–238) of the mercenaries after the end of the First Punic War, some of their coins carried a legend in Greek, ΛΙΒΥΩΝ 'Libyans'.

10. Livy, xxviii.46 fin.

11. Aristotle, *Politics* viii.3.1338a15–17; Harris 1989, 25–26.

12. Herodotus, *Histories* iv.77–80.

13. Powell 1991, 219–20.

14. Plutarch, *Crassus* fin.

15. Thucydides, iii.38: *sophistôn theataîs*.

16. Pelliot 1912, 105. The skeptical point is made by Skaff 2003, 475–76 (footnotes).

17. Walter 2006, 15–18; Pulleyblank 1952, 324–25.

18. Sims-Williams 1996, 52–56.

19. Menandros Protēktōr 'Menander the Guardsman', fragment 10, reported and discussed in de la Vaissière 2002, 222–33.

20. See, e.g., Babayarov and Kubatin 2009.

21. *Shiji* 史記 123, p. 3174 (tr. Watson 1993, 245).

22. *Da tang xiyu ji* 大唐西域記 Book 1, trans. Beal 1884, 26–27.

23. *Tang hui-yao* 唐会要 'Important Documents of the Tang' (Chinese Annals), as cited in Mori 1979, 30; also Watson 1983, 553.

24. Skaff 2003, 493–94.

25. *Hanshu* 漢書 'Book of the Han' 96A, 3893.

26. *Sanguozhi* 三國志 'Records of Three Kingdoms' 4, 895.

27. Sims-Williams 1996, 49–51.

28. Schafer 1963, 61, 295n29, quoting Richard Frye's statement that this was a Sogdian word. Sims-Williams 1996, 61n77, concurs with Frye, noting that the Chinese version 吃撥 (now *chībō*) would have then been pronounced *tcʰit-pat*. Sogdian *čerðpaðu* 'four-foot' appears in the *Vessantara Jātaka* story at lines 1178 and 1484.

29. De la Vaissière 2002, 267. A dirham was a silver coin (weighing just under three grams), and twenty were worth a *mithqāl* (4.4 grams) of gold, coined as a dinar.

30. Schafer 1963, 64

31. An-Lushan, as reported by de la Vaissière 2002, 213–14; Kang Senghui per Walter 2006, 23–26.

32. Foltz 1999, 13.

33. Tremblay 2001, 99–100; Foltz 1999, 74, 78.

34. Also, one fragmentary medical text is in Brahmi script, bilingual in Sanskrit and Sogdian. Sims-Williams 1989b, 178.

35. Tremblay 2001, 15, 54–55; Compareti et al. 2006 (especially papers by Osawa, Stavisky); Babayarov and Kubatin 2009.

36. De la Vaissière 2002, 200, citing ultimately *Suishu* 隋書 'Book of the Sui' 67, 1582.

37. See Pelliot and Chavannes 1911~1913 for the whole story. The Arabic word for the planet Saturn is *keyvān*, not a god at all. It is ultimately borrowed from the Akkadian name *kaiamanu* 'steadfast'. The phonetics given here assign the pronunciation reconstructed for the eight century (Late Middle Chinese) (as per Pulleyblank 1991) to the characters (themselves unchanged till 1956).

38. Henning 1939; de la Vaissière 2002, 286.

39. Lifshits 2004, 17.

40. Hourani 1995, 36; Gervase 1963, 97; Daryaee 2003. The trade may have been pioneered (outside royal auspices) by the Bażrāngi clan from the first century BC. The Bażrāngi, originally from Zrāngi (known in Greek as Drangiana), in southern Iran, apparently established Persian colonies in Mazun on the southern shore of the Persian Gulf from the second century AD, then (feeling pressure from the Parthians) farther afield on the African coast. Bażrāngi activities became detached, and known as the Kilwa Empire, after Ardashir I had expelled its parent state from southern Persia in AD 224, and his son Shahpur I had taken the remaining possessions in Oman and Muscat.

   *Zangīg* certainly became a widespread Perso-Arab term for negroids, picked up as *zanj* or *zinj* (pl. *zunuj*) in Arabic and used all over the Indian Ocean, even in China as *sēngqí* (a word for black slaves). It is even possible that *zangīg* was a back-formation from *Zangibar*, and that that was a deformation of *Bażrāngi-bār* 'coast of the Bażrāngi'.

41. Schafer 1951, 407, 410, 413–16.

42. Ibid., 403; Curtin 1984, 106.

43. Pelliot 1913, 185, quoted and commented on by Schafer 1951, 405.

44. Baker 1996, 654, refers this to Ḥasan 1928, 80; it is said to occur in an Arabic text before AD 564, but both words occur in Steingass's Persian dictionary, meaning 'boat, skiff'. The term *buzi*, in thirteenth-century Venetian Italian, meant a round ship (Martin 2001, 207).

45. Ferrand 1924. *Nāmag* is the Pahlavi original of Modern Persian *nāmeh* 'book'.

46. Ibid., 238–44; Yule and Burnell 1886, s.vv.; *necodá* passim in Fernão Mendes Pinto's *Peregrinação* (1614). It is also used, in the form *nākhū* (of a Muslim captain Firūz), in a Sanskrit inscription at Veraval, on the Gujarati coast, from 1264 (Sircar 1960, 143).

47. De la Vaissière 2002, 179.

48. Somadeva, *Kathāsaritsāgaram* vii.3.36; Gode and Karve 1957, s.v. *Tājika;* Monier-Williams 1899, s.v. *Tājaka*; Mahmud al-Kashgari, *Dīwānu l-Luġat al-Turk*, s.v. *Tejik.* The history of this word, with all those responsible for inferring it, can be read in Sundermann 1993, 165–67.

49. Minorsky 1913–36.

50. Huang et al. 1992

51. Pelliot 1913, 185, quoted by Schafer 1951, 405.

52. *Archivum Secretum Apostolicum Vaticanum (ASV), Archivum Arcis, Armoria i–xviii,* 1802 (2). This multilingual document had a preface in Turkic, and the date in Arabic, as well as an official seal in Mongol. The fact that Persian was not universally seen as the obvious lingua-franca at the time is shown in that the pope's original message (written presumably in Latin or Greek) had laboriously had to be translated via versions in Russian and Arabic, before being read to the khan in Qara Qorum. As surviving records show (*ASV, A.A., Arm. i–xviii,* 1801), when the Mongol Il-Khans of Persia later wrote to European addressees (Arghun to King Philippe le Bel of France in 1289 and to Pope Nicholas IV in 1290, Ghazan to Boniface VIII in 1302, Öljeitü to Philippe in 1305), their letters were delivered in the original Mongol, and the vertical Uyghur script. (http://asv.vatican.va/en/doc/1246.htm and asv.vatican.va/en/arch/mongolian.htm, with more details from www.silk-road.com/artl/carrub.shtml)

53. Huang et al. 1992. The "passports" or "tablets of authority" were badges of office issued to high officials, and also known in Chinese as *paizi* 牌子. Dillon 1999, 18–23; Allsen 2000, 31. The quote is from Dillon, 1999, 156.

54. Allsen 2000, 36–37, quoting *Yuanshi* 元史 'Yuan History' 39, p. 839, and Huang 1986.

55. The paizah authorizes the bearer to work at night. The Persian inscription (on the left) reads: *itimād mānand bar lauḥ-i šab gašt* 'credential valid as tablet for night patrol'. (Rachewiltz 1982, 417). The other two inscriptions say something else in two orthographies for Mongolian, the pan-Mongol 'Phagspa script (center) and the Uyghur script (on the right): *jar t'uŋqaq ma·uni seregdek'u* 'official declaration: of-villains beware!' (Poppe 1957, Text X, with transcription and translation, and notes 71–73). Chinese text occupies the other side: 宣慰使司都元帥府　公務急速 持此夜行 'Pacification Commission and Chief Military Command: official business, urgent - bearer of this (may) travel at night'. (Rachewiltz 1982, 415). Since this paizah was discovered close to Beijing, the Chinese version may in this case have been the most useful to the bearer.

56. Allsen 2000, 42–44. The other languages beside Persian were Mongolian, Jürchen (Manchu), Tibetan, Uyghur, Sanskrit, Burmese, and Shan, and later on Vietnamese, Siamese, and Malay.

57. Flecker 1923, act 3, scene 4.

# Chapter 6: God's Own Language

1. Krishnaswamy 2006, 11. Those who defined their identity by their faith naturally saw foreigners' religion as their distinctive feature. So Omar Ibn Said, a Muslim from Senegal sold into American slavery ca 1795, refers to English, in his memoir originally in Arabic (Jameson 1925), as "the Christian language." And "Christian tongue" is what the villagers are still calling the English language in Raja Rao's 1938 evocation of Indian village life, *Kanthapura* (p. 46).

   The term was taken up in English too. It was a pompous synonym for *English* in colonial journalism of the mid-nineteenth century. For example, "They were, however, to say the mildest thing of them, barbarians; for they could not speak the Christian tongue, but uttered gibberish, and laughed one with the other as they left the shop" (*Sydney Gazette and New South Wales Advertiser*, March 31, 1836); and "Imagination can hardly conceive the realities of their desolate condition in parts of the world that may be regarded as the peculiar scene of nations professing the Christian religion, and speaking the Christian tongue" (*Courier* (Hobart, Tasmania), April 1, 1845).

2. Bradley 1976, 76.

3. Mundus, "London Missionary Society," www.mundus.ac.uk/cats/4/251.htm.

4. Howatt 2004, 137–38.

5. Ibid., 143.

6. Bradley 1976, 77.

7. The figures are derived from Wikipedia's "Protestantism by Country" (relating to 2004~2005), supplemented by *New York Times Almanac 2001* (for Christians and Muslims). They are given in the form "Protestants/Christians (Muslims)": Sierra Leone 6.1/10% (60%); Liberia 20/40% (20%); Ghana 33/68% (15%); Nigeria 26.5/40% (50%); Cameroon 20/40% (20%); Namibia 68/85% (0%); Botswana 41/50% (0%); South Africa 68/80% (2%); Lesotho 20/80% (0%); Swaziland 66/66% (0%); Zimbabwe 33/75% (2%); Zambia 27/66% (33%); Malawi 35.5/80% (20%); Tanzania 14/45% (35%); Uganda 35/66% (16%); Kenya 38/66% (7%).

8. E.g., Todd M. Johnson, *Christianity in Global Context: Trends and Statistics*, pewforum .org/uploadedfiles/Topics/Issues/Politics_and_Elections/051805-global-christianity.pdf

9. Geiger [1916] 1943, 6–7, referring to *Cullavagga* v.33.1. This reads, in full, *na bhikkhave buddhavacanaṃ chandaso āropetabhaṃ yo āropeyya, āpatti dukkaṭassa. anujānāmi bhik-khave sakāya niruttiyā buddhavacanaṃ pariyāpunitun ti* 'O Monks, do not render the word of the Buddha into Sanskrit language. Whoever does so, is guilty of an offence. I give you, O Monks, permission to learn the word of the Buddha in own dialect' (*Vinaya Piṭakaṃ 2:139*). The phrase is actually singular (so literally 'dialect' not 'dialects'); and there is no explicit pronoun, so whose 'own' dialect is not stated.

10. *ettha sakā nirutti namā sammāsambuddhena vuttappakāro Māgadhikavohāro* (*Samantapāsādikā* 1214:18–19). Buddhaghosa's date is estimated by Hinüber 1996, 102–3.

11. Salomon 1998, 73–75.

12. Ashoka's Rock-Edict 13 (line 10) claims that throughout Andhra (as well as the un-known Parimda) they are conforming to the instruction in his dharma (*Aṃdhra-Palideṣu savatra Devanaṃpriyasa dhramanuśasti anuvaṭaṃti*).

13. Ashoka's Rock-Edicts 2 and 13. On the identification of Satiyaputa, see Burrow 1947.

14. Collins 2003, Hinüber 1996, 297.

15. Winternitz 1987, 2:80; Conze 1993, 85.

16. Nilakanta Sastri 1975, 90, 93, 130.

17. Ibid., 382, 386, 394.

18. De Silva 1997, 59–60.

19. Cosmas Indicopleustes, *Christian Topography* xi (137). This all describes the island of *Taprobanē*: cf. Ashoka's *Tamrāparṇi*.

20. Majumdar 1975, 13.

21. Jacob 1993, 151.

22. Hall 1981, 158–61. This is the interpretation of Gordon H. Luce, published in *JBRS* 36(1953) and *JRAS* 1–2 (1966).

23. Sirisena 1978, 70. The record is in the Pali chronicle *Culavaṃsa* 80:6–7.

24. Hall 1981, 137. This is the interpretation of Lawrence Palmer Briggs, *The Ancient Khmer Empire*, 1951, which has become standard. Cf. Goonatilake 2003, 201. If there is dissent, it is that royal patronage for Theravada Buddhism in Cambodia may have begun earlier. Note the inscription in Pali by a preceding king, Śrīndravarman, com-memorating the building of a monastery and of an image of Buddha in 1309, two years after his abdication (Coedès 1936).

25. Jacob 1993, 149–66.

26. An overview of the differences between the national styles of pronunciation can be found in Eisel Mazard's *Resources for Learning Pali (with special reference to problems of indigenous orthography and phonology)* at www.pali.pratyeka.org. See also Busyakul 2003.

27. *Regesta Pontificum Romanorum* 3319 (*Industriae tuae*), 3407 (*Quia te zelo*).

28. The details are in 2 Kings, chapters 17:6 and 24.

29. Sáenz-Badillos 1993, 112–13.

30. E.g., the incident in Luke 7:1–10, with the Roman centurion who requested a cure for his slave: the sympathetic Roman is anxious to spare Jesus the indignity of visiting his own house.

31. Sawyer 1999, 15.

32. Foltz 1999, 62.

33. Al-Biruni, *Chronology of Ancient Nations*, [1879] 1983, tr. Edward Sachau, 282.

34. Foltz 1999, 69–70.

35. Ibid., 68.
36. Bugge 1995, 42.

## Chapter 7: Regenerations

1. Cuevas 1914, 159.
2. Kazakevich and Kibrik 2007, 246–47.
3. *Para que de una vez se llegue a conseguir el que se extingan los diferentes idiomas de que se usa en los mismos Dominios, y sólo se hable el Castellano . . .* , quoted in Triana y Antorveza 1987, 511.
4. Payton 2000, 112–13; but Cornish is now being actively revived.
5. Athanasius, *Historia Arianorum* 75.
6. *Philosophantem rhetorem intellegunt pauci, loquentem rusticum multi.* Gregory of Tours, preface to *Historia Francorum, Monumenta Germaniae Historica, Scriptorum* i, l.31.14.

## Chapter 8: Ruin and Relegation

1. Anquetil du Perron, *Recherches historiques et géographiques sur l'Inde*, 2:xii–xiii, quoted by Lopes 1936, 60.
2. Holden Furber, *Bombay Presidency in the Mid-Eighteenth Century*, 2, cited in Sinha 1978, 6.
3. Adams 2003, 209, citing Amadasi Guzzo 1990, 81. The inscription is puzzling in that it uses an obsolete Punic alphabet and is dated in terms of suffetes (the ancient Punic magistrates). It might be a work of conscious archaism, by a well-informed antiquarian.
4. Lancel 1997, 436–38.
5. Elimam 2004.
6. Lewis 1995, 185, translating ʿAbd-al-Ḥamīd, *Risāla ilaʾl-kuttab* 'Letter to Secretaries'.
7. Braudel 1993, 72, quoting the Arab historian Baladhori.
8. Lewis 1995, 184–6
9. Wexler 1996, 78–79. The geographer was Abu ʿAbdullah Muḥammad ibn Muḥammad al-Idrisi.
10. Guichard 2000, 29.
11. From Abbé Grégoire's speech to the Committee of Public Instruction on September 30, 1793, reported in Abalain 1991, 115.
12. Rahman 1999, 49.
13. Ibid., 49, 53–54.
14. Ibid., 54.
15. Ibid., 50.
16. Beames 1961, 80.
17. Rahman 1999, 54.
18. Ibid., 58.
19. Ibid., 55.
20. Roy 2000, 32.
21. Rahman 1999, 56–57. The captain's name was A. R. Fuller.
22. *Draft of a humble account by General-Adjutant K. P. Kaufman I of the civil regulation*

and organization in the regions of the Governorate-General of Turkestan, 7 Nov. 1867–25 Mar. 1881, St. Petersburg, p. 438, cited and translated by Pierce 1960, 213–14.

23. Pierce 1960, 293, citing Frank Lorimer's *Population of the Soviet Union* (1946), which estimates the total loss from Turkestan between 1914 and 1918 as 1,230,000. Others assess the proportion of émigrés among these as about a quarter, three hundred thousand.

## Chapter 9: Resignation

1. De la Vaissière 2002, 282, 310–15.
2. Ibid., 211. The Chinese did not distinguish the different groups of Iranians who came to them as merchants. All, including Sogdians and Persians, were lumped together as *hú* 胡.
3. Huang 1997, 118–19.
4. Krippes 1991, 68.
5. Lurje 2003.
6. Savory 1953, 152.
7. Ammon 1998, 1–5; Ammon 1999, 669–71.
8. Abramsky 2008, 4.
9. Ammon 1998, 10–11, gives a list of twenty-two Nobel Prize winners in chemistry, physics, physiology, and medicine from 1903 to 1937, all nonnative users of German who had had key graduate training in German-speaking countries. They include Britons, Americans, Dutchmen, and Scandinavians as well as a Frenchman, a Russian, and a Hungarian.
10. Charpa and Deichmann 2007 (itself a German book produced in English) gives, on 275ff, a list compiled by Simone Wenkel of approximately one thousand Jewish émigrés who distinguished themselves in the sciences. In this section's introductory statistical analysis, she notes that Jewish scientists made up 7.7 percent of the known German scientists between 1800 and the present, including 9.1 percent of chemists, 10 percent of mathematicians, 10.5 percent of physicists, and 12.7 percent of medical researchers. In medicine itself, 10 percent of German-speaking scientists were Jewish in 1876–1900, 19 percent in 1901–25, and 25 percent in 1926–50. For comparison, the proportion of Jews in the German population, according to the census of 1933, was 0.5 percent.
11. Reid 1996, 205; Abramsky 2008, 3, quoting Amos Eilon, *The Pity of It All*, 393.
12. Stern and Rudowski 1968. This was the statement of three German Nobel Prize winners, Rudolf Mössbauer, Karl Ziegler, and Feodor Lynen.
13. Sachau [1910] 1983, 1:17–19.
14. Ibid., 1:19–20.
15. Koran 53:20.
16. Thapar 1999, 9–10.
17. Sircar 1960; discussed in Thapar 1999, 7–8.
18. Sachau [1910] 1983, 2:104; Thapar 1999, 4.
19. Thapar 1999, 8.
20. Pollock 1993, 285.
21. Desai 1953, 226–27.
22. Rahman 2002, 126–27. The information on Todar Mal comes from the *Ain-i-Akbari*,

a contemporary Persian-language description of the administration of Akbar's empire.

23. On description and analysis of this, see especially Pollock 2006, chapters 9, 10, and 12. There increasingly indirect ultimate causes are suggested, including the expansion of world trade, Muslim influence, and more specifically the intervention of Muslim poets to make new use of vernacular languages.

24. Ibid., 311–13.

25. Ibid., 423, notes the political theorist Kaviraj expressing this view, as well as some feminists (Tharu and Lalitha) as well as a European historian (Feldhaus).

26. Grierson 1927, vol. 1-1, p. 127.

27. Deshpande 1993, 27, although the evidence is rather elusive. Formal events (where Sanskrit would have been used) seem to have been closed to women. *katham strī nāma sabhāyām sādhvī syāt* 'How indeed should a woman be fitting in an assembly?' (Patanjali's *Mahābhāṣya* (K.) 2:108).

28. Speaking of the ninth century AD, Rājaśekhara insists that a good poet should have a wife fluent in Sanskrit and Prakrit (*Kāvyamīmāṃsā*, 50, according to Deshpande 1993, 16.) In Sanskrit drama, which flourished from the second century BC to the seventh AD, it was deemed proper for all high-class (*ārya*) characters (including women) to use Sanskrit, while the commoners used a variety of local Prakrits. Salomon 1995, 297, argues that Sanskrit as used by Kṣatriyas (i.e., non-Brahman nobles) is the language of the epic poems *Rāmāyaṇa* and *Mahabharata*.

29. Pollock 2006, 28–29.

30. Febvre and Martin 1976, 248–49.

31. Waquet 2001, 96.

32. Burke 1993, 52.

## Chapter 10: Big Beasts

1. Figures for ca 1880, derived from McEvedy and Jones 1978, 69, 206, 216.

2. Topan 2008, 255. In 1924, the visiting commission of the American philanthropist Anson Phelps-Stokes reported, "Instructor qualifications, curricula, textbooks, teaching materials, all met standards unmatched anywhere in tropical Africa . . . In regards to schools, the Germans have accomplished marvels. Some time must elapse before education attains the standard it had reached under the Germans." (Wikipedia, "German East Africa")

3. There is a congeries of stories and quotations from Lingua Franca in all these regions by Roberto Rossetti attached to Alain Corré's glossary of the language at www.uwm .edu/~corre/franca/go.html.

4. Nadeau and Barlow 2008, 259–62.

5. The statute is at www.iranculture.org/en/about/aghmari/farsi.php.

6. www.domain-b.com/economy/general/20091008_pratibha_patil.html.

7. Yunus Khalikov 2006, "Uzbekistan's Russian-language conundrum," www.eurasianet.org/departments/insight/articles/eav091906.shtml; and Marina Kozlova 2008, "Uzbekistan: Do you speak Russian?" chalkboard.tol.org/uzbekistan-do-you-speak-russian.

## Chapter 11: The Jungle Is Neutral

1. Laitin 1989, citing *Report of the Official Language Commission (Kher Report)* 1956, ch. 7.
2. Danzin et al. 1990.
3. ixa2.si.ehu.es/saltmil/en/activities/workshops/review-by-nicholas-ostler.htm.
4. These statistics are obtained from "Internet World Stats by Language" (at www .internetworldstats.com/stats7.htm).
5. This story was constructed by applying the Internet Archive Wayback machine at www.archive.org to the Google Language Tools site at www.google.com/language_ tools. Details of the Babel Fish site are at babelfish.yahoo.com, and of Microsoft Bing Translator at www.microsofttranslator.com.

## Chapter 12: Under an English Sun, the Shadows Lengthen

1. Wilson and Purushothaman 2003.
2. Lewis 2009, 556.
3. Horrocks 1997, 322–24.
4. Waquet 2001, 96.
5. Sebes 1961, Twitchett 1963.
6. Kay 1834, 263.
7. Reported by the then English ambassador, Bulstrode Whitelocke, in his *Journal of the Swedish Embassy* 1855, 1:300, cited in Burke 1993, 52.
8. See, e.g., Sharifian 2009, especially pt. 1, "Native/non-native divide." Graddol 1999 provides a useful statistical account of the long-term decline of the native speaker among English-speaking communities, but raises only briefly and inconclusively the future problem in selecting an authoritative standard for learners.
9. Prodromou 1988.
10. Personal communication 2007, but discursively discussed throughout Graddol 2008.
11. Max Weinreich originally wrote this saw in Yiddish as *A shprakh iz a diyalekt mit an armey un a flot* 'A language is a dialect with an army and a navy' in the article *Der yivo un di problemen fun undzer tsayt* 'Yivo' and the problems of our time' in the periodical *Yivo-bleter* 25, no. 1 (1945).
12. Indian National Knowledge Commission, *Final Report, 2006–2009*, ed. Sam Pitroda, 14, 185. This is available at knowledgecommission.gov.in/reports/report09.asp. The report, however, suggests overcoming the barrier of restricted access through English not by diversifying the languages of higher education, but by teaching English from year one in Indian primary schools, and (as a halfhearted afterthought) instituting a National Translation Mission.

    The anglophone beliefs of Macaulay's *Minute of 2 February 1835 on Indian Education*, to wit that "whoever knows that language has ready access to all the vast intellectual wealth, which all the wisest nations of the earth have created and hoarded in the course of ninety generations," evidently lives on in official thinking and probably more widely in the Indian elite—and this even after sixty years of independence.

# Bibliography

Abalain, Hervé. 1991. *Histoire des langues celtiques.* Paris: Jean-Paul Gisserot.

'Abd al-Ghani, Muhammad. 1929. *A History of the Persian Language and Literature at the Mughal Court.* Allahabad: Indian Press.

Abramsky, Oded. 2008. *Science, Jews and Germans (German-Israeli Conference on Science).* Jerusalem: www.gist2008.com/_media.

Adams, J. N. 2003. *Bilingualism and the Latin Language.* Cambridge: Cambridge University Press.

Adler, Elkan Nathan. 1987. *Jewish Travellers in the Middle Ages: 19 Firsthand Accounts.* New York: Dover.

Allsen, Thomas T. 2000. "The Rasûlid Hexaglot in Its Eurasian Cultural Context." In Golden, ed., 25–49.

Amadasi Guzzo, Maria Giulia. 1990. *Le iscrizioni fenicie e puniche in Italia.* Rome: Istituto Poligrafico dello Stato.

Ammon, Ulrich. 1996. "The European Union . . . Status change of English during the last fifty years." In Fishman et al., eds., 241–70.

———. 1998. *Ist Deutsch Noch Internationale Wissenschaftssprache?* Berlin: de Gruyter.

———. 1999. "Deutsch als Wissenschaftssprache: Die Entwicklung im 20. Jahrhundert, und die Zukunftsperspektive." In H. E. Wiegand, ed., *Sprache und Sprachen in den Wissenschaften: Geschichte und Gegenwart,* 668–85. Berlin: de Gruyter.

Babayarov, Gaybulla, and Andrey Kubatin. 2009. "Role of Sogdian Language in the Western Turkic Qaghanate." In Elnazarov and Ostler, eds.

Baker, Philip. 1996. "The potential for the development of Arabic-based and other contact languages along the maritime trade routes between the Middle East and China, from the start of the Christian era." In Wurm et al., 2:637–72.

Beal, Samuel. [1884] 1995. *Si-Yu-Ki: Buddhist Records of the Western World.* Delhi: D.K. Publishers.

Beames, John. 1961. *Memoirs of a Bengal Civilian.* London: Chatto and Windus.

Beckwith, Christopher. 2009. *Empires of the Silk Road.* Princeton, NJ: Princeton University Press.

Blunt, C. E. 1961. "The Coinage of Offa." In *Anglo-Saxon Coins*. London: Methuen.

Borah, M. J. 1934. "The nature of the Persian language written and spoken in India during the 13th and 14th centuries." *Bulletin of the School of Oriental and African Studies* 7, no. 2: 325–27.

Bradley, Ian. 1976. *The Call to Seriousness: The Evangelical Impact on the Victorians*. London: Jonathan Cape.

Braudel, Fernand. 1993. *A History of Civilization. Grammaire de civilizations*, trans. Richard Mayne. New York and London: Penguin.

Briquel-Chatonnet, Françoise, ed. 1996. *Mosaïque de langues mosaïque culturelle: Le bilingüisme dans le Proche-Orient ancien*. Paris: Jean Maisonneuve.

Brooke, James. 2005. "For Mongolians, E Is for English, F Is for Future." *New York Times,* national ed., February 15, 2005, A1, A9.

Bugge, Henriette. 1995. *Mission and Tamil Society: Social and Religious Change in South India (1840–1900)*. London: RoutledgeCurzon.

Bulliet, Richard W. 1994. *Islam: The view from the edge*. New York: Columbia University Press.

Burke, Peter. 1993. *The Art of Conversation*. Ithaca, NY: Cornell University Press.

Burrow, T. 1947. "Dravidian Studies VI." *Bulletin of the School of Oriental and African Studies* 12, no. 2: 132–47.

Busyakul, Visudh. 2003. "Changes of Pali-Sanskrit loan-words in Thai." In *Sanskrit in Southeast Asia: The harmonizing factor of cultures: Proceedings of International Sanskrit Conference, May 21–23, 2001, Bangkok, Thailand*, 519–22. Sanskrit Studies Centre, Silpakorn University.

Charpa, Ulrich, and Ute Deichmann, eds. 2007. *Jews and sciences in German contexts: Case studies from the 19th and 20th centuries*. Tübingen: Mohr Siebeck.

Christian, David. 1998. *A History of Russia, Central Asia and Mongolia: Vol. 1, Inner Asia from prehistory to the Mongol empire*. Oxford: Blackwell.

Clausen, Sir Gerard. 1962. *Studies in Turkic and Mongolic Linguistics*. London: RoutledgeCurzon.

Coedès, G. 1936. "La plus ancienne inscription en Pâli du Cambodge." *Bulletin de l'École Française d'Extrême-Orient* 36: 14–21.

Collins, Steven. 2003. "Review of *Subodhālaṅkāra (Porāṇa-ṭīkā, Abhinava-ṭīkā)* by Padmanabh S. Jaini." *Journal of the American Oriental Society* 123, no. 1 (January–March): 215–16.

Compareti, Matteo, Paola Raffetta, and Gianroberto Scarcia, eds. 2006. *Eran ud Aneran. Studies presented to Boris Il'ič Maršak on the occasion of his 70th birthday*. Venice: Libreria Editrice Cafoscarina. (Also updated at /www .transoxiana.org/Eran/.)

Conze, Edward. 1993. *A Short History of Buddhism*. London: George Allen and Unwin.

Cribb, Joe, Barrie Cook, Ian Carradice, and John Flower. 1999. *The Coin Atlas.* London: Little Brown & Co.

Crystal, David. 2003. *English as a Global Language.* 2nd ed. Cambridge: Cambridge University Press.

Cuevas, Mariano. 1914. *Documentos inéditos del siglo XVI para la historia de México.* Mexico City.

Curtin, Philip D. 1984. *Cross-cultural Trade in World History.* Cambridge: Cambridge University Press.

Dale, Stephen Frederic. 2004. *The Garden of the Eight Paradises.* Leiden: Brill.

Daniels, Peter T. 1996. "Aramaic scripts for Iranian languages." Section 48 in Daniels and Bright, eds., 499–535.

Daniels, Peter T., and William Bright, eds. 1996. *The World's Writing Systems.* New York and Oxford: Oxford University Press.

Dankoff, Robert, ed. 1983. *Yūsuf Khāṣṣ Ḥājib 'Wisdom of Royal Glory' (Kutadgu Bilig): A Turko-Islamic Mirror for Princes.* Chicago: University of Chicago Press.

Danner, Victor. 1975. *Arabic Literature in Iran.* Ch. 18 in Frye, ed., 566–94.

Danzin, A., S. Allén, H. Coltof, A. Recoque, H. Steusloff, and M. O'Leary. 1990. *Eurotra Programme Assessment Report.* (French original: *Rapport Danzin: Document COM [90] 289 final*). Luxembourg: Commission of the European Communities, DG-XIII.

Daryaee, Touraj. 2003. "The Persian Gulf Trade in Late Antiquity." *Journal of World History* 14, no. 1.

de la Vaissière, Étienne. 2002. *Histoire des marchands sogdiens.* Paris: Collège de France, Institut des Hautes Études Chinoises.

Desai, Z. A. 1953. "Arabic and Persian Inscriptions." *Ancient India* 9: 224–32.

Deshpande, Madhav M. 1993. *Sanskrit and Prakrit: Sociolinguistic Issues.* Delhi: Motilal Banarsidass.

de Silva, Chandra Richard. 1997. *Śri Lanka: A history.* New Delhi: Vikas.

Devereux, Robert, ed. 1966. *Muhākamat al-lughatain, by Mīr 'Ali Shīr.* Leiden: Brill.

Dharmadasa, K. N. O. 2007. "Sri Lanka." In Simpson 2007, 116–38.

Diakonoff, I. M. 1979. "Elamite Language" (in Russian). In *Yazyki Azii i Afriki* (Moscow) 3: 37–49. Also at www.philology.ru/linguistics4/dyakonov-79.htm.

Dillon, Michael. 1999. *China's Muslim Hui Community.* London: Routledge.

Doerfer, Gerhard. 1963–75. *Türkische und Mongolische Elemente im Neupersischen, I–IV.* Wiesbaden: Steiner Franz Verlag.

———. 1998. "The influence of Persian language and literature among the Turks." In Hovannisian and Sabagh, eds., 237–49.

Eckmann, János. 1966. *Chagatay Manual.* Bloomington: Indiana University Press.

Edgerton, Franklin. 1951, *Buddhist Hybrid Sanskrit Grammar and Dictionary.* New Delhi: Munshiram Manoharlal.

Elimam, Abdeljlil. 1977. *Le maghribi, langue trois fois millénaire.* Algiers: ANEP.

Elimam, Abdou. 2004. *Le maghribi alias "ed-darija."* Oran, Algeria: Éditions dar
    El gharb.

Elnazarov, Hakim, and Nicholas Ostler, eds. 2009. *Endangered Languages and
    History.* Bath: Foundation for Endangered Languages.

Ermers, Robert. 1999. *Arabic Grammars of Turkic.* Leiden: Brill.

Eurobarometer. 2006. "Europeans and Their Languages." *Eurobarometer* 243.
    http://ec.europa.eu/public_opinion/archives/ebs/ebs_243_en.pdf.

Febvre, Lucien, and Henri-Jean Martin. 1976. *The Coming of the Book.* London:
    New Left Books.

Ferrand, Gabriel. 1924. "L'élément persan dans les textes nautiques arabes de XVe
    et XVIe siècles." *Journal asiatique,* April–June 1924, 191–257.

Fishman, Joshua A., Andrew W. Conrad, and Alma Rubal-Lopez, eds. 1996.
    *Post-Imperial English: Status Change in Former British and American Colonies,
    1940–1990.* Berlin: Mouton de Gruyter.

Flecker, James Elroy. 1923. *Hassan: The Story of Hassan of Baghdad and How He
    Came to Make the Golden Journey to Samarkand.* London: Heinemann.

Foltz, Richard C. 1999. *Religions of the Silk Road.* New York: St. Martin's Griffin.

Fragner, Bert G. 1999. *Die „Persophonie": Regionalität, Identität und Sprachkontakt
    in der Geschichte Asiens.* Berlin: Das Arabische Buch.

Fränzel, Walter. 1939. *Die lebenden Sprachen im Sprachunterricht der Welt.* Interna-
    tionale Zeitschrift für Erziehung 8, no. 2: 104–28.

Frye, Richard N., ed. 1975. *The Cambridge History of Iran.* Vol. 4. Cambridge:
    Cambridge University Press.

———. 1995. *The Heritage of Central Asia.* Princeton: Markus Wiener.

———. 1996. *Bukhara: The Medieval Achievement.* Costa Mesa, CA: Mazda.

Gandjei, Tourkhan. 1986. "Turkish in Pre-Mongol Persian Poetry." *Bulletin of the
    School of Oriental and African Studies* 49, no. 1: 67–75.

Geiger, Wilhelm. [1916] 1943. *Pāli Literature and Language.* Trans. Batakrishna
    Ghosh. New Delhi: Munshiram Manoharlal.

Gershevitch, Ilya. 1979. "The alloglottography of Old Persian." *Transactions of the
    Philological Society,* 114–90.

———. ed. 1985. *The Cambridge History of Iran.* Vol. 2. Cambridge: Cambridge
    University Press.

Gervase, Mathew. 1963. "The East African Coast until the Coming of the
    Portuguese." In M. Gervase and R. Oliver, eds., *History of East Africa,*
    94–127. Oxford: Oxford University Press.

Giles, Howard, Justine Coupland, and Nikolas Coupland. 1991. *Contexts of
    Accommodation: Developments in Applied Sociolinguistics.* Cambridge,
    Cambridge University Press.

Glasenapp, Helmuth von. 1925. *Jainism*. Trans. Shridhar B. Shrotri. Delhi: Motilal Banarsidass.

Gode, P. K., and C. G. Karve, eds. 1957. *Revised and enlarged edition of V. S. Apte's The Practical Sanskrit-English Dictionary*. Pune: Prasad Prakashan.

Goh, K. S., et al. 1979. *Report on the Ministry of Education, 1978*. Singapore: Ministry of Education.

Golden, Peter B. 1998. "The Turkic Peoples: A historical sketch." In Johanson and Csató, eds., ch. 2, 16–29.

———. ed. 2000. *The King's Dictionary: The Rasūlid Hexaglot*. Leiden: Brill.

Goonatilake, Hema. 2003. "Sri Lanka–Cambodia Relations with Special Reference to the Period 14th–20th Centuries." *Journal of the Royal Asiatic Society of Sri Lanka* 48.

Graddol, David. 1999. "The decline of the native speaker." In Graddol and Meinhof, eds., 57–68.

———. 2008. *English Next*. British Council. www.britishcouncil.org/learning-research-english-next.pdf.

Graddol, David, and Ulrike H. Meinhof, eds. 1999. *English in a Changing World*. Milton Keynes: Catchline/*AILA Review* 13.

Greenfield, J. C. 1985. "Aramaic in the Achaemenian Empire." Ch. 15 in Gershevitch, ed., 698–713.

Grierson, Sir George. 1927. *Linguistic Survey of India*. Vol. 1, pt. 1 (of 19). Calcutta: Government of India Central Publication Branch.

Guichard, Pierre. 2000. *Al-Andalus, 711–1492*. Paris: Hachette.

Hadi, Nabi. 1995. *Dictionary of Indo-Persian Literature*. Delhi: Indira Gandhi National Centre for the Arts, Shakti Malik.

Hale, Mark. 2004. "Pahlavi." In Woodard, 764–76.

Hall, D. G. E. 1981. *A History of South-East Asia*. London: Macmillan.

Harris, W. V. 1989. *Ancient Literacy*. Cambridge, MA: Harvard University Press.

Haṣan, Hādi. 1928. *The History of Persian Navigation*. London: Methuen & Co.

Henning, W. B. 1939. "Sogdian Loan-Words in New Persian," *Bulletin of the School of Oriental Studies* 10, no. 1: 93–106.

Hinüber, Oskar von. 1996. *A Handbook of Pāli Literature*. Berlin: De Gruyter.

Hoban, Russell. 1980. *Riddley Walker*. London: Jonathan Cape.

Horrocks, Geoffrey. 1997. *Greek: A History of the Language and Its Speakers*. Harlow: Longman.

Hourani, George F. 1995. *Arab Seafaring*. Princeton, NJ: Princeton University Press.

Hovannisian, Richard G., and Georges Sabagh, eds. 1998. *The Persian Presence in the Islamic World*. Cambridge: Cambridge University Press.

Howatt, A. P. R., with H. G. Widdowson. 2004. *A History of English Language Teaching*. 2nd ed. Oxford: Oxford University Press.

Huang, Ray. 1997. *China: A Macro History*. Armonk NY: M. E. Sharpe.

Huang Shi-Jian. 1986. "The Persian Language in China during the Yuan Dynasty." *Papers on Far Eastern History* 34: 83–95.

Huang Shi-Jian and Ibrahim Feng Jin-Yuan. 1992. "Chinese-Iranian Relations (Persian Language and Literature in China)." Encyclopaedia Iranica Online. www.iranica.com.

Humbach, Helmut. 1989. "Choresmian." Ch. 3.2.2 in Schmitt, ed., 193–203.

Irwin, Robert. 1994. *The Arabian Nights: A Companion*. Harmondsworth: Allen Lane.

Jacob, Judith. 1993. *Cambodian Linguistics, Literature and History*. Ed. David Smyth. London: Routledge.

Jameson, John Franklin, ed. 1925. "Autobiography of Omar ibn Said, Slave in North Carolina, 1831." *American Historical Review* 30, no. 4: 787–95.

Johanson, Lars, and Eva Á. Csató, eds., 1998. *The Turkic Languages*. London: Routledge.

Jones, G. M., and C. K. Ozóg, eds. 1993. *Bilingualism and National Development*. Clevedon: Multilingual Matters Ltd.

Kachru, Braj. 1985. "Standards, codification and sociolinguistic realism: The English language in the Outer Circle." In R. Quirk and H. Widdowson, eds., *English in the World*, 11–30. Cambridge: Cambridge University Press.

Kahane, Henry and Renée. 1976. "Lingua Franca: The Story of a Term." *Romance Philology* 30, no. 1: 25–41.

Kay, Joseph H. [1834] 2008. *Journal Kept by the Midshipman Joseph Henry Kay During the Voyage of HMS* Chanticleer, *1828–1831*, ed. Ann Savours and Anita McDonnell, in Herbert Beals et al. eds., *Four Travel Journals: America, Antarctica and Africa 1775–1874*. The Hakluyt Society, third series, 18.

Kazakevich, Olga, and Aleksandr Kibrik. 2007. "Language endangerment in the CIS." In Matthias Brenzinger, ed., *Language Diversity Endangered*, 233–62. Berlin: Mouton de Gruyter.

Kennedy, Paul. 1988. *The Rise and Fall of the Great Powers*. London: Unwin Hyman.

Kent, Roland G. 1934. "More Old Persian Inscriptions." *Journal of the American Oriental Society* 54: 34–52.

Khanlari, P. N. 1979. *History of the Persian Language*. Trans. N. H. Ansari. New Delhi: Mohammad Arhad for Idarah-i-Adabiyat-i Delli.

King, Linda. 1994. *Roots of Identity: Language and Literacy in Mexico*. Stanford, CA: Stanford University Press.

Kirkpatrick, Andy. 2007. *World Englishes*. Cambridge: Cambridge University Press.

Kretzenbacher, Heinz L. 2004. *German: The Language of Science*. Goethe-Institut. www.goethe.de/kue/lit/dos/dds/en146304.htm.

Krippes, Karl. 1991. "Sociolinguistic Notes on the Turcification of the Sogdians." *Central Asiatic Journal* 35: 67–80.

Krishnaswamy, N., and Lalitha. 2006. *The Story of English in India*. Delhi: Foundation Books.

Laitin, David D. 1989. "Language policy and political strategy in India." *Policy Sciences* 22: 415–36.

Lancel, Serge. 1997. *Carthage: A History*. Trans. Antonia Nevill. Oxford: Blackwell.

Lazard, Gilbert. 1975. "Rise of the New Persian Language." Ch. 19 in Frye, ed., 595–632.

———. 1989. "Le persan." Ch. 4.1.1 in Schmitt, ed., 263–93.

———. 1993. "The Origins of Literary Persian." Foundation for Iranian Studies, Noruz Lecture. www.fis-iran.org/en/programs/noruzlectures/literary-persian.

Lehmann, Winfred P. 1967. *A Reader in Nineteenth-Century Indo-European Historical Linguistics*. Bloomington and London: Indiana University Press.

Lemaire, André, and Hélène Lozachmeur. 1996. "Remarques sur le plurilinguisme en Asie Mineure à l'époque perse." In Briquel-Chatonnet, 91–124.

Lewis, Bernard. 1991. *The Political Language of Islam*. Chicago: University of Chicago Press.

———. 1995. *The Middle East*. London: Phoenix Press.

Lewis, Geoffrey. 1967. *Turkish Grammar*. Oxford, Clarendon Press.

Lewis, M. Paul, ed. 2009. *Ethnologue: Languages of the World*. 16th ed. Dallas: Summer Institute of Linguistics.

Lifshits, Vladimir. 2004. "A Sogdian precursor of Omar Khayyám in Transoxania." In *Iran and Caucasus. Research Papers from the Caucasian Centre for Iranian Studies* 8, no. 1: 15–18. Leiden: E. J. Brill.

Lopes, David. 1936. *A Expansão da Língua Portuguesa no Oriente durante os séculos XVI, XVII e XVIII*. Barcelos: Portucalense Editora.

Lurje, Pavel B. 2003. "How long was Sogdian spoken in Transoxiana?: A Toponymical Approach." *Proceedings of the 5th European Conference of Iranian Studies*. Abstract at http://www.societasiranologicaeu.org/Sito%20 Conferenza/pdf/abstract/thursday/mi_Lurje.pdf.

Majumdar, Ramesh Chandra. 1975. *The Study of Sanskrit in South-East Asia*. Calcutta: Sanskrit College.

Martin, Lillian Ray. 2001. *The Art and Archaeology of Venetian Ships and Boats*. College Station: Texas A&M University Press.

Martinez, A. P. 1991. "Changes in chancellery languages and language changes in general in the Middle East, with particular reference to Iran in the Arab and Mongol periods." *Archivum Eurasiae Medii Aevi* 7 (1987–91): 103–52.

Masica, Colin. 1991. *The Indo-Aryan Languages*. Cambridge: Cambridge University Press.

McAlpin, David. 1981. "Proto-Elamo-Dravidian: The evidence and its implications." *Transactions of the American Philosophical Society* (Philadelphia) 71, pt. 3.

McEvedy, Colin, and Richard Jones. 1978. *Atlas of World Population History*. Harmondsworth: Penguin.

McWhorter, John. 2007. *Language Interrupted: Signs of Non-native Acquisition in Standard Language Grammars*. New York and Oxford: Oxford University Press.

Meierkord, C. 2004. "Syntactic variation in interactions across international Englishes." *English Worldwide* 25, no. 1: 109–32.

Minorsky, V. 1913–36. "Tāt." In Martijn Theodor Houtsma, ed., *First Encyclopaedia of Islam*, 697–700. Leiden: E. J. Brill.

Monier-Williams, Sir Monier. 1899. *A Sanskrit-English Dictionary*. Delhi, Varanasi, and Patna: Motilal Banarsidass.

Mori, Masao. 1979. *Shiruku rōdo to sogudojin* (The Silk Road and the Sogdians). *Tōyō gakujutsu kenkyū* 18.

Mufwene, Salikoko. 2001. *The Ecology of Linguistic Evolution*. Cambridge: Cambridge University Press.

———. 2008. *Language Evolution*. London and New York: Continuum.

Nadeau, Jean-Bénoît, and Julie Barlow. 2008. *The Story of French*. London: Portico.

Nilakanta Sastri, K. A. 1975. *A History of South India*. New Delhi: Oxford University Press.

Nornes, Markus. 2007. *Cinema Babel: Translating Global Cinema*. Minneapolis–St. Paul: University of Minnesota Press.

Omar, Asmah Haji. 2004. *Encyclopedia of Malaysia: Languages and Literature*. Singapore: Didier Millet, Archipelago Press.

———. 2007. "Malaysia and Brunei." In Simpson 2007, 337–59.

Ostler, Nicholas. 2005. *Empires of the Word: A Language History of the World*. London and New York: HarperCollins.

———. 2007. *Ad Infinitum: A Biography of Latin*. New York and London: Walker; HarperCollins.

Pakir, A. 1993. "Two Tongue Tied: Bilingualism in Singapore." In Jones and Ozóg, eds., 73–90.

Payton, Philip. 2000. "Cornish." In Glanville Price, ed., *Languages in Britain and Ireland*, 109–19. Oxford: Blackwell.

Pelliot, Paul. 1912. "Les influences iraniennes en Asie Centrale et en Extrême-Orient." *Revue d'histoire et de littérature religieuses*, n.s., 3: 97–119.

———. 1913. "Les plus anciens monuments de l'écriture arabe en Chine." *Journal asiatique*, series 11, no. 2: 185.

Pelliot, Paul, and E. Chavannes. 1911, 1913. "Un traité manichéen retrouvé en Chine." *Journal asiatique* (1911): 499–617; (1913): 99–199, 261–392.

Pierce, Richard A. 1960. *Russian Central Asia, 1867–1917.* Berkeley and Los Angeles: University of California Press.

Pollock, Sheldon. 1993. "Rāmāyaṇa and Political Imagination in India." *Journal of Asian Studies* 52, no. 2 (May): 261–97.

———. 2006. *The Language of the Gods in the World of Men—Sanskrit, Culture and Power in Premodern India.* Berkeley: University of California Press.

Polotsky, Hans Jacob. 1971. *Aramäisch prš und das „Huzvaresch".* In E. Y. Kutscher, ed., *Collected Papers,* 631–43. Jerusalem: Magna Press, Hebrew University.

Poppe, Nicholas N. 1957. *The Mongolian Documents in Hpʻagspa Script.* Göttinger Asiatische Forschungen, Band 8. Wiesbaden, Germany: Harrassowitz.

Powell, Barry. 1991. *Homer and the Origin of the Greek Alphabet.* Cambridge: Cambridge University Press.

Prodromou, Luke. 1988. "English as cultural action." *ELT Journal* 42, no. 2.

Pulleyblank, Edwin G. 1952. "A Sogdian Colony in Inner Mongolia." *T'oung Pao,* 2nd ser., 41, livr. 4/5: 317–56.

———. 1991. *Lexicon of Reconstructed Pronunciation in Early Middle Chinese, Late Middle Chinese, and Early Mandarin.* Vancouver: UBC Press.

Rachewiltz, Igor de. 1982. "Two Recently Published Pai-tzu Discovered in China." *Acta Orientalia Hungarica* 36: 413–17.

Rahman, Tariq. 1999. "Decline of Persian in British India." *Journal of South Asian Studies* 22, no. 1: 47–62.

———. 2002. *Language, Ideology and Power: Language-learning among the Muslims of Pakistan and North India.* Karachi: Oxford University Press.

Reid, Constance. 1996. *Hilbert.* New York: Springer.

Richter-Bernburg, Lutz. 1979. "Linguistic Shuʻūbiya and Early Neo-Persian Prose." *Journal of the American Oriental Society* 94, no. 1: 55–64.

Roy, Olivier. 2000. *The New Central Asia.* London: I. B. Tauris.

Sachau, Edward C. [1910] 1983. *Alberuni's India.* Delhi: Munshiram Manoharlal.

Sáenz-Badillos, Angel. 1993. *A History of the Hebrew Language.* Cambridge: Cambridge University Press.

Salomon, Richard. 1995. "On drawing socio-linguistic distinctions in Old Indo-Aryan." In George Erdösy, ed., *The Indo-Aryans of Ancient South Asia: Language, material culture and ethnicity,* 293–306. Berlin: de Gruyter.

———. 1998. *Indian Epigraphy.* New York: Oxford University Press.

Savory, Theodore H. 1953. *The Language of Science.* London: André Deutsch.

Sawyer, John F. A. 1999. *Sacred Languages and Sacred Texts.* London: Routledge.

Schaeder, Hans Heinrich. 1930. *Iranische Beiträge I, Schriften der Königsberger Gelehrten Gesellschaft, Geisteswissenschaftliche Klasse, Jahr 6, Heft 5.* Halle (Saale): Max Niemeyer. Reprinted 1972 by Georg Olms.

Schafer, Edward H. 1951. "Iranian Merchants in T'ang Dynasty Tales." In Walter J. Fischel, ed., *University of California Publications in Semitic Philology*. Vol. 11. Berkeley and Los Angeles: University of California Press.

———. 1963. *The Golden Peaches of Samarkand Tales*. Berkeley and Los Angeles: University of California Press.

Schleicher, August. 1871. *Compendium der vergleichenden Grammatik der Indogermanischen Sprachen*. Weimar: Hermann Böhlau.

Schmitt, Rüdiger, ed. 1989. *Compendium Linguarum Iranicarum*. Wiesbaden: Dr. Ludwig Reichert Verlag.

Sebba, Mark. 1997. *Contact Languages: Pidgins and Creoles*. London: Palgrave Macmillan.

Sebes, Joseph. [1961] 1962. *The Jesuits and the Sino-Russian Treaty of Nerchinsk (1689): The Diary of Thomas Pereira, S.J.* Bibliotheca Instituti Historici Societatis Iesu, Vol. XVIII. Rome: Institutum Historicum S.I.

Sharifian, Farzad, ed. 2009. *English as an International Language: Perspectives and Pedagogical Issues*. Bristol: Multilingual Matters.

Simpson, Andrew, ed. 2007. *Language & National Identity in Asia*. Oxford: Oxford University Press.

———. ed. 2008. *Language & National Identity in Africa*. Oxford: Oxford University Press.

Sims-Williams, Nicholas. 1989a. "Bactrian." Ch. 3.2.4.1 in Schmitt, ed., 230–35.

———. 1989b. "Sogdian." Ch. 3.2.1 in Schmitt, ed., 172–92.

———. 1996. "The Sogdian merchants in China and India." In Alfredo Cadonna and Lionello Lanciotti, eds., *Cina e Iran*, 45–67. Florence: Leo S. Olschki.

Sinha, Surendra Prasad. 1978. *English in India*. Patna: Janaki Prakashan.

Sircar, D. C. 1960. "Veraval Inscription of Chalukya-Vaghela Arjuna, 1264 A.D." *Epigraphia Indica* 31, no. 21: 141–50.

Sirisena, W. M. 1978. *Sri Lanka and South-East Asia*. Brill Archive.

Skaff, Jonathan Karam. 2003. "The Sogdian trade diaspora in East Turkestan during the seventh and eighth centuries." *Journal of the Economic and Social History of the Orient* 46, no. 4: 475–524.

Skalmowski, Wojciech, and Alois van Tongerloo. 1993. *Medioiranica*. Leuven: Peeters.

Skjærvø, Prods Oktor. 2002. "An Introduction to Old Persian." MS. http://www .fas.harvard.edu/~iranian/OldPersian/index.html.

Stern, Guy, and Victor Rudowski. 1968. "Ph.D.'s, Nobel Prize winners, and the foreign language requirement." *Modern Language Journal* 52, no. 7: 431–35.

Suárez, Jorge A. 1983. *The Mesoamerican Indian Languages*. Cambridge: Cambridge University Press.

Sundermann, Werner. 1989. "Mittelpersisch." In Schmitt, ed., 138–64.

———. 1993. "An early attestation of the name of the Tajiks." In Skalmowski and van Tongerloo, 163–72.

Szemerényi, Oswald. 1981. "Sprachverfall und Sprachtod besonders im Lichte indogermanischer Sprachen." In Yoel L. Arbeitman and Allan R. Bomhard, *Bono Homini Donum: Essays in Historical Linguistics in Memory of J. Alexander Kerns*, 281–310. Amsterdam: John Benjamins.

Tavernier, J. 2007. *Iranica in the Achaemenid Period (ca. 550–330 B.C.): Lexicon of Old Iranian Proper Names and Loanwords, Attested in Non-Iranian Texts*. Leuven: Peeters.

Tekin, T. 1968. *A Grammar of Orkhon Turkic*. Bloomington: Indiana University Press.

Thackston, Wheeler M. 1994. *A Millennium of Classical Persian Poetry*. Bethesda, MD: Ibex.

Thapar, Romila. 1999. "Somanatha and Mahmud." *Frontline* 8 (April 10–23) Published with *The Hindu*. www.thehindu.com/fline/fl1608/16081210.htm.

Thompson, Roger M. 2003. *Filipino English and Taglish*. Amsterdam and Philadelphia: John Benjamins.

Topan, Farouq. 2008. "Tanzania." In Simpson 2008, 252–66.

Tremblay, Xavier. 2001. *Pour une histoire de la Sérinde*. Vienna: Verlag der Österreichischen Akademie der Wissenschaften.

Triana y Antorveza, H. 1987. *Las lenguas indígenas en la historia social del Nuevo Reino de Granada*. Bogotá: Instituto Caro y Cuervo.

Tsunoda, Minoru. 1983. *"Les langues internationales dans les publications scientifiques et techniques." Sophia Linguistica* 13: 144–55.

Twitchett, D.C. 1963. Review of Sebes 1961. *Bulletin of the School of Oriental and African Studies* 26, no. 1: 234–35.

Waldmeir, Patti. 1998. *Anatomy of a Miracle*. New York: W.W.Norton.

Walter, Mariko Namba. 2006. "Sogdians and Buddhism." *Sino-Platonic Papers* 174 (November). www.sino-platonic.org.

Waquet, Françoise. 2001. *Latin, or the Empire of a Sign*. London and New York: Verso.

Ware, James R., and Roland G. Kent. 1924. "The Old Persian Cuneiform Inscriptions of Artaxerxes II and Artaxerxes III." Transactions of the American Philological Association 55: 52–61.

Watson, Burton. 1993. *Records of the Grand Historian: Han Dynasty I*. 2nd ed. New York: Columbia University Press.

Watson, W. 1983. "Iran and China." In Yarshater, ed., 537–58.

Wexler, Paul. 1996. *The Non-Jewish Origins of the Sephardic Jews*. Albany: State University of New York Press.

Wilson, D., and R. Purushothaman. 2003. *Dreaming with BRICs: The path to 2050*. New York: Goldman Sachs, Global Economics paper 99.

Windfuhr, Gernot. 1979. *Persian Grammar: History and state of its study.* Berlin: Walter de Gruyter.

Winternitz, Moriz. 1987. *History of Indian Literature.* Vols. 1–20 Delhi: Motilal Banarsidass.

Woodard, Roger D., ed. 2004. *The Cambridge Encyclopaedia of the World's Ancient Languages.* Cambridge: Cambridge University Press.

Wurm, Stephen A., Peter Mühlhäusler, and Darrell T. Tryon. 1996. *Atlas of Languages of Intercultural Communication in the Pacific, Asia, and the Americas.* 3 vols. Berlin and New York: Mouton de Gruyter.

Yarshater, E., ed. 1983. *The Cambridge History of Iran.* Vol. 3. Cambridge: Cambridge University Press.

Yule, Colonel Henry, and A. C. Burnell. [1886] 1986. *Hobson Jobson.* New ed. William Crooke. New Delhi: Rupa & Co.

# Index

Note: Page numbers in italics indicate a map or illustration.

# He just wanted a decent book to read ...

Not too much to ask, is it? It was in 1935 when Allen Lane, Managing Director of Bodley Head Publishers, stood on a platform at Exeter railway station looking for something good to read on his journey back to London. His choice was limited to popular magazines and poor-quality paperbacks – the same choice faced every day by the vast majority of readers, few of whom could afford hardbacks. Lane's disappointment and subsequent anger at the range of books generally available led him to found a company – and change the world.

*'We believed in the existence in this country of a vast reading public for intelligent books at a low price, and staked everything on it'*
**Sir Allen Lane, 1902–1970, founder of Penguin Books**

The quality paperback had arrived – and not just in bookshops. Lane was adamant that his Penguins should appear in chain stores and tobacconists, and should cost no more than a packet of cigarettes.

Reading habits (and cigarette prices) have changed since 1935, but Penguin still believes in publishing the best books for everybody to enjoy. We still believe that good design costs no more than bad design, and we still believe that quality books published passionately and responsibly make the world a better place.

So wherever you see the little bird – whether it's on a piece of prize-winning literary fiction or a celebrity autobiography, political tour de force or historical masterpiece, a serial-killer thriller, reference book, world classic or a piece of pure escapism – you can bet that it represents the very best that the genre has to offer.

**Whatever you like to read – trust Penguin.**